United States–Vietnam Reconciliation

ADST MEMOIRS AND OCCASIONAL PAPERS SERIES
Series Editor: LISA TERRY

In 2003, the Association for Diplomatic Studies and Training (ADST), a nonprofit organization founded in 1986, created the Memoirs and Occasional Papers Series to preserve firsthand accounts and other informed observations on foreign affairs for scholars, journalists, and the general public. Through its book series, its Foreign Affairs Oral History program, and its support for the training of foreign affairs personnel at the State Department's Foreign Service Institute, ADST seeks to promote understanding of American diplomacy and those who conduct it. Desaix Anderson, author of the 34th volume in the series, spent most of his 35-year Foreign Service career specializing on Asia, culminating in becoming America's first envoy to the Socialist Republic of Vietnam.

RELATED TITLES FROM ADST SERIES

CHARLES T. CROSS, *Born a Foreigner: A Memoir of the American Presence in Asia*

JOHN GUNTHER DEAN, *Danger Zones: A Diplomat's Fight for America's Interests*

ROBERT WILLIAM FARRAND, *Reconstruction and Peace Building in the Balkans: The Brčko Experience*

DONALD P. GREGG, *Pot Shards: Fragments of a Life Lived in CIA, the White House, and the Two Koreas*

ROBERT E. GRIBBIN III, *In the Aftermath of Genocide: The US Role in Rwanda*

DENNIS JETT, *American Ambassadors: The Past, Present, and Future of America's Diplomats*

ROBERT KEMP, *Counterinsurgency in Eastern Afghanistan 2004–2008: A Civilian Perspective*

JOHN G. KORMANN, *Echoes of a Distant Clarion: Recollections of a Diplomat and Soldier*

TERRY MCNAMARA, with Adrian Hill, *Escape with Honor: My Last Hours in Vietnam*

ARMIN MEYER, *Quiet Diplomacy: From Cairo to Tokyo in the Twilight of Imperialism*

ROBERT H. MILLER, *Vietnam and Beyond: A Diplomat's Cold War Education*

WILLIAM MORGAN and CHARLES STUART KENNEDY, eds., *American Diplomats: The Foreign Service at Work*

DAVID D. NEWSOM, *Witness to a Changing World*

HOWARD B. SCHAFFER, *Ellsworth Bunker: Global Troubleshooter, Vietnam Hawk*

For a complete list of series titles, visit <adst.org/publications>

United States–Vietnam Reconciliation

Through Wars to a Strategic Partnership

Desaix Anderson

ASSOCIATION FOR DIPLOMATIC STUDIES AND TRAINING
MEMOIRS AND OCCASIONAL PAPERS SERIES

NEW ACADEMIA PUBLISHING · VELLUM

Washington, DC

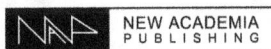

Library of Congress Control Number: 2021919569
ISBN 978-1-7333980-2-2 paperback (alk. paper)

VELLUM An imprint of New Academia Publishing

New Academia Publishing, 4401-A Connecticut Ave. NW, #236,
Washington, DC 20008
NEW ACADEMIA
PUBLISHING
info@newacademia.com - www.newacademia.com

To my Princeton students in the original Princeton Global Summer Seminars in 2007–2009 in Hanoi, without whose enthusiastic participation and perceptive insights these magical educational events could not have succeeded.

Contents

Contents

Abbreviations and Acronyms

APEC	Asian-Pacific Economic Cooperation
ARVN	Army of Vietnam
CAP	Combined Action Platoons
CDC	Center for Disease Control
CDP	Liberal Democratic Party of Japan (Jin Min To)
CEMA	Council for Mutual Economic Assistance
CIA	Central Intelligence Agency
CIP	Commodity Import Program
COMUSMACV	Commander of U.S. Military Assistance Command and Vietnam
CORDS	Civil Operations and Revolutionary Development Support
COSVN	Communist Party's Southern Region
DIA	Defense Intelligence Agency
DMZ	Demilitarized Zone
DPP	Democratic Progressive Party
DPRK	Government of Democratic Kampuchea
DRV	Democratic Republic of Vietnam
FBIS	Foreign Broadcast Information Service
FDI	Foreign Direct Investment
FIA	Foreign Investment Agency
FSO	Foreign Service officer
FUNCINPE	The United National Front for an Independent, Neutral, Peaceful, and Cooperative Cambodia
GDP	Gross Domestic Product
GVN	Government of Vietnam
ICC	International Control Commission
ICP	Indochinese Communist Party
IMF	International Monetary Fund

INR	Intelligence and Research Bureau (of the U.S. Department of State)
JCS	Joint Chiefs of Staff
JUSPAO	Joint United States Political Affairs Office
KMT	Kuomintang
KPNLF	Khmer People's Liberation Front
MAAG	Military Assistance Group
MACV	Military Assistance Command Vietnam
MFN	Most Favorable Nation
NA	National Assembly
NLF	National Liberation Front
NPAC	National Peace Action Coalition
NSC	National Security Council
NSA	National Security Advisor
OSS	Office of Strategic Services
PAVN	People's Army of Vietnam
PCPJ	People's Coalition for Peace and Justice
PF	Popular Forces
PIIRS	Princeton Institute of International and Regional Studies
PNTR	Permanent Normal Trade Relations
POW/MIA	Prisoner of War/Missing in Action
PRC	People's Republic of China
PRI	Institutional Revolutionary Party
PRG	Provisional Revolutionary Government
PXs	military stores
SEATO	Southeast Asian Treaty Organization
SEG	State Economic Group
SOE	State Owned Enterprise
SVN	South Vietnam
TPP	Trans Pacific Partnership
UNTAC	United Nations Transitional Authority in Cambodia
USAID	U.S. Agency for International Development
VA	Veterans' Administration
VNQDD	Nationalist Vietnam Quoc Dan Dang

Acknowledgments

I wish to acknowledge my indebtedness to Princeton University President Shirley Tilghman and Princeton Institute of International Relations (PIIRS) Director Michael Centano, who entrusted me to organize a new program to enhance the strategic perspective of Princeton undergraduates. This became the Princeton Global Seminar, which I proposed, organized, and conducted in Hanoi 2007–2009. These seminars formed the basis for this book, *United States–Vietnam Reconciliation: Through Wars to a Strategic Partnership.*

I am profoundly indebted to Secretary of State Warren Christopher and Assistant Secretary Winston Lord, who sent me to open the U.S. Embassy in Hanoi from 1995 to 1997. Ambassador Lord and the late Ambassador Richard Solomon, whom I regard as great friends as well as bosses, have their own recollections in the Library of Congress American Memory collection of Oral Histories and in the Foreign Affairs Oral History archive of the Association for Diplomatic Studies and Training <adst.org/oral-history>. I am also indebted for inspiration to friends and authors, the late Stanley Karnow and Don Oberdorfer, whose writings supplied the structure on which I drew in organizing the Princeton seminar. Historians K. W. Taylor, Fredrik Logevall, David Marr, and Kai Bird provided invaluable insights into Vietnam's history. Harvard Professor Hue-Tam Ho Tai provided superb insights into the intellectual-political development of Vietnam's emerging leaders. Of utmost importance was Archimedes Patti's *Why Vietnam: Prelude to America's Albatross,* which provided profound insights into Ho Chi Minh's intentions and hopes.

I was blessed enormously with three professors from the University of Economics and Social Studies, Vietnam National University, as the core group of professor/lecturers and my supporters: Vice Rector and Professor of History Pham Quang Minh, history professor Dr. Pham Hong Tung, and social science professor Do Thu Ha. Of crucial importance was assistance by my good friend Mme Ton Nu Thi Ninh, an influential chair of the Foreign Affairs Committee of Vietnam's National Assembly. Mme Ninh arranged participation of many of the special guest speakers who were instrumental in the success of the seminar, allowing the students to hear directly from and question influential figures in the Vietnamese establishment and society. I was deeply indebted to them for providing open access for the students to Vietnam's leaders like the late General Nguyen Dinh Uoc, a close confident of General Vo Nguyen Giap; a Communist Party operative; the writer Bao Ninh (*The Sorrows of War*); Vietnam's vice president Nguyen Thi Binh, chief representative of the Provisional Revolutionary Government (Viet Cong) at the Paris Peace Talks; Ambassador Nguyen Khac Huynh, also a member for the North Vietnam delegation to the Peace Talks; historian Huu Ngoc; and friend Le Dang Doanh, Vietnam's leading economist.

I am also deeply indebted to ADST Publishing Director Margery Thompson and her diligent editors Lisa Terry and Madeline Doctor, as I am to Princeton student and friend Kent Kuran for excellent editing.

Finally, I am indebted for the great moral support, advising, and cheering on of my sisters Elizabeth Aldridge in editing and Florri DeCell in superbly managing graphics and technical matters, and strong support from Ken DeCell, and my brother, Buford Anderson.

Prologue

My Rendezvous with Vietnam

Except as a distant historic footnote or an idle comparison to a possible quagmire in Iraq or Afghanistan, what does the Vietnam War evoke in the minds of Americans? A fight against global communism? An effort to support democracy in a distant land? Napalmed villages? Free-fire zones? Search-and-destroy military tactics? Mass antiwar protests? Student riots? American defeat?

These vivid images have become subliminal, but I surmise that the national memory is of a bloody, misguided war that could never have been won on any politically acceptable basis, into which we stumbled without realizing, either then or now, the strength of nationalist or popular determination of a people who had struggled for a thousand years to achieve independence.

In South Vietnam, Washington was attempting to help establish a free-market democracy, which our leaders hoped would best protect American interests, keep the Vietnamese from the depredations of a communist system, and prevent the spread of communism to the rest of Southeast Asia. As noble as this cause may have seemed to many Americans, the spectacular Vietcong offensive during the Lunar New Year, "Tet Mau Tan," on January 31, 1968, shocked policymakers and onlookers alike, exploding skepticism about the chances of American success. Tet intensified the struggle of those opposed to the war, channeling the growing anguish being felt by the nation.

The Tet Offensive of February 1968 spanned the breadth of South Vietnam and demonstrated a pervasive Vietcong capability throughout the cities and countryside to a degree almost no one had thought possible. On the Vietnam Working Group in the State

Department in Washington D.C., where I worked, the shock was intense as the news rolled over the wires revealing the intensity and scope of the Tet attacks. I recall the entire edifice that General William Westmoreland and the U.S. government had constructed collapsing in a single night. As if to signal the changing mood in the country, the most trusted man in America, CBS commentator Walter Cronkite, sounded the cost of Tet, solemnly declaring on February 27 that he was "more certain than ever that the bloody experience of Vietnam is to end in a stalemate."[1]

After a few confused, bloody weeks, the Tet Offensive was crushed militarily at great cost to the Vietcong cadres. However, from a political perspective, it was a stunning victory by the Vietcong and Hanoi against the U.S. and South Vietnamese governments. Tet dismayed Washington. Doubt about the success of the war against the Vietcong reflected the high political cost.

It took five more years for Nixon to extricate the nation from that quagmire. It took almost twenty more years for us to erase Vietnam from our national psyche and for Americans to claim that the Vietnam War was finally over. Was it over? Did we really learn the lessons of the Vietnam War, or the "American War," as Vietnamese refer to it? How had American leaders so misjudged the nature of the struggle in Vietnam, the strength of nationalist sentiment, the determination of North Vietnam's leaders, and Hanoi's attitude toward China and the Soviet Union? Were none of the American leaders aware of Vietnam's history? How did we come to expect that a corrupt regime in Saigon could earn the respect and support of the population? Was it understood that the widespread sympathy in South Vietnam toward the Vietminh (Vietcong)[2] did not reflect support for communism as an economic or political system, but rather for the unfinished struggle for national independence?[3] How did American military leaders believe that search-and-destroy operations, bombing villages, punitive bombing in Northern Vietnam, and the massive presence of U.S. military personnel throughout the country was a productive strategy for handling this "people's war?"

Like most tragedies, there was nothing inevitable about the American fiasco in Vietnam. President John F. Kennedy asked Secretary of State Dean Rusk and Secretary of Defense Robert

McNamara five questions for which he wanted answers. McNamara described in his book, *In Retrospect: The Tragedy and Lessons of Vietnam*, with considerable chagrin, Dean Rusk's analysis, which was, in his words, "inadequate": "We failed to address the five most basic questions that were never asked: Was it true that the fall of South Vietnam would trigger the fall of all Southeast Asia? Would that constitute a grave threat to the West's security? What kind of war—conventional or guerrilla—might develop? Could we win it with U.S. troops fighting alongside the South Vietnamese? Should we not know the answer to all these questions before deciding whether to commit troops?"[4]

President Kennedy never received answers to these questions, but, after having been poorly advised by the Pentagon during the ill-fated Bay of Pigs Operation and the handling of the Cuban Missile Crisis in 1962, Kennedy bucked the generals' recommendations. On the eve of his assassination in November 1963, he again rejected the Pentagon's request to send 200,000 combat troops to Vietnam, as the Pentagon had regularly recommended since November 1961.[5]

In contrast, President Lyndon B. Johnson, facing political pressure from conservatives, neglected to ask the questions Kennedy had asked his secretaries of State and Defense and instead accepted his civilian advisors' and military leaders' advice to steadily escalate the war. By the end of Johnson's presidency, South Vietnam was swarming with more than 500,000 U.S. soldiers.

To many Americans, the Vietnam War is a painful memory of military defeat and wasteful sacrifice. To North Vietnamese, the American War was just one episode in a centuries-long nationalist struggle against foreign domination. Hanoi committed Vietnam to this struggle despite the horrors of the war—a death toll in the millions, hundreds of thousands of Vietnamese soldiers unaccounted for, and a devastated country—in order to deliver a proud victory over the Americans, as had been their victory over the French after 100 years. This was all the more true in Vietnam's 1,000-plus years' struggle against the Chinese, which temporarily ended when the Chinese first accepted the independence of Vietnam in 1428. However, China would return repeatedly to reassert control over Vietnam from the 14th to 18th centuries. At every opportunity the Vietnamese repelled Chinese occupation.[6]

Hanoi's ultimate victory was one of history's few wars in which the winner received no reparations or compensation but struggled alone with the poverty and devastation of war. To make matters worse, the reunification of Vietnam was followed not by the representative government envisioned by early Vietminh figures but by the strict Marxist-Leninist authoritarianism imposed by leaders such as the Communist Party of Vietnam's General Secretary, Le Duan, who replaced Ho Chi Minh after his death in 1969.

The rigid ideological system began to lift and give way to a period of *Doi Moi* (renovation), and Vietnam began to define itself in the contemporary world, only in 1986—eleven years after the war concluded and national reunification was achieved.

Not until 1995, nine years later, and more than two decades after America's complete withdrawal of troops, did the United States begin reconciliation with Vietnam. Then, as *chargé d'affaires*, I opened the U.S. Embassy in Hanoi a month after President Bill Clinton established diplomatic relations with Vietnam in July 1995.

The arc of my life and career in the U.S. Foreign Service followed closely the trajectory of the Kennedy brothers—John, Robert, and Edward. A fervent supporter of John Kennedy's bid for president, and as part of the throng at his inauguration in Washington in January 1961, I heard him declare, "Ask not what your country can do for you, but what you can do for your country." Like many of my generation, I heeded his call: I joined the U.S. Foreign Service, where I worked for forty years, virtually always in or dealing with Asia. Robert Kennedy structured his 1968 campaign in significant part on opposition to the Vietnam War. Edward Kennedy, in his memoir, *True Compass*, focused on the dilemma regarding Vietnam with which President Kennedy struggled. He recounted how, "Jack's antenna was set to find a way out. He just never got the chance." Senator Kennedy later based his opposition to the Iraq War, at least in part, upon his perceptions of Vietnam.[7]

After my initial assignment to Kathmandu, Nepal—at the time, the enchanting Shangri-La in the Himalayas—State Department personnel came to Kathmandu in June 1964 and asked about my aspirations for future assignments. Mesmerized by the stunning beauty of the Himalayas emblazoned across the northern sky, the feudal kingdom nestled in the Kathmandu Valley, and certainly by the Nepali people themselves, I first asked for an extension of my time in Kathmandu. At their insistence, I reluctantly responded, "If I must move, I wish to go anywhere in Asia, except Vietnam, because I do not like war!" Within a couple of weeks, the State Department ordered me to return to Washington to study Vietnamese and assigned me in 1965 to the rural U.S. Agency for International Development (USAID) program working to support the provincial governments' efforts to strengthen the South Vietnamese government. In early 1967, I was assigned as an evaluator for Deputy Ambassador William Porter, traveling to contested areas to explore the effectiveness of the newly established revolutionary development program of the South Vietnamese government.

From Vietnam, I was assigned from mid-1967 to mid-1968 to the Vietnam Working Group, the State Department's Vietnam Desk, during which the 1968 Tet Offensive occurred. In 1968–70, I studied Chinese in Washington and then in Taichung, Taiwan, and acted as a political officer to the U.S. Embassy in Taipei, recognized at the time by the United States as the Government of China. I was selected in early 1973 as one of forty Foreign Service officers (FSOs) to return to Vietnam to evaluate security, political, military, and other developments in the wake of the departure of American forces after the signing of the Paris Accords. I was assigned to the pretty Mekong Delta town of My Tho. I will describe these experiences as the story progresses.

After my second assignment to Vietnam, I was assigned to Japan from 1973 to 1976 in the political section as the "China Watcher." After Japan, I was assigned from mid-1977 to 1980 to Thailand, where I interviewed Khmer refugees on the Thai-Cambodian border and Vietnamese in refugee camps for "boat people." I reported on the conditions and developments under the heinous Pol Pot regime in Phnom Penh and the results of the Vietnamese invasions and occupation of Cambodia in December 1978 and 1979. At the same time, I reported on developments in Vietnam itself that I learned from refugees: the preparations for attack on Cambodia, the movement towards an alliance with the Soviet Union, the deterioration in Hanoi's relations with Beijing, and China's "teaching Vietnam a lesson" by its punitive invasion of Vietnam in February 1979. Through refugees I learned of Vietnam's movement toward reunification in 1976 and "socialist transformation," including the anti-Chinese policies in North and South Vietnam from 1977 to 1979.

In reward for my work on Indochina, the assistant secretary of state for East Asia and the Pacific, Richard Holbrooke, chose me to be country director for Vietnam, Laos, and Cambodia from 1980 to 1983. In 1981 I was shocked and elated when the Reagan administration selected me to approach Vietnam about the possibility of normalization—predicated upon Vietnam's withdrawal from Cambodia. I also was an active participant in the Conference on Kampuchea (Cambodia), which devised a formula for resolution of the Vietnamese withdrawal from Cambodia, the template for their ultimate withdrawal in 1988–89 and the resolution to the Cambodian issue in 1991.

After a two-year stint in 1983–85 as country director for Japan, Ambassador Mike Mansfield selected me as his deputy at the U.S. Embassy in Tokyo from 1985 to 1989. Although Senator Mansfield in 1954 admired Ngo Dinh Diem, his assessment gradually evolved.[8] When President Kennedy sent Majority Leader Mansfield to Vietnam in 1962, he was brutally frank in his conclusion that the United States had spent two billion dollars in seven years, yet "the same difficulties remain, if, indeed, they have not been compounded." The fault lay, he said, with U.S. policy and with Diem for his failure to share power with non-Catholic factions of South Vietnamese society, e.g., Buddhists. Mansfield expressed fears that the United States was falling inexorably into a position in Vietnam formerly occupied by the French.[9] Subsequently, I learned of Senate Majority Leader Mansfield's nineteen memos to President Johnson arguing against escalation in Vietnam and of President Kennedy's private comments to the Majority Leader about his intention to withdraw from Vietnam after the 1964 elections.

Serving as principal deputy assistant secretary for East Asia in the first Bush administration from 1989 to 1992 and on President Bill Clinton's State Department policy-planning staff in 1994–95, I followed negotiations with Vietnam closely.

Thus, with six assignments in or on Vietnam (probably the most of any FSO), in 1995 I opened the U.S. Embassy in Hanoi as *chargé d'affaires* and embarked on one of the most rewarding assignments an individual can have in diplomacy—reconciliation with a former enemy. Just prior to my departure in August for Hanoi, Deputy Secretary Warren Christopher emphasized that the resolution of the Prisoner of War/Missing in Action (POW/MIA) issue and human rights were at the top of my agenda, but he also stressed that I was to build a new relationship with Vietnam through reconciliation, a wonderfully open-ended instruction.

The day before I departed Hanoi at the conclusion of my assignment in May 1997, I called on Vietnam's wartime premier, Phan Van Dong, one of Ho Chi Minh's closest comrades. We discussed Vietnam's history from the 1940s through the American War and the junctures at which different policies might have produced vastly different outcomes. That conversation, buttressed by many more, is carried in full in this book, as it was the most exquisite moment of my career as a public servant.

Several years later, Princeton University's president, Shirley Tilghman, made clear that she found Princeton students too isolated from the contemporary world and urged the faculty to identify ways to overcome this situation. As a member of the Advisory Council of the Princeton Institute for International and Regional Studies, I suggested that I conduct a summer seminar in Hanoi entitled "The Vietnam War: Origins, Implications, and Consequences."

Princeton agreed.[10] But why undertake a retrospective on events that occurred fifty years ago and which scholars have dissected hundreds of times? Why is this history relevant today?

My desire to equip the next generation of leaders with the tools and knowledge to navigate our country's increasingly complex security challenges motivated me to recommend the in-depth study of Vietnam and the exploration of the lessons of the Vietnam War.

These are my perceptions from my fifty-year engagement with Vietnam.

1

The Impact of Chinese Imperialism on the Vietnamese Psyche

Opening my Princeton Global Summer Seminar in Hanoi with a lecture, which he also gave to visiting European kings, queens, and other dignitaries, Vietnamese historian Huu Ngoc discussed "Three-Thousand Years of Vietnamese History and Culture." Huu Ngoc gave his lecture in a prayer hall in the Van Mieu Confucian Temple. The Temple was built in 1070 as a Temple to Confucius, but it soon became Vietnam's first university—charged with instilling in the minds of young royalty and Vietnamese Mandarins the tenets of Confucianism. The Temple has become the spiritual and intellectual epicenter of Vietnam; President Clinton visited the Temple in 2000, President Bush in 2006, and President Obama praised it during a state visit to Vietnam in 2016 as "a great Temple of Literature that stands as a testament to your pursuit of knowledge."

In Huu Ngoc's description of Vietnam's genesis, "the land of the South Vietnam was a Southeast Asian wet rice culture, akin to Cambodia, Laos, Thailand, and the Philippines." Over time, however, "Vietnam, while preserving its Southeast Asian attributes, also enriched itself with different grafts. Over 2,000 years, Vietnam was absorbed in the cultural orbit of East Asia, imbued with Confucianism, like Korea and Japan." The impact of Chinese culture "came from two directions, at different times. It was forcibly imposed during the period of Chinese occupation from 179 BC to 938 AD and was subsequently emulated and embellished by the Vietnamese themselves during the era of national independence from 938 to 1884."[1]

"The relations between Vietnamese and Chinese followed a particular dynamic. On the one hand," Huu Ngoc told the seminar,

"Vietnamese reject the culture of Chinese aggression and aspire to preserve their Southeast Asia roots. On the other, Vietnamese feel attracted by a culture—the Chinese—that seemed richer in many ways and stronger than the Viet culture. They borrowed from the culture the elements they saw as capable of enriching their own society. Rejection and attraction characterize this ambiguous relationship, even in the present time." Huu Ngoc compared Vietnam to a banyan tree with Chinese, Confucian, and, to a lesser but important extent, India, with its Buddhist and Hindu religious and cultural influence. In Huu Ngoc's view, "while Han China gave critical technologies to Vietnam, such as the manufacture of paper and glass, river and sea navigation, China's intellectual and spiritual legacy was equally important, enriching Vietnam stock without altering it."

"Confucianism is the moral and political creed of the learned man, the intellectual, the 'superior man,'" Huu Ngoc said, "and projects itself morally to manage one's family, to govern the country, and to establish order in the world. In a word, it is a set of very strict rules about social behavior intended to maintain order and harmony in a strongly hierarchical society."

He continued to tell us that "this doctrine [Confucianism] is perfectly suited to the East Asian feudal societies: agricultural, autarchic, stationary, and subject to despotic monarchic regimes which gave the king the proprietorship over all the land."[2]

In his excellent and meticulously researched description of this same process, K. W. Taylor explains that for tens of thousands of years Vietnam encompassed a much broader plain, which also included the land now under the Tonkin Gulf and the South China Sea. About eight- to twelve-thousand years ago, quarries and caves, with the melting of the Ice Age, were covered due to rising sea levels. Gradually the seas receded and the chains of mountains, valleys, and plains in present-day northern Vietnam emerged.[3]

At that time, several Bronze Age cultures existed on the Asian continent and one such culture began to assert rule over current northern Vietnam, extending to the Yunnan Plateau in present-day southern China. Over the next millennium, the political culture of the great power to the north, then associated with ancient China, led to the incorporation of current northern Vietnam into the Chinese realm.

The Dong Son Culture, present in northern Vietnam during the next four to five centuries, produced "distinctive bronze drums, decorated with boats, men and women copulating, beheadings, warriors, musicians, dancers, feathered garments, birds, animals, reptiles, and amphibians." Conquest by the Han Chinese in the mid–first century brought the area firmly under Chinese authority.[4]

The Historical Emergence of Vietnam

Some events are established from the mythical early Hung king history of the area of present-day southern China. Han Dynasty General Lu Bode in 111 BC conquered the local Nan Yue (Nam Viet in Vietnamese), but allowed the Au Lac Nam Viet to rule. Thus, the great Han Dynasty emerged to control China and Nan Yue, although Lac lords ruled the latter, and the land became a province of Han China, called Giao Chi. The local prefectures were put in the hands of the area Au Lac lords, who received imperial "seals and ribbons" (symbols of their tributary status) in return for what the lords viewed as tribute to the suzerain but which over time began to be viewed as a tax. The Imperial Authority would ensure security; local leaders were to maintain domestic tranquility and nurture trade and agriculture to produce a taxable surplus and encourage northern immigration to Nan Yue. The Imperial Authority also sought to educate locals in Chinese norms of education and social reform, meaning Confucianism. However, the Chinese also attempted to reconcile their customs with the practices of residents.[5]

In 940 a young woman, Trung Thach, a descendent of Lac lords, and her sister, Trung Nhi, led a revolt against the Chinese rulers, who fled to southern China. Supporters installed Trung Thach as queen of Nam Viet; the Han retaliated in 943 and overthrew the Trung Trach rule. Both Trung sisters committed suicide or were beheaded, according to alternate sources. Because they were revered as heroic martyrs of national resistance, streets in almost every city, including Hanoi and Saigon, are named "Hai Ba Trung" in honor of the two sisters.[6]

After restoration of Han rule, the indigenous cultures and institutions remained largely intact, but in the first century, Han China undertook to reform the culture of the Nan Yue and enforced China's more rigid, authoritarian system on Vietnam.

Although there were occasional periods of renaissance of native traditions, as well as repeated outbreaks of armed revolt, this Sinicized Vietnam lasted seven-hundred years, through both the Han and Tang dynasties. The Han Dynasty collapsed in 220, and several lesser dynasties ruled from then until the Tang Dynasty emerged. Ad interim, the lesser dynasties achieved relative prosperity.[7]

The Tang Dynasty, founded in 618, was arguably one of the most glorious periods in China's history. Until it collapsed in 907, the Tang state became the most powerful and prosperous in the world. It too enforced the Chinese influence and customs on the Vietnamese.

Indpendent Vietnam Established

Early in the tenth century, as the southern Han's rule of China weakened, successive lords from the Vietnamese Nan Yue family ruled under Tang sovereignty. The first, Duong Dinh Nghe, ruled Giao Chi autonomously under the Tang. Ngo Quyen, the son-in-law of Duong Dinh Nghe, defeated the southern Han fleet in 938 and proclaimed himself King Ngo of the Le Dynasty. Ngo Quyen's sudden death after a short reign resulted in a power struggle for the throne—the country's first major civil war, which lasted until 960.[8] But this date in history, 938, when Vietnam first established independence from China, remains a sacred, celebrated date for Vietnam.

From 960 to 1279 China's Song Dynasty leaders attempted to exercise suzerainty over Vietnam but were effectively repulsed, and the border was demarcated by the end of the thirteenth century. The situation stabilized when Ly Cong An established the Ly Dynasty (1009–1225). King Ly Cong Anh (posthumously Le Thai Tho) moved the capital to Thang Long ("Rising Dragon"), where Hanoi is today.

Four Vietnamese dynasties stand out for their strong, influential rule. The Ly Dynasty established a stable, independent Vietnam and built on myths, legends, and practices drawn from the Dragon

Ages of the earlier Chinese-influenced Hung and Lac kings. Buddhism flourished during this period.[9] There was also a resurrection of Confucianism. As noted previously, the Van Mieu Temple of Literature was constructed in 1070. National examinations and a national university were established there, reflecting institutions from China's Confucius tradition; however, some Vietnamese traditions diluted them.

Following the strong Ly Dynasty came the Tran Dynasty (1225–1400), which continued the development of institutions common in China—an army, bureaucracy, and examination system of the Confucian tradition. At about this time, Mahayana Buddhism swept into Vietnam. During the Tran Dynasty, China's Kublai Khan's rule (the Mongols), seeking trade routes to Indonesian spices, invaded Vietnam three times. Under the leadership of another great Vietnamese general, Tran Hung Dau, the Vietnamese defeated the Mongols in 1287. As before and since, Tran Hung Dao used "mobile methods of warfare, abandoning the cities, avoiding frontal attacks, and harassing the enemies, leaving the enemies confused and exhausted. The Vietnamese routed 300,000 Mongol troops."[10]

During the early fifteenth century, weak Vietnamese leadership, economic crisis, and peasant revolts led the Chinese Ming Dynasty to reassert control over Vietnam in 1407. Ming rule was draconian, enforcing a rigorous system of political, economic, and cultural control down to the village level and regulating everything from religious ceremonies to language, hairstyles, dress codes, and literature.

Following resumption of Chinese control of Vietnam under the Ming Dynasty in 1407–28, another great Vietnamese leader, Le Loi, began a revolt in 1418. The Chinese fortified towns with walls protected by large battalions, but Le Loi devised a strategy of evasion insurgency until he developed a new strategy and struck directly, defeating the Chinese. Le Loi then expelled the Chinese and established the Le Dynasty, which lasted until 1772.[11] The Le Dynasty achieved considerable reform in the administration of the country, setting up examination systems for the civil service and developing agriculture, trade, and other economic activities.[12]

During the Le Dynasty, Vietnam expanded to take control of the Champa Kingdom, Gia Dinh (Saigon), and the Mekong Delta from

Cambodia. Vietnam annexed central and southern Vietnam from the Chams by 1735. The encroachment by the Vietnamese against the Khmer continued between 1705 and 1735, by which time the Vietnamese had established control of the Lower Mekong towns of contemporary Ha Tien, Rach Gia, Camau, and the large island of Phu Quoc, thus achieving the borders of contemporary Vietnam.[13]

During the second half of the eighteenth century, the introduction of a Vietnamese writing script—the *nom*—as an alternative to Chinese characters produced a vibrant culture that emphasized literature. This new script allowed Vietnam to distance itself culturally from China and reinforce its own native culture. But an atmosphere of discontent with corruption, Chinese intrigue, religious ferment, and renaissance of Vietnamese traditions led to the Tay Son Rebellion. The rebellion broke out in 1772 when merchant and peasant leaders appealed to peasants and seized control of the entirety of Vietnam within a few years. The rebels introduced an equitable tax system and agrarian land reform that gave the land from feudal lords to peasants. The Tay Son Rebellion also wiped out the commercial Chinese classes in Gia Dinh, killing tens of thousands of ethnic Chinese.[14]

Wearying of emerging Tay Son corruption by 1797, another great Vietnamese leader, Gia Long, founded the Nguyen Dynasty in 1802, which, in effect, remained the predominant Vietnamese leadership until Emperor Bao Dai abdicated to Ho Chi Minh in 1945. Gia Long was a particularly colorful and cruel ruler. When "his soldiers exhumed the bones of a deceased Tay Son leader, Gia Long urinated on the bones before the eyes of the Tay Son's son, whose limbs were then bound to four elephants and ripped apart."[15]

Despite this lurid report, Nguyen Phuc Anh (Gia Long's original name) played a decisive role in the Thirty-Year War against the Tay Son. From his base in Saigon he built perhaps the largest navy in Asia, which helped overwhelm the Tay Son. Nguyen Phuc Anh also directed the forces in this war that took place mostly in the northern part of southern Vietnam. He enlisted the Thai, Khmer, and Lao to fight with his forces.[16] Subsequently, he ousted the Thai from their dominant position in Cambodia. As the war ended, Gia Long established a new dynasty, which he located in Hue, where his predecessors in the seventeenth century had resided and been buried. Gia Long was a highly effective ruler, accomplishing, for example, the first uniform code of law written for Vietnam and the construction of the Vinh Te Canal, which today separates Vietnam from Cambodia. Literature also flourished.

China's Return to Relevance

As the modern era brought intense currents of independence movements and radical, competing social visions, in 1858 the French and nearby nations influenced Vietnam. As early as 1868, the Meiji Restoration in Japan inspired some political figures, including Vietnamese revolutionary Phan Boi Chau, who operated from Japan and southern China. The collapse of the Manchu Dynasty in China in 1912 brought Sun Yat-sen to authority in a republican form of government in China. This dramatic event happened at a time when Vietnamese intellectuals and politicians were looking to Asia and elsewhere for new models of anticolonial resistance and reform. Others, including Ho Chi Minh, looked to Sun Yat-sen's experience as a leader against the Manchu Dynasty, as the "Father" of modern China, and the first president of the Republic of China as a model.[17]

China's role in East Asia represented a threat to Vietnam from its birth as a nation to the present day. While borrowing its system of governance, education, and writing initially, Vietnam has felt the threat of occupation and domination by its immense northern neighbor. Vietnam likewise has striven to preserve its unique culture—not easy, as the Han persistently expanded their territory and influence into the far reaches of much of the region.

The encroachment by China and the resulting armed struggle became the defining motif of Vietnamese history—even before the modern struggles against France and the United States. To outsiders, Ho Chi Minh is the iconic symbol of Vietnamese national resistance, but most Vietnamese consider the Trung sisters—Ngo Quyen, Ly Thai To, Tran Hung Dao, Le Loi, Le Thanh Tong, and Gia Lam—to be the classic resistance heroes, all of whom fought against the Chinese existential threat. Vietnam struggled to establish its independence from China for more than a thousand years.[18]

So deeply rooted in its history and popular imagination is Vietnamese resistance to China, in my view, Vietnamese policy will certainly strive to maintain independence from China. The Vietnamese are not likely surrogates for China.

Reflecting on this history, I witnessed the exuberant celebrations of the one-thousandth anniversary of Hanoi on October 10, 2010. As I took a taxi into Hanoi from Noi Bai Airport, the driver told me that because of the throngs of Vietnamese celebrating, cars could not enter the inner city and I would have to walk from the outskirts of Hanoi to the Metropole Hotel in the city's center. This did not happen, but for the three days of my visit, automobile traffic was almost impossible because of the thousands of young Vietnamese with painted faces joyously marching and celebrating in the streets, jubilantly saluting the independence of Vietnam.

2

The Impact of French Colonialism on Vietnam

The French were not the first European traders and colonialists to arrive in Asia; Marco Polo returned with tales of "Burmese temples covered with gold a full finger thick" and Indian shores whose "sands sparkled and glittered with gems and precious ores." However, the prime treasures for the European masses were pepper, nutmeg, clove, and other spices essential to preserving food, not the silk and gems longed for by French elites.[1]

Coupled with spices, religion was the other impelling force that led Europeans to Asia via the Silk Road and sea. Europe was in the late phases of pushing Muslims out of Iberia after Islam's occupation of Spain and Portugal for seven centuries. At the same time, Europeans sought to overcome the Muslim monopoly on lucrative Eastern trade routes and outflank Islam in East Asia by sailing around Africa.

The dynamic city-state of Venice would lead the way in the late fourteenth century, but the Portuguese left the strongest European mark on Asia in the first centuries of the Age of Exploration. Prince Henry the Navigator received "exclusive franchise" in Asia from the Pope to "bring under submission the pagans of the countries not yet inflicted with the plague of Islam and give them knowledge of the name of Christ." Columbus's perceived discovery of America led to the Vatican-brokered Treaty of Tordesillas in 1494—allocating areas east of a line at Meridian 370, east of Cape Verde, to Portugal and areas west of the line to Castille, interpreted very roughly to mean Asia (and eventually Brazil) to Portugal and the Americas to Spain. No other European powers recognized this treaty.[2]

Vasco da Gama reinforced Portuguese claims by landing in India in 1498, forcing trade concessions from Siam and Burma, and even entering xenophobic Japan. The Portuguese built a base at Macao, China, and established in 1516 the first European outpost in Vietnam, just fifteen miles south of Tourane (Danang), called Faifo by the Portuguese explorer Antonio da Faria. Vietnam offered fewer gems or spices than other Asian markets, but the new age of European trade with Asia brought inevitable contact.

Vietnamese emperors pursued often-contradictory policies toward the European missionaries. They welcomed the missionaries' technical advice and connections to European suppliers of weapons and merchandise but usually abhorred their efforts to convert Vietnamese to Catholicism, in part because it lessened their dependence upon the Confucian system and the emperor.

A young French Jesuit priest, Alexandre de Rhodes, arrived in the seventeenth century under Portuguese auspices and mastered Vietnamese in six months.[3] He perfected the simplified *quoc ngu*, which transcribed Vietnamese into the Roman alphabet, making the language more accessible to Europeans. Although a hero today, Rhodes was feared by the emperors because of his effectiveness in promulgating Christianity. In 1664, four years after Rhodes's death, the Vatican agreed to support his earlier proposal for spreading Christianity in Asia. As a result, the French government and business community agreed to support the spread of Christianity and trade in Asia by establishing the *Société de l'Extrême Orient* (Society of the Far East).

Despite the establishment of a bridgehead company to promote French commercial interests and Christianity in Vietnam, the French government vacillated for two-hundred years in its attitude toward Vietnam, in part because of the financial cost of supporting its efforts.

In 1802, after defeating the Tay Son rulers, Nguyen Phuc Anh crowned himself Emperor Gia Long. Gia Long's takeover marked a hiatus in European attempts to colonize Vietnam, and Gia Long, as noted above, showed no mercy to the defeated Tay Son leaders.[4]

The Opium War of 1840 and Great Britain's efforts to establish a major commercial presence in China renewed French interest in pursuing a stronger presence in Asia and Vietnam, since Great

Britain already dominated India, Singapore, Malaya, Burma, and Dutch-controlled Indonesia. France hoped to participate in the scramble for Asian colonies, and the militant Catholic clergy renewed hopes of promoting Christianity.

In the face of increasing aggression from industrialized powers, Gia Long's son, Emperor Minh Mang, and the latter's son and successor, Trieu Tri, vacillated between negotiations, often taking a very hard line toward European negotiations and in response to Christian proselytizing.[5]

Several military incidents involving French naval vessels, and the succession of Emperor Tu Duc to the throne in 1847, led to increased repression and an edict to kill Christian missionaries on the spot. Tu Duc concluded that, to preserve Vietnam's security, he must defend the feudal system, and he undertook a fierce campaign to eliminate Christians. The colonial movement received a boost in 1852 when Louis Napoleon, with the support of the Church, seized power in France by a *coup d'état*, declaring himself emperor of France. Napoleon, encouraged by his devoutly Catholic wife, who lobbied him for missionaries in Asia and Africa, readily agreed.[6]

French Colonialism Arrives

In 1858, France attacked the city of Tourane (now Danang) with gunboats, claiming a right to seize Vietnamese territory under a 1787 treaty.[7]

In 1861 an expedition of 2,000 men, led by Admiral Leonard Victor Joseph Charner, succeeded in overrunning and claiming Gia Dinh, the province around and including Saigon. A year later Emperor Tu Duc, after unsuccessfully attempting to persuade President Abraham Lincoln to help save Vietnam, ceded Gia Dinh and three surrounding provinces to the French in 1862 by the Treaty of Saigon. After the capitulation to the French, Emperor Tu Duc lost credibility with his subjects, and protracted resistance to the French presence erupted.[8]

Between 1862 and 1874, Vietnamese efforts to negotiate the departure of the French naval forces failed, and the French continued to occupy Gia Dinh and annexed the rest of the plain to create the colony of Cochinchina.[9]

With his throne crumbling, Tu Duc then offered a French protectorate containing all six provinces of Cochinchina, full French control of Saigon, trade privileges with Vietnam, and an annual tribute. Ignoring Emperor Napoleon II's instructions to end expansion,
French commanders in Gia Dinh occupied Cambodia and seized
the remaining three provinces of southern Vietnam, a *fait accompli*
that completed French rule over Cambodia and Cochinchina.[10]

During this period, the Taiping Rebellion raged across southern
China before being brutally crushed, sending thousands of armed
Taiping insurgents to seek refuge in northern Vietnam. France
feared the United Kingdom, Germany, or the United States would
make a play to seize Tonkin amid the chaos, thus losing their toe-
hold in Asia. A French gunrunner, Jean Depuis, utilizing the pretext
that salt-monopoly officials were thwarting his honest, commercial
activities, seized control of Hanoi, the capital of Tonkin. Without
Paris's consent, the French governor general of Cochinchina, Admiral Marie-Jules Dupré, sent forces to join Dupuis, and within a
month they had taken control of Hanoi, the port of Haiphong, and
the land in-between.

Emperor Tu Duc in Hue sued for peace and negotiated the
Treaty of 1874 that gave France undisputed control of Cochinchina, implicitly recognized a French protectorate over Tonkin, a loose
protectorate over the monarchy of Hue, gave French access to the
Red River for commerce, and allowed for joint Franco-Vietnamese
custom stations in Hanoi, Haiphong, and Qui Nhon. Emperor Tu
Duc's domain had shrunk to garrisoned administrative centers,
primarily in Hanoi, Son Tay, Bac Ninh, Hai Duong, Hon Gai, Nam
Dinh, and Ninh Binh.[11]

At Tu Duc's death in 1883, French gunboats appeared at the
Imperial City of Hue. The French demanded and received formal
recognition of a French protectorate over Tonkin and Annam, virtually all of Vietnam; Western nations stopped using the name
"Vietnam."

After Tu Duc's death, the Vietnamese monarchy deteriorated into factional strife, with regents unwilling to relinquish their
influence. Subsequently, various relatives of Tu Duc ascended,
were overthrown, and killed until a pliant younger brother of Tu
Duc was installed as Emperor Hiep Hoa. Within a month of his

installation, Hiep Hoa signed the Treaty of Harmand, which met all the French demands outlined for a protectorate over Hue, although Paris would never sign it. Two of the three regents then deposed Hiep Hoa, who was killed, and installed fourteen-year-old Kien Phuc. During a supposed moment of harmony after signing the Tientsin Accord in May 1884, the French ambassador to China, Jules Patenotre, visited Hue with a new treaty, the Patenotre Treaty, almost identical to the Harmand Treaty. In early June 1884, at the signing of the Patenotre Treaty, the gold and silver seal of investiture given to Hue by the Chinese Qing Dynasty was melted down to symbolically end the centuries of Vietnamese vassalage to Chinese dynasties.[12]

At the end of July, King Kien Phuc was likely poisoned, so the anti-French regent, who had regularly engaged in the murder of youthful Hue kings, placed a twelve-year-old half-brother of Kien Phuc, Ham Nghi, on the throne. France prepared to exercise its new authority under the Patenotre Treaty after the brief Franco-Russian war. An uprising against the French erupted and led to the installation by the French of the last surviving adopted nephew of Tu Duc, Dong Khanh, as king of Hue.

Enraged by the French maneuverings, the Vietnamese unleashed a wave of violence and killed an estimated forty- to fifty-thousand Vietnamese Christians. The French Army, debilitated by a cholera epidemic, could do little to protect the Christians. At the same time, the governor general in Saigon, seeking to enhance French authority in Cambodia, stirred up an anti-French riot among the Khmers. These events created strong disgust in Paris and the approval needed for continued action in Indochina was only narrowly passed.[13]

The French understood a new policy initiative was needed to sustain colonial policy in Indochina, and they selected Paul Bert, a scientist, professor of physiology, and staunch anticleric, to devise the new policies for Indochina. Pursuing Bert's idea, as the new governor general to Indochina in 1891, Jean Marie Antoine de Lanessan, believed "the only justifiable purpose of colonialism was to bring defenseless, out-of-date countries up to the highest possible level of administrative order and technical efficiency, working through existing structures of authority."[14]

De Lanessan understood that "the problem of pacifying the North was political as much as military. Operations must be conducted in close collaboration with efforts to build a civil administration." Two French military officers developed an "oil spot" approach to pacification by which military operations proceeded incrementally and no faster than the pace at which civil government could be realized. By 1896 pacification was completed.[15]

De Lanessan also seized Laos and Cambodia from Siam (Thailand). He sent troops to Laos and naval forces from the Gulf of Thailand to Bangkok to confront the Royal Siamese government. As a result, the Siamese ceded by treaty all provinces east of the Mekong to Laos. With a more stable society and budget, subsequent Governor General Paul Doumer undertook extensive infrastructural development throughout Indochina and, at the same time, pursued cultural and educational advancements. The framework for governing Indochina and fiscal stability he achieved endured. French dominance of Indochina ensued for the next seventy-plus years, ending definitively in July 1954.[16]

3

French Colonialism after 1900

By 1938 just 27,000 French officials dominated at least 18 million Vietnamese. Although Tonkin and Annam were protectorates of the Nguyen emperor, still holding court in Hue, the French wielded the real power. Only sixteen years later, 450,000 French forces could not avoid defeat at Dien Bien Phu at the hands of the highly motivated Vietnamese resistance movement. In the intervening years, hundreds of thousands of Vietnamese, seemingly passive French subjects, changed into pith-helmeted *bo doi* (foot solders) dedicated to driving out the French and establishing a strong, independent, and egalitarian Vietnam.[1]

This transformation did not occur overnight. For sixty years after the French occupation began, Vietnamese largely accepted French rule as the Darwinist result of the superiority of Western technology over a poor, weak Confucian society. Without external pressures, the Mandarins of the royal family, literate foreign-language experts, merchants, educated Catholics, or the French colonial administration might have undertaken internal reforms to try to bring Vietnam into the modern world without the trauma that occurred. Unfortunately, Western powers found strategic reasons to intervene—often violently.[2]

By 1897, armed resistance to the French ended. Governor-General Doumer introduced the system that was to dominate Vietnam, Laos, and Cambodia for the next forty years. The mercantilist system was hierarchical, with the French dominating the political and economic structures and Vietnamese given subservient positions under the strong authority of French officials. Education was expanded, with a few promising students sent to

France for higher education, and infrastructure was improved so as to promote exports to France. Security forces kept the Vietnamese under strict control, and the French continued to control financial resources. Under this system few Vietnamese earned or obtained any substantial wealth.[3]

The educated elite, trained in French schools, began assimilation, but questions began to arise. A consciousness began to emerge among second- and third-generation Vietnamese in the 1920s, reflecting a torrent of literary and other publications that brought Western thought into Vietnam. They raised profound questions about Vietnam's existential condition and the French occupation. Patriotism and anger emerged. International support stirred questions, but the Vietnamese themselves began to develop new, comprehensive intellectual frameworks for resistance. Vietnamese responses varied and led to the complicated political ambiance that characterized the 1920s in Vietnam.

Under these circumstances, the systemic changes became increasingly onerous. As described by David Marr in his excellent *Vietnamese Tradition on Trial, 1920–1945,* the French established a centralized and top-heavy administration and expanded the heavy tax and *corvée* labor system. They established a near monopoly status for French financial capital and product imports. They undertook construction of an impressive, although not necessarily financially viable, network of railroads, roads, and canals. Their French rulers rigorously and efficiently enforced the traditional obligations of taxes, labor, and military service. Unlike prior periods of repression, there was no unmonitored hinterland to which the disaffected could flee—the French had the capacity to control and coerce Vietnamese as no rulers of Indochina ever had before. Although rich, land-owning Vietnamese families emerged in the south, the French paid little attention to their grievances, conciliation, compromise, or sharing power with Vietnamese.[4]

Vietnamese who collaborated with the French could achieve some degree of wealth and self-esteem but little authority. They also could ignore the anger felt by the rest of the population and the lack of ethics in French colonial society.

The French policy of granting large land concessions to French companies and Vietnamese collaborators, along with French concepts of private property and individual legal responsibility, introduced fundamental changes to village economic and social life. There was a sustained movement toward concentrated wealth and the loss of traditional land for farming driven by the French officials and their Vietnamese collaborators, leading to a growing number of landless, disaffected poor.

The colonial power summarily evicted peasant families who had spent a generation or more clearing and tilling land. Small-business owners were frequently outmaneuvered by means of usurious loans, cadastral manipulations, seizure for back taxes, and duplicitous officials. There was no redress.

The French also seriously undermined the traditional village system. Communal lands that had supported social welfare institutions such as schools and temples increasingly became the private property of well-placed Vietnamese families. The selection of local notables, religious festivals, weddings, funerals, and other traditional ceremonies became subject to the discretion of the wealthy.[5]

The gap between the poor and wealthy widened into a chasm. Frequently, local wealthy moved away and served as absentee landlords to the impoverished locals who had no means of appealing. By 1937, absentee landlords, entrepreneurs, and a few high officials—the indigenous bourgeoisie—totaled 10,500 families, or just 0.5 percent of the population.[6] Thus, while the French colonial period brought technological and institutional changes that enriched a collaborative elite, much of the population benefited little from the changes.[7]

Finally, the introduction of a cash economy brought unanticipated changes. An impersonal commercial exchange system replaced traditional, multiple, and personal forms of interaction. Cash payment of taxes replaced in-kind contributions. Marketing, stamps, consumer goods, transit, entrepôt, navigation, and other indirect taxes replaced traditional exchanges. The government also controlled and enforced salt and liquor taxes.[8]

Peasants bartered and traded for a living and, although they might have considered themselves subsistence farmers, trading for what few nonfood items they might need, taxes and cash payments drew them into the harsh and alien world of the money economy.

The primary objective of the French was to develop a modern

export sector, focusing originally on rice and mining, later rubber, then ultimately coffee and tea plantations. A flood of cheap French imports wiped out the traditional artisan producers of diverse domestic goods. A clear majority of Vietnamese found that the capital and contacts required for business were unattainable.[9]

On top of other vexations, after the outbreak of the First World War in 1914, the French forced the Vietnamese to fight the Huns in Europe. The government encouraged Vietnamese to buy war bonds, which became yet another onerous tax.

The liberal, French governor-general, Albert Sarraut (1911–14 and 1916–19), spun all these changes into a vision of Franco-Vietnamese collaboration, including "Liberty, Equality, and Fraternity" for good measure. France, Sarraut said, was acting as the "elder brother" in transmitting all the advantages of modern civilization (*mission civilisatrice*). At some unspecified point in the future he held out the possibility of native self-rule. This charitable attitude, however, came from a weakened French government offering concessions during a wartime crisis. After the defeat of Germany, the French government quickly returned to a harder line in the administration of Indochina. As France recovered from the war, huge investment flowed into Indochina—in the 1920s, three billion francs, or close to 60 percent of the total since French arrival, was invested in Indochina to expand export capabilities. The colonial government conscripted huge numbers of Vietnamese to establish rubber plantations in the south. Conditions were horrible: Malaria, contaminated and insufficient food and water, long hours, low wages, and severe punishment were common.[10]

Conditions for miners were equally harsh. At the Hong Gay coal pits northeast of Hanoi, intense profit-making dictated dirt-cheap labor, company stores, twelve- to fourteen-hour shifts, physical brutality, and few safety precautions.

Coffee and tea plantations created in the south had similar conditions. Land was also cleared to expand rice production and exports.[11]

The Great Depression hit Indochina hard as the bottom fell out of the rice and rubber markets. By 1931 landowners were defaulting on loans and companies were going bankrupt, leading to the sacking of thousands of Vietnamese tenants, agricultural laborers, plantation hands, miners, and factory workers. While French officials leaned on the government for assistance, the indigenous laborers struggled without any official safety net. Only in 1936 did the economy begin to improve.[12]

Accelerating earlier trends, hundreds of thousands more subsistence farmers lost their land or were hanging on to scraps of land that were too small for subsistence and insufficient to support families. Poor farmers, tenants, and agricultural laborers made up 70 percent of the population in the late Thirties.

During the Thirties, Vietnamese political forces began to use conditions for recruitment that opened the path to success. For example, the Indochinese Communist Party (ICP) promoted mutual-aid societies among subsistence farmers. The Communist Party recruited some farmers, while others joined the Vietminh in the early Forties during the First Indochina War. Subsistence farmers comprised the bulk of the Communist Party cadres.

By the late Thirties, between 93 and 95 percent of all Vietnamese still lived in rural areas, but their village lives had changed drastically.[13]

In 1940, after Nazi Germany occupied France, the Vichy government in Indochina subordinated Indochina to the Japanese. However, the Japanese left administration in the hands of the French, so conditions did not change.

In the winter of 1944–45, a tragic but avoidable dislocation of rice stocks led to mass famine and death. Neither the French nor the Japanese sent the hundreds of tons of rice, which remained in storehouses in the south and could have averted starvation in the north, where an estimated one- to two-million Vietnamese starved to death.[14] The Japanese shipped the rice to China and elsewhere to feed their army. This terrible famine contributed directly to political disaffection just before the end of the Second World War.[15]

Education

While the French brought investment into export-oriented infrastructure such as railways and ports, their investment in social infrastructure was minimal, particularly in education. French officials received repeated requests by Vietnamese to improve the education system but did little to improve conditions.[16]

Almost 90 percent of all children who entered first grade between 1920 and 1938 did not get beyond the third grade. Poverty, distance to walk to school, and stiff exams kept these numbers down.

Six percent of all students were in the fourth to sixth grades, but this fell to 0.3 percent in the seventh grade. From 1920 to 1938 total enrollment increased from 126,000 to about 287,000, yet at no point were more than 10 percent of school-age children in school. In the upper primary schools (years seven to ten), enrollment increased from 2,430 in 1920 to 22,552 in 1938. In 1923 only 83 Vietnamese enrolled in secondary schools (ages 11 to 13), and in 1939 there were still only 465 Vietnamese enrolled. Perhaps this same number of Vietnamese attended the private French schools, or *lycées*, meaning a total of only 900 in all secondary schools and *lycées*.

The French established in 1902 the University of Indochina, called the University of Hanoi, featuring technical, medical, and vocational training. By 1937 there were 631 Vietnamese students enrolled. By 1944 there were 1,209 students studying at the University of Hanoi–681 from the North, 216 from central Vietnam, and 212 from the South.

A prime reason for the upgrading of the University of Hanoi in the 1930s was the evident radicalization of the students who studied abroad, the most popular destination being Paris, followed by Japan, or Canton, China, where Ho Chi Minh instituted classes at one point. French authorities hoped that keeping most students in Vietnam would avoid the contamination of foreign ideas. Disturbed by this radicalization from study in France, especially on the Left Bank in Paris, France ended Vietnamese study in France in 1930.[17]

The Role of the Intelligentsia

In the first half of the twentieth century, Vietnam produced three generations of intellectuals. The scholar gentry, or intellectuals, of the turn of the century understood that Vietnam was being transformed whether they liked it or not. They tried desperately to come to terms with and gain from the changed environment.

By the end of World War I, these intellectuals had not been able to formulate a comprehensive new worldview or a realistic plan of action. Even the most sophisticated scholar-gentry remained suspended between Neo-Confucian classics, about which they had serious doubts, and the ideas of Montesquieu, Rousseau, Adam Smith, and Herbert Spencer, which they vaguely assumed would be more pertinent to Vietnam's future. Nonetheless, as Stanley Karnow wrote, "they were able to convey to the next generation a sense of historical crisis, a profound respect for knowledge, a commitment to action, and faith in the perfectibility of humankind."[18]

The intellectuals who emerged in the 1920s faced many of the same problems as their predecessor scholar-gentry, but the social and economic context had changed significantly, and they sought different intellectual sources to cope with the change.

Despite being intellectuals, they were not alien to the villages, small farmers, and handicraft workers, but were very much a product of the colonial system, with its big landlords, miners, and plantation workers. The young intelligentsia frequently graduated from French and French-Vietnamese schools and sought employment as clerks, interpreters, primary-school teachers, or journalists—a highly aware, if not wealthy, *petite bourgeoisie*.[19]

Since career opportunities were sharply circumscribed even for the few lucky enough to receive an education, there was widespread disenchantment and unrest. However, many Vietnamese, even those opposed to the French regime, compromised their ideals for the sake of expediency. Many joined the French administration or worked for French economic institutions—as colonial police, overseers for landlords, mine supervisors, and plantation administrators—despite their opposition to the French. Thus, a large portion of the backbone of the colonial regime simmered with discontent, leading to decay and weakening of the French system once unrest broke out in the wake of the Second World War.[20]

Whether or not the colonial regime absorbed the young intellectuals, the growing class of Vietnamese intellectuals was only vaguely familiar with Neo-Confucianism but highly impatient to assimilate learning from Europe in a relatively short time. Even though their parents believed in ghosts, arranged marriages, social harmony, and still had ties with rural Vietnam, the young, educated

Vietnamese were increasingly urban and Westernized. They were familiar through their studies "with cameras, germs, galaxies, free love, class struggle, and evolution" and encountered these things and ideas every day from living in an urban environment.[21]

Their parents urged a practical approach to urban life, encouraging them to ignore the colonial injustices, study hard for exams, and get a good job thereafter. This only compounded the young intellectuals' frustration. They wanted to understand contradictions and to construct a new consciousness for themselves and the nation. Many elders judged the youths' enthusiasm for the search for new meaning and their aggressive curiosity to be repulsive, but the changes occurring also made them feel impotent to reassert authority over the youths. Consequently, young intellectuals seized the lead.[22]

Traditionally, Vietnamese elites regarded foreigners, including Europeans, as barbarians. Nonetheless, Vietnamese began to have difficulty in distinguishing universal insights in the European and Asian experiences. Vietnamese had accepted their model of reality well into the twentieth century, but as Europeans exerted themselves technologically, economically, culturally, and intellectually across the world, this forced Vietnamese to acknowledge that the "Eastern spirit" no longer had justifiable claim to universality. At the other extreme, many participants in the French colonial schools began to believe that, in fact, Europeans were the civilized ones and Asians barbarians. The French did not accept as equals those who adopted French customs, and all young, urban Vietnamese did so to a certain degree. Nor were they emulated by the mass of Vietnamese. Thus, they were alienated by both sides and struggled to find ideologies to suit their circumstances.

The traditional fallback of Confucianism was no longer an option. With China disintegrating before their eyes, Japan emulating the West to beat the Europeans at their own game, and the Vietnamese emperor accepting a salary from the French government, Neo-Confucianism appeared absurd. Buddhism and Taoism still offered inner peace, but knowledge of the two religions was not deep or broad. At the same time, Europeans had just brutally torn the world apart in the First World War, an event that made a lot of colonial peoples question the ultimate desirability of the Western model.[23]

During the 1920s, Vietnamese began to look beyond the East-West paradigm for ideas that would resolve their emotional and intellectual turmoil. They studied the social revolution underway in China, political turmoil in postwar Europe, revolutionary developments in Russia, and nonviolent resistance in India as potential models. Vietnamese writers began to look at historical processes as a central explanation of reality, wrestled with the question of Vietnam's place in the universal historical process, and sought to determine how to improve Vietnam's role therein.[24]

Vietnamese thinkers concluded that to win independence and national dignity it was not sufficient to simply exhort people to be patriotic, unite, and help save the country. Other peoples around the world engaged in similar processes and loved their homelands as much as the Vietnamese. There were similar patterns for resisting foreign domination, yet in the interwar years, the pinnacle of European colonialism, nearly every non-Western nationality had been crushed and thoroughly absorbed into an empire. There were not yet many success stories for national resistance—only inspiring but futile failures. Many Vietnamese thinkers concluded that knowledge and technology had no moral roots.

They soon realized they must relate their new knowledge and techniques to Vietnam itself, and to do this they needed to know much more about Vietnam. This was difficult in the repressive colonialist environment, but several writers attempted to learn, particularly in the 1930s.

Some Vietnamese began to write about the lives of Vietnamese functionaries, landlords, intellectuals, shopkeepers, and peasants in a realist style not previously attempted in Vietnam. By the late 1930s, critics and writers increasingly expanded their focus on the lives of poor peasants, tenants, proletarians, beggars, and prostitutes. Collectively, these writings built and reflected an indictment of both traditional Vietnamese society and the colonial system.[25]

Although these new works were highly critical of modern Vietnamese society at large, many increasingly discovered and celebrated the underlying strength and wisdom among the Vietnamese masses. These Vietnamese focused on the village, whether for preserving the authentic communal character, suggesting institutional reform, or convincing the peasants to seize control of their destiny.[26]

These insights occurred at momentous political times: the collapse of the Popular Front in France (1939), the formation of the Japanese-Vichy alliance (1940), and the formation of the communist-led Vietminh in Vietnam (1941). Combining a new appreciation of both the good and bad aspects of Vietnamese society with a dramatically changing political environment gave intellectuals hope and jump-started a moribund opposition movement.[27]

4

The Emergence of Political Radicalism in Vietnam

What transpired in the Vietnamese psyche during these complicated years of the 1920s that tipped Vietnam toward radicalism? What led Vietnam, a traditional, rural Asian nation to turn toward Marxism? To many, Vietnamese radicalism arrived via the Soviet Union and China. These movements had a profound influence on Vietnam's political development, but they represent only part of the story. The Vietnamese increasingly developed a deep dissatisfaction with both their own society and French versions of European society and were eager for a "third way"—one that would confer both national independence and revitalization on Vietnam.

The Vietnamese were by no means united on what the third way should be or if there should even be one. Various Vietnamese sects or organizations, such as the Cao Dai and Hoa Hao religious sects, Catholic militias, and even the Binh Xuyen criminal elements, developed tenuous ties with Emperor Bao Dai and offered various proposals. Some of these elements even achieved a degree of success in struggling against the National Liberation Front (NLF), a communist organization set up in 1960. Communist movements typically established such front organizations to attract support, disguising the communist background of the front. The NLF had little influence until it was resurrected by Ho Chi Minh in 1940 as the Vietnam Independence League (Vietminh), his vehicle for achieving power. However, many Vietnamese, though by no means all, increasingly viewed more radical ideas, including Marxism, as the solution.

Vietnamese radicalism stemmed from foreign conquest and influences. Conquest was not novel for Vietnam; a 2,000-year struggle with China had forged the people, nation, and culture of Vietnam. Vietnam had borrowed liberally from China's political, social, and cultural institutions and values. But the West posed an altogether different challenge. At first, the Confucian Mandarins of Vietnam tried to preserve the social and political order they had inherited, but eventually realized they would not restore national integrity and strength through force of arms and Confucian principles.[1]

Harvard Professor Hue-Tam Ho Tai, in a seminal work on the role of radicalism (as opposed to simply communism), brilliantly describes setting the stage in the 1920s for profound intellectual and political turmoil in Vietnam. In her compelling book, *Radicalism and the Origins of the Vietnamese Revolution*, Dr. Ho Tai explores the "the rhetoric of [the French-created] *mission civilisatrice* and the realities of colonial life: in the yawning gap between the two lay the breeding ground of radicalism and revolution" in Vietnam. Many Vietnamese intellectuals were attracted to Social Darwinism, which suggested that ideals of peace and harmony could not handle effectively the West's emphasis on struggle and competition. While rising powers in the West might see Darwinism as a spur to conquer new territories, some Eastern intellectuals saw it as evidence of the decline and irrelevance of Eastern societies. The Vietnamese literati imagined Vietnam as a small, weak society cannibalized by the stronger and fitter France.[2]

New ideas and information compounded the profound change colonialism had brought to the political, economic, and social environment of Vietnam. This undermined the power of Confucian orthodoxy and the moral authority of traditional values.

Intellectuals sought information about what was occurring in the rest of the world as they attempted to move beyond the simplistic divide between East and West. Increasingly Vietnamese began to conclude there were no qualitative differences between Vietnamese and Europeans. National particularities were superficial. Because of this perception, rather than explore philosophical and cultural systems, Vietnamese intellectuals began to explore whether there were historical processes that assumed increasing importance as central elements in determining reality.[3]

Traditional revolutionary Vietnamese organizations, like the Nationalist Vietnam Quoc Dan Dang (VNQDD), which had previously led the progressive movement, now offered no conceptual framework for historical development and lost credibility.[4]

An additional source of radicalism was the increasing influence of anarchism in Vietnam derived from student and intellectual contacts in France, China, and Japan. Anarchism, both in its collective and individualist strains, had been introduced into Vietnamese politics in the 1890s but enjoyed its greatest influence in the 1920s. "Unlike Social Darwinism, anarchism was preoccupied not with survival and competition but with freedom and the relationship between the individual and society. Anarchism inspired many acts of violence, but it was also responsible for the humanistic tone in the revolutionary discourse [in Vietnam] of the 1920s."[5]

Marxist-Leninism introduced yet another branch of thinking. "Whereas radicals conceived of independence as arising organically from their struggle toward self-emancipation, Marxists established a new symmetry between national liberation and pursuit of social justice along class lines."[6]

To many, especially the young, "revolution came to seem the only possible solution to the existential predicament that bound their personal concerns to those of the nation."[7]

Revolutionary Organizations in Vietnam

In this context of intellectual and political turmoil, the earliest reformist political organization in Vietnam following colonialization emerged in the 1880s as the "Aid the King Movement" (*Can Vuong*). The movement mounted an indirect attack on the puppet ruler under French aegis. Since it was peripheral in focus and did not come to grips with the real problems of feudalism and colonialism Vietnam faced, the movement withered quickly.[8]

Of more lasting importance were the intellectuals Phan Boi Chau and Phan Chu Trinh, who were leaders of the major movements that emerged later in the early twentieth century.[9]

Phan Boi Chau, born in 1867 in Nghe An Province (a hotbed of radicalism that would produce numerous radicals, including Ho Chi Minh), was a principal leader of the Reform Movement. Chau advocated foreign learning to strengthen oneself and encouraged use of the romanized script developed by French missionaries in the seventeenth century, rather than Chinese characters, to bridge the gap between elite scholars and the masses. The romanized script also reduced the importance of classical learning and, therefore, the importance of the Confucian tradition. Chau was an early example of a Vietnamese intellectual who embraced the liberal Western philosophies of thinkers such as Rousseau, Montesquieu, Mazzini, and Cavour, while also drawing inspiration from Chinese reformers such as intellectuals Liang Chi-chao and Kang Yu-wei.[10]

Chau, not unlike other contemporary nationalist figures, such as the African American Booker T. Washington or the Indian Jawaharlal Nehru, believed assimilation and education were the best means for long-term liberation. To address this goal, Chau launched the Eastern Travel Movement in 1905 to enable Vietnamese students to go to China and Japan to study Eastern and Western ideas—with the aim of eventually overthrowing French rule. In his early days he did not oppose violence to promote political change, but his main weapon was the building of political awareness and confidence through modern, liberal Western education.[11]

Phan Boi Chau inspired the traditional patriotic parties, notably the VNQDD, in the 1920s. Elitist patriots, including students, older literati, rural notables, landlords, interpreters, government office clerks, and military men who tended to assume all Vietnamese were patriots, constituted his supporters.[12]

Phan Chu Trinh, from the Quang Nam Province of central Vietnam, developed a more cultural approach. Trinh advocated a more gradualist effort toward change, opting to "defer independence until . . . the Vietnamese had undergone a thorough cultural and social transformation." Trinh admired French culture and political institutions. He accepted the notion of French tutelage before independence. Trinh tended to accept the judgment of relatively liberal French figures, such as Governor-General Albert Pierre Sarraut, who served from 1912 to 1914 and 1917 to 1919. Sarraut, a popular and liberal deputy in France, argued that the Vietnamese were not ready for independence, but after a period of French rule, the Vietnamese could achieve the goal of self-government. Phan Chu Trinh would have countered that the march toward independence should be defined and attainable in a shorter period than even French liberals, such as Sarraut, contemplated. In contrast, Phan Boi Chau sought and fought for independence as an immediate goal.[13]

These two leaders, still revered today, framed early debate. Trinh was a true reformer through French tutelage and education, and Chau was the pioneer of revolution.

Southern Vietnam emerged as the primary center of revitalization and resistance, where by the turn of the century they had already adopted the romanized script. Reformers in the south were therefore able to spread their ideas to a wider audience. As a matter of patriotism, southerners also pursued commerce, both to compete with Chinese and French merchants and as a platform through which to support reformist ideas. "They opened rice mills, fish-sauce plants, hotels, restaurants, serving shops, and grocery stores" to spread new ideas. This contrasted with central and north Vietnam, where commerce was regarded as demeaning—beneath the dignity of an intellectual. The more international, prosperous, and progressive southerners also encouraged the young to study in Japan and China, as well as France.[14]

Southerners also adopted cultural changes to reflect their more progressive orientation. In Vietnamese tradition, long hair was the gift of their fathers and something to be preserved. Many southerners began to keep their hair short, both as a hygienic measure, but also to distance themselves from patriarchal customs. Familial relationships began to reflect changing political views, but few parents initially realized the depth of their children's frustration over receiving an inferior education that led to menial positions in the colonial administration. Despite fine titles, most of their work was meaningless. Paradoxically, the graduates of the most prestigious schools were the most alienated because they experienced broader thinking, more ideas, and more analytical training.[15]

The introduction of metal currency in 1908 sparked a wave of anti-tax protests and led to a crackdown on those linked to reform. France jailed Phan Chu Trinh on Con Son Island. Phan Boi Chau escaped to Japan, but eventually the French Sureté stopped the movement of students to Japan and had Chau deported from Japan. Therefore, the Reform Movement was temporarily repressed as a political force, but the cultural transformation continued.[16]

French officials supported the crackdown, but the French Government in Paris thought they needed to reform the colonial system. As noted above, Paris had sent as the new Governor-General Albert Sarraut. France instructed Sarraut, and he heartily agreed, "to streamline the relationship between the Governor-General of Indochina and its five constituent states (Cochinchina, Annam, Tonkin, Laos, and Cambodia) as a precondition to giving more autonomy to Indochina." They also instructed Sarraut "to enlarge the native representation in various legislative and advisory bodies, revise procedures for naturalization, and introduce educational reforms."[17]

However, even as Sarraut and the French undertook these progressive reforms, resistance to their rule steadily grew. Not surprisingly, the taste of a slightly improved role whetted Vietnamese appetites for more autonomy. After the overthrow of the Manchu dynasty in China in 1911, "Phan Boi Chau created the League for the Restoration of Vietnam (Viet Nam Quang Phuc Hoi) among Vietnamese expatriates in southern China."[18] Although Chau advocated an overthrow of the French and the establishment of a Republic of Vietnam, his southern supporters who provided the money insisted on a monarchical government led by a descendent of the Nguyen Dynasty, Prince Cuong De. Despite these anomalies, the League for the Restoration of Vietnam set up a provisional revolutionary government in 1912 and named Chau prime minister.[19]

Though operating from China, the League for the Restoration of Vietnam brought direct, physical resistance back to Indochina after a decade of relative calm. Chau masterminded a series of terrorist incidents in Vietnam to give the league visibility. Two French army officers in Hanoi and the Vietnamese governor of Thai Binh Province were killed in 1913. At the same time, secret societies staged attacks on the French police headquarters in Saigon.[20]

As protests grew, Sarraut conceded that the French had established control over the Vietnamese "against their will, and through much violence," and therefore were not legitimate in the long term. However, he contended the issue was whether or not the Vietnamese were capable of self-rule, and he believed that they were not. Like many Frenchmen, Sarraut concluded that Vietnamese "customs, institutions, level of education, their mentality put them in the category of backward people who would profit from the firm guidance of a Western nation."[21]

Sarraut took pride in advocating this period of tutelage. France would bestow independence on Vietnam after it accomplished this *mission civilisatrice.* One could interpret this, logically, to mean "the Vietnamese would not be fully mature" or capable of running their own affairs "until they had become exactly like the French in their thinking, their customs, and their institutions."[22]

During the First World War, forced recruitment of thousands of peasants and workers resulted in widespread protest and riots in Cochinchina, led by these same secret societies, such as Chau's Restoration League. A plot against the French garrison was uncovered. Phan Boi Chau was thought to be behind the plot, as was the 16-year-old emperor, Duy Tan, whom the French summarily replaced with the more reliable Khai Dan. French administrators and conservatives "clamored for blood. Military tribunals were convened . . . . Thirty-eight men were publicly executed" by French authorities in Cochinchina, and another 1,000 detained.[23]

Because of the outcry from officials over growing unrest, Sarraut was unable to further expand his reforms. He did, however, abolish Confucian exams in 1919 and tried to reform the education system. He also established two premier secondary schools in Hue—the Imperial College for boys and the Dong Khanh School for girls. Each village in Vietnam was ordered to establish a new school at its own expense. Nonetheless, even after these reforms, only about 10 percent of school-aged children attended school.[24]

Before departing his post in 1919, Sarraut gave a rousing farewell speech at the Van Mieu Confucian Temple of Literature, in which he promised to continue "fighting for their interests in his new position [as Minister of Colonies] in the 'mother country.' " He promised: "A Father does not abandon his children." But Sarraut's replacement, Martial Merlin, reversed many of his reforms.[25]

The French arrested Phan Boi Chau and tried him in 1925 for a history of revolutionary activities. In the closely watched trial, Chau was spared the death penalty but sentenced to life in prison. Another relatively liberal governor-general, Alexandre Varenne (1925–28), commuted Phan Boi Chau's sentence and left him under house arrest. Nonetheless, Chau remained an object of security concern to the French *Sureté.*[26]

Phan Chu Trinh's untimely death in 1926 unleashed two years of unrest, which would have been much more appropriate following the death of Phan Boi Chau than Trinh. Unrest and dissension was growing steadily, and dissenters seized on Trinh's death to reflect their dissatisfaction. Waves of strikes hit businesses, factories, and the Banque d'Indochine.[27]

The VNQDD appointed a young Vietnamese, Nguyen Thai Hoc, chairman of the group for six months in December 1927; the party swerved to the left during his chairmanship, advocating violence to overthrow the French administration. At the same time, the more revolutionary Youth *(Thanh Nien)* of Ho Chi Minh and New Vietnam *(Tan Viet)* merged to form the Vietnamese Communist Party that subsequently became the ICP in 1930. Nguyen Thai Hoc was arrested and executed at 28 years old after being implicated in a mutiny in the Yen Bai Prison and assorted terrorist actions in February 1930.[28]

Depression and Marxism in the 1930s

The Great Depression in 1929, the peasant revolts in Vietnam in 1930–31, and the absence of satisfactory alternative theories pushed activists, both in Ho Chi Minh's Youth League and the VNQDD, toward a Marxist frame of reference. Hue-Tam Ho Tai develops an interesting analysis of the reorientation of the VNQDD toward a Marxist interpretation of historical change. She writes, "The introduction ... of a class-based social analysis outlined a drastic intellectual reorientation. ... This reorientation involved a rethinking of the role of the revolutionary party (and of the individual within it) and of the social processes that give rise to revolution. It substituted the masses for the individual, class for generation, society for family, and economics for culture." It also represented a radical new approach in political analysis.[29]

The context of this shift was quite important. By the end of the 1930s, Marxist-Leninism's emergence in Vietnamese revolutionary thinking coincided with the collapse of the United Front in China and the struggle between the Nationalists and the Communists in China. At the same time, the Moscow-based Comintern, originally more focused on sowing revolution in the industrialized countries of the West, adopted a revolutionary strategy more sympathetic to the movements of decolonization in agricultural countries such as China and Vietnam.[30]

As this shift took place, the history of radicalism in Vietnam focused on several basic concerns: "freedom, security, the needs of the individual, and the interests of the community. Both supporters and foes of the colonial status quo defined their political choices in terms of freedom and security." If security ranked higher, then pro-colonial figures promoted traditional institutions, even oppressive ones, and the colonial system. Those who favored freedom looked to "liberation of the nation from colonial rule and emancipation of the individual from the patriarchal family system, outdated moral values, and authoritarian institutions."[31]

Professor Hue-Tam Ho Tai argues that the link between radicalism and Marxism was tenuous. She writes: "Whereas radicals had believed that a . . . struggle for the liberation of the nation as a whole would serve as an operational framework for the emancipation of the individual, Marxists cast the struggle against imperialism in terms of conflicts between classes. Marxism downplayed the importance of the individual."[32] In effect, she states, "they addressed different concerns. ... The central issue of radicalism was freedom; Marxism provided a solution to the dilemma of survival" in the face of the Darwinistic challenge posed by Western civilization. She continues, "These two issues came together at the level of the nation which was battling for both its freedom and survival." But beyond that, underlying goals "did not fully coincide. Radicalism operated at the level of the individual, Marxism at the level of the group. The radicalist critique conceived of society in terms of institutions such as the family. Marxism addressed problems of social justice; it spoke of economic forces and conceived of society in terms of class."[33]

In Ho Tai's view, "The Marxist historicism thus acted as a counterbalance to the fears of national annihilation that had spurred every Vietnamese reformer and revolutionary since the notion of Heaven's Will [the divine right of kings] was superseded by the Social Darwinism theory of the perpetual struggle between strong and weak nations, races, cultures as the source of historical change and the explanation of colonial conquest." Ho Tai adds: "The appeal of Marxism derived ... from its perceived parallelism with Social Darwinism. Both ... laid claim to scientific truth. Both combined elements of determinism and voluntarism in their theories of history. Both were based on the idea of struggle as the motive force for progress. ... Marxist theory of history promised redemption instead of endless struggle. Instead of the real possibility of extinction [as pessimistic Vietnamese feared], Marxism offered the prospect of a workers' utopia," [turning] Social Darwinism, which offered no hope for the survival of small nations, "on its head. ... Marxism promised victory to the oppressed masses of Vietnam through its historical determinism."[34] But Marxism did not address a core concern of Ho Chi Minh and his closest cohorts: nationalism.

With freedom, however derived, came uncertainty; and even revolutionaries wanted reassurance that their sacrifices and transgressions in fighting against conventional morality would not be in vain. Despite the "vagaries of revolutionary life, the Marxist promise of certain victory seemed irresistible" to some. In the meantime, the Leninist Party cleverly balanced iron discipline with comradely warmth and acted as a substitute for the despised patriarchal family.[35]

New recruits to the Vietminh took seriously the French words "liberty, equality, and fraternity." Membership in a revolutionary organization permitted them to act somewhat autonomously as individuals rather than cogs in a family unit. The party became a quasi-family, more supportive of equality and more nurturing than their own.

The language of family also characterized their relations. They used the terms *anh*, *chi*, and *em* (older brother, older sister, and younger sibling), to address each other, reinforcing the idea of the party as family.[36] They also possessed feelings of moral and intellectual superiority over the masses, and a trace of ingrained elitism was evident.[37]

Marxism's appeal was based on the inevitability of historic change, even though this change required ending the special role of the bourgeoisie before it could succeed. Vietnamese pursued Marxism before they had decided on revolution rather than reform. Marxism, as opposed to Leninism, provided a map of the world and an itinerary.[38]

As Vietnamese revolutionaries gravitated toward Marxist-Leninism in the 1930s, the concerns of the 1920s—self-realization, emancipation of the individual from the tyranny of the group and from ideological conformity—remained unaddressed, unrealized, and served as goals for the future.

5

The Emergence of Ho Chi Minh and the Communist Agenda

After working as a sailor on merchant ships and washing dishes in New York and London, Nguyen Ai Quoc (later Ho Chi Minh) finally arrived in France in 1916 at the age of 26.[1] When he arrived in France he was an advocate of Woodrow Wilson's principle of self-determination for colonial peoples. However, he soon concluded that Western nations were not serious about self-determination and instead were committed to "business as usual" in Asia and Africa.[2]

Britain was promoting weak vassal states in the Muslim parts of the Russian Empire, but only to weaken its rival. France was interested in Eastern European satellites and the Middle East. To pander to domestic ethnic constituencies, the United States backed the Irish and Czechoslovak nationalist movements. Italy focused on catching up with the other colonial powers by building an empire in Libya, Albania, and Ethiopia. None of the European nations supported Asian nationalists such as Gandhi, Nehru, Haile Selassie, or the Vietnamese revolutionary Ho Chi Minh.[3]

While Ho Chi Minh was disappointed by the West, he lobbied the United States for support on several occasions. While working menial jobs in Paris at the end of World War I, Ho Chi Minh attempted to personally lobby President Wilson to fulfill America's putative goal of self-determination for all peoples, including the Vietnamese, at the peace conference in Versailles. In a secondhand clothing store he rented a pinstriped suit, pinch-waisted overcoat, derby hat, and a light tan muffler and went to Versailles. Ushers and busy-looking secretaries shunted Ho around, and he was unable to see Wilson. There was no official record of a petition from

the "Annamite" (a French term for Vietnamese). Ho saw other petitioners, led by the Irish, mutter: "Armed revolution was the answer,
the road to power via the terrorist's bombs and the guerrilla's gun
barrel." All the petitioners were talking about a big country, Russia,
that had overthrown its monarchy through revolution.[4]

Ho Chi Minh left Versailles in despair, his hopes dashed for a
"liberal" solution to Vietnam's colonial condition. Rather than beginning a process of "self-determination," as Ho hoped, Versailles
instead reinforced European colonialism. At the same time, radicalism was on the march across the West, and many expected the Bolshevik Revolution in Russia to spread. Europe was seething from
the World War; anarchists were throwing bombs in the United
States; red flags were flying in Milan; huge strikes racked Britain.[5]

As a young radical, Ho Chi Minh's time in Paris and other European intellectual centers exposed him to various European revolutionary theories; however, he was attracted to the French Communist Party in the 1920s. The party was ideologically grounded in
Lenin's advocacy of the struggle against colonization and viewed
self-determination as a component of global revolution. Ho's emphasis was on Leninist organizational lines rather than Marxist
theory of history. The implications of Marxist-Leninism intrigued
Vietnamese revolutionaries and groups, including Ho Chi Minh's
own Youth League, but those ideas were not their focus until a decade later, in the 1930s.[6]

Frustrated by what he considered retrograde colonial policies in
Washington, London, and Paris, Ho Chi Minh became increasingly
attracted to the Russian-led communist movement. His personal
epiphany occurred in Tours, France, on Christmas Day 1920. As the
delegate representing Indochina, Ho Chi Minh attended the Tours
Congress of the Socialist Party and voted to join the Comintern
Third International, "becoming a founding member of the French
Communist Party," persuaded by Lenin's call at the Third International to support anti-colonialist movements around the world.
He pleaded with the delegates to include the "colonial question,"
promising to "help the oppressed colonial peoples to regain their
liberty and independence" in their manifesto.[7] Ho Chi Minh went
to Moscow in 1923, where, despite Lenin's lofty rhetoric, the Soviets ignored the plight of colonial peoples. Vietnam was unknown to

the leadership—at best, an appendage of China, where the growing Chinese communist movement was beginning to capture Russian attention. After a little more than a year in Moscow, Ho Chi Minh followed communist agent and weapons supplier Mikhail Borodin to Canton in 1925. Mikhail Markovich Borodin (1884–1951) was a chief Comintern agent in China in the 1920s who built the loosely structured Nationalist Party (Kuomintang) of Sun Yat-sen into a highly centralized Leninist-style organization. As an advisor to Chinese nationalist Sun Yat-sen, Borodin convinced him and the Kuomintang (KMT) to allow communists to attend the Whampoa Military Academy.[8] This nefariously linked the Nationalists with the Communists in China.

Ho Chi Minh found little political sophistication or interest in communism as an economic or social ideology. In 1925 he created the League of Oppressed People of the East. Focusing on Vietnamese, he founded a nine-member cell called the Communist Youth Corps (*Thanh Nien Cong San Doan*), all but one of which came from his native Nghe An Province. Publicly, the group was called the Vietnamese Revolutionary Youth (*Viet Nam Cach Mang Thanh Nien*).[9]

Ho Chi Minh benefited from the very public sentencing of Phan Boi Chau, which occurred three days before his *Youth* began publishing on June 21, 1925. *Youth* was published for five years and was not theoretical but hortatory, advocating uniting for revolution. It was clearly left-wing, but its ideological underpinnings were not so clear. Ho specifically did not advocate terrorism and stressed, instead, political organization and struggle.[10]

The Youth League quickly became popular for dissidents from Vietnam, and the prestigious Albert Sarraut School in Hue became one of its chief recruiting grounds. Phan Van Dong, the son of a Mandarin, joined the organization in 1927.

Communist ideology achieved remarkable success in Vietnam: From Ho Chi Minh's cell of nine men in 1925, the nationalist revolutionaries took power in Hanoi in the August 1945 revolution, and the organization grew to 1.5 million members in 1975, mostly in North Vietnam.

A remarkable feature of the communist movement in Vietnam was the unlikely fusing of two very different movements—the Marxist-Leninist, proletarian, anti-imperialism, and Vietnamese patriotic traditions—into a single force. Another notable feature was that Vietnamese Communism evolved to serve the anti-imperialist struggle and was frequently at odds with the leadership and colonial strategy in Moscow and, later, Beijing. Despite communist dogma, class struggle was not a prominent component of the Vietnamese struggle. Vietnam's struggle was a petit bourgeois–peasant alliance, organized and led by the urban petite bourgeoisie and rural gentry. This reality created tensions between the Vietnamese communists and their Moscow backers, which in turn created divisions within the Vietnamese leadership. For example, Vietnamese communists, who followed Moscow's ideology of international proletarianism and class struggle, shunted Ho Chi Minh aside during most of the 1930s.[11]

In 1930 the ICP was formed under the direction of the Comintern, but it brought together numerous revolutionary organizations operating in Indochina. Moscow chose cadres to lead the ICP who had trained in and were close to Moscow and those who adhered to the Comintern's international proletarian stance. Moscow rejected a role for Ho Chi Minh, whom they regarded as too nationalist and not devoted to international proletarianism. Ho spent the decade on the sidelines in Canton, Hong Kong, and the Soviet Union, where he lived from 1934 to 1938.[11]

Phan Boi Chau had inspired the traditional patriotic parties, notably the VNQDD, in the 1920s. Elitist patriots—including students, older literati, rural notables, landlords, interpreters, government office clerks, and military men who tended to assume all Vietnamese were patriots—constituted his supporters.[12] After some time in Jingxi, China, Nguyen Ai Quoc adopted the name Ho Chi Minh and undertook recruiting efforts for the Independence League, forged a questionable alliance with the Vietnamese Nationalist Party, and formed the Vietnamese Liberation League (*Viet Nam Gia Phong Dong Minh Hoi*). Phan Van Dong and Vo Nguyen Giap joined and remained Ho Chi Minh's closest comrades until his death in 1969. From Jingxi, Ho established contact with Truong Chinh of the Indochinese Communist Committee in Tonkin. Trung Chinh, considered pro-Chinese, became a stalwart member of the ruling party after the revolution. In May 1941, Ho Chi Minh and his allies convened what became known as the Eighth Plenum of the

Indochinese Communist Party, subsequently called the Pac Bo Plenum, since Pac Bo was the liaison office inside Vietnam.[13] At the Pac Bo Plenum the ICP Central Committee inaugurated a new revolutionary strategy to seize power after the Pacific War ended. The political centerpiece of the new approach was the establishment of a new, united front—the League for the Independence of Vietnam, or the "Vietminh." The communist direction of the new front would be disguised to attract patriotic elements from all social classes. The organization avoided radical social measures, such as the nationalization of industry and the collectivization of agriculture, and they would adopt a moderate program calling for social reforms and democratic freedoms. The primary focus of the new front would be on the struggle for independence.[14]

Supplementing the new political manifesto was a new military strategy, borrowed from the Chinese Communist Party, which would rely on a people's war to mobilize peasants and workers and establish liberated bases in isolated areas of the country. At the end of the war, through a combination of guerrilla tactics and popular uprisings, they would seize power in key urban centers. For the next four years, communists meticulously built up the new Vietminh front in villages throughout northern Vietnam, especially in areas near the Chinese border. In 1944 the Vietminh leadership set up the first units of what would eventually become the Vietnam Peoples Liberation Army.[15]

After a year of supervising propaganda, training recruits, and establishing bases in Cao Bang, in August 1942 Ho Chi Minh left for Chungking to try to attract support from allies. On the way, Chinese Nationalist forces arrested and jailed him in Liuzhou, China, for carrying false documents. Guilin provincial authority, Zhang Fakui's operation, had been attempting to assemble Indochinese intelligence and discovered Ho Chi Minh's identity. They then released him from jail and allowed him to return to Cao Bang in August 1944.[16]

After Ho Chi Minh's return to Vietnam, in the winter of 1944–45, Tonkin (northern Vietnam) faced severe famine, which killed an estimated one to two million Tonkinese. Insects, a typhoon, and shifting production from rice to crops desired by the Japanese, such as hemp, ramie, cotton, peanuts, and castor oil, reduced the size of the rice crop. American attacks on coastal shipping also impacted shipments of rice from the south to the north. Most important, the Japanese and French armies stockpiled rice in the south to circumvent political uncertainties, and a wartime economy led to the imminent collapse of the Vietnamese economy from inflation, speculation, and hoarding.

Ho Chi Minh predicted that Japan would go to war with the United States and lose. Japan's defeat, Ho Chi Minh imagined, would create a vacuum in Indochina, and the anticipated Allied occupation of Indochina would provide an opportunity for favorable developments in Vietnam, during which the revolutionary forces might seize control.[17]

In March 1945 the Japanese occupation forces, suspicious of growing support for the Gaullist Free French movement among civilians and military officials in Indochina, deposed and incarcerated the French colonial administration and set up a pro-Japanese puppet government under Emperor Bao Dai. The Japanese coup encouraged the Vietminh, since not only was the French administration deposed, but the Japanese did not bother to replace it in rural areas, left wide portions of the country open for Vietminh expansion and proselytizing.[18]

After the Vietminh took control of Hanoi in the August Revolution in the wake of Japanese surrender, on September 2, 1945, Ho Chi Minh addressed his compatriots, echoing the words of Thomas Jefferson: "All men are created equal. They are endowed by their Creator with certain inalienable rights; among those are Life, Liberty, and the Pursuit of Happiness." However, Ho Tai explains, Ho Chi Minh's Declaration of Independence "stress[ed] the theme of freedom rather than equality, which had come to symbolize class conflict." Initially, Ho Chi Minh attempted to bring elements of Vietnamese society together but avoided such words as 'equality,' as it had come to signify the individual in communist parlance." But it was the collective, not individual, freedom he was talking about, as Ho Tai notes and as Ho Chi Minh made clear in his closing words: "Vietnam has the right to enjoy freedom and independence, and, in fact, has become a free and independent nation. The whole Vietnamese people are resolved to bring its spirit and its power, its life, and its possessions to preserve the right to freedom and independence."[19]

Ho Chi Minh's careful avoidance of the word "equality" marked another instance in which he broke from orthodox Marxist-Leninists. Ho's nationalist impulses trumped Marxist-Leninist ideological terminology, hinting at the perennial question of whether Ho Chi Minh was more a nationalist than a communist. In any case, in the heady days of 1945, few Vietnamese could have predicted that full, united, national independence would require three more decades of struggle.

6

America's Early Engagement with Vietnam, 1946–1954

The United States pursued a tortuous trajectory in its relationship with Vietnam and Indochina. In the aftermath of the Second World War, the revived anticolonial struggle against the French drew the United States to the region, leading to a thirty-year conflict, and the first major military defeat in U.S. history. This tragic path, which in hindsight spirals to disaster, was not inevitable.

Among the developed, capitalist nations, the United States was, by the 1940s, the leading voice of anti-colonialism. President Roosevelt had been skeptical of colonialism, questioning both its morality and efficacy to the United States, a position he had taken in the 1920s.[1]

The Atlantic Charter, signed by Franklin Roosevelt and Winston Churchill in the summer of 1941, which pledged the two "to see sovereign rights and self-government restored to those who have been forcibly deprived of them," encouraged Ho Chi Minh. Churchill presumably regarded this language as idealistic rhetoric. But not Roosevelt. In January 1943, he commented in Casablanca to his son Elliott, "Don't think for a moment that Americans would be dying in the Pacific tonight if it had not been for the short-sighted greed of the French, the British, and the Dutch." As envisaged by Roosevelt and his Secretary of State, Cordell Hull, after the United States extended independence to the Philippines in 1946 our European allies would follow our lead with their colonies.[2]

As Archimedes Patti notes in *Why Viet Nam? Prelude to America's Albatross*, "Roosevelt went out of his way to single out France in Indochina and often cited French rule there as a flagrant example of onerous and exploitative colonialism," and suggested in 1942 that

France could repossess the territory by pledging eventual independence.[3]

In his excellent *Embers of War*, Fredrik Logevall describes Roosevelt as a "committed anti-colonialist" who believed that colonialism had contributed to both world wars. Roosevelt told the White House Correspondents' Association in March 1941: "There never has been, and there isn't now, and never will be, any race of people on earth fit to serve as masters over their fellow men. . . . We believe that any nationality, no matter how small, has the right to its own nationhood." More officially, Roosevelt wrote a memorandum to Secretary Hull on January 24, 1944, indicating that after the war Indochina should be administered by an international trusteeship. Roosevelt, "wrote a note-taker, 'remarked that after 100 years of French rule in Indochina, the inhabitants are worse off than they had been before. The people of Indochina are entitled to something better than that.' "[4]

Roosevelt advocated trusteeship for Indochina at meetings in Cairo and Teheran and the Yalta Conference, received the endorsement of Chiang Kai-shek and Stalin, but after repeated rebuffs from British Prime Minister Churchill, a conservative pro-empire stalwart, he resisted raising the issue again with him in public.[5] UK Foreign Minister Anthony Eden, like Churchill, supported French return because of its implications for Britain in India and elsewhere. In Cairo, during his first meeting with Stalin, Roosevelt stressed the importance of preparing the people of Indochina for self-rule. Stalin concurred. Likewise, Chiang Kai-shek agreed, but as time went on, reflecting a low opinion of Charles de Gaulle, Roosevelt's position hardened. The more de Gaulle's position strengthened, the more Roosevelt opposed French colonialism in Indochina.[6] Roosevelt, Logevall wrote, "continued to push his trusteeship plan and his opposition to a French return to Indochina, but with less urgency as 1944 progressed."[7] The U.S. and European allies began to have doubts in 1944 about both Stalin and Chiang Kai-shek—Stalin because of his focus on dominating Eastern Europe after the war, and Chiang Kai-shek since he seemed to be losing China's civil war. As France began to play a more serious role, senior U.S. officials began to suggest a review on the issues. At the Yalta Conference in February 1945, Roosevelt backed off his theretofore resolute position on the subject and said that, apart from Japanese-mandated territories, internationalization would happen only with the consent of the colonial power. But then he shifted again, stating that colonial powers would act as trustees, remaining in control only long enough to prepare the colony for independence. He specified France could return only as a trustee with a set date for independence.[8]

France's position, under both the Vichy puppet regime and de Gaulle's Free French rule, was that agreements should restore French authority and sovereignty over overseas territory. This was contrary to the principles of the Atlantic Charter and America's anticolonial policy.[9]

After Roosevelt's death in April 1945, it was American concerns over the spread of communism in Western Europe rather than Indochina that tilted U.S. policymakers toward the French position. While Asian experts in the U.S. government continued to support Roosevelt's position, the majority moved to support de Gaulle, especially as Stalin cracked down on Poland, Romania, and Bulgaria in 1945. As socialist elements exerted influence in the chaotic months of postliberation France, many thought by stripping France of her empire, the United States would tilt France towards the Soviet camp. Churchill and General de Gaulle's adamant positions, Eurocentric officials in the State Department, and the eastern establishment brought Truman and Washington around.[10]

The Truman administration dispatched State Department Southeast Asia Division Chief Abbot Low Moffat to Hanoi in 1945 to assess the situation. As David G. Marr recounts in *Vietnamese Tradition on Trial, 1920–1945*, Moffat assured Ho Chi Minh that the United States supported greater Vietnamese "autonomy within the framework of democratic institutions, and warned him against using force to achieve those objectives." Moffat also sought to determine the degree to which communists dominated Ho's government and its loyalty to Moscow. Ho Chi Minh, apparently, assured Moffat that "national independence, not communism was his first objective. Maybe in fifty years, things would be different"—a line he also used with journalists in Paris. He asked for U.S. assistance and "through an associate" offered the use of Cam Ranh Bay as a naval base. A State Department report to "President Truman on June 2, 1945, acknowledged that 'Independence sentiment ... is believed to be increasingly strong,' but declared that 'the United States recognizes French sovereignty over Indochina.' "[11]

On December 17, 1945, the State Department sent out a circular to missions abroad "noting the Vietminh's Communist character and saying a continued French presence in Indochina was imperative not only as an antidote to Soviet influence, but to protect Vietnam and Southeast Asia from future Chinese imperialism." There was no mention of sympathy for Vietnamese national independence. When Truman met Chiang Kai-shek a few weeks later, Truman himself dismissed any notion of trusteeship.[12]

Logevall concludes eloquently: "In historical terms it was a monumental decision by Truman, but like so many decisions that U.S. presidents made in the decades to come, it had little to do with Vietnam itself, it was all about American priorities on the world stage. France had made her intentions clear, and the administration did not dare defy a European ally, for the mere sake of honoring the principles of the Atlantic Charter."[13] French stability overrode principles.

U.S. Intelligence and Liaison Teams in Indochina

By the time American diplomats made the decision to back France's colonial ambitions, U.S. forces already had years of experience with anti-French insurgents in Indochina. Two prominent teams, the Office of Strategic Services (OSS), forerunner to the Central Intelligence Agency (CIA), and the military's "Deer Team," both operating out of the China Theater, became heavily involved in relations with Ho Chi Minh and the Vietminh.

An OSS team, led by Archimedes Patti, attempted from 1942 to 1945 to conduct intelligence work and to recruit natives of China, Korea, Indochina, and Burma and locate pilots shot down in Indochina. Their mission was not to promote anticolonial goals, but was part of the broader wartime effort against the Japanese.[14]

As noted earlier, Ho Chi Minh returned to Vietnam from China in early 1941 for the first time in ten years to establish his field headquarters in Pac Bo, fifty miles northwest of Hanoi, deep in the densely forested "liberated area" of the Tuyen Quang Province.

The OSS negotiated the insertion of a military Deer Team, led by Major Allison Thomas, into Ho Chi Minh's base at Kim Lung and near his base at Tan Trao, Tuyen Quang. The Deer Team provided small arms and some training for Ho Chi Minh's guerrillas.[15]

Despite this assistance, the United States instructed the OSS and Deer Teams to remain neutral vis-à-vis French efforts to restore their sovereignty to Indochina. Early on, the State Department and OSS referred to the Vietminh as pro-Allies, anti-colonialist, anti-Japanese, and only much later, after the Japanese surrendered, did they begin to call them communists.[16]

The United States knew little of Ho Chi Minh, but he regularly provided the OSS with highly useful information on downed pilots and the status of Vietminh relations with the French, Japanese, and Vietminh plans. Patti developed a close relationship with the former Boston-based busboy and regarded him with great respect, but remained careful not to mislead Ho regarding possible long-term support from the U.S. government.

The Vietminh recovered a downed U.S. pilot in February 1945 whom Pham Van Dong, one of Ho Chi Minh's closest comrades and prime minister of Vietnam during the war, escorted back to the Americans in China. After this gesture, Ho Chi Minh prevailed upon the Deer Team to arrange a visit in Kunming with Major General Claire Chennault, the senior U.S. air officer in China. By Patti's account, the arrangement was predicated on the condition that Ho would not seek support or supplies.[17]

After a friendly meeting with Chennault, Ho Chi Minh asked for a photograph of the general, which Chennault produced and signed, "Yours sincerely, Claire Chennault." When Ho returned to Pac Bo, he used the photo to claim U.S. support and edge his way to the leadership of resistance activities. The assumption that Ho Chi Minh had the support of the Americans also played well among moderate Vietnamese, who saw Ho as favorably balanced between the Soviet Union, where he had trained, and the United States, where he claimed support. In another version of the story, Chennault gave Ho Chi Minh two pistols with the same impact.[18]

With the boost from Chennault, Ho Chi Minh put his other closest comrade, Vo Nguyen Giap, in charge of building the fledgling military forces. With little support, funding, or weapons, Giap managed to develop an effective guerrilla force capable of attacking exposed French and Japanese positions.

In December 1944, General Giap formed an armed propaganda team, his first major unit, of thirty-four local men that became the Vietminh's military organization. On Christmas Eve 1944 he overwhelmed two remote French posts and captured arms and ammunition. He then strengthened his force and attacked larger French posts. Within months the gold-starred red flag flew over communities throughout the northern zone.[19]

March 9, 1945, Japanese Coup

In 1940 Japan had occupied Indochina with the consent of the pliant French Vichy government, but the French continued to administer the colony.[20] One cannot understate the importance of food and minerals in Indochina to France.

This arrangement lasted until March 9, 1945, when the Japanese suddenly demanded the French join them in defending Indochina against an expected Anglo-American invasion. The French were to accept the Japanese terms unconditionally and within two hours. However, the French stalled. Anticipating this tactic, Tokyo then unleashed a military coup, ending French control of Indochina. The French administrative apparatus was largely jailed.[21]

As a consequence of the Japanese coup in Indochina and the liberation of France, the complex network of rivalries shifted. Nations assumed Americans were supporting the Vietminh against the Japanese, but increasingly the French believed the Americans were trying to prevent French return.

The Chinese KMT, who had supported the Vietminh, were concerned about the perceived communist inclinations of the Vietminh and looked for noncommunist alternatives among the Vietnamese.[22]

The Soviets, for their part, assumed the Americans were supporting the Vietminh, and thus withheld support. In a conversation with Archimedes Patti, the Soviet representative in Indochina, Stephane Solosieff, echoed Franklin Delano Roosevelt's vision for Indochina. As Karnow recounts, Solosieff said that "the days of French colonialism were over. The Indochinese would have to assume a role of responsible nationalism, although they might not be able to handle the reins alone. Perhaps with enlightened French help and American technical assistance, they could achieve national independence in a few years." Regarding a Soviet role, Solosieff said, "I do not believe that the Soviet Union will be in a position to interpose itself in Southeast Asia. 'Mother Russia,' after the Nazi onslaught, would need time to rebuild."[23]

The War Ends

World War II ended four days after American nuclear bombs devastated Hiroshima and Nagasaki. The rapid Japanese surrender complicated American decision-making in Indochina. Not only was Indochina still in the hands of Japanese forces, but Roosevelt had died just weeks before and Truman had little understanding of faraway Indochina.

The Potsdam Agreement of late July 1945 called for the British to accept the Japanese surrender in South Vietnam and for the KMT to accept surrender in the North. With its own colonialist equities at stake, Britain supported French return to Indochina.

Ho Chi Minh sporadically tried to contact and negotiate with the French, but the French response was invariably vague. The French insisted that their sovereignty be restored but claimed that they and Ho Chi Minh could make arrangements to pave the way for eventual Vietnamese self-determination within the French Union or various other permutations, which meant the return of French control.[24] Ho Chi Minh sent eleven letters seeking U.S. support and recognition to President Truman and Secretary Hull. None of the letters received a response.[25]

Ho Chi Minh masterfully orchestrated his relationship with the small Deer Team and with the OSS, allowing him to feign the stature necessary to lead the resistance movement. But his success also reflected the remarkable political and propaganda efforts he made in bringing the entire nation to support independence under his leadership, including the nationalist parties and virtually all social classes.[26]

Patti's assessment of Ho Chi Minh was insightful: Patti told French delegate Jean Sainteny that Ho was not a wild-eyed revolutionary. He was a moderate who was cognizant of his limitations and liabilities. He recognized the nation was bankrupt, had no assurances of outside support, and his people lacked the technical expertise to govern skillfully or establish an economic base.

Patti also outlined Ho Chi Minh's important assets: He had disciplined followers and a sound political organization among the peasant, worker, and intellectual classes, who were motivated by a common goal. Ho had described the depth of the popular support Vietnam's independence and himself. Just prior to a farewell dinner, Ho Chi Minh "assured me [Patti] he had absolute confidence in the people, regardless of political affiliation, and was certain that they were totally with him in their desire for independence, even the Catholics."[27]

Patti thought Ho Chi Minh would try to maintain and build the revolution but believed he would rather negotiate than fight.

A Last Farewell

Archimedes Patti received his final orders September 29 to close his mission and depart Hanoi on October 1, 1945. Ho Chi Minh invited him to join a few aides, Vo Nguyen Giap, and himself for a private dinner on September 30, 1945. After dinner, the aides departed and General Giap, whom Patti had regarded as a "hard-line communist," expressed his appreciation for Patti's "understanding of the Vietnamese cause." He also expressed his personal appreciation for the "tremendous assistance the Americans in Kunming had provided him during the early days of the revolution." With a friendly "Bon voyage" and hopes that Vietnam would soon have a friend in Washington, Giap departed.[28]

Alone, Ho Chi Minh, for the first time, asked Patti if the United States was going to allow France to return to Vietnam.

Patti commented that American policy, as conveyed to him "when I was first assigned to my mission, was one of hands off Indochina, to be completely 'neutral' except for intelligence operations directed at the Japanese." Patti noted that President Roosevelt, on numerous occasions, expressed no support for French colonial ambitions. Since Roosevelt's death there had been no statement of U.S. policy regarding Indochina.

Ho Chi Minh listened attentively, shook his head, and told Patti he "could not reconcile the United States position in Washington, Quebec, Tehran, and Potsdam, where the 'United States had been a champion of anti-colonialism,' with its passivity in letting England and China assist France in re-imposing colonial rule in Laos, Cambodia, Annam, and even Tonkin." He claimed the United States and Britain, who fought World War II for lofty goals, as incorporated in the Atlantic Charter and the United Nations, now stood idly by while France violated those principles.[29]

"He [Ho] suddenly came out of his emotional reverie" and asked Patti to "forgive his impassioned musings." Patti wrote that Ho said "it was difficult to express his inner feelings with strangers, but that he considered me a very special friend with whom he could confide."

After discussing the maneuvering by the French, Chinese, and noncommunist Vietnamese political factions, noting the repeated duplicities in French proposals, he discussed his travels to France, Portugal, Spain, and Africa.

Patti then asked Ho Chi Minh what made him decide communism was the way for him.

Ho Chi Minh responded that he "had not decided directly but had come upon the communist philosophy through socialism. In fact," he said, he still did not consider himself a "true communist" but a "national socialist." Explaining that his realization of the plight of the downtrodden in Vietnam and his political life had arisen from that concern, he said that "despite all his political activity, he was really following a single nationalist purpose for reforms to better the lot of his own people." At that time, he was "not interested in international movements or politics. He understood nothing of socialism, communism, or trade unionism." In a socialist political meeting to discuss various international movements and the Bolshevik Revolution in Russia, a participant gave him a copy of Lenin's *Thesis on the National and Colonial Question*. Attracted by Lenin's attention to these questions, his literary talents, and understanding, Ho Chi Minh accepted Lenin as the champion of anti-colonialism and joined in forming the French Communist Party in Tours in December 1920.[30]

Ho Chi Minh then commented that he found little interest in the Soviet Union, Britain, and France in the anti-colonial movement, and noted that, in all the years that followed, none of the so-called liberal elements came to the aid of the colonials. Stunningly, he added: "I place more reliance on the United States to support Vietnam's independence before I could expect any help from the USSR."[31]

Ho said, "The Americans consider me a 'Moscow puppet,' " because he had been in Moscow, but in fact he was not a communist in the American sense. The Americans had given him more material and spiritual support than the Soviets. Why should he feel indebted to Moscow? He would have to find allies if any were to be found; otherwise, the Vietnamese would have to go it alone.

Ho concluded the evening by asking Patti "to carry back to the United States a message of warm friendship and admiration for the American people." He wanted Americans to know "the people of Vietnam would long remember the United States as a friend and ally. They would always be grateful for the material help received but most of all for the example the history of the United States had set for Vietnam in its struggle for independence."[32]

This poignant moment foretold the path America would follow. Rather than follow President Roosevelt's vision, outlined in the Atlantic Charter, which championed anti-colonialism, as evidenced in our granting of independence to the Philippines, we ceded the anti-colonialist role to the Soviet Union and China. This was, sadly, a critical strategic error.

Ho Chi Minh's Declaration of Independence

On August 25, 1945, Emperor Bao Dai abdicated and recognized the political power Ho Chi Minh had developed and his own weakness as a ruler. He handed over of the instruments of power, the seal and sword, to Ho Chi Minh, transferring the "mandate of heaven" to the popular leader.[33]

Ho Chi Minh's declaration of Vietnam's independence on September 2, 1945, in Ba Dinh Square in Hanoi was remarkable. The hard, political work in the countryside meant the country was his and the Vietminh's. In his own declaration of independence, delivered to an overflowing crowd in Hanoi, Ho Chi Minh cited the central lines from the American Declaration of Independence: "All men are equal. The creator has given us certain inalienable Rights, the Right to Life, The Right to be Free, and the Right to Achieve Happiness."[34]

Northern Vietnam, central Vietnam, and Cochinchina erupted in support for the Vietminh; Vietminh flags appeared everywhere. An American airplane flew over the event, and crowds perceived it as a sign of U.S. support.

7

The French Return: The Indochina War and the Geneva Accords

Within days of Ho Chi Minh's declaration of independence, the French arrived in South Vietnam with the support of the British military, many on American ships.

At the same time, under the Potsdam Agreement, 200,000 KMT troops under Nationalist Chinese General Lu Han descended on Hanoi. Having ravaged villages all along the way, the troops were sick, clothed in rags, dragging along pillaged ducks, chickens, and even cattle, along with their wives and children. They stole everything in sight.[1]

Ho Chi Minh cleverly appeased Lu Han. Having urged citizens to hand in their gold to finance the new government, he gave a portion to Lu Han to curry favor with him. On the political front, Lu Han worked out an agreement he thought would favor the VN-QDD, the chief political challenge to the Vietminh. In the deal, Ho Chi Minh dissolved the ICP, joined forces with the VNQDD, and set up a cabinet that included Catholics, VNQDD figures, and communists under another name,[2] the Marxist Research Association in League with the Vietminh.[3]

Meanwhile, the French were negotiating with Chiang Kai-shek, Lu Han's nominal overlord, who urged him to withdraw his troops from northern Vietnam in favor of France. In exchange, France agreed to drop its concessions in Shanghai and other ports in China. An agreement was reached by the KMT government in Chungking in February 1946, and KMT forces withdrew by August.

At this point, General de Gaulle named an arrogant Frenchman, Admiral Georges Theirry d'Argenlieu, high commissioner in Saigon.[4]

Concurrently, a lieutenant of Ho Chi Minh's, Tran Van Giau, installed himself as the ruling official of the Vietminh's Provisional Executive Committee in Saigon, but faced violent competition. The Cao Dai, Binh Xuan Elements, Trotskyites, religious, criminal, and political groups in South Vietnam also attempted to seize power. The ensuing chaos in Saigon terrified the French community.[5]

Suddenly, Vichy French paratroopers and Foreign Legionnaires were released from jail on September 22 and went on a rampage. "[T]hey poured into Saigon's city hall and ousted [Tran Van Giau], took over police stations ... raising the French flag from the rooftops. ... Angry French civilians" joined the fray, "break[ing] into Vietnamese homes and shops and clubb[ing] men, women, and even children. ... Saigon was paralyzed without electricity or water. ... Vietminh squads attacked the airport, burned the central market, and stormed the local prisons to release Vietnamese prisoners. The French barricaded themselves in their residences or fled in a panic to the old Continental Palace hotel" barracks, hoping for protection by French and British soldiers. Gunfire and mortars were widespread. "Binh Xuan terrorists ... massacred one hundred and fifty French and Eurasian" men, women, and children, mutilating many.[6]

A Beleaguered Ho Chi Minh Seeks Negotiations

Despite Ho Chi Minh's repeated pleas and constructive relations with the OSS, the U.S. supported France. The Soviet Union, preoccupied with rebuilding at home, regarded Vietnam as an appendage of China and offered no support. Even the Communist Party of France's secretary general, Maurice Thorez, declared he "did not intend to liquidate the French position in Indochina."[7] Ho Chi Minh concluded he had no choice but to seek accommodation.

Despite bitter criticism within Vietminh ranks, Ho negotiated agreements with France in 1945 and in 1946 attempted to broker an agreement that would have temporarily restored French administration but put Vietnam on a rapid path to independence. France's representative in Hanoi, Jean Sainteny, signaled that France would recognize Vietnam as a free state within the French Union if Ho Chi

Minh would allow the posting of 25,000 French troops in Hanoi for five years. While Sainteny's plan might have averted war, approval of Sainteny's plan never came from Paris.[8]

"Ho Chi Minh came under heavy criticism for this tentative deal. He responded in exchange for recognition of Vietnam's legitimacy, it would only allow the small French force into Hanoi and it would give the Vietminh time to strengthen their hold and rid Vietnam of Chinese troops, which Ho Chi Minh considered to be a primary threat. He vigorously countered his Vietminh critics, 'Don't you realize what it means if the Chinese remain? Don't you remember your history? The last time the Chinese came, they stayed for a thousand years. Colonialism is dying. The white man is finished in Asia. But, if the Chinese stay now, they will never go.' "[9]

French colonials also severely criticized the deal. De Gaulle's new high commissioner, ardent nationalist Admiral George Thierry d'Argenlieu, obfuscated big issues, such as Cochinchina's status and Vietnam's sovereignty, claiming higher-ranking officials needed to handle those issues.

Ho Chi Minh left for Paris on May 31, 1946, to conclude the deal Sainteny had proposed. No sooner had he left than d'Argenlieu violated the supposed understanding without informing Paris and proclaimed a Republic of Cochinchina. Ho Chi Minh's delegation was sent to Biarritz to await the outcome of French elections, and talks shifted to Fontainebleau to avoid demonstrations by Vietminh supporters.[10]

The French in Biarritz and Paris warmly greeted Ho Chi Minh, inviting him to attend events on Bastille Day. To ease concerns about his political views, "Maybe in fifty years, Vietnam would be ready for Communism, he told a group of journalists in Paris the week before, 'but not now.' Any change in the economy would be gradual and the Vietnamese constitution—modeled he emphasized, on the American one—contained safeguards for private property. 'If capitalists come to our country, ... they will make money.' "[11]

The French finally produced a draft agreement, but it strengthened France's position economically in Northern Vietnam and left the status of Cochinchina unresolved.

After initialing the "modus vivendi," Ho Chi Minh commented to his bodyguard, "I've just signed my death warrant." Back in

Hanoi in October, hardline Vietminh critics accused Ho Chi Minh of a sellout, but the masses acclaimed him. Rumors of a French *coup d'état* and skirmishes heightened tensions, as fears grew that a new phase of the war was imminent.[12]

Seizing on a minor customs dispute in November 1946, the French commander of the northern port of Haiphong ordered the Vietnamese to evacuate their troops within two hours. Shortly thereafter, the French attacked with aircraft and naval guns, demolishing whole neighborhoods. Between 6,000 and 20,000 Vietnamese were killed. Tensions, of course, exploded, and Vietnam was effectively at war.

The French also attacked Vietnamese in Hanoi. On December 19, the Vietminh militia sabotaged a municipal power plant in Hanoi, then broke into homes to murder or abduct French occupants. The French counterattacked, and Hanoi became a battlefield with Vietnamese corpses lining the boulevards. Ho Chi Minh escaped before he could be captured.

In the face of this bloodshed, General Giap issued a virtual declaration of war: "I order all soldiers and militia in the center, south, and north to stand together, go into battle, destroy the invaders, and save the nation. The resistance will be long and arduous, but our cause is just and we will surely triumph." Ho Chi Minh "had fled to Hadong, a town six miles south of Hanoi, where he echoed Giap's call to arms—and also appealed to the Western allies to restrain the French." He later promised that in the budding conflict between the West and the Communist bloc, Vietnam would remain neutral.[13]

As Fredrick Logevall concludes: "Yet, if it takes actions by two sides to make a war, both sides are not always equally culpable. And if it's true that the Vietnamese fired the first shots on December 19, 1946, ultimately France bears primary responsibility for precipitating the conflict."[14]

In Paris, French provisional premier Andre Leon Blum stressed his commitment to Vietnam's independence within the French Union but insisted that "order must be restored" as a precondition for talks. D'Argenlieu said talks with Ho Chi Minh were impossible and called for the return of Bao Dai to the throne. Paris recalled d'Argenlieu, but the situation quickly spun out of control.[15] Finally, after repeated efforts by the French, Bao Dai initially rejected the settlement until it included "independence." But Bao Dai acceded on March 8, 1949, to the French "Elysée Accord," which confirmed Vietnam's autonomy and status as an "Associated State of Vietnam within the French Union." Laos received the same status in July, and Cambodia in November. Bao Dai's "State of Vietnam" would have its own army, supplied and directed, in effect, by the French. Not surprisingly, Ho Chi Minh denounced Bao Dai's French agreement and insisted he would continue the struggle until Vietnam won complete independence.[16]

While maintaining contacts with Ho Chi Minh, the French continued to contact Bao Dai, dangling, cynically, various permutations of Vietnamese independence in the French Union, but no agreements were finalized. The ultimate proposal arrived just on the eve of the Geneva Conference, and, for the first time, the French did not insist on Cochinchina remaining a colony, but the parties never signed an agreement.[17]

The legal status of Cochinchina was finally established in June 1949, and Bao Dai declared the establishment of the State of Vietnam in Saigon. His actions opened the way for the United States and other Western nations to recognize the State of Vietnam; the United States established a military assistance group (MAAG) in Saigon in February 1950, after which the United States expanded its role quickly, to the chagrin of the French.

The World Divides: Communism Versus the Free World

There was no help for Ho Chi Minh from Washington. Secretary of State Dean Acheson declared the question of whether Ho Chi Minh was a communist or nationalist "irrelevant" because "all Stalinists in colonial areas are Nationalists."[18]

By this time, scarcely a year after a joint Allied and Soviet victory over Nazi Germany, American policymakers were already viewing most world events through an anticommunist lens. By the time Ho Chi Minh fled Hanoi, Churchill had delivered his famous "Iron Curtain" speech in Missouri in March 1946, and George Kennan had composed the "Long Telegram," laying out the strategic threat posed by the Soviet Union. In the years to come, events in Asia would heighten American concern about communist expansion and shred any hope of a constructive relationship with the Vietminh. In October 1949, Mao Zedong took control of China. In June 1950, North Korean forces invaded South Korea and four days later captured Seoul.

The United States mobilized the United Nations to counter the North Korean invasion and to "contain" communist expansion.[19] China quickly set up an advisory military group, which provided crucial supplies and support for the Vietminh.[20]

China recognized the Democratic Republic of Vietnam on January 18, and Moscow followed suit on January 30, 1950. Ho Chi Minh requested a treaty of alliance with Moscow, as the Soviet Union had signed with China. The Soviets declined Ho's proposition during a secret mission to Moscow.[21]

During his trip home, Ho Chi Minh must have felt enormous ambivalence, since recognition by the great communist powers would certainly damage his relations with other Southeast Asians and reduce his international maneuverability. Ho Chi Minh must have poignantly remembered his twenty years of appeals for support from the United States.

The United States adjusted its approach to French Indochina. In 1949 Washington announced it would deploy its resources to "preserve Indochina and Southeast Asia from further Communist encroachment." The domino theory clearly influenced American strategy, and in seeking ways to block the fall of the dominos, Washington rapidly became more adamant than France that Indochina must be "saved."

The irony, recognized by few Americans at the time, was that the Vietminh under Ho Chi Minh might have offered the best barrier to continued Chinese and Soviet expansion in Southeast Asia. The Vietminh had substantial ideological differences with the USSR and the Chinese communists, and as a national resistance movement it was keen on maintaining its independence from these new "Second World" powers. Unfortunately, the blinding, black-and-white intensity of the early Cold War prevented Washington from perceiving the clear signs that the Vietminh was significantly different from enemies in Moscow or Peking. For example, when in 1950 Ho Chi Minh established diplomatic relations with Tito's Yugoslavia, then an enemy of Moscow, American policy experts noted the event, but tragically no one in authority appears to have concluded that the Vietnamese anti-colonial forces were independent from their supposed masters in Moscow and Peking.[22]

Washington's ability to judge objectively the budding anti-colonial movements of the world would only diminish as the Cold War intensified. During the early 1950s, anti-communist witch trials led by Senator Joseph McCarthy and fear of the "Red Menace" reached a fever pitch, and any attempt to take a fresh look at some Third World communist movements could be a career-ending proposition.[23]

Against this backdrop, American support for the French in Indochina was increasingly resolute and substantial. By 1954 American aid accounted for 80 percent of French expenditures on the Indochina conflict. The United States, under Eisenhower, contributed three billion dollars in 1953–54 to support the French in Indochina—a staggering sum in the early Fifties.[24]

The French Indochina War Ensues

In preparing for the struggle against the French, Ho Chi Minh and Vo Nguyen Giap decided on a three-phase approach: to start with hit-and-run strikes, then mount larger actions, and, finally, as the balance of force tilted in their favor, stage conventional battles. They judged that time was on their side, assuming that protracted struggle would exhaust the French and public opinion would force an end to the conflict.

By the end of 1946, however, French forces had reoccupied the Red River Delta and begun building ubiquitous towers and blockhouses for defense, which one can still see today. They skirmished constantly with the Vietminh. The Vietminh emerged at night to assault the French outposts and then disappeared into the hamlets or jungles. They plagued French forces, constantly conducting ambushes on mountainous, twisting roads of North Vietnam. Giap bought time to enlarge his main force units. In late 1947 and 1948 the Vietminh internally began to harden its ideological lines, became slightly less inclined to empathize with the NLF, and tightened restrictions on new recruits into the party structure. In 1951, they changed the name of the party to Labor Party (*Lao Dong*), possibly in deference to China's narrower definition of the party's former inclusiveness of bourgeois and more moderate membership and ideology. One must view these moves in the context of the evolving international cleavage dividing the West and the communist and socialist worlds. Spurned by the West, the Vietminh sought new allies in the East, especially China. This might also have reflected a growing influence of the secretary general of the party, Truong Chinh, with his known attachment to Chinese dogma. The new trends began to alienate more moderate bourgeois and professional figures, such as Ngo Dinh Diem, who increasingly advocated nationalist and anti-communist positions.[25] Internally, the Vietminh continued to try to project an inclusive stance to bolster its position, considering growing moderate opposition.

With the victory of the communists in China, a dramatic change ensued for the Vietminh. The long Sino-Viet border became a means of escape but, more important, it augmented access to resources to fight against the French. Giap shifted tactics gradually in 1949 by harassing the most isolated French garrisons, bottling up the French, and leaving the countryside open to the resistance. The French insisted in maintaining widespread garrisons, but they were frequently overrun, especially in the remote mountain areas. In one engagement in 1949, 6,000 French troops were killed trying to maintain the outposts on the Chinese border. The French hold on Indochina was frequently described as precarious.[26]

Although retaining flexibility, Giap, based on Chinese advice, shifted to conventional strikes in 1951 in the Red River Delta and was mauled. At times Giap was reckless with his forces, overestimating their capabilities.[27]

In December 1950, France appointed military hero Jean de Lattre de Tasigny commander-in-chief of the French expeditionary forces. For a little over a year, his powerful, if arrogant, behavior significantly improved French hopes until he died of cancer in January 1952.[28] In 1952, the French attempted to expand their forces by bringing in large numbers of Vietnamese to bulk up in a process Nixon would later try to emulate and label "Vietnamization."

However, at such a late stage in the conflict, the impact was minimal. By late 1952, 90,000 French soldiers had been lost in Indochina while their hold over territory continued to slip, leading the French public to oppose the war.

In 1953 Giap decided to mount attacks in Laos against the pro-French king, Sisavang Vong, in Luang Prabang, hoping to divert French forces to distant Laos along dangerously overextended and isolated supply lines. To counter these efforts, the French decided to fortify an outpost at Dien Bien Phu as a barrier to Vietminh access to Laos.[29]

International political forces were edging closer to a negotiated settlement of Asian crises. After three years the Korean War ended in an armistice. Following Stalin's death, the Soviet Union moved to reduce tensions worldwide. French politicians openly called for a negotiated settlement in Indochina.[30]

Paradoxically, China was fearful that France might abandon its efforts and Americans might enter the conflict in Indochina, risking establishment of an American military presence on China's southern border, a perpetual fear. China also hoped to expand its own international role by moving away from exclusive dependence on the Soviet Union.

The United States and Ho Chi Minh were wary of negotiations. Washington feared a neutralist solution might emerge, which in the Washington political climate would be anathema. Hanoi was concerned that France might again betray Vietnam through negotiations, as it had in 1945–46.[31]

In the lead-up to the battle of Dien Bien Phu in March 1954, the French forces were one-third of the garrison—25 percent were legionnaires, 22 percent were mainland French, and 20 percent were African (mostly Moroccan). During battle five more paratroop battalions—one Vietnamese, French, German, and other legionnaires, and three Airborne Surgical Detachments—parachuted into battle. Among the legionnaires, a sizeable number were Germans in their mid-twenties from the Wehrmacht who had conquered France in 1940 and knew nothing but war.[32]

K.W. Taylor points to several reasons the French established a strong point at Dien Bien Phu: It would inhibit movement of resistance forces from Vietnam into Laos; establish a base for taking the battle to resistance-infested areas; energize the Montagnards, who frequently supported the French; and attract resistance to suicide attacks, which could be easily destroyed by French airpower. In addition, it would promote French control of the opium trade, centered in Dien Bien Phu, and deny financial support for the resistance. Finally, and most important, it would restore a sense of mobility and offensive character the French had lacked.[33]

French General Henri Navarre replaced General Raoul Salan at the urging of Washington, even though he was unknown to the Americans. Navarre, with no experience in Vietnam, underestimated Giap's strategy.[34] Instead of reinforcing Dien Bien Phu, Navarre massed forces in central Vietnam because he thought Giap would attempt a headlong attack at Dien Bien Phu. A Chinese advisor had recommended to Giap such a "human wave attack"; however, after its start Giap realized its folly and the risk of huge losses. He decided instead to encircle and strangle the French at Dien Bien Phu.

The French attempted to get the Americans to come to the rescue, and Eisenhower, in his inaugural address, described the situation in Indochina as extremely perilous.

U.S. Secretary of State John Foster Dulles embroidered in a nationwide broadcast, "If they [the Soviets] could get this peninsula of Indochina, Siam, Burma, and Malaya they would have the rice bowl of Asia. ... And you can see that would be another weapon which would tend to expand their control into Japan and India." Eisenhower knew that he would need congressional support, and Dulles briefed a joint group of senators, outlining the dangers and threats and seeking agreement on a resolution that would authorize the President, "in the event that he determines such action is required to protect and defend the safety and security of the United States, to employ U.S. Naval and Air Forces to assist the forces which are resisting aggression in Southeast Asia."[35]

Dulles contended that such a resolution might deter the Vietminh and, more seriously, China from entering the battle, which was central to Dulles's concerns.

The senators were receptive but insisted that any action not be unilateral and that it include, notably, the UK, France, Australia, New Zealand, the Philippines, Thailand, and others. Dulles informed the president and sought allied support for a defense coalition.[36]

In an extraordinary diplomatic tour de force in early April, Dulles, Eisenhower, and Joint Chiefs of Staff (JCS) Admiral Arthur Radford attempted to gain support from allies and calm calls from France for urgent action. Eisenhower knew that "greater efforts by the Western powers would be required to save Indochina from Communism." In contact with Churchill, he noted that the "loss of Indochina could lead to a disastrous shift in the power ratio 'throughout Asia and the Pacific' and severely undermine the global strategic position of both the United States and Britain. ... Following a defeat in Vietnam, Southeast Asia could swiftly fall, and Australia and New Zealand would be threatened. Japan would be deprived of non-Communist markets and sources of food and would almost certainly have to make an accommodation with the Communist world. 'This has led us . . . to the hard conclusion that the situation in South Asia requires us urgently to take serious and far-reaching decisions.' " Australia, New Zealand, and Britain consistently declined, including Churchill himself. Various options, from bombers, which were sailing on carriers from the Philippines, to nuclear weapons, bruited in the Pentagon, to additional planes and U.S. pilots, were all thrown into the mix. In the end, Eisenhower and Dulles could not assemble support.[37]

Simultaneously, Giap's strangling of Dien Bien Phu proceeded.

In the final days before Dien Bien Phu's collapse, on April 4 President Eisenhower assembled a small group to discuss the situation. The president agreed to send American forces to Indochina under strict conditions: the action must be united, including the UK; France must agree to maintain its commitments in the area; and France must grant full independence to the Associated States so there would be no hint of colonialism.[38]

Two days earlier, the French Laniel government requested heavy U.S. bomber air strikes to try to save Dien Bien Phu. General Navarre first worried that this might cause the Chinese to enter the war but changed his mind and agreed. Eisenhower refused without coalition support (UK), but then acceded to a follow-up request for French pilots to fly U.S. aircrafts from the Philippines. Since French pilots had no experience with B-29s, Eisenhower offered corsairs and light Navy bombers instead, subject to approval by Congress.[39]

Dulles then undertook a six-day trip to London and Paris to

garner Prime Minster Anthony Eden's support for the principle of united action and to convince Foreign Minister Georges Bidault to grant independence to the Associated States. Bidault replied, "What would be the point if Indochina was no longer associated with France?" Dulles then returned to Washington to assemble a meeting of ambassadors of prospective allies to create a new defense arrangement, including the UK, France, Australia, New Zealand, the Philippines, Thailand, and the Associated States. At this point, Eden declined to participate. In a meeting after April 30 the minister of state, Lord Reading, and Dulles continued to talk with Eden about a united action. Dulles alluded to the possibility of maintaining a "bridgehead," or foothold for two years until the South Vietnamese troops could train to defend their country. "To Eden and Reading's ears, this sounded unmistakably like a plan to take over military operations from the French. When Reading remarked that the bridgehead notion 'meant that things remain on a boil for several years to come,' Dulles retorted: 'that would be a very good thing.' "[40] These ideas forecast eventually the Southeast Asian Treaty Organization's (SEATO) treaty and a U.S. determination to continue the battle beyond, and regardless of the outcome in, the Geneva Accords.

As Dulles was pursuing his idea of united action, the U.S. Congress was paying close heed to a proposal. Freshman Senator John F. Kennedy made a speech at a colloquium with remarkably perceptive insights. Kennedy first demanded candor from the administration, then qualified his position. As Logevall explained:

> While he favored the concept of United Action proposal, Kennedy feared where such a policy would lead the nation: "to pour money, matérial, and men into the jungles of Indochina without at least a remote prospect of victory. This would be dangerously foolish and destructive." Would the United States ever be able to make a difference in that part of the world? "No amount of American military assistance can conquer an enemy which is everywhere and at the same time nowhere, 'an enemy of the people' which has the sympathy and covert support of the people." No satisfactory outcome was possible, Kennedy concluded, unless France

accorded the Associated States full and complete independence.[41]

Over the next months, the Vietminh constructed miles of tunnels and advanced sometimes only a few meters a day, tightening
their strangling grip around the French forces. Movement of Vietminh artillery to commanding heights overlooking the French in
the valley and low clouds were the decisive factors at Dien Bien
Phu. In one of the most extraordinary battles in history, General Giap defeated the French Expeditionary Forces under General
Christian Marie Ferdinand de la Croix de Castries, who was, in full
regalia, taken captive. Roughly 6,000 in French uniforms and 10,000
Vietminh died at Dien Bien Phu.

On May 7, 1954, the gold-starred red flag was hoisted at the
command bunker at Dien Bien Phu. The Geneva talks opened the
next day.

The Geneva Accords

In Paris, French Premier Pierre Mendes-France gave the negotiations on Asian issues four weeks, after which he promised, if the
talks were unsuccessful, he would resign. Since 1953, Mendes-
France had called, Logevall wrote, for France to "guarantee . . . full
independence to the Indochinese states and should set a definite
time schedule for the withdrawal of French forces. . . . France would
then propose an armistice to Ho Chi Minh, subject to nationwide
elections for a constituent assembly to establish a constitution for
a free and independent Vietnam."[42] He did not consider himself
bound by any previous French commitments or negotiating tactics.[43] In the talks, the Vietminh showed no flexibility, and noncommunist Emperor Bao Dai appointed the inflexible Ngo Dinh Diem
as his prime minister in Hue.[44] The talks appeared stalemated from
the start.

Ho Chi Minh was under pressure from Beijing and Moscow to
achieve a settlement at Geneva. The Soviet Union wanted improved
relations with the West and for France to reject the European Defense Committee pushed by the United States. China wished to be

recognized as a major power and to prevent the United States from intervening on its southern borders. Moscow clearly came down for partition to reflect France's position in Cochinchina and Vietminh strength in Tonkin and Annam. The Soviet ambassador had already raised this possibility of partition with the French, and the French did not reject the idea. Zhou Enlai had told Ho Chi Minh by wire that conditions were ripe for pursuit of a diplomatic struggle and that a fixed demarcation line would create the base for such a struggle. He suggested that the 16th parallel was a possibility. In his meetings in Beijing and Moscow, Ho Chi Minh must have been deeply disappointed that both his principal allies were urging him to accept a half loaf, after seven years of struggle and the enormous victory at Dien Bien Phu. Ho Chi Minh and Zhou Enlai continued to Moscow, where the Russians emphasized the European aspects of their geostrategic considerations.[45]

In the Geneva meetings, China's foreign minister, Zhou Enlai, intervened through a secret meeting with Mendes-France. China's principal goal was peace in the region without U.S. bases on China's borders. Zhou informed the premier, in contrast to the Vietminh, that he favored a ceasefire first and political accord afterward, violating the Vietminh's basic demand for reunification. Zhou also urged the Vietminh to respect the sovereignty of Laos and Cambodia, to both of which France had granted independence in 1953. Zhou Enlai proposed the idea of two zones in Vietnam, and Mendes-France was receptive. This was anathema to Hanoi. Under fierce pressure from the Chinese and Soviets, Phan Van Dong agreed to the two zones but insisted that they be at the 13th parallel, giving two-thirds of Vietnam to the North. Mendes-France suggested the 18th parallel. Zhou persuaded the Vietnamese to drop demands for the Pathet Lao and Free Khmer to occupy parts of Laos and Cambodia, and Phan Van Dong called for nationwide elections to reunite Vietnam and to determine Vietnam's future in six months.[46]

In the judgment of K.W. Taylor, "it was obvious to all the major powers that the only way to avoid the likelihood of Vietnam again becoming a place of crisis in the Cold War was to separate the two Vietnam governments, each in its own territory. The Vietnamese of all persuasions opposed any permanent partition of the country."

The idea of subsequent elections was contrived to deal with this issue.[47]

U.S. Secretary of State John Foster Dulles suspected French subterfuge with secret protocols that would turn Vietnam over to the communists immediately and threatened to withdraw from the Conference. Although this boycott never came to fruition, the United States was sidelined and offered little at the talks. U.S. Ambassador Bedell Smith and Bao Dai's delegate were excluded from the negotiations. They invited Russian Prime Minister Vyacheslav Mikhailovich Molotov to mediate among Mendes-France, Zhou, British Prime Minister Anthony Eden, and Phan Van Dong. Arguing the location of the partition, Phan Van Dong argued for the 16th parallel. Mendes-France stuck to the 18th. Suddenly Molotov declared, "Let's agree on the 17th," then moved on to the subject of when the elections would be held. Again, Molotov suddenly declared, "Shall we say two years?" The subject was settled.[48]

With the help of Zhou and Molotov, Mendes-France had won a major achievement by thwarting Hanoi's most ambitious hopes and preserving, at least temporarily, a noncommunist, Western-oriented component in the settlement. Phan Van Dong, furious with Zhou, walked away and muttered to an aide, "He has double-crossed us." China's complicity in the partition of Vietnam and the ensuing twenty years of conflict to reunite the country haunts Chinese-Vietnamese relations to this day.[49]

The Geneva Accords papered over the threat of broader conflict and postponed a settlement of the underlying issues of the future of Indochina by dividing Vietnam at the 17th parallel and called for a nationwide election in 1956 to determine the future of Vietnam. While the other participants expressed vocal agreement to the accords, the United States pledged to abide by the Geneva Agreement. But, fatefully, U.S. representative Bedell Smith made the following unilateral U.S. statement, in part: "The United States would 'view any renewal of the aggression in violation of the aforesaid agreements with grave concern and as seriously threatening international peace and security.' " President Kennedy used this statement to justify later actions in Vietnam.[50]

8

Post–Geneva Accords: South and North Vietnam Diverge

In the days before the French defeat at Dien Bien Phu and the Geneva Accords, the French had killed, arrested, or exiled many of the nationalist figures in South Vietnam.

The Mandarin family of Ngo Dinh Diem, who became South Vietnam's prime minister in 1954 under Emperor Bao Dai, was an exception. In 1933 Diem's father, Ngo Dinh Kha, was appointed minister of the interior for the Mandarin court of Emperor Bao Dai; he and his brothers had been prominent political and religious figures. Diem insisted that the French give real influence to the Vietnamese legislature. He resigned after three months out of frustration with the lack of power conceded to the Vietnamese by the French. Thus, Ngo Dinh Diem had legitimate anti-colonial credentials in the eyes of many Vietnamese.

In the wake of the Geneva Accords and the partition of Vietnam, the United States chose Diem to lead South Vietnam with American support, as John Foster Dulles asserted, "because we knew of no one better."[1] More seriously, the Ngo Dinh family had been conservative leaders for some time. Ngo Dinh Diem, the younger brother, had gone to school with Bao Dai. Bao Dai knew Diem but regarded him as too anti-French to be part of a solution. Ngo Dinh Phuc was a prominent cleric, eventually appointed archbishop in Hue, where his role was markedly unhelpful to the government during the Buddhist crisis of 1963. Nonetheless, Diem was from a prominent family, and he himself was regarded as an experienced, strong nationalist and anticommunist, which, of course, appealed to Dulles.[2]

Diem perceived the challenges ahead to be primarily military and ignored the widespread support of Ho Chi Minh—even by noncommunists—for his patriotism in the anticolonial struggle. Diem, like most observers, understood Ho Chi Minh, with his charisma and popularity, would win in a free election, so he, with American support, immediately rejected the notion of elections in 1956, claiming free elections could not be held in the North.[3]

Washington mischaracterized the Geneva Accords as establishing two Vietnams with an international boundary at the demilitarized zone (DMZ), a position contradictory to the boundary established by the Geneva Accords, which had created the temporary military demarcation line until 1956 elections could settle the matter. Washington persisted in this fabrication, and it took the United States to war.

The language of the accords could not have been clearer, yet the new Diem government and its American backers found the armistice line to be politically expedient, albeit with tragic consequences.

This was the prelude, in effect, to a U.S. rejection of the Geneva Accords. John Foster Dulles acknowledged the accords, but did not accept them, did not insist on holding elections in 1956 as outlined, and lost the momentum for the settlement built into the accords. SEATO constructed an alliance to contain North Vietnam and, in contravention of the accords, began the process that established the DMZ as a political demarcation of two separate states. President Kennedy violated the strict limits on introduction of personnel and equipment into South Vietnam. President Johnson constructed U.S. policy based on these steps to contend that North Vietnam had committed aggression by sending troops to South Vietnam, eventually allowing him to invade a sovereign state. These major sleights of hand successively rejecting the Geneva Accords were the second great strategic error in Indochina, which, of course, led inexorably to the Vietnam War.

Washington also accepted Diem's analysis that the struggle in Vietnam was principally a military struggle and sent some 600 military advisors to Vietnam to provide support.

Diem's Early Rule

Ngo Dinh Diem was authoritarian, convinced of the correctness of his views and policies, and demanded obedience and loyalty.

Under political attack by military figures, religious sects such as the Cao Dai (an eclectic religion with saints ranging from Jesus to Victor Hugo), the reform Buddhists known as Hoa Hao, and criminal elements such as the Binh Xuyen (who operated in the jungle marshes just south of Saigon), Diem turned inward to his close family and friends, especially his younger brother Ngo Dinh Nhu, his closest political advisor. Diem believed his rectitude and moral authority should prevail despite the widespread popularity of the charismatic Ho Chi Minh. Isolated among a small clique of agreeable insiders, Diem became increasingly removed from the realities of his country.

In the United States, the frequent differences between the Department of Defense and State Department were stark: The Joint Chiefs of Staff argued in 1954 against providing military support to Diem until he established stability in South Vietnam; Secretary of State John Foster Dulles countered that training Diem's army was the best way to strengthen Diem's regime. Despite pessimism, especially in the CIA (about Diem's prospects in Vietnam), Eisenhower split the difference, telling Diem that America's support would depend on "standards of performance." At the same time, plans for military and other support proceeded without regard to Diem's performance. Nonetheless, his early years were judged satisfactory from the U.S. standpoint.

But American military advisors complained that Diem paid no heed to their advice. He feigned interest in discussions with Colonel Edward G. Lansdale, who had served as an advisor to Philippine President Ramon Magsaysay as he crushed the communist rebels, the Hukbalahap, in the late 1940s. Lansdale was the model for William Lederer in Eugene Burdick's *The Ugly American* and for Alden Pyle in Graham Greene's *The Quiet American*. Lansdale urged Diem to employ "psychological warfare," which seemingly amounted to simplistic, ineffective propaganda gimmicks.[4]

As Lansdale later argued in his counterinsurgency training course for American military going to Vietnam: "Just remember this: Communist guerrillas hide among the people. If you win the people over to your side the Communist guerrillas have no place to hide. With no place to hide, you can find them. Then, as military men, fix them . . . finish them!!"[5]

This somewhat spiritual approach appealed to the religious and aloof Diem, who appeared to have little understanding of the problems he was to deal with, the peasants he ruled over, or the context of his challenges.[6] Lansdale's simplistic approach, too, reflected an absence of clear understanding of the historic, cultural, and political context in which he was operating. Diem's village councils, *agrovilles*, and later strategic hamlets were no match for the patriotic appeals of the Vietminh.

Following the Geneva Accords, some 600,000 to 1 million Vietnamese moved from the North to the South, while about 150,000 went from the South to the North.

Diem did not prepare for elections in 1956, declaring vaguely that he could not hold elections until it could be ascertained that the elections would be fair.

At the same time, Diem held a rigged referendum by which he deposed Bao Dai as emperor, and consequently assumed the position of head of state. The proponent of "absolutely fair" elections won this referendum with 98.2 percent of the vote. American advisors had urged a more plausible vote of 60 to 70 percent, but Diem would not tolerate any indication of a challenge to his rule.[7]

On Vietnamese elections, the United States took the position that the Vietnamese themselves should decide, while simultaneously supporting Diem. China and the Soviet Union did nothing to promote elections, and Moscow even proposed in early 1957 that the United Nations accept North and South Vietnam as "two separate states" with different political and economic systems. The United States rejected this solution since, as a principle, it was unwilling to recognize a communist regime, although the status quo suited it. Diem proceeded ruthlessly to eradicate communists in the South. As a result of torture and other extreme measures, some 90 percent of the communist cadres were thought to have been eliminated by the end of 1956.[8]

Diem also instituted *agrovilles*, later in the American era known as "strategic hamlets," which sought to isolate the rural population from the communists. But the peasants viewed the *agrovilles* as little more than prisons, which further alienated the rural population. Saigon separated peasants from their land, homes, and graves of their ancestors, whom they worshipped. Many judged that the strategic hamlets were thus a counterproductive failure. Strategic hamlets were an improvement over the *agrovilles* and designed to modernize, bring the rural society under control, and encourage cooperative efforts and self-reliance that would make the peasants resistant to Vietcong enticements. But the implementation was strict, forced to develop too fast, and had many of the same problems as the *agrovilles*. Moreover, the regime compelled villagers to leave their land and build the strategic hamlets, which amounted to forced labor reminiscent of the French *corvée* system. Such an approach reflected Diem's belief that Vietnam's issues were fundamentally security-based, and his goal was to ensure his own control of the population. He also saw the hamlets as a means to curtail American influence, which he strongly wished to avert. The United States enthusiastically supported the strategic-hamlet program as an imaginative method of isolating the Vietcong.[9]

The use of strategic hamlets led to widespread animosity among peasants. While they did not necessarily become communists, the disaffection seriously undermined support for Diem and his government.

To sum up the state of affairs in South Vietnam, on May 25, 1961, President Kennedy, in his second State of the Union address, commented that communists had killed 4,000 officials from April 1960 to 1961. Overall, about 10,000 village chiefs were killed in a country with about 16,000 hamlets.[10]

Drawing on the successful counterinsurgency efforts in the Philippines and Malaysia and Diem's own *agroville* program, the United States (under President Kennedy and his advisors) advocated a new "strategic hamlet" program to move villages to fortified, armed hamlets and, thereby, to isolate the villagers from the Vietcong. Established in 1962, roughly 8,500 strategic hamlets were constructed. By 1963 only 20 percent were judged by the United States as satisfactory. By late 1963, only 1,400 of the 8,500 strategic hamlets survived. This concept, associated with the oil slick theory employed successfully by the French in 1888–94, was intended to eliminate insurgency in an area and allow counterinsurgency forces to enlarge the pacified area. In fact, the "oil slick" merely pushed the Vietcong into the next province, and as the counterinsurgency efforts moved on, the Vietcong returned to the original province.[11]

Despite finding themselves on the same side of the Cold War conflict, American relationships with Diem strained as he ignored U.S. calls for reform. Saigon siphoned funds for economic development to projects building political support. Diem used funds intended to strengthen the army and resist an invasion of the North to build a conventional army to protect him from rivals. Many believe Diem mistakenly designated the funds for counterinvasion from the North. In late December 1960, a group of Vietnamese military units (three paratrooper battalions and a marine unit) surrounded the palace, demanding reform. Diem managed to outfox the officers by going on the radio and agreeing to free elections and other liberal measures, but he reneged on the promises. Just as the measures were to take effect, the loyalists routed the dissidents, killing 400 and exiling the leaders to Cambodia.

Meanwhile in the North: Radical Land Reform

While Diem was eliminating political rivals in the South, the North undertook forced land reform between 1953 and 1956—a process that engendered violent resistance from traditionalist Vietnamese peasants. Contrasting with Ho Chi Minh's attempts to bring all classes and political forces together in a united front, the land-reform program pitted the party and poorer peasants against landlords and rich peasants, adopting social policies from both the Soviet Union and China. Moreover, the process often victimized whoever happened to fall under the ire of local authorities, not just those who were wealthy and could be labeled "exploiters." In 1955, cadres set up Agricultural Reform Tribunals and were charged with quotas to arraign certain numbers of landlords, even in districts where there were few. Trumped-up charges were ubiquitous and atrocities were common. Many cadres charged their neighbors or relatives and seized the land for themselves.[12] Faced with chaos and popular resentment in the countryside, the party abandoned the land-reform program in 1956.

In a conversation the author had at a restaurant in Hanoi on July 12, 2010, with University of Social Sciences and Humanities, VNU, professors Dr. Pham Quang Minh and Dr. Pham Hong Tung, who led the Princeton Seminars, the professors offered a more nuanced view of land reform in North Vietnam in 1953–56. I asked how Saigon implemented the drastic land reform program, since it seemed to go against Ho Chi Minh's fundamental approach of trying to unite the Vietnamese people in the struggle for revolution. How did such a flawed policy move forward under the watch of Uncle Ho? Was Secretary-General Truong Chinh, who implemented the land-reform program, more powerful than Ho? Did Ho acquiesce because of pressure from Mao and Stalin? Were Giap's and Ho's apologies to the Vietnamese people in 1956 about the drastic and divisive nature of the land-reform program a reflection of their doubts all along?

Dr. Tung took the lead in responding, although Dr. Minh had conducted the Princeton seminar session on land reform. Tung said the Politburo split along lines of Truong Chinh on one side and Ho Chi Minh, Vo Nguyen Giap, and Phan Van Dong on the other (of whom Ho and Giap were the most powerful). While Ho had spent several years in the Soviet Union and China, he attempted to try to keep both at bay. Truong Chinh had also been in both the Soviet Union and China, but he was openly and uncharacteristically pro-Chinese, in contrast to others, including Ho, who tried to maintain politically correct positions toward both. Nonetheless, the Vietnamese had to be solicitous of both Moscow and Beijing because of their dependence on both for financial, political, diplomatic, and, in the case of China, military support. However, Stalin put more pressure on Vietnam regarding land reform. Stalin chided the Vietnamese for struggling since 1946 to throw out the French; in all those years they had not undertaken any policies to consolidate socialist leadership. The time was then, the early 1950s, to rectify this. [13]

K.W. Taylor reports that Truong Chinh and Vo Nguyen Giap had, in fact, written a joint study on land reform and published it during the 1937–38 Popular Front period. Taylor describes the study as portraying five categories of peasants that became the targets for land reform in the Fifties. It described a system of landholdings, taxation, and indebtedness that made the peasants' lives very difficult and indoctrinated them to accept exploitation through religious belief and an irrational respect for private property. With myriad problems faced early on, Truong Chinh nonetheless pushed for rent and debt controls, radical reforms; in 1951 he promoted land reform as a priority.[14]

Continuing Dr. Tung's analysis, the Politburo in Hanoi succumbed to the pressure and Party Secretary-General Truong Chinh led the Reform Movement in North Vietnam. But Chinh's mentors were the Chinese, and the plan he implemented was straight from the Chinese playbook. The Chinese even provided an advisory group to guide the program. As a matter of practice, when the Vietnam Politburo decided on an action, usually all the leadership acceded. Thus, Truong Chinh had the lead and others who might have had reservations, such as Giap and Ho, left the implementation of the program to Truong Chinh. While they had agreed to undertake land reform, as the program proceeded Giap and Ho became increasingly concerned about the implementation. Finally, Giap first and then Ho apologized to the Vietnamese people about the drastic nature of the reform. Under criticism for the land-reform disaster, they ousted Truong Chinh as party secretary general and temporarily replaced him with Ho Chi Minh in 1957 until they appointed Le Duan. In 1960 Le Duan returned to Hanoi to become party leader. Thereafter, he and Le Duc Tho, polished and upper-class, were the chief decision makers until Le Duan died in 1986. Truong Chinh, however, returned to the top leadership tier again as secretary general in 1986, but southern moderate Nguyen Van Linh replaced him later the same year.[15]

In K.W. Taylor's view, despite criticism of the land-reform policies, it achieved a basic aim of the party by eliminating revolutionary class enemies in rural society, implementing a more equitable distribution of land, and it "traumatized the rural population into obedience."[16]

In 1957, reacting to Diem's attempt to exterminate the Vietminh in South Vietnam, Hanoi instructed its agents in the South to form armed companies in the jungle and marshes in the western edge of the Mekong Delta. In reaction to Diem's denunciation campaign, coupled with muted reaction to Nikita Khrushchev's denunciation of Stalin's cruelty and personality cult, Le Duc Tho teamed up with the unpolished Le Duan to abandon the nonviolent struggle in the South and pursue a much more aggressive policy against South Vietnam. Their approach was a direct challenge to Truong Chinh, who espoused Chinese advice to build socialism in the North and postpone dealing with the southern question.[17] Le Duc Tho in 1961 also helped organize the communist party's southern region, which the United States would later refer to as COSVN.[18.]

While Le Duan was consolidating his position in the party, Ngo Dinh Diem had successfully dealt with communist policy and smashed their infrastructure in the South in the late Fifties.[19]

In May 1959, Hanoi formed the 559 Group to enlarge and improve the route that became known as the Ho Chi Minh Trail to South Vietnam. Shortly thereafter, Group 759 formed to study how to send men and material into the South. Within a few months, they had constructed the communication and transportation system to the South and thousands of southerners, regrouped in 1954, returned to the South to fight the government.[20]

Until May 1959, Ho Chi Minh discouraged political activity by communists in the south, fearing that calls for an uprising could lead to a crippling of the communist elements.

However, in part because of the absence of political opportunities, and since they were more effective, assassinations of local officials grew from 1,200 in 1959 to 4,000 in 1961, leading Diem to appoint military officials as village chiefs, once again playing into Vietminh hands. Diem concentrated on security rather than supporting traditional village chiefs. While these were not mutually exclusive, Diem's reliance on the military cost him political support and helped galvanize the communist movement in the South.

In December 1960, Hanoi announced the formation of the National Liberation Front (NLF), which used the classic communist method of creating front organizations to promote its agenda. Using the same ploy the party had adopted in 1941, establishing the League for Independence of Vietnam (the Vietminh), and espousing a moderate agenda, the NLF had widespread appeal among disaffected intellectuals, religious sects, and rural peasants who opposed Diem. Headed by Saigon lawyer Nguyen Huu Tho, Hanoi claimed the NLF did not violate the Geneva Accords, since southerners organized and ran it, thereby disguising the real power in Hanoi.

There are other perspectives. A daughter of a wealthy Saigon family left South Vietnam to study literature at the Sorbonne in Paris and joined the NLF there. After graduation, she taught English literature at the Sorbonne and at Cambridge University in Great Britain. In 1972, she returned to teach English literature at the University of Saigon even as she worked as an undercover agent for the NLF. She has subsequently risen to high-level positions in the Vietnamese government. Each year she spoke on the NLF for my Princeton Global Summer Seminar in Hanoi.[21]

In her presentations she described the NLF as "fundamentally a southern entity which served as coordinator with Hanoi." Although Hanoi had dispatched several of its agents to the South after the 1954 Geneva Accords, many supporters of the NLF had been in and remained in the South throughout. Villagers tended local matters in the south. Consequently, many observers thought the Vietcong were principally rural peasants, but in fact, from the start, many were working to gain a foothold in the cities, particularly among the middle class, intellectuals, and students. She herself returned to Saigon from Paris in July 1972, just months before the Paris Accords ended the war, anticipating the struggle would be fought in the urban political arena. Her task was to attract recruits and motivate them for the political struggle.[22]

She emphasized "the broad rallying character of the National Liberation Front (NLF). This was the 'Third Force' whose driving advocacy was to end the war and achieve reunification of the country. They did not support the GVN [Government of South Vietnam], nor were they Vietminh." What was its appeal? My friend described the process as follows:

> Why did a diverse group support the NLF? Most Americans at the time believed the NLF drew its support from its Communist ideology, but these observers missed the point amidst the Cold War backdrop under the rubric in which the United States operated. To most Vietnamese the ideological economic struggle (i.e., capitalism vs. communism) of the NLF resistance movement was irrelevant. Most cadres did not support communist political and economic goals. Their prime motive was opposition to the war and the division of their country, but they directed the brunt of their opposition at the United States. Rarely did cadres think both sides must

stop the fighting. They thought without U.S. intervention, there would have been no war. Without U.S. intervention, Vietnam could have implemented the Geneva Accords and held the elections in 1956, which Ho Chi Minh would certainly have won.

Vietnamese are fiercely nationalistic, which motivated them to fight the Americans, the French, and Chinese. Their motivation was not pro-war but pro-reunification and nationalism. Reconciliation between the various factions could be achieved within this context.

The U.S.-Vietnam relationship unfortunately became entangled in the French Colonial epoch and the crisis deepened partly due to a misunderstanding of each other's history. Ho Chi Minh, like many other Vietnamese leaders, had studied U.S. history, and he even quoted the U.S. Declaration of Independence in the Vietnamese Declaration of Independence. The U.S. had become a nation by severing its ties with British colonial power. Ho Chi Minh wrote several letters to President Truman, but there was no response. U.S.-Vietnam relations started with this major and tragic lost opportunity. If the U.S. had been less obsessed with its Cold War ideology and truer to its own ideals of freedom and popular sovereignty, relations between Vietnam and the U.S. could have developed much more differently.

9

From Mass Destruction
to Counterinsurgency: The Kennedy Years

President Kennedy came to power having promoted a strong and positive leadership role for America. In his inaugural address he asserted that America would "pay any price, bear any burden, meet any hardship, support any friend, and oppose any foe to assure the survival and success of liberty." As noted earlier, his famous call to service, "Ask not what your country can do for you but what you can do for your country," led me to join the Foreign Service in 1962.[1]

As a student of 1930s history, Kennedy vigorously and regularly supported traditional American foreign-policy goals. Despite his favor of national independence and his support for self-determination for the Algerians against France, the new president also supported, as a senator, funding the French War in Indochina, asserting that the United States must ensure that communism did not "engulf all of Asia." This approach quickly embedded Vietnam into the Cold War.

Among leaders, President Dwight D. Eisenhower, however, first enunciated the domino theory—if South Vietnam fell to communism then the rest of Southeast Asia, including populous Indonesia, would promptly fall like dominoes.

As Karnow wrote, President Kennedy maintained that South Vietnam was the "proving ground for democracy in Asia" and a "test of American responsibility and determination." He denounced the "menace of monolithic Communism directed from Moscow and its wars of liberation," and the "relentless pressure of the Chinese Communists."[2] Kennedy saw South Vietnam as the "proving ground for democracy in Asia" and a "test of American responsibility and determination." On NBC's *Huntley-Brinkley*

Report on September 9, 1963, David Brinkley asked the president if he had any reason to doubt the "Domino Theory"—that "if South Vietnam falls, the rest of Southeast Asia will go behind it?"

The president replied, "No, I believe it. I believe it. I think that the struggle is close enough. China is so large, looms so high just beyond the frontiers, that if South Vietnam went, it would not only give them an improved geographic position for a guerrilla assault on Malaya, but would also give the impression that the wave of the future in Southeast Asia was China and the Communists. So, I believe it."[3]

Nonetheless, President Kennedy's comments were at times much more nuanced. Asked about the domino theory at a press conference on April 24, 1963, Kennedy responded:

> The population of Laos is 2 million and it is scattered. It is a very rough country. It is important as a sovereign power. The people desire to be independent, and it is also important because it borders the Mekong River and, quite obviously, if Laos fell into Communist hands it would increase the danger along the northern frontiers of Thailand. It would put additional pressure on Cambodia and on South Vietnam, which, in itself, would put additional pressure on Malaysia.
>
> So, I do accept the view that there is an interrelationship in these countries and that is one of the reasons why we are concerned with maintaining the Geneva Accords as a method of maintaining stability in Southeast Asia.[4]

This is less than a full-throated support of the theory, driven, at least in part, by the anticipation of a tough fight in the 1964 elections, but also by skepticism about the validity of the domino theory. Having drawn a clear line, these were tough stances from which to back away. But there was a steady stream of questioning, doubts, and intentions that Kennedy's comments on the domino theory were political, not representative of his real assessment or intentions.

Reflecting those same questions, Kennedy's close advisor, McGeorge Bundy was later dismissive of the theory. "I always lose my temper," Bundy said, "at the notion that a series of complex political organisms can be understood by comparing them to an inanimate set of black tiles." He understood Vietnam was a gamble, not really a nation. Bundy understood the hazards of white men fighting a war in Asia and that the odds were poor that the United States could achieve what the French had been unable to do.[5]

Despite President Kennedy's lip service to the importance of maintaining the status quo in South Vietnam, the young president was cautious about U.S. commitment to the country. In a National Security Council (NSC) discussion of Vietnam in November 1961, Kennedy gave short shrift to proposals to send combat troops to Vietnam.[6] In a speech the next day, November 16, 1961, at the University of Washington he dramatically recast his inaugural speech activism, replacing it with a new realism, no doubt learned in his first year in power. President Kennedy said, "We must face the fact that the United States is neither omnipotent nor omniscient. We are only 6 percent of the world's population, and we cannot impose our will on the 94 percent. We cannot fight every wrong or reverse every adversary. Therefore, there cannot be an American solution to every world problem."[7]

Ted Sorenson, Kennedy's speechwriter, said, "Kennedy's emphasis on pragmatic realism and recognition of the limits of American power was the quintessential expression of Kennedy's foreign-policy beliefs."[8]

The Eisenhower Administration–conceived CIA Bay of Pigs fiasco, Kennedy's problematic meeting in Vienna with Nikita Khrushchev, and confrontation with the Soviets over Berlin overshadowed Kennedy's foreign policy principles and posed serious challenges to the perception of him as competent to manage foreign affairs.[9]

Kennedy faced two other crises: in Laos, where Eisenhower urged Kennedy to send troops, and a deteriorating situation in South Vietnam. Eisenhower recommended that Kennedy concentrate on protecting Laos from communism. Going against the advice of Eisenhower, Kennedy appointed trusted family advisor Averell Harriman to promote a neutral and independent Laos, as was subsequently mandated by the 1962 Geneva Accords.[10] Harriman was a major force in the Democrat Party, a significant financial contributor, and a former governor of New York.[11]

But regarding South Vietnam, Kennedy, who had met Ngo Dinh Diem while a senator, resisted neutrality, though he was not willing to "bear any burden, pay any price" to rescue the country. He wanted to save South Vietnam from the communists without committing American combat forces.

Kennedy also did not agree with Eisenhower's reliance on "massive retaliation" for dealing with threats. He felt instead that the United States should, in general, meet the challenges with carefully tailored responses. Defense Secretary Robert McNamara's conservative business background at Ford Motor Company reinforced Kennedy's natural inclination to prefer limited action to large-scale military involvement in Vietnam. The counterinsurgency doctrines promoted by General Edward Lansdale fascinated Kennedy. Among other things, this led Kennedy to establish the "Green Berets," covert units trained to fight third-world insurgencies.

In contrast, Vice President Lyndon B. Johnson favored a robust approach. Kennedy dispatched Johnson to Vietnam in May 1961. Johnson called Diem "the Asian reincarnation of Winston Churchill" and proclaimed that the loss of Vietnam would compel America to fight "on the beaches of Waikiki!" Bluntly, he warned: "The battle against Communism must be joined in Southeast Asia or the U.S. must surrender the Pacific and take up its defenses on its own shores."[12]

With such a resounding recommendation, Diem evidently concluded that Washington considered him indispensable. His constant rejection of advice from the United States and unwillingness to undertake necessary reforms plagued U.S. policies in South Vietnam and led to U.S. complicity in Diem's overthrow.

Even during Johnson's hectic 1961 visit, Diem rejected the notion of U.S. combat forces in Vietnam, fearing it would undermine his authority as a nationalist and subject him to greater American leverage over his policies—both of which were true. This issue arose frequently during that year. In mid-1961 there was much talk internationally of a "neutralist solution." French President de Gaulle, amid coup-plotting in Saigon, issued invitations on August 29 to all parties in North and South Vietnam to meet in Paris and negotiate reunification of Vietnam based on national unity and neutralism.

While de Gaulle's approach might have offered Kennedy an escape from the Vietnam dilemma, his aides—the Bundy brothers—dismissed de Gaulle's proposal as meddling, impractical, and even mischievous."[13]

Kennedy sent his close advisor, General Maxwell Taylor, to Saigon in October 1961 and sought his advice on how to deal with Diem's requests. As Karnow reported, Kennedy told Taylor to go to Saigon with State Under Secretary for Political Affairs Eugene Rostow to determine how "to avoid further deterioration of the situation, but to remember that the initial responsibility lay with the South Vietnamese government."[14] Kennedy steadfastly opposed the introduction of American combat troops in Vietnam, although he voiced no intention of accepting defeat that permitted communist takeover of South Vietnam. As Taylor said later, "the question is how to change a losing game and begin to win, not how to call it off."[15] Besides proposing bombing of the North, Taylor otherwise offered few concrete proposals for his winning game.

Prior to Taylor's arrival, the Vietcong launched large attacks on South Vietnamese army posts in Phuoc Thanh and Darlac provinces. Deciding "real war" was emerging, Diem changed his mind and said he would welcome American combat soldiers as a "symbolic gesture" of support. He also proposed a bilateral defense pact between South Vietnam and the United States.

After a two-week tour of Vietnam, Taylor and his team went to the Philippines to review his visit to Vietnam and then urged President Kennedy to approve eight thousand U.S. combat troops to South Vietnam, labeling them "logistical legions," sent to help cope with flooding in the Mekong Delta, retaining the option of increasing the number, if necessary. Taylor asserted these could be an advance party for additional troops, should they be needed to fight in Vietnam. Ignoring the potential adverse consequences, this recommendation for escalation foreshadowed Taylor's urging President Johnson to bomb North Vietnam without the expectation of a serious response from the North, a position Kennedy, as president, would not contemplate. The JCS, however, rejected Taylor's proposals as inadequate and advocated the deployment of six divisions, roughly two hundred thousand troops. Juggling concerns about alienating the Pentagon and their supporters in Congress,

Kennedy persuaded Rusk and McNamara to draft a less aggressive posture. He was also very reluctant to assume the aggressive role envisioned by the Pentagon.[16]

Countering these proposals, other Americans (especially in the State Department, but also journalists) cited Vietnamese sources as saying South Vietnamese officials, soldiers, and ordinary citizens had "lost confidence" in Diem. These American dissenters emphasized that the war was waged in Vietnamese villages where "foreign forces cannot win," and warned it would be a mistake for the United States to commit itself irrevocably to the defeat of the communists.[17]

Kennedy sent two younger advisors to Vietnam, Mike Forrestal and Roger Hilsman from the NSC and State, respectively, who issued critical reports on the government of Vietnam's and its U.S. advisors' habit of using enormous firepower against the Vietcong, which destroyed villages and alienated the villagers.[18]

Karnow reported that Kennedy weighed these competing viewpoints and leaned against heavy American troop intervention in Vietnam, while still maintaining American engagement in the country. The NSC formulation that emerged with Kennedy's guidance did not mention providing combat troops or a formal commitment to defend South Vietnam from communist takeover. Kennedy tailored his response to the existing circumstances in Vietnam. He rejected withdrawal but was unwilling to commit full-scale combat forces to save the South. But he mocked George Ball, a persistent dissenter about escalation in Vietnam, when Ball speculated it would take perhaps three hundred thousand troops to contain the threat. Kennedy laughed and retorted, "Well, George, you're supposed to be one of the smartest guys in town, but you're crazier than hell. That will never happen."[19]

His advisors were split on the issue. In contrast to George Ball, Secretary of State Dean Rusk, Defense Secretary Robert McNamara (at that point, in deference to his hawkish JCS), and National Security Advisor McGeorge Bundy supported a vigorous defense. Kennedy demonstrated a pattern of resisting the advice of the JCS. During the tense days of the Cuban Missile Crisis, Kennedy, as in the disastrous Bay of Pigs Fiasco, did not accept the advice of the JCS to bomb missile sites in Cuba. Instead he opted for a quarantine to prevent ships carrying additional nuclear weapons and missiles to Cuba. As we now know, this allowed for secret discussions with Khrushchev, who agreed to withdraw the missiles with a secret understanding that the United States would withdraw its Jupiter missiles from Turkey, which were considered both obsolete and provocative.[20]

This triumph regarding Cuba, along with the mounting and sustaining of the Berlin blockade, established the credentials of the young president as a tough and wise defender of American national interests. His newfound credibility and stature allowed him later to reject the advice of military and civilian advisors when dealing with Vietnam decisions.[21]

Kennedy, while refusing to quit Vietnam, was wary of escalation. Prophetically, he confided to Arthur Schlesinger: "The troops will march in, the bands will play, the crowds will cheer, and in four days everyone will have forgotten. It's like taking a drink. The effect wears off, and you have to take another. . . . The war in Vietnam could be won only so long as it was *their* war. If it were ever converted into a white man's war, we would lose as the French had lost a decade before."[22]

In another telling vignette, Kennedy's ambassador to India, John Kenneth Galbraith, sent a note to the president in early 1962 expressing concern about the danger of drifting into combat and an ever-widening war. He urged Kennedy to "keep open the door to a political solution."[23] This led to a discussion with senior advisor Averell Harriman and Michael V. Forrestal, Mac Bundy's new deputy for Far Eastern affairs. According to Forrestal's notes from the meeting, the President and Harriman agreed "it is important that the overt association of the United States with military operations in Vietnam be reduced to absolute minimum." While not in favor of Galbraith's suggestion to reconvene the Geneva Conference and disagreeing with Galbraith's implied notion of seeking a "neutral solution," Kennedy expressed interest in Galbraith's notion that the Indian government might be a channel for negotiations with Hanoi. "The meeting ended," according to Forrestal's notes. "The President observed generally that he wished us to be prepared to seize upon any favorable moment to reduce our involvement, recognizing that the moment might yet be some time away." Kai Bird concludes: "Clearly—at least at this moment in early 1962—

Kennedy was seeking an escape route out of Vietnam."[24]

But the dilemma remained. After emphasizing his resolve to stop the spread of communism, Kennedy could not entirely withdraw from Vietnam without jeopardizing American prestige or his own political future. This fact became the driving force behind U.S. decisions. Troop numbers grew to 16,000 within two years, and U.S. pilots began to fly combat missions—disguised as training missions—from Bien Hoa Air Base in 1962.[25] The U.S. government, however, attempted to maintain secrecy about its growing involvement both because it violated the Geneva Accords and to hide the truth from the American public.[26]

The introduction of U.S. helicopters onto the scene provided yet another dangerous component.[27] At first they ferried Vietnamese troops to battle, but increasingly they undertook combat activity themselves. Their strafing, damage to villages, and killing of civilians further increased disaffection among Vietnamese with their government and its American backers.

The United States began to import vast quantities of weaponry into Vietnam, convincing Diem he was fighting a conventional war, but it also made the South Vietnamese increasingly dependent on the United States.

Deterioration

Despite the deteriorating circumstances, Washington estimated larger investments of men (now 16,000), money, and materials in 1962 would yield results. Washington managers envisaged a phased withdrawal, taking the number down to 12,000 by 1964. But the word "victory" began to pop up, in parallel with the notion that troop withdrawals might begin in 1964, but this did not square with reality.

In late 1962 President Kennedy sent Senate Majority Leader Mike Mansfield, who earlier had strongly supported Diem, on a survey of Vietnam. His conclusions were unequivocal: The United States had spent 2 billion dollars in seven years, yet the conditions remained unchanged or even worse. He laid the blame not just on the Vietcong but on counterproductive policies of the Americans and Ngo Dinh Diem, who had failed to share political power with other political forces.

"Mansfield recommended a careful reassessment of American interests in Southeast Asia to avoid deeper involvement in South Vietnam, where the primary responsibility rested with the Vietnamese themselves. His belief was 'it is their country; their future is at stake, not ours. To ignore that reality will not only be immensely costly in terms of U.S. lives and resources but may also inexorably draw the U.S. into the unenviable position of the French.' "[28]

According to Karnow, Kennedy told his aide Kenneth O'Donnell, "I got angry with Mike for disagreeing with our policy so completely, and I got angry with myself because I found myself agreeing with him."[29]

Karnow said Kennedy also intimated to O'Donnell and others that he would have the Americans withdraw from Vietnam after his reelection in 1964, even at the risk of being "damned everywhere as a Communist appeaser."[30]

President Jimmy Carter later appointed Majority Leader Mike Mansfield ambassador to Japan in 1977, and President Reagan asked him to stay on from 1981 until 1989. I served as Ambassador Mansfield's fourth and final deputy chief of mission in Tokyo from mid-1985 until December 1989, when the ambassador left Japan for health reasons. I stayed on until June as *chargé d'affaires*, introduced the new ambassador, Michael Armacost, when he arrived in June, and remained as deputy until August. Ambassador Mansfield and I frequently talked about politics and history on Saturday mornings. The ambassador was eager to discuss anything and everything. He was invariably relaxed and thoughtful. Ambassador Mansfield often told me he considered President Kennedy his closest political friend in Washington. Once in discussing Vietnam, the ambassador told me President Kennedy had told him he would withdraw from Vietnam after the 1964 election. Ambassador Mansfield was the essence of integrity and certainly this reflected his understanding of President Kennedy's intentions.

Ted Kennedy's *True Compass* expressed John F. Kennedy's changing attitude toward Vietnam, about which Ted wrote:

> I must speak of another tragic outcome of the bullets fired
> in Dallas that November. Toward midsummer 1963, I was

aware that my brother had qualms about Vietnam. He felt that we needed a new and different direction. He had a growing understanding that he could not resolve the conflict militarily and felt strongly that he certainly would not have escalated it. I witnessed elements of this process unfolding, and Jack affirmed it to me in private conversations. The situation troubled him. He said that Vietnam must belong to the Vietnamese. He had spoken with McNamara about a plan for withdrawal in two to three years.

Ted Kennedy continued, "Jack's antenna was set to find a way out. And I am convinced that he was on his way to finding that way out. He just never got the chance."[31]

Bobby Kennedy, the president's other brother and closest advisor, was perhaps better positioned than Senators Mansfield or Ted Kennedy to understand the president's intentions in Vietnam after the 1964 election. But Bobby's record was not entirely clear. He frequently said that the administration was not sending combat troops to Vietnam, but in 1962 he commented, "We are going to win." There are numerous reports of the President's resisting sending combat troops to Vietnam and his desire not to "Americanize" the war. After a meeting with Averell Harriman in 1962, Mike Forrestal wrote in his notes, "The President observed generally that he wished us to be prepared to seize on any favorable moment to reduce our involvement, recognizing that the moment might yet be some time away."[32] Kenneth O'Donnell asked the president how he could withdraw the American forces, to which the president responded, "Easy, put a government in there that will ask us to leave." In retrospect, however, Robert Kennedy told Daniel Ellsberg in October 1967, "Of course no one can know what my brother would have done in 1964–65."[33] However, the subsequent coup and assassination of Ngo Dinh Dem made any withdrawal more difficult.

Shortly before his assassination, in a relaxed moment President Kennedy instructed Forrestal to prepare a "profound review" of the policy and situation in Vietnam. He told Forrestal, "I even want to think about whether or not we should be there."[34]

Despite his predilections, we cannot know with confidence

what President Kennedy would have done if faced with the rapid deterioration of conditions in Vietnam in 1964–65. The comment by Robert Kennedy is probably the most apt. However, based on the personal accounts of those closest to him, we can suspect that American policy might have taken a more fortuitous direction in Indochina.

The Buddhist Crisis

Diem's army's weakness was demonstrated at a village called Ap Bac in the Mekong Delta in January 1963 when an inferior Vietcong contingent mauled a South Vietnamese division led by an incompetent protégé of Diem.[35]

Ngo Dinh Diem's brother and Ngo Dinh Nhu's wife, "Madame Nhu," as Americans called her, became symbolic of the aloof, corrupt regime in Saigon. Justified or not, Americans and French critics laid all sins and faults on Mme Nhu. Stanley Karnow, for example, wrote that Mme Nhu came from a corrupt family, lived a lavish lifestyle, issued edicts abolishing divorce, made adultery a crime, and banned abortions, contraceptives, beauty contests, and boxing matches—even as her family profited from many of these activities. Her hypocrisy and lack of understanding of the Vietnamese people appalled ordinary citizens.[36]

Vietnamese have traditionally accepted an eclectic mix of religions, but they genuinely venerated scholars over priests. Traditionally, most Vietnamese considered themselves Buddhists, with Confucianism, Daoism, Catholicism, and animism tossed in.

The French favored Catholics during the colonial period, and the Catholic Church became the largest landowner in Vietnam under Diem. The French imposed a "private status" on Buddhists, meaning that in contrast to the Catholic Church, which had "public support and status," the Buddhists received no such support. These laws remained under Diem, a devout Catholic. Hundreds of thousands of Catholics migrated south following the Geneva Accords of 1954 and reinforced the core constituency of Ngo Dinh Diem.

On May 8, 1963, Buddhists assembled in Hue to celebrate the 2,527th birthday of Buddha. The Catholic province chief enforced an old decree prohibiting them from flying Buddhist flags, although he had allowed Catholics to display their blue and white papal colors a week before. The celebrating Buddhists assembled before the radio station to hear an address by Buddhist leader Thich Tri Quang. The station director cancelled the speech, saying it had not been censored, and the province chief dispatched armed cars to the scene, where they fired and killed a woman and eight children.[37]

Diem blamed the incident on the Vietcong, which was patently false. The Buddhists were not communists, but adopted their techniques to protest. They formed three-person cells and mobilized with amazing speed and effectiveness, issuing communiqués and organizing protests.

Meanwhile, Thich Tri Quang, a monk who had studied in Ceylon, spoke elliptically with great mystic power. He was also a shrewd political operator. The French had jailed him as a communist, but he was not, and, in fact, was somewhat right-wing. Tri Quang had approached the U.S. Embassy in Saigon, asserting that the United States must either make Diem reform or get rid of him. If not, the situation would deteriorate and the United States would be the principal victim.[38]

In the wake of the Hue shooting, the United States urged Diem to operate more conciliatorily toward the Buddhists, but Diem refused to abandon his allegation that the Vietcong had caused the Hue incident. He only appointed a committee to investigate the incident. Madame Nhu aggravated the situation when she contradicted Diem by proclaiming that Americans were manipulating the Buddhists.

The U.S. embassy warned Diem that the regime might lose the support of the United States if repression of Buddhists continued, but Diem procrastinated.

On June 11, a motorcade drove up to a busy intersection in Saigon. An elderly monk emerged, sat on the street with his legs crossed, surrounded by monks and nuns. One doused him with kerosene and another ignited the monk with lighter fluid. The monk, Quang Duc, pressed his arms together in prayer. The yellow flame and his yellow robes enveloped him. Passersby, even a policeman, prostrated themselves in astonished awe.[39]

Quang Duc's last words were a respectful plea to Diem to show "charity and compassion" to all religions. Despite American efforts and Quang Duc's symbolic self-sacrifice, Diem refused to back off. His "committee" agreed with Diem that the Vietcong had caused the Hue incident. More monks immolated themselves. Mme Nhu exacerbated the crisis, calling the "self-immolations a barbeque." She told one reporter to "let them burn and we will clap."[40]

The Assassination of Ngo Dinh Diem

President Kennedy announced on June 27, 1963, the replacement of Ambassador Frederick Nolting—who had constantly but unsuccessfully attempted to placate Diem—with Republican Henry Cabot Lodge. Within a week, Kennedy summoned Lodge and his other close advisors. They all agreed that Madame Nhu was the chief spoiler in the Diem regime and that Diem would never jettison Ngo Dinh Nhu. For the first time in Kennedy's presence, according to Karnow, they speculated about a *coup d'état* to replace Diem.[41]

Coup talk and planning by various Vietnamese generals and colonels emerged independently in Saigon. The CIA chief was involved in cautious, veiled discussions on the subject. As the plots developed, the Vietnamese generals sought U.S. support, or at least acquiescence. Some foresaw disaster in a coup; other Americans saw disaster if Diem remained. Lodge, initially opposed, gradually came around, but the president remained wary of U.S. involvement in a coup.

The generals urged Diem to declare martial law to get the situation under control, but they secretly wanted a highly questionable display of centralized authority to justify a coup. Ngo Dinh Nhu saw martial law as a means to smash the Buddhists. Diem concurred and a crackdown on Buddhists in Saigon ensued, exacerbating the political crisis.[42]

Eventually, President Kennedy approved Lodge's recommendations, giving him complete discretion to suspend aid to Diem. Thus, Kennedy gave Lodge a mandate to run policy in Saigon, and Lodge interpreted his mandate to include acquiescence in a coup. The president allowed the CIA chief to tell General Duong Van Minh, the prospective coup leader, that the "U.S. would not attempt to thwart a coup, although the U.S. would not be involved in planning, reviewing, or advising on any operational plans, or any other act that might identify the U.S. too closely."[43] The assistant secretary for Intelligence and Research (INR), Roger Hilsman, replaced Averell Harriman in the fall of 1963 as assistant secretary for Far Eastern Affairs when Harriman was elevated to the position of undersecretary for Political Affairs. Reportedly, Hilsman and Harriman wrote the cable that allowed the CIA chief to give the go-ahead for the coup, as described above.[44]

In the final, confusing event, the generals offered exile to Diem and Nhu but murdered both in the end.

Following the coup, Ambassador Lodge celebrated with the successful generals in Saigon and cabled President Kennedy: "The prospects now are for a shorter war."[45]

President Kennedy remained ambivalent about the coup and, certainly, the assassination of Diem. This may have stemmed from deep moral convictions or practical wariness of what the new order would bring. In any event, we will never be able to sort out the president's thoughts, since Lee Harvey Oswald assassinated Kennedy three weeks later in Dallas, Texas.

10

President Lyndon Baines Johnson's War

Lyndon Johnson was a giant of a man, physically and politically. He dominated any room he entered, and as Senate Majority Leader from 1955 to 1961 he dominated the institution as no one has before or since. He had great dreams for America and, to build on the legacy of his hero Franklin D. Roosevelt, vigorously promoted his Great Society, an effort to overcome racial differences and poverty and to achieve social and economic equity.[1]

After the assassination of President Kennedy, President Johnson intended to pursue both Kennedy's goals and his own, but Vietnam stood in the way of his objectives and eventually overwhelmed his presidency. Initially, however, Johnson distanced himself from the conflict and rejected escalation. To defeat Republican Barry Goldwater in the 1964 presidential election and to consolidate political support to achieve his goals, Johnson committed himself to peace. The emblem of his bid for election was the poster of the little girl with a flower threatened by a nuclear mushroom cloud, a menacing ad that suggested his presidential opponent, Barry Goldwater, would lead the nation to war.

Johnson was torn from the start. He knew war in Vietnam could jeopardize his Great Society and his presidency. But, like Kennedy, he also knew failure in Vietnam would allow the right wing to accuse him of being weak on communism, of having allowed the dominoes to topple.

Despite his pacifist posturing during the election, Johnson did not want to be the first American president to lose a war to communists. America did not surrender; as a Texan, such would be unthinkable. In *The Color of Truth*, Kai Bird wrote, "Johnson was at war with himself, tormented and feeling trapped by the issue [of Vietnam]. . . . "He told Senator Richard Russell, 'I'm confronted. I don't believe the American people ever want me to run [abandon Vietnam]. If I lose it, I think they'll say I've lost it. . . . At the same time, I don't want to commit us to a war.' "[2]

As Stanley Karnow noted, with the Munich Conference with Hitler in mind, "Johnson would not reward 'aggression' with 'appeasement.' But Johnson had little appreciation of the nature of his adversary Ho Chi Minh. Ho bamboozled Johnson when he rejected his proposal in 1965 for a giant economic project to develop the Mekong Delta in exchange for unspecified concessions in Vietnam. "Old Ho can't turn me down," Johnson reportedly asserted.[3]

Johnson was disdainful of the "elitist," Eastern-establishment administration he inherited from Kennedy. Despite tolerating and listening to the various policy experts and military men with whom he constantly consulted, he made clear Vietnam was his war and he was in charge. Two days after succeeding Kennedy, he gathered his advisors to confer with Ambassador Henry Cabot Lodge, whom he recalled for consultations following Diem's assassination. Johnson stated that he would not "lose Vietnam." He instructed Lodge to tell the ruling generals in Saigon that the "U.S. will stand by our word." Formally, Johnson signed a memorandum emphasizing that "the United States would assist the South Vietnamese to win their contest against the externally directed and supported communist conspiracy."[4]

At the same time as the new president was publicly and privately confirming the American commitment to Vietnam, all signs were that the situation had continued to deteriorate since the coup that toppled Diem, especially in the Mekong Delta.[5] Strategic hamlets were rapidly destroyed, even in supposedly pacified areas. Village chiefs were killed in worrisome numbers. Government cadres and the Army of Vietnam (ARVN) troops were dispirited. Reports indicated in the wake of Diem's assassination that a new crop of military cronies had replaced his inner circle—many more corrupt than Diem's people. Washington feared the new South Vietnamese government might be secretly undertaking talks with the Vietcong about a neutralist settlement, anathema to Washington.

The generals who overthrew Diem were paralyzed by ineptitude and ousted in January by General Nguyen Khanh, who seemed equally incompetent to hand-wringing American observers.[6]

Americans were increasingly exasperated. They could not understand how, in the face of the mounting challenges in Vietnam, the generals seemed either unable to grasp the dangers to South Vietnam or unwilling to marshal the effort and resources to counter the situation.

The spring and summer saw a seesawing of coups and counter-coups—seven in 1964 alone. An abortive 24-hour coup in September 1964 against the government of General Nguyen Khanh resulted in the first appearance on the political scene of the younger generation of military leaders, popularly labeled the Young Turks.[7] One thoughtful observer and Young Turk leader was Air Force wing commander Nguyen Cao Ky. He later explained in his remarkable book, *How We Lost the Vietnam War*, the dynamic following the assassination of Diem, an era of many coups:[8]

> By insisting that the hated President Diem should remain in power for so long and then discarding Diem so abruptly, the Americans created a political vacuum which only the Communists were able to exploit. We were not capable of filling that vacuum because we did not know what to do. We had jumped from being a colony ruled by the French to being a country dependent on America, and the transition from independence French-style to independence American-style was so swift that we never had the opportunity to learn the art of governing ourselves unaided and uninfluenced.

Ky went on to recall,

> This problem was bad enough, but another problem compounded the malaise. Had the Americans arrived in our country with clear-cut ideas, we might have learned. However, they arrived with good intentions but without any real understanding of the problems involved, without any real policy, and so took refuge in makeshift accommodations. And there is a world of difference between pursuing a policy and taking measures. We never learned

how to pursue a policy, only the doubtful art of taking measures. Improvisation, usually in the form of a coup, was all we could think of in a country dominated by another race. If the Americans had arrived and taught us the art of government, especially the art of compromise in governing, how different the end might have been.

Ky pointed to yet another problem on the Vietnamese side. The lack of stability stemmed from "the lack of unity in the Military Revolutionary Council," in whose name the original coup against Diem had been undertaken. "The council, responsible for electing government leaders, was not sufficiently united to select effective leaders and then to give full support to the leaders."

The revolving coups finally led to installing a former school-teacher, Tran Van Huong, as prime minister, but Huong proved no more effective than the military leaders. His three months in power were chaotic, and another general soon replaced him.[9]

Political Maneuvering in Washington

As the situation continued to deteriorate in South Vietnam, Johnson sought to prepare the political landscape for the trials ahead. He was keenly aware that demagoguery could result from any failure or loss to the communists, such as occurred in the early Fifties when Senator Joe McCarthy terrorized Washington by charging that communists and fellow travelers had "lost China."

Johnson also recalled the nearly unanimous support Eisenhower achieved from Congress in January 1955 mandating that he deploy U.S. forces "as he deems necessary" to protect Taiwan and the shore islands Quemoy and Matsu against communist assault. Johnson sought such a mandate as he considered how to deal with the conflict in Vietnam.[10] Rightly, there was considerable concern that Congress might not pass such a congressional resolution and might be unwilling to give Johnson a "blank check." Consequently, considerable political calculations went into the effort to gain congressional support and cover.[11]

Four hypothetical questions-and-answers were formulated to counter any objections that Congress might have:

1. "Does this resolution imply a blank check for the president to go to war over Southeast Asia?"

    Answer: "The resolution will indeed permit selective use of force, but hostilities on a larger scale are not envisaged and, in any case, any large escalation would require a call-up of reserves and thus a further appeal to the Congress. . . ."

2. "What kinds of force, if any, are possible under this authorization?"

    Answer: "No force will be used if the president can avoid it. If the continued aggression of others should require a limited response, that response will be carefully aimed at installations and activities that directly support covert aggression. . . ."

3. "What change in the situation requires such a resolution now?"

    Answer: "This answer should include a candid account of the existing situation and hazard and growing dangers both in Laos and in South Vietnam [and] refer to the need for international awareness that the United States is not immobilized by a political campaign. . . ."

4. "Does Southeast Asia matter all that much?"

    Answer: "Yes, because of the rights of the people there, because of our own commitments, because of the far-reaching effect of a failure, and because we can win if we stay."

A very interesting set of questions and answers. Their dishonesty was palpable.

The administration composed the draft resolution by June 1964 and prepared to advance it to Congress as it was ready to escalate the conflict to include North Vietnam. Even before the Gulf of Tonkin incident, the Pentagon had identified 94 bombing targets in North Vietnam and prepared to suppress anti-aircraft dissension, rescue downed pilots, and handle other associated issues. However, Johnson postponed the action out of concern that he would look like a warmonger prior to the presidential election. He wanted hard evidence that North Vietnam deserved the massive bombing before proceeding.[12]

In the meantime, U.S. naval vessels were moving closer to monitor the situation in the Gulf of Tonkin off Haiphong and Hanoi, a sea filled with small fishing and commercial boats as well as cargo ships from the Soviet bloc and China. Two American vessels—destroyers *Maddox* and *J. Turner Joy*—sailed into the Gulf of Tonkin.[13]

On August 2, 1964, the *Maddox* sailed within ten miles of the Red River Valley, which lies inside the accepted twelve-mile limitation, although Vietnam had never formally redefined its French-era zone of three miles off the coastline. The *Maddox* cruised among myriad North Vietnamese junks, intercepted a hostile North Vietnamese message, and radioed in that the *Maddox* expected "hostile enemy action." Three Vietnamese vessels headed straight for the *Maddox*. In range, the Vietnamese fired torpedoes that missed. The *Maddox* disabled two of the three vessels and sank the third during a 20-minute skirmish.

Johnson announced the United States had "no wish to widen the conflict with North Vietnam, but hoped North Vietnamese vessels would not 'molest' American ships in international waters." The Pentagon ordered the *Maddox* and other vessels to return to the Gulf and attack any force that attacked them. "Johnson also approved the first ever diplomatic note to Hanoi warning 'grave consequences would inevitably result from any further unprovoked offensive military action.' "[14]

In the Gulf of Tonkin, violent thunderstorms are frequent in the summer months. The evening of August 4, 1964, was no exception. As the destroyer *J. Turner Joy* edged toward the Vietnamese coast, lookouts and radar technicians perceived attackers amidst the turbulent waves and hazy lights of boats. In the official report, sonar detected 23 torpedoes racing toward the *Turner Joy*, although none struck the destroyer. The *Turner Joy* launched a counterattack, sinking two or three North Vietnamese vessels.[15]

In retrospect, no one on the *Turner Joy* was sure any North Vietnamese attack boats and torpedoes were launched, and they immediately conveyed these doubts to Washington. Pentagon and White House reports erased those doubts and served as the pretext to launch a planned raid on North Vietnam, which was too attractive to discard. The White House calculated the domestic political reaction to these events, agreed they were testing Johnson, and he would have to respond firmly to defend himself against Goldwater and the Republican right wing. The world could not perceive Johnson as weak.

The White House described the reprisals as "limited in scale," as U.S. aircraft conducted 64 sorties against four North Vietnamese patrol-boat bases and a major oil-storage depot. Twenty-five North Vietnamese vessels were thought to have been destroyed. Johnson sent his resolution to Congress for approval, bolstered by an 85-percent public-approval rating and supported by most newspaper editorial boards. The Senate roundly approved it, with only Oregon's Wayne Morse and Alaska's Ernest Gruening voting against the measure. Even Chairman J. William Fulbright of the Senate Foreign Relations Committee initially supported a vigorous defense of South Vietnam and complimented President Johnson on his "moderate" actions with the proposed Gulf of Tonkin Resolution. However, Fulbright shifted to dissent, as did Frank Church of Idaho and George McGovern of South Dakota, as the president escalated with combat troops in the spring of 1965.[16]

Kennedy's and Johnson's defense secretary, Robert McNamara, visited me in the embassy in Hanoi in the summer of 1996, fresh from a visit to General Vo Nguyen Giap, his Vietnamese counterpart during the Vietnam War. McNamara was giddy with excitement because, he told me, "General Giap just agreed that there was no second attack by the Vietnamese on August 4!" This was even though Johnson's reprisal against North Vietnam was predicated on a second North Vietnamese attack.

This is astonishing for two reasons. Most important, McNamara's own Navy had serious reservations at the time that there had been a second North Vietnamese attack. Surely the first source of important evidence for McNamara should have come from an investigation by his own Navy through thorough examinations of the ship's logs, interviews, and other intelligence. And second, why would General Giap want to undermine the story that there was no second Vietnamese attack, even if there had been one? Denying a North Vietnamese attack on the U.S. ship shifted the blame squarely on the U.S., as opposed to North Vietnam.

When I met with Lieutenant General Nguyen Dinh Uoc in January 2007 to discuss his conducting a Princeton seminar, he told me he had attended McNamara's meeting with General Giap. General Uoc expressed surprise at McNamara's reaction to General Giap's denial of the second attack. "McNamara had erupted in glee when Giap confirmed McNamara's question, and McNamara told Giap that he was going to send a message immediately to Washington to correct the record on the question of the second attack!"

This meant the war that came to define McNamara's life, which continued to torment him, had been started on false pretexts.

The Tonkin Gulf attacks convinced Hanoi that Washington had crossed a major threshold and would now commit its military might. Until this point, Hanoi had carefully avoided provocative actions that would give Washington a pretext to attack North Vietnam. Thus, Hanoi later in the fall of 1964 dispatched its first organized military units to the South, also crossing a major threshold. The cautious new president, intent on focusing on social policy, had crossed the Rubicon toward war in Indochina.[17]

Johnson's Dilemma

President Johnson won a landslide victory in the November 3, 1964, elections, topping Goldwater's popular vote by 16 million votes and significantly increasing the Democratic majorities in Congress.[18]

His campaign for the Great Society managed to obscure the Vietnam conflict so that it had not become the crucial issue in the campaign. His bombing of North Vietnam had immunized him from rightwing criticism for being "soft on communism," while his pledge "not to send American boys nine- or ten-thousand miles away from home to do what Asian boys should be doing for themselves" in turn insulated him from criticism from the left and camouflaged his intentions regarding Vietnam.[19]

As Stanley Karnow postulated, "Some historians hold that events enveloped Johnson in the war. Others portray him as the victim of duplicitous aides, while others contend that he consciously chose involvement." No single theory, according to Karnow, tells the entire story, yet each contains a grain of truth.[20]

In the historical tradition of Truman, Eisenhower, and Kennedy, Johnson could not yield to communism. Communism had to be stopped on all fronts. Johnson's unwillingness early on to accept the advice of French President Charles de Gaulle and Majority Leader Mansfield to negotiate a "neutral" solution to the issues involved in Vietnam left him with only one other option—war.

However, Johnson insisted he would pursue only "limited war," but the definition of limited war was not spelled out, except that he would act so as not to provoke Chinese or Soviet direct intervention against America. He was not prepared to "bomb Vietnam back into the stone age" as General Curtis Lemay demanded.

Although shocked that Ho Chi Minh would not bite on his bait of "a massive electrification project for the Mekong Delta," Johnson and his close advisors did not believe poor, backward Vietnam would ever jettison Ho Chi Minh's determination to achieve Vietnam's independence. His "limited war" was designed to turn up the heat gradually, to inflict just enough pain to ensure Ho Chi Minh would capitulate. Had Johnson and his advisors been more attuned to Vietnamese history and seen the conflict against the backdrop of centuries of resistance to foreign domination rather than simple, state-backed communist aggression, the decision to pursue a limited war might have been quite different. It is one of many examples where appreciation of foreign culture as well as understanding history is critical to decision-making.

Military Strategy and Tactics

By 1964 Eisenhower's domino theory had become an article of faith in Washington, although President Kennedy's national security advisor, McGeorge Bundy, acknowledged to colleagues he did not subscribe to the theory. CIA and State Department INR studies both concluded this theory was questionable. In June 1964, the CIA's National Board of Estimates released a report widely circulated in the intelligence community, including INR, stating, "We do not believe that the loss of South Vietnam and Laos would be followed by rapid, successive communization of the other states of the Far East. With the possible exception of Cambodia, it is likely that no other nation in the area would succumb quickly to communism."[21]

NSA Bundy's unwillingness to incorporate this study in his presentations to the president was based on his acceptance of Cold War parallels to the Korean War. The loss of South Vietnam to communism ran against the prevailing conviction that no country could fall to communism. His unwillingness to question publicly the domino theory led him to conclude that extrication by diplomatic negotiations was not possible and, therefore, that only stark military options remained: either a sustained bombing campaign against the North to undermine Hanoi's support for the Vietcong insurgency or the deployment of U.S. combat forces to reinforce the South Vietnamese Army. Bombing would precede the more dramatic and consequential Americanization of the war, in Bundy's conception. The predilection to find a tough but straddling consensus, neither dovish nor as aggressive as the Pentagon's, demonstrates that these recommendations were a matter of judgment rather than blatant political expediency.

As the debate on how to proceed heightened in the spring of 1964, President Johnson insisted on removing Kennedy's assistant secretary of state for Far Eastern affairs, Roger Hilsman, who earlier had advocated getting tougher with Diem and a more political approach rather than a bombing strategy.[22] McGeorge Bundy's brother, William Bundy, who replaced Hilsman as assistant secretary for East Asia in the spring of 1964, advocated the latter approach, which prevailed in the Johnson administration.[23] As recounted by Karnow, Bundy outlined his proposed approach:

1. During the first phase running until August 1964, the United States would avoid belligerent actions to keep the focus on Communist aggression and escalation.
2. Thereafter the United States would proceed to tougher actions, including resumed South Vietnamese forays against North Vietnamese coastal bases, redeploying U.S. Naval patrols in the Tonkin Gulf, undertaking U.S. and South Vietnamese air strikes against the Communist infiltration routes in southern Laos (in ways not to embarrass neutralist Laotian Prime Minister Prince Souvanna Phouma).

3. The next escalation would start in January 1965—regular U.S. bombing of North Vietnamese bridges, railroads, oil storage facilities, and mining the Haiphong Harbor. Bundy did not think it would be necessary to go beyond these measures at the time.

My Involvement Begins

As deliberations regarding U.S. policy in Vietnam intensified, Washington curtailed my assignment to Kathmandu and I received orders to go to Washington to study Vietnamese, after which I would be dispatched to Vietnam to work for USAID in the provinces. With four other Foreign Service Officers (FSOs) I began an intensive course in the Vietnamese language, followed by survival training at the counterinsurgency school at Fort Bragg, North Carolina, in the spring before being sent to Vietnam in June 1965. This was the first such State Department program for Vietnam. We were not aware of the government's discussions, but we could read from the newspapers that South Vietnam's government was deteriorating rapidly due to increasing Vietcong attacks on government forces and positions, with bridges blown and strategic hamlets attacked. War was in the air, and the heightened rhetoric from the U.S. government and media darkened the horizons.

In Vietnam, Ambassador Maxwell Taylor was concerned about the possibility that Bundy's tactics might drive the United States to send combat troops to Vietnam, which he strongly opposed for strategic reasons. Taylor commented, "We should not get involved militarily with North Vietnam and possibly with Red China if our base in South Vietnam is insecure and Prime Minister Khanh's army is tied down everywhere by the Vietcong insurgency."[24] Some Pentagon leaders shared Taylor's concern and favored vigorous bombing of North Vietnam to provide "relief and a psychological boost" to the Saigon government. Johnson summoned his chief military and civilian aides in September 1964 and asked if Vietnam was worth the price. He knew the answer he wanted, but he also prided himself on being willing to listen to all opinions before making final decisions. He likely wanted to validate his own inclinations at that point. The answer, of course, was "yes," because even though President Johnson sought the views of others, he had made clear the war was his and he would make the final decisions, after which he demanded support.[25]

According to Karnow, the JCS wished to start bombing immediately, Rusk wanted to wait to explore other options first, and Ambassador Taylor warily mused that in September 1964 "only the emergence in South Vietnam of a leader like George Washington could salvage the situation and none was in sight." Taylor added, however, "If we leave Vietnam with our tail between our legs, the consequence of this defeat in the rest of Asia, Africa, and Latin America would be disastrous."[26] Thus the domino theory let escalation become the default policy position, even for those informed enough to understand its consequences.

Johnson's Fateful Decision

Three months after discussions, the United States moved a squadron of B-57s from the Philippines to the Bien Hoa Airbase just north of Saigon. On November 1, 1964, about 100 black-pajama-clad Vietcong surrounded the airbase and launched a barrage of mortars. Gasoline tanks erupted, spewing flames and debris widely, destroying six B-57s, killing five Americans and two Vietnamese service members, and wounding nearly 100 persons.[27]

Ambassador Taylor demanded that Washington retaliate against North Vietnam, but President Johnson, with the election only three days away, demurred. He did, however, mention to the JCS that he was considering sending U.S. combat troops to Vietnam to protect American personnel and installations.

The attacks on Bien Hoa shifted the debate in Washington. Discussions no longer concerned Vietnam's importance to U.S. security interests—that had already been agreed upon. Now policymakers addressed the tactical question of what to do with the nation. Bill Bundy represented the majority view that "the Johnson Administration was on trial before the world, its credibility hinging on its determination to take risks, if necessary, to maintain our position in Southeast Asia."[28]

But there were more pessimistic views. Some CIA analysts

foresaw "stalemate" as the best achievable outcome. Others believed the Vietcong could continue the insurgency even if North Vietnam were severely damaged or incapacitated by bombing.

Bill Bundy's interagency group refined its position and suggested three options: (1) to continue the policy of moderation; (2) to undertake bold air attacks against North Vietnam immediately; or (3) to make gradual military moves initially in Laos and then against North Vietnam to allow the United States flexibility to escalate or scale back, as it might wish. Under the "Goldilocks principle," the group selected the "middle" option.

By November 1964, as Johnson's administration weighed these military options, one advisor, Under Secretary of State George Ball, emerged again as a significant dissenter, opposing direct U.S. military involvement with Vietnam. He had conferred with France's President de Gaulle, who warned against becoming involved with "the potpourri," as he called Vietnam. Ball dictated a 67-page memorandum to Dean Rusk, Bob McNamara, and McGeorge Bundy outlining his reservations.[29]

"Once on the tiger's back, we cannot be sure of picking the place to dismount." Ball wrote. "An air offensive against North Vietnam would induce escalation on both sides. The Communists would step up their attacks on the weak Saigon government, which could only be rescued by U.S. forces. But the U.S. cannot substitute its presence for an effective South Vietnamese government over a sustained period of time."[30]

"The spreading conflict," Ball thought, "would set in train a series of events leading, at the end of the road, to the direct intervention of China and nuclear war." The sanest approach, according to Ball, was an immediate political solution that would avoid deeper U.S. involvement. "What we might gain by establishing the steadfastness of our commitments, we could lose by an erosion of confidence in our judgment."[31]

The dissenting opinion shocked McNamara, who also worried that the memo might leak. Rusk and Bundy regarded it as an "idiosyncratic diversion" from the main job of "how to win the war."

By the end of 1964, Johnson's advisors had reached no consensus on how to proceed. Rusk, General Westmoreland, McGeorge Bundy, and Walt Rostow argued that a bombing campaign against the North would significantly alter the dynamics of the war in the South; Bill Bundy, McNamara, and Defense's John McNaughton also favored some bombing in the North, but thought the United States could only win the war with a stable and viable government in the South. In the administration, Ball stood nearly alone in his outright opposition to American military action in Indochina.

Johnson concluded the session with the decision: The United States would react, as appropriate, against North Vietnam in retaliation for any "communist attack" against American units in Vietnam. This language retained some ambiguity about what the United States might do, leaving the door open to gradual escalation.[32]

America wandered, without clear definition, into the quagmire.

President Johnson Goes to War

On February 6 and 7, 1965, an attack on a U.S. base near the mountain market town of Pleiku jarred Johnson from his indecision. Eight Americans died, more than 100 others were injured, and ten U.S. aircraft were destroyed in the barrage of mortar and ground attack. Bundy, in Vietnam for another survey, cabled the president that the Pentagon's retaliation plan—"Punitive and Crippling Reprisal Actions on Targets in North Vietnam"—should be the response. Bundy's message also noted that "prospects were grim" and the Vietcong's energy and persistence were "astonishing."[33]

Johnson convened his national-security advisors and included Senate Majority Leader Mike Mansfield and House Speaker John McCormack. Johnson had already made up his mind and thundered, "I've had enough of this." Only Mansfield and Vice President Herbert Humphrey dissented and, consequently, Humphrey was banished from such deliberations for a year as punishment.[34]

The bombing started promptly. Within hours, U.S. aircraft from the carrier *Ranger* attacked the coastal town of Dong Hoi, about 60 miles north of the DMZ.

Bundy also urged the president to shoot straight with the American people and tell them this was going to be a long, rough struggle. The president ignored this advice and continued to tell visitors to ignore the histrionic headlines and TV broadcasts. A poll indicated 70 percent support for the president, partially because 80 percent believed American withdrawal would open Southeast Asia to communist domination.[35]

Even as the president called the retaliation "appropriate and fitting," he warned of "air operations" designed to stop the "pattern of aggression," which he referred to as "rolling thunder"—devastating attacks that were to last for "eight weeks" but lasted for three years.

In the American tradition "more is better," and the United States soon added napalm and cluster bombs to its devastating mix. Between then and the bombing halt in 1973, the United States dropped three times the amount of explosive tonnage on Texas-sized North Vietnam than it did in the whole of Europe, Asia, and Africa during the Second World War.[36]

The United States did not, however, bomb the dikes in the Red River Valley, since doing so would have flooded and killed hundreds of thousands of Vietnamese. Nor did the U.S. carpet-bomb North Vietnamese cities in the manner of Dresden and Tokyo. Experts estimate that by 1966, 23,000 to 24,000 North Vietnamese were killed by the bombing, 80 percent of whom were civilians—small for a population of 18 million but significant nonetheless.[37]

Far from diminishing the Vietcong insurgency in the South, the American bombing campaign resulted in the escalation of attacks, perpetuating the cycle of tit-for-tat violence. Another communist attack followed against American barracks in Qui Nhon, resulting in yet another retaliatory attack by the United States, which morphed into "Operation Rolling Thunder," the American campaign of sustained air warfare.

After a month-long bombing campaign, Johnson concluded that bombing alone would not prevent the collapse of the South Vietnamese government in Saigon. With the Korean experience in mind, he was concerned that further expansion of the bombing campaign alone, especially near the Chinese border, might provoke the entry of China into the war, a circumstance that he, like others, viewed as a potential disaster.[38]

The situation on the ground continued to deteriorate. South Vietnamese were pleading for more U.S. troops. President Johnson had by now read the Ball memo and asked Ball and McNamara to produce papers with specific policy descriptions.

McNamara presented a memo on June 30, 1965, recommending that the number of U.S. forces be raised to whatever levels were necessary to persuade the Vietcong they could not win. This meant, he specified, an additional 200,000 troops, a tripling of sorties against the North, and a naval blockade of Northern ports.

McGeorge Bundy responded that McNamara's proposals would be rash to the point of folly, saying that the notion of making this kind of commitment without extracting political reforms from the South Vietnamese that would make the war winnable, would be "the slippery slope toward total U.S. commitment and corresponding fecklessness on the Vietnamese side."[39] Bundy questioned where the ceiling was on American liability. Could U.S. troops wage an anti-guerrilla war, since the "central problem" was in South Vietnam? And what was the real object of the exercise? To get to the conference table? If so, what results did we seek there? Or was the investment simply intended to cover the eventual retreat? If that was the case, could we not do that just as well where we were?[40]

In contrast, McNamara's views were more aggressive. Karnow goes on to explain that McGeorge Bundy's younger brother, William, State Department assistant secretary for East Asia, who had been handling the running deliberations of the interagency group, was not so critical of his friend McNamara. He shared McNamara's view that Vietnam was vital to America's interests, but he took a more moderate middle position—e.g., 100,000 troops. He also thought the president himself should make such a decision after discussions with the Cabinet. After reading the various proposals, the president shunted most aside and chose a position between the recommendations of assistant secretary Bill Bundy and McNamara.[41]

As my fellow FSOs and I were finishing our Vietnamese studies and preparing to go to Vietnam in June, U.S. troops began pouring in—first, 3,500 Marines in Danang in June, then tens of thousands more elsewhere.

Johnson made the final decision in late July without announcing the policy change. The U.S. would send in more troops, and General Westmoreland would be authorized to use them for offensive "search and destroy missions," first near bases in Danang and Bien

Hoa, then into the remote reaches of South Vietnam's border areas. By September Westmoreland would ask for 35,000 more troops, with the expectation of having 325,000 by July 1966 and 410,000 by July 1967.[42]

The die was cast: We had crossed the Rubicon into Americanizing and totally militarizing the conflict.

Meanwhile, the Vietcong and the South

While the United States was calibrating what to do vis-a-vis the North, the Vietcong were actively expanding their influence in the southern countryside, recruiting, and stepping up their terrorist campaigns against southern officials and outposts.

Vietcong strength doubled in 1964 to roughly 175,000 men. Approximately 30,000 more were incorporated into corps battalions equipped with World War II weapons from the North—mortars, rocket launchers, AK-47 automatic rifles, and machine guns. Their goal was to grind up the South Vietnamese army troops, hope pressures would increase, and force the establishment of a coalition government to create a neutralist state that could eventually link with the North.[43]

North Vietnam was building for the longer struggle, constructing the elaborate Ho Chi Minh Trail to the south to supply weapons and material to the Vietcong and eventually to transport North Vietnamese troops, logistical equipment, and material for their main force units.

Subsequently, Vietcong guerrillas lacked the skill and experience to wage the conventional war Hanoi envisaged they would wage against the ARVN. Hanoi hoped Saigon would fall before the U.S. ground forces escalated the conflict. Northern troops were already infiltrating into the South to enlarge the Vietcong units, strengthen the southern command structure, and provide political commissars, communications experts, ordnance technicians, and other specialists. Moreover, we learned later, one full division of the People's Army of Vietnam (PAVN), the 325th, was infiltrated into the South in December 1964.

Concurrently, the Central Office of South Vietnam (COSVN)

was discovered in the Parrot's Beak area along the Cambodi-an-Vietnam border, there to coordinate and command the southern theater. As noted earlier, Le Duc Tho set up COSVN in 1961. Americans thought of a Pentagon-like headquarters that could be overrun and destroyed. While Nixon later invaded Cambodia to eliminate COSVN, there was in fact no Pentagon on the border, but a labyrinth of tunnels and mobile hideouts from which Hanoi directed its southern operations.

The Southern Campaign

In the south, 135,000 more troops headed ashore at Danang on March 8, 1965, and by the end of 1965 a total of 181,000 troops would be in the area, as General Westmoreland had requested. That same morning of March 8, an aide to civilian Prime Minister Phan Huy Quat, Bui Diem, later ambassador to Washington, summoned Diem and told him to draft a communiqué welcoming the Marines. Bui Diem later wrote that he had asked Quat if he had known ahead of time that the U.S. Marines would arrive. "Not exactly," replied Quat, "although there had been a general discussion."[44]

Although the Marines and other forces were slated to protect U.S. bases, Westmoreland deployed them otherwise. "A good offense is the best defense," he explained.[45]

By June 1965, South Vietnam had lost many of its best mobile forces in battle. The South Vietnamese military seemed to be crumbling. General Nguyen Khanh replaced Prime Minister Huong in mid-1964, and turmoil reigned. Members of General Khanh's cabal, including General Nguyen Van Thieu and Air Marshall Nguyen Cao Ky, immediately began to plot the downfall of Khanh. Near-continuous strikes and protests by Buddhists and Catholics characterized the era, adding to the chaos. To restore order, Khanh appointed a civilian prime minister—Harvard-educated and genial Nguyen Xuan Oanh, whom the Americans called "Jack Owen." Khanh retained Phan Khac Suu, a figurehead civilian, as chief of state. By February, Khanh had replaced Oanh as prime minister with Phan Huy Quat—a physician, decent man, experienced, and devoted to bringing democracy to Vietnam, but without a power base. Khanh continued in control of the army.[46] A combination of religious protests and military maneuvering resulted in Khanh's final ouster, then Quat's in June 1965, just as I arrived in Vietnam. General Nguyen Van Thieu became president, and Air Marshall Nguyen Cao Ky served as prime minister.[47]

Westmoreland asked for 180,000 additional forces and announced that Vietnam would likely require another 100,000 troops in 1966 to avert imminent catastrophe.[48]

On the ground, General Westmoreland first planned to deploy American forces to protect U.S. air and supply bases along the South Vietnamese coast and around Saigon. He would also send forces to the highlands to block any attempt to sweep across and divide the country.

Having gained the initiative, he intended to launch search-and-destroy operations whereby the vastly superior mobility and firepower of U.S. forces would destroy the enemy.

This strategy would require two additional components—intensive bombing of the North and success in the pacification program. While Americans, including Westmoreland, spoke of "winning the hearts and minds" of the Vietnamese people through the South Vietnamese government, in fact, Westmoreland and the United States were relying on might to win.

The massive U.S. military operations, especially the helicopter raids and bombing, devastated much of the countryside. The famous comment from the 1968 Tet Offensive, "We had to destroy Ben Tre to save it," accurately reflected the American military mindset but did not win many hearts and minds.

The bombing and spread of herbicides to destroy vegetation turned vast areas of South Vietnamese farmland into toxic dumps and jungles into wastelands. The rural economy was steadily destroyed.

Pacification Programs: My Role in Bien Hoa Province

During this period, sensitive to charges of neocolonialism, U.S. army units and civilian aid workers, of whom I was one, distributed building materials for schools and health stations, handed out piglets, and promoted self-help projects to urge peasants to support the South Vietnamese government. However, the military destruction of the lives and economy of South Vietnam outweighed these efforts. I was assigned in June 1965 to Bien Hoa province, a relatively peaceful province on the outskirts of greater Saigon. The sprawling Bien Hoa Airbase, with thousands of airmen, was on the edge of the town of Bien Hoa and, despite occasional rocket attacks, provided security to the province. An Australian battalion was also part of the airbase's defenses. Following the First Indochina War, tens of thousands of refugees from the northern and central regions of Vietnam—a large portion of whom were Roman Catholics—resettled in Bien Hoa. They settled along Highway One, just outside Bien Hoa City; they were fiercely anti-communist and therefore added to the stability of the province. USAID provided cooking oil, pigs, and building materials to the refugees.

In my role as assistant province representative of USAID, I traveled regularly around the province, carrying out my responsibilities to promote support for the South Vietnamese government among the population. The villagers welcomed me with smiles and were appreciative of the supplies I distributed. Children followed me around as I called on village officials and checked on projects in the village. Remarkably, old women, frequently with betel-blackened front teeth, would engage in conversation in Vietnamese with me and, after a few minutes, often erupted in broad smiles and would say in Vietnamese, "*Ong Noi tieng Viet*" ("Oh, you speak Vietnamese!"). I occasionally accompanied U.S. advisory forces, also stationed in Bien Hoa, as they also made community-service visits. They, too, were usually followed around the villages by an adoring trail of tiny Vietnamese children shouting, "*Nguoi My*" ("American"), to summon friends to join the parade.

Only one district, Nhon Trach (in the southeast of Bien Hoa), was considered dangerous and in genuine competition with the Vietcong. During daylight I visited the district town and villages nearby, but I did not visit at night. The Vietcong took over the countryside after dark. In 1967, as an embassy evaluator, I did visit villages in Nhon Trach to evaluate the programs of the Government of Vietnam (GVN) Revolutionary Development Program. I will later describe the very different security situation outside the district town after dark, when the Vietcong attacked the village.

I concluded that the USAID programs and work were worthwhile in improving the status of the South Vietnamese government and building goodwill toward America. Young, unarmed Americans arriving in the villages with cement, corrugated roofing, piglets, food, and other help to construct a new school or medical station were positively perceived by villagers. We supplied food and clothes to orphanages, schools, and *Chieu Hoi* refugees resettling from communist-controlled areas. Our efforts were a positive contrast to American or ARVN soldiers on search-and-destroy operations. Villagers saw the difference and appreciated the positive role we were playing. This reflected well on the provincial officials, as well as on the United States. They also appreciated the fact that we spoke Vietnamese. My two Filipino assistants, who traveled daily through more dangerous villages than I dared visit, became known even better than I as "USAID," thus spreading the word of the U.S. role in helping the Vietnamese government build a better life for the villagers. Our Filipino assistants had strong backgrounds in agriculture and advised Vietnamese on new crops, crop rotation, and other ways they could improve agricultural production. The Vietcong never accosted us as we traveled around—perhaps an implicit sign that the Vietcong acknowledged the positive role USAID was playing in their lives.

The province chief and deputies often invited me to visit villages with them, indicating that they thought the connection with USAID was a positive element in their attempts to cultivate better relations with the villagers. To bolster our role, the province chief invited me to join his morning meetings with his officials, both military and civilian. After vigorous exchanges on activities, toasts with small glasses of cognac empowered our efforts. Unfortunately, our work was only a small part of the strategic policies of the U.S. and South Vietnamese governments.

One result of those policies was that the escalating role of the U.S. military emasculated the South Vietnamese military's sense of self-respect. The more the U.S. military took the lead, the less responsibility the South Vietnamese military assumed. U.S. public criticism of the succession of South Vietnamese government leaders also inhibited the emergence of a popular figurehead for the Vietnamese to support. Both aspects robbed the South Vietnamese of self-respect and, therefore, effectiveness.

Political Developments in the South

Bui Diem, who, as a former student activist in the Dai Viet Party (in disfavor during Diem's regime) had established a newspaper called the *Saigon Post* and became a principal advisor in the Phan Huy Quat government, was eventually brought into Nguyen Cao Ky's entourage. Diem's strong noncommunist, nationalist credentials were a plus for Ky's image, but Bui Diem's strong preference for a civilian, democratic government, at odds with Nguyen Cao Ky's military background, made a favorable impression on the progressive, democratic elements in South Vietnam.

Bui Diem was appointed Vietnamese ambassador to Washington, serving from 1967 to 1972. After the war, he wrote a book, *In the Jaws of Victory*, a thoughtful insider's report on political developments from 1964 on. He describes the political situation from the standpoint of someone who longed for a good, uncorrupt, democratic, civilian government in South Vietnam—the only government that he believed could outperform the communist challenge.

He gave telling commentary about "lost opportunities" in South Vietnam, writing:

> In retrospect, the regime of Prime Minister Nguyen Khanh in 1964–65 put an end to the idea of bringing alive in South Vietnam a democracy vital enough to ward off the political and military challenges of the Vietnamese Communist Party. As I saw it then, Vietnamese nationalists, the only bearers of this torch, had had several opportunities to make this dream a reality. The first came in 1948, when the French offered a "Bao Dai solution," the second arrived in 1954, when the Geneva conference created an independent South Vietnam. The third opened in 1963, when the generals brought down Ngo Dinh Diem. In each of these instances, Vietnam's leaders themselves aborted the prospects. Just as the Vietnamese Communist party seemed to be blessed in its leaders, its opponents—those responsible for the fate of a free Vietnam—were burdened by flaws and weaknesses that made them unequal to the struggle.[49]

Nurturing democracy was not only a Vietnamese concern; it was a concern of the United States, as well. "Just as the Vietnamese failed, so did the Americans," Bui Diem concluded.

The United States always seemed to be tiptoeing along a delicate tightrope between intervention and nonintervention. It never could figure it out and thus brought the Vietnamese the worst of both positions.[50]

On the one hand, American policymakers believed that geopolitical realities required one set of actions: support for French colonial policies and for Diem's consolidation of power. On the other, moral and idealistic considerations seemed to call for a strong anti-colonialist stance and for nourishment of a national democracy. It was as if the United States could never decide quite what policy to pursue. In Karnow's view: "From the beginning, they had been unwilling to put themselves squarely on the line for democracy and national unity in South Vietnam—and for the sincere social and economic reforms that could derive only from a democratic government."[51]

Bui Diem placed great faith in and worked for the civilian government of Dr. Phan Huy Quat, who he found had experience in government and possessed an unusual intelligence, determination, and sense of decency. In Diem's judgment, a deep commitment to social justice and democratic procedures characterized Quat's politics.[52]

Under the Quat government, the United States began its massive build-up—from the Marines in Danang in March 1965 and upwards thereafter, with only pro-forma, after-the-fact consultations with South Vietnamese civilian or military authorities. The Marines' role as "protectors of the Danang airbase" transformed into an aggressive enclave strategy, undertaken without the approval of Quat. Even U.S. Ambassador Taylor was scarcely better informed. Bui Diem wrote, "From air strikes to 'passive base defense' to a general combat role—the next steps led from one to the next with a relentless logic. Within the next nine months, the original embryonic unit of Marines would be transformed into an army of over 200,000 American and allied troops, all there according to the demands of the same reasoning."[53]

Bui Diem made clear he concluded the U.S. military was going

around the civilians in Washington and Saigon and going directly
to President Johnson for approval of the precipitous escalation and
expansion of the role of U.S. forces introduced into Vietnam. In
that vein, Diem thought Ambassador Taylor was also sidestepped,
inasmuch as he had, in Diem's perception, objected strenuously
and repeatedly to the build-up in South Vietnam. Bui Diem cites the
widely known view that the U.S. military was in late 1964 urging
President Johnson to send 200,000 U.S. combat forces to Vietnam,
despite Ambassador Taylor's advocacy for a bombing campaign
in the North. Such a strategy would avoid a huge troop build-up
of U.S. combat forces in South Vietnam and inspire forceful action
on the part of Saigon's leadership. This is a prime example of the
U.S. military's circumventing the civilians to influence President
Johnson.

According to Bui Diem, Quat opposed an Americanization
of the war but saw it develop before his eyes, after which he was
expected to honor the *fait accompli*.[54] "The Americanization of the
war," Bui Diem wrote, "took place abruptly and imperiously in the
spring of 1965. This followed an extended failure of American diplomacy to foster a vital South Vietnamese democracy capable of
handling its own affairs and worthy as a partner for common struggle. However, it was not just the Americans who were responsible,
the Vietnamese who held power bear the prime responsibility."[55]

Regarding Westmoreland's strategy, one Vietnamese general
told Bui Diem, "The Vietnamese military did not press its views on
the Americans." Diem mused: "The fact is that though it was our
war and our country that was at stake, we were such a junior partner that our voices carried no weight. Undoubtedly, one reason for
this was this was an inferiority complex we brought to the alliance.
Another was our blind confidence in the U.S., which suggested that
however grave our doubts about the policy, in the larger scheme,
they were probably not consequential. The U.S. possessed such vast
power and resources that it would do what it wanted regardless,
and we believed it would be successful."[56]

In June 1965, the military put an end to "civilian government,"
but the growth of American power continued unabated. Nguyen
Van Thieu became president and Nguyen Cao Ky assumed the role
of prime minister. But this did not change the increasingly lopsided

dynamic in the relationship between the Vietnamese government and the United States.

Summit in Honolulu

A first Thieu-Johnson summit was scheduled for Honolulu in February 1966.

For his part at the meeting, President Johnson spoke not just of winning the struggle but also of health, education, textbooks, fertilizer, and rural electrification—subjects that were important to Vietnamese nationalists committed to building a prosperous, democratic system in South Vietnam.

Bui Diem concluded this was the opportunity for his new boss, Nguyen Cao Ky, to make a major statement of policy that would move Vietnam decisively toward establishing a democratic government concerned with social justice and the welfare of its citizens— the goals for which Bui Diem had worked all his life.

President Thieu allowed Ky to make the major policy remarks at Honolulu. Bui Diem drafted Ky's remarks as ambitiously as he hoped Ky might use. The speech focused on social and economic reform and promoted constitutional government. He emphasized social justice, education, economic opportunity, religious liberty, and other human rights—all occurring alongside real democratization.[57]

A major threshold of maturity was crossed. Ky's remarks represented the first time in history a South Vietnamese government leader expressed such a progressive and ambitious set of proposals. For the first time since the Geneva Accords, in Bui Diem's view, there appeared to be possibility for stability and political progress in South Vietnam. The Americans were very impressed. President Johnson praised the speech, saying Ky "talked like an American," his highest praise.[58]

The Battle of Danang

Driven by his sharp political instincts—and confounding some of the Americans who had heard his thoughtful and progressive remarks—the intrepid Prime Minister Ky decided to crack down in May 1966 on what he saw as infiltration by the communists into Buddhist organizations in Danang, Hue, and the South Vietnamese government and military structure in central Vietnam.

Ky fired the commander of the central Vietnam region, General Nguyen Chanh Tri, whom he accused of being in league with the communists and Buddhists. Ky calculated he could use General Tri's connections to bring the Buddhists under control, especially the militant Buddhist leader Thich Tri Quang. The Buddhists were demanding Ky's resignation after his meeting with President Johnson in Honolulu, charging that the United States and the Thieu-Ky regime were in league to dominate and destroy Vietnam and its culture.[59] In reaction, Buddhists began demonstrations in Hue; civil servants and even some military forces in Danang joined them. A full-scale revolt seemed to be brewing in central Vietnam.

Chaos ensued when Ky announced he would "liberate Danang." Ambassador Lodge lent him an aircraft to ferry 4,000 troops to do the job; but when Ky landed, dissident troops prevented him and his forces from entering Danang. The U.S. commander of the base intervened to avert a clash, deadlocking the standoff. Ky abandoned his efforts and flew back to Saigon. This led Buddhists in Danang, Hue, and their supporters to denounce the Americans, Lodge, and the Thieu-Ky regime.

Returning to Saigon, Ky finally, in May 1967, acquiesced to resigning within five months. The demonstrations subsided, but Ky, without informing the U.S. Embassy or President Nguyen Van Thieu, reversed his policy, flew back to Danang, and led a battle against Buddhist dissidents that lasted all day. The U.S. commander launched six jets to protect the airport and keep Ky from rocketing the remaining dissidents.

Ky then moved to quell the Buddhists in Hue, gripped by chaos and demonstrations, complete with a self-immolation of a Buddhist nun reminiscent of the Buddhists under Diem in 1963. However, Ky's agents cracked down, arresting hundreds of students and activists. Thich Tri Quang was jailed. The Buddhists never recovered politically, but the sympathy demonstrated toward the communists in 1966 may have influenced the decision to make Hue a focal point of the January 1968 communist Tet Offensive.

Second Summit in Guam

A new, democratic constitution was written and approved by the South Vietnamese Council of Ministers in March 1967. A second Thieu-Johnson summit was planned for later in March, at which point a much more confident Thieu and Ky would note fulfillment of their commitments and outline future plans.

But the mood was not as upbeat as earlier. American support for the war was slipping. Despite the presence of 400,000 U.S. troops in South Vietnam, there was no end in sight. But as Bui Diem reported, "The only bad news at Guam concerned the faltering pacification program—the effort to keep the countryside under government control and strengthen the allegiance of the rural villagers to the government. Vietcong influence seemed to be expanding." General Nguyen Duc Thang reported on the program, indicating that rapid expansion of the Army had detracted from the hoped-for performance of the pacification program.[60]

The newly appointed U.S. ambassador, Ellsworth Bunker, was introduced, as was Robert Komer, newly appointed in charge of the U.S. pacification advisory team in Vietnam, which covered numerous U.S. agencies, also adding some confusion.

President Johnson wanted progress and was frustrated by the bureaucratic impediments and general lack of progress. In Washington, there were differences among his closest advisors. There was a ragged consensus among proponents of the war for expanding military troop commitments and bombing of the North, but also, at the same time, calls by others for negotiation. Johnson's disappointment over the differences showed in his demeanor. But differences were even greater in Vietnam. Nonetheless, with few perceived policy options, the Americans and South Vietnamese continued the present course—prosecuting the war, promoting pacification, and continuing constitutional development. The last would culminate with the September 1967 elections of a new government in Saigon.

Bui Diem perceptively pointed to several relevant issues. The South Vietnam military had rapidly expanded, but the large number of newly trained soldiers had not been well integrated and the ARVN often remained ineffectual. There was no clear delineation of responsibility between the regular Vietnamese army and local forces, nor among their American counterparts. There was a proliferation of overlapping programs and competition for limited resources. "Everybody got in everybody's way" Bui Diem wrote. There were so many U.S. agencies involved in the countryside— Military Assistance Command, Vietnam (MACV), USAID, Joint United States Public Affairs Office (JUSPAO), CIA, and Defense Intelligence Agency (DIA)—with programs that overlapped and duplicated one another; agencies spent a great deal of time in traditional rivalries and bureaucratic games, making the results of pacification predictably deplorable.[61]

Bui Diem also noted: "The American perception shifted toward bolstering South Vietnam politically and economically, as well as militarily. This change of emphasis derived in part from a slowly ripening frustration with the lack of military progress." Bui Diem foresaw this movement as a preview of Nixon's Vietnamization policy.[62]

Demoralization in the South; Determination in the North

Over the next months, demoralization increased. The ARVN was suffering steady casualties, losing many of its best units. Political direction was weak and elicited little support for the elected leaders. The military virtually forced Thieu and Ky onto a single ticket in the September 1967 elections, but Thieu-Ky received only 37 percent of the votes, with the remainder spread among nine other candidates.

The leader of the opposition in the National Assembly, Truong Dinh Dzu, came in second, winning 17 percent, a result more reflective of resentment toward military rule than support for an unsavory lawyer. Dzu was known more favorably by others, including

American insurgency expert John Paul Vann. Dzu was, nonetheless, a surprise winner. The countryside was devastated, with a quarter of the population having fled to the cities and towns to escape the bombing and destruction. The society was being radically undermined and changed for the worse. Traditional life was being utterly uprooted, and traditional values had become meaningless in the throes of constant military action and intrusion.

Bombing and fighting seriously disrupted the economy. Although South Vietnam had been the traditional supplier of grain to the country, poor distribution of land and the devastation of bombing reduced the South's output, requiring the importation of rice by 1965. As sons were conscripted into the military and others joined the Vietcong, families were torn apart. The urban economies were scarcely less affected. Huge influxes of refugees from the provinces moved into the cities. Cities were hosts to inevitably disruptive U.S. military forces. The urban economy suffered enormous disruption from the importation of huge quantities of foreign goods through the Commodity Import Program (CIP) to ease inflationary pressures. Similarly, the United States brought shiploads of consumer goods to Vietnam to soak up the extra funds to avoid inflation.

At the same time, the American-led war economy contributed to the development of a rentier class of merchants, landlords, and many senior ARVN officers. Those with property to rent to Americans became fabulously rich, while average soldiers, government workers, and peasants fought to get essentials. The traditional society succumbed to a new morality of dance halls, prostitution, and loss of sons and brothers in battle. Saigon's *Tu Do* Street became the center of the universe for GIs, with tawdry bars and beautiful, seductive young Vietnamese women, and functioned as a foreigners' paradise as Vietnamese society crumbled. The country seemed under the aegis of foreign forces. The government and its military were subservient to the Americans and thereby emasculated in the eyes of ordinary Vietnamese. These factors were abundantly clear to any perceptive American working in Vietnam.[63]

Meanwhile, the communists moved decisively, with high morale in the ranks. North Vietnam had mobilized the masses despite the hardship, struggled to build the network of roads known as the Ho Chi Minh Trail, manned antiaircraft guns, survived on less and less, and sent their sons steadily to battle in the South—all inspired by Ho Chi Minh's exhortation that "nothing is more precious than independence and freedom." Northerners and their southern communist comrades were above all fired with a faith that they represented the "patriots" fighting to liberate their country, part of a tradition going back 2,000 years.

The devastating bombing that Washington hoped would lead to capitulation instead backfired, feeding determination, acceptance of sacrifice, and renewed zeal to fight for the country's independence. Even many of those who opposed the "communist policies" of the government rallied to the cause of liberation.

Another Perspective

I have already described in Chapter 7 my experience from July 1965 until June 1966 as assistant provincial representative for USAID. From June 1966 until January 1967 I was a USAID advisor to a project in one of Saigon's poorest districts, District Eight. Despite the seemingly corrupt state of the Vietnamese government, there were many young Vietnamese who yearned, like Ambassador Bui Diem, for an open, uncorrupt, responsive, and democratic government. I do not know the precise origins of this project, but the central government and the Saigon government responded to appeals by known young leaders to give them a chance to show that an uncorrupt, energetic, and responsive government would work. I met and admired the leader of the project, Doan Thanh Liem, a Northerner who moved South in 1955 after the Geneva Agreement came into force. He graduated from the Saigon Law School in 1958, became a legal analyst of the South Vietnamese parliament, and in 1960–61 received a scholarship for further legal training in Washington, D.C.

Liem and his friends started Project 8, but as it proved successful, it quickly expanded to two other poor districts, Six and Seven. The young leaders met with the leaders and people of the districts, listened to what they wanted done, discussed options, and proceeded to carry out what was agreed upon to promote economic development, health care, education, or self-help projects. As it had been in Bien Hoa Province, my function was to provide cement, tin roofing, and other supplies to construct whatever the leader and people decided was needed for these projects. The young Vietnamese leaders demonstrated strong interest in listening to and working with the people to promote their goals. Widely applauded for its success and the enthusiasm and idealism of the young leaders, the project would have served as a model for expansion throughout South Vietnam, but time, vested political interests, and the war prevented the expansion of this promising approach to governing. The projects collapsed, of course, when the communists took over in 1975.

In 1996, as *chargé d'affaires* of the embassy, I was informed, through the intervention of mutual friend Richard Hughes, that the government had released one of the former top young South Vietnamese leaders from prison after six years. To my amazement, it was Doan Thanh Liem, the leader of the District Six, Seven, and Eight Project, with whom I had worked in 1966. After 1975 Liem did odd jobs and tutored, but mainly read. However, he had been arrested as a political prisoner in 1990 and sentenced to twelve years in prison. The tragedy and waste that had befallen the idealistic and effective young leader stunned and saddened me. With gratification I agreed that the United States should accept him immediately.

In my final six months, I served as one of four "evaluators" for Deputy Ambassador William Porter. My responsibility was to travel, visit, and spend overnights with the Revolutionary Development Cadres working in places contested by the government of South Vietnam and the Vietcong, of which there were many. I traveled throughout South Vietnam and discovered mixed success of the program, which was, in effect, an attempt to transfer the success of the Saigon Youth Project throughout the country.

On one occasion, I went unannounced to Nhon Trach village in Bien Hoa Province, where the Revolutionary Development cadres were working, asked permission to join them a day or so, and they accepted me without question. The cadres worked diligently with the townspeople to repair homes, build medical facilities, and more, and each night they lay in rows on the ground. I joined the row and at about midnight was awakened by rifle fire, mortars, and artillery firing over our heads. Eventually, the barrage ended and we returned to our row of blankets on the ground.

On another excursion, I joined an ARVN colonel on a tour of the Revolutionary Development projects near Hue. We stayed at a nice hotel on the banks of the Perfume River, which winds through Hue. Exactly one week later, several nude Vietcong swam across the river and blew up the hotel with satchel charges.

11

Assessment from 1966: Facing the Facts

Toward the end of my assignment to Vietnam in the fall of 1966, the FSOs with whom I had studied and gone to Vietnam exchanged our assessments of the state of American policies towards Vietnam. They included Ray Riemer, who had been in Pleiku Province, Steve Ledogar and Rich Brown in Quang Tri Province, Clay Nettles in Lam Dong Province, and Bob Myers in Kon Tum Province. We integrated our assessments of U.S. policies and developments in Vietnam and, following our return to Washington, presented and discussed the paper with the State Department undersecretary for political affairs, Eugene Rostow.[1] The main points and conclusions were as follows:

- The basic danger facing the United States in Vietnam is losing sight of the struggle's essential truth: that the war in South Vietnam is a Vietnamese political and civil war.
- Secretary McNamara has stated that it cannot be won in the North, bomb as we will. What he has not made clear is that it is equally sure that the war can never be won by force of arms alone in the South.
- Units of the North Vietnamese Army were first sent South late in 1964 to give a speedy coup de grace to an already all-but-vanquished South Vietnamese state. Their arrival did not affect the real danger—that is the Vietcong infrastructure, which remained largely intact throughout South Vietnam.
- To be sure, terrorism and other applications of brute force were and continue to be widely used by the

Vietcong in securing its influence in South Vietnam. But banditry pure and simple (that is, violence without popular roots and support) could not long exist in a state with a military and police structure as developed by the South Vietnamese regime.

- The Vietcong are able to gain support initially and continue to flourish essentially because of grievances among the Vietnamese people. Vietcong terrorism was effective because there remained behind it a vision of a "just society" affording equality of opportunity for the "masses."
- The Government of South Vietnam has not yet remedied these grievances, nor has it given the Vietnamese peasant or intellectual any vision to counter that of the Communists.
- The South Vietnamese governmental system is seen essentially as a successor government to the colonial regime, with a privileged class of urban Vietnamese replacing the French in the hierarchy, supported by a Western power.
- The South Vietnamese government continues to be unrepresentative and unresponsive, increasingly corrupt, hopelessly bureaucratic, and paternalistic. A very lethargic program of evolutionary change has been started, but at a pace which is unlikely to inspire and win the allegiance of the rural population.
- Belief in a military solution can only earn frustration and eventually overwhelming impatience in America, and seriously threatens the ability to maintain this presence for as long as necessary.
- The United States should concentrate on assisting the Vietnamese government and people to fight the only war that can destroy the Communist threat, the political struggle against the Vietcong.
- The Vietcong infrastructure remains at the heart of the Vietnam struggle.

Several areas need urgent attention:

- An expanded system for full primary, secondary, and vocational education and a greatly expanded scholarship program based on need and merit, not connections.
- A primarily youth-oriented District Six, Seven, and Eight program in Saigon [the program with which I worked the second half of 1966] should be multiplied many times over throughout the country so that as many young people as possible may take part in the building of their society.
- South Vietnam should restore elections of local officials and progressive institute elections throughout the political structure of South Vietnam.
- Building a society is not only social programs, however, it is also expanded political activity, real economic development, to which little attention has been given in South Vietnam. An urgent expansion of economic development is an essential component of success.
- We cannot, for example, hope to destroy the enemy's total military capacity, as in the two World Wars. The United States does not propose to conquer the territory of North Vietnam. We trust it is not our goal to best the Communists in a war of attrition. These are traditional military goals and in Vietnam neither of them is worth the price they would impose. What mission then is left with the military?
- The mission of the U.S. military in Vietnam should be an essentially defensive one of neutralizing the enemy's military support for his political effort—that is to say, securing the base of operations for our real offensive effort—which must be for revolutionary development. This has to be, for revolutionary development concerns the people—not unpopulated, empty real estate.
- What is needed is a military strategy suitable to aid the South Vietnamese military and police apparatus in securing populated areas—all populated areas, not just coastal or defensive "enclaves"—for a period of time, long enough for the proposed social reforms to really

take hold among the Vietnamese and thereby weaken the popular appeal of the Vietcong and destroy their ultimate strength.

We proposed the following considerations:

1. If our military purpose is, as we have suggested, "not to destroy the enemy" per se, then there is no point in ground attacks against enemy defensive positions in unpopulated areas. Pacification should be conducted wherever there are people—including the central Highlands.

While the best defense (of an area) is certainly often a good offense (conducted around its periphery), we feel that the logic of this doctrine has been extended too far. A combination of bombing and aggressive patrols, with the possibility of immediate large-unit response if correspondingly large enemy units are encountered, would serve the purpose of keeping large Communist military units off balance and at a safe distance from areas being pacified.

We do not believe the nature of the war justifies the sacrifice of hundreds of men in ground attacks against remote Communist positions to destroy even larger numbers of the enemy, proving once again that no place is safe for them, and then withdraw again. Even when such operations result in killing 500 or even 800 Communist soldiers at the cost of 100 Americans KIA, they are but Pyrrhic victories. They represent needless losses of life that only bring domestic patience closer to the breaking point.

2. Bombing of "strategic targets" in North Vietnam, such as power plants, factories, oil depots, and cement plants, is unjustifiably expensive in terms of planes, men, and international and domestic public opinion. It does little to diminish the Communists' real strength in South Vietnam and serves to divert attention—in the U.S. government and among the people—away from the only area in which the war can be won—among the people of South Vietnam.

3. Competition among the U.S. military in publicizing their contributions to the total war effort is seriously harmful in that it distorts the nature of the struggle and, depending on the attitude of the individuals at whom the publicity is directed, either serves to arouse further foredoomed hopes of military "victory" or further increase abhorrence and rejection of the entire U.S. effort in Vietnam.

4. Another facet of the present misdirected emphasis in the U.S. effort in Vietnam is that MACV has downgraded the role of advisor in Vietnam to below that of the officer serving in a main force U.S. combat unit. We have for years berated ARVN for neglecting pacification support in favor of military operations often unrelated to this task but producing good will among superiors and hence decorations and promotions, rather than promoting effective government.

By subordinating the advisory to the combat role, we encourage exactly the same thing among Vietnamese. As among the civilians, grossly expanded but mediocre MACV advisory teams should be replaced with lean teams of first-rate officers—officers who should, if they merit it, receive the highest honors and acclaim given for military service in Vietnam. Combat units too can and should perform an instructive role. The system of combining U.S. and ARVN or RF/PF units, as employed in I Corps, should be expanded to all of Vietnam.

5. If the above suggestions result in a possibility of reducing U.S. troop strength in Vietnam, so much the better. The full paper, drafted in late 1966, suggests that it will. (See Annex 1)

The Importance of Being Honest

The vast collection of quantitative reports does not reflect the reality of what was happening in South Vietnam. It is essential that, from the president on down, we face the situation in Vietnam honestly.

I felt as though the State Department ignored our recommendations. Undersecretary Rostow listened sympathetically but made no commitments, and we could not detect any change in policy related to our comments. Only months later, after the Tet Offensive, did they discover many of the realities we had described. At that point, the hollowness of American efforts was exposed. We had Americanized and militarized a political conflict, seeking to win a political war through foreign military force. That was unlikely to lead to success anywhere, and in Vietnam, with its long legacy of anti-colonial struggle, it was failing. There were some policy changes consistent with our proposals when General Creighton Abrams replaced General Westmoreland on June 10, 1968. These included reemphasizing counterinsurgency and the withdrawal of 49,000 U.S. troops in 1969 to turn the fight back to ARVN forces. I attribute these changes to the broad realization that existing policy was failing and not to U.S. efforts.

Photo Gallery

Early U.S. Cooperation with Ho Chi Minh

Figure 1: In the late stages of World War II, the U.S. sent Office of Strategic Services (OSS) and special Deer Team personnel to Kunming, China, and northern Vietnam to rescue American pilots shot down, particularly in southern China. In 1945 OSS leader Lt. Col. Archimedes Patti led the team, which provided small-arms training to the Viet Minh in exchange for assistance in rescuing American pilots. OSS team member Pvt. Henry Prunier, a former Berkeley student of Chinese language (pictured center above), worked directly with Ho Chi Minh (in shorts) and Vo Nguyen Giap (in white suit). Pham Van Dong (not pictured) rescued and delivered one downed pilot to the OSS team. Patti himself developed a close relationship with Ho Chi Minh.

President Roosevelt strongly opposed the return of Indochina as a colony to France after the war. He later shifted to the possibility of "Trusteeship." Following FDR's April 1945 death, President Truman, under heavy pressure from General Charles De Gaulle and Europeanists in the State Department, shifted support to Vietnam's return to the French and ended support for independence on October 1, 1945.

Patti, not informed of the decisions being made in Washington, had a farewell dinner alone with Ho Chi Minh, who asked whether the United States was going to allow the return of Vietnam to France. Patti professed neutrality, which Ho Chi Minh interpreted as a negative answer. As Patti recounted in his book, *Why Vietnam?* (pages 266–274), that in parting, Ho Chi Minh asked him "to carry back to the United States a message of warm friendship and admiration for the American people. He wanted Americans to know that the people of Vietnam would long remember the United States as a friend and ally. They would also be grateful for the material help received, but most of all for the example the history of the United States has set for Vietnam in its struggle for independence." *Public Domain U.S. Government*

Vietnam 1945 Independence

Figure 2: Hanoi Ba Dinh Square, where Ho Chi Minh declared independence in 1945. Inspired by the U.S. Declaration of Independence, the Vietnam Declaration of Independence begins with "All men are created equal." *Author's Photo, 2007*

Figure 3: Uniformed students carry a portrait of President Ho Chi Minh during a parade in Hanoi in 1965. The U.S. began its serious military build-up in South Vietnam in March of that year. *PhotoQuest/Archive Photos via Getty Images*

War: Indochina War 1946-1954 and American War 1965-1975

The following four photos represent themes and facts that thread throughout the civil and foreign wars that Vietnam endured from 1946 until 1975.

Figure 4: Weapons and supplies were transported by bike and on foot by a peasant army endlessly slogging through rough terrain. *Marc Riboud/ Magnum Photos, 1969*

150

Figure 5: The Vietminh planted poison-tipped punji traps extensively along the trails. These and similar efforts were ultimately effective in achieving Vietnam's independence. On the darker side, the French at Hoa Lo Prison tortured, guillotined, and starved their Vietnamese opponents. After 1954, the Vietnamese maintained the prison but also used it as a training facility. During the American War, Hoa Lo again became a full-time prison where American pilots were tortured, starved, and deprived of decent medical treatment. *Author's Photo, 2007*

Figure 6: Numerous American planes were shot down, including B-52s, during the punitive Christmas bombing of Hanoi to force the Vietnamese to accept a peace treaty in 1972. Most of the prison was demolished in the Nineties, replaced with a modern Singaporean Hotel, but the gatehouse and entry became the Hoa Lo Museum. *Author's Photo, 2007*

Figure 7: Skeletal plaster figures reflect the miserable torture, starvation, and medically deprived conditions under French colonial rule. *Author's Photo, 2007*

Hoa Lo Prison (Hanoi Hilton)

Figure 8: Ho Tay (West Lake), where then-Lt. John McCain crashed in 1967 and was saved by a Vietnamese despite strong opposition from other fishermen, who shouted, "Kill him!" In 1996, Senator McCain visited Hanoi, where he met and thanked the man who had saved his life. *Author's Photo, 2007*

Figure 9: Senator John McCain's flight suit at Hoa Lo prison. *Author's Photo, 2007*

154

Figure 10: A Princeton seminar student stands beside the Hoa Lo (Hanoi Hilton) guillotine. *Author's Photo, 2007*

South Vietnam, 1965–1967

Figure 11: Author with U.S. Advisory Team. Bien Hoa, 1965. *US Advisory Team*

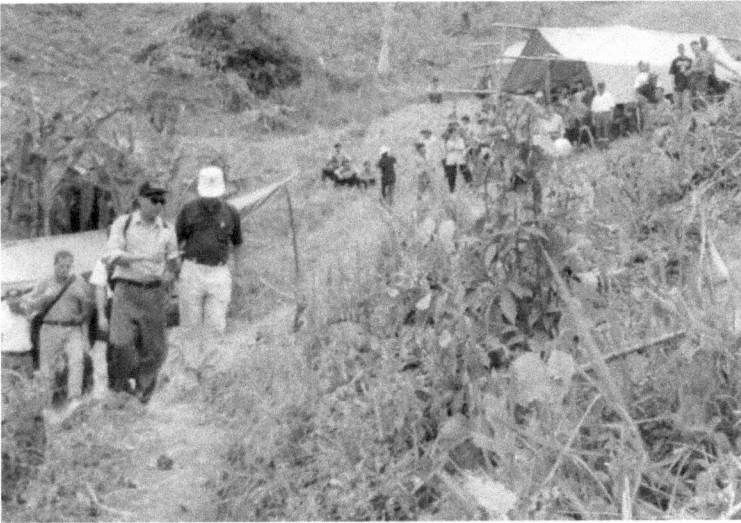

Figure 12: U.S. military team searching for MIAs. With strong U.S. government interest, before and after normalization, Vietnamese cooperation has been diligent. *Author's Photo, 1965*

Figure 13: Author with village children, who typically followed him wherever he went, chattering in Vietnamese, 1965. *USAID*

Saigon, South Vietnam

Figure 14: Former South Vietnam Presidential Palace. A chief Vietcong objective during "Tet" in 1968 was to attack the Presidential Palace to demonstrate South Vietnamese vulnerabilities. Similarly, the takeover of the Palace in 1975 was a definitive signal of the downfall of the Thieu regime and victory over the South. *Author's Photo, 2008*

Figure 15: Catholic Cathedral. Pro-Catholic President Diem denigrated and alienated Buddhists, politically lethal to majority-Buddhist South Vietnam. *Author's Photo, 2008*

Figure 16: Former Opera House, then South Vietnam National Assembly, now "People's Hall." *Author's Photo, 2008*

South Vietnam Buddhist Uprising, 1963

Figure 17: Thich Quang Duc, a Buddhist monk, immolated himself in opposition to Diem's policies. Saigon, June 11, 1963. *AP Photo/Malcolm Browne*

Figure 18: Morris Minor driven by Buddhist monk Thich Quang Duc. *Author's Photo, 2007*

Democratic Republic of Vietnam (DRV),
North Vietnam Leaders

Figure 19: Vo Nguyen Giap with Ho Chi Minh, 1941. *Photo 12/UIG via Getty Images*

162

Figure 20: Comrades Ho Chi Minh and Pham Van Dong during the struggle for independence, 1968. *Marc Riboud/Magnum Photos*

Figure 21: Ho Chi Minh's mausoleum in Ba Dinh Square, Hanoi. *Author's Photo, 2008*

Figure 22: Ho Chi Minh's home, Hanoi. *Author's Photo, 2008*

Post-1954 North Vietnam

Figure 23: Ba Dinh Square Presidential Palace, Hanoi. *Author's Photo, 1996*

Figure 24: Communist Party Headquarters, Hanoi, 2012. In 1996, the Communist International Affairs Chief asked the *Chargé* to have U.S. Embassy officers explain to party political cadres how multi-party democracy functioned in the United States, Singapore, Mexico, and Japan. This was readily done. To further their education, the *Chargé* invited the political cadres as well as American Democrats and Republicans to the Embassy Residence to watch the November U.S. election returns. They eagerly joined the election-watch. *Author's Photo, 2008*

Figure 25: Hanoi Opera House, built between 1901 and 1911 by architects Broyer, V. Harley, and Francois Lagisquet, modeled after Garnier Opera House in Paris. *Author's Photo, 2007*

Contemporary Streets of Hanoi—the "36" Streets

Figures 26 and 27. *Author's Photos, 2008*

Popular Sights in Hanoi

Figure 28: One-legged pagoda built by aging Emperor Ly Thai Tong in 1049 in honor of answered prayers to Buddha for a son. *Author's Photo, 2008*

Figure 29: Thap Nước Hang Dau (Water Tower) on Hang Dau Street.
Author's Photo, 2008

Figure 30: Huc Bridge, Hoan Kiem Lake, Hanoi. *Author's Photo, 2008*

170

Princeton Global Seminar in Vietnam

Figure 31: Van Mieu Confucian Temple, built in 1070 to educate royal youth, later became Vietnam's first university. At the site, the Princeton Seminar received an excellent introductory lecture by historian Huu Ngoc on "Three Thousand Years of Vietnamese History" in one hour. Huu Ngoc has provided the same lecture to visiting European royalty. *Author's Photo, 2007*

Figure 32: General Nguyen Dinh Uoc, close confidant of Vo Nguyen Giap, and Desaix Anderson, founder of the Princeton seminar. *Princeton Seminar Student Photo, 2007*

Princeton Students Visit Dai Bai Lo Village for Public Service

Figure 33: Princeton students cleaning graves in a soldiers' cemetery at Dai Bai Village, North Vietnam, in 2009. *Photo courtesy Duane Hynes*

Figure 34: Student smokes a peace pipe with a man who was shot point-blank by a U.S. soldier and whose daughter was afflicted by Agent Orange. *Author's Photo, 2009*

Figure 35: Vietnamese students ready for dance class led by a Princeton student. *Princeton Seminar Student Photo, 2007*

Figure 36: University of Social Sciences and Humanities, Vietnam National University (VNU) professors for the Princeton Global Seminar with author Desaix Anderson (center): Vice Rector Pham Quang Minh, and Dr. Do Thu Ha. Not shown: Dr. Pham Hong Tung. *Princeton Seminar Student Photo, 2007*

Princeton Global Seminar Visit to Hue and Hoi An

Figure 37: Hoa Lo Bridge, Hoi An. *Photo courtesy Duane Hynes, 2007*

Figure 38: Tomb of Emperor Minh Mang who ruled 1820–1841, Hue. *Author's Photo, 2007*

Figure 40: Thien Mu Buddhist pagoda near Hue. *Author's Photo, 2007*

Figure 41: Unrestored ruins in Hue damaged in 1968 Tet Offensive.
Author's Photo, 2007

Figure 42: Thai Hoa (Supreme Harmony) Palace near Hue, home of Nguyen emperors for 100 years. *Author's Photo, 2007*

Princeton Global Seminar Excursion to Ha Long Bay

Figure 43: *Author's Photo, 2007*

Figure 44: *Author's Photo, 2007*

Figure 45: *Author's Photo, 2007*

Reconciliation

Figure 46: U.S. Embassy Hanoi, opened in 1995. *Author's Photo, 2007*

Figure 47: President Bill Clinton and author Desaix Anderson in Hanoi July 2, 2015, for the 20th anniversary of the normalization of U.S.-Vietnam relations. *Photo courtesy U.S Embassy Hanoi*

Figure 48: U.S. Ambassador Mike Michalak, *Chargé d'Affaires* Desaix Anderson, Ambassador Pete Peterson and wife Vi, Mr. Clayton Bond, and Ambassador Ted Osius at the 20th anniversary celebration in 2015. *Photo courtesy Bond/Osius*

12

The 1968 Tet Offensive

After two years in the villages of Vietnam, in the summer of 1967 I was assigned to the Vietnam Working Group of the State Department's Vietnam Desk in Washington. On the morning of January 31, 1968, messages flooding in from the Embassy in Saigon and the press tickers revealed a massive Vietcong offensive unfolding in Saigon and throughout South Vietnam.

The best and most extensive report on the events of Tet is *Tet!: The Turning Point in the Vietnam War*, by the *Washington Post*'s premier East Asian journalist, Don Oberdorfer, and I will draw on his writings extensively in discussing those events.

Although there had been ominous reports of impending Vietcong attacks and sharp attacks in some provinces in the far north of South Vietnam before Tet, the Vietnam Working Group had no inkling of the massive uprising that was about to occur. We were as shocked as the rest of the nation by the breadth of the attacks.

First reports were from the embassy under attack, indicating a Vietcong sapper unit, perhaps fewer than 20 men, had entered the embassy compound and were likely within the embassy itself. Reports of similar attacks at numerous points around Saigon began flowing in, as did press-ticker reports from provincial capitals.[1]

While we were accustomed to attacks on provincial and district capitals, the strike at the heart of Saigon at the new, fortress-like U.S. embassy on Thong Nhut Boulevard, just down the street from the sparkling new presidential palace, was astonishing.

Only six weeks earlier, on December 15, 1967, with growing confidence in the ARVN forces, the United States had turned over defense of Saigon and the U.S. embassy to the Vietnamese. The

Saigon embassy, however, still had the largest Marine security contingent of any embassy, an 85-man rotating force housed on the grounds of the embassy itself. Because of the Tet holiday the Marines were on maximum alert, with additional Marines stationed in and around the Chancery building.[2]

Oberdorfer describes the opening attack:

> The sapper unit rolled down Thong Nhut Boulevard in a small Peugeot truck and a tiny taxi, opened fire on the two Marines standing guard on the side street, and then stopped just outside the high embassy wall on the boulevard. The Marines fired back and slammed shut the heavy steel embassy gates.

> Wearing neckerchiefs, armbands, and black pajamas, the sappers unloaded, placed rockets and explosive charges against the Embassy outer wall, and blew a large hole in the wall. The two U.S. Marines fired and killed the first two sappers through the wall, but they themselves were then killed as the other sappers poured through the hole.

> One of the two Marines just inside the Embassy raced to slam the huge teak front doors of the Chancery building and raced back to his desk to call for help. A sapper rocket demolished the teak doors and the Vietcong were inside the Chancery. The rockets wounded one of the two Marines and demolished the radio sets they were attempting to use.

> The Embassy duty officer, an economic officer tracking rice imports, subsequently a friend, Allan Wendt, raced to the code room on an upper floor, locked himself with a small staff within, and remained the Embassy contact with the Political Counselor and Washington throughout the sapper attack. Wendt was obviously fearful that the Vietcong would force their way into the code room at any minute.[3]

Of the wire services, the *Associate Press* reported first and most often: "The attack on Saigon started around 3 am, following on seven large provincial cities and the second largest city of Danang."

The long-planned "uprising" throughout South Vietnam would strike more than one hundred cities and towns—the capital city of Saigon, 39 of the 44 provincial capitals, and 71 district capitals. The specific targets included the U.S. embassy, the presidential palace, the Joint General Staff headquarters in Saigon, and the headquarters of all four military regions.

The Vietcong committed 67,000 of their military and political cadres out of an estimated 240,000 Vietcong and North Vietnamese forces in the South, one-fourth of its forces. Against them were 492,000 Americans; 61,000 South Koreans, Thais, and other free world troops; 342,000 South Vietnamese ARVN regulars; and 284,000 regional and popular force units. The U.S. forces were armed with 2,600 planes, 3,000 helicopters, and 3,500 armored vehicles.[4] Vietcong killed in the attacks totaled 40,000–44,000.

The communists hoped to catch the United States and ARVN off guard, scattered around the country, and stretched thin in myriad locations. They hoped the Saigon regime would collapse, its leaders would be assassinated, and its military officers off-duty during the Tet holiday. They anticipated ARVN and local governmental forces would join the uprising, turn their arms against the governmental forces, and create a "general uprising" with demands for formation of a coalition government including the NLF.[5]

Lieutenant General Nguyen Dinh Uoc, a close confidant of General Vo Nguyen Giap, told me the communists aimed to sap the will and hopes of the American and South Vietnamese forces. Ho Chi Minh was aware of American quadrennial elections and held large offensives in those years, General Uoc told me. "The major push in 1964, Tet in 1968, the offensive against northern South Vietnam 1972, and the final battle were slated to have been in 1976—for maximum political impact in the United States on presidential elections," he said.

Southern communist forces would carry the main burden of the offensive. Northern forces would create diversions as they had been doing at Khe Sanh in central Vietnam and provide reserves for battles such as at Hue.[7]

This was the first time the war entered directly into the big cities—heavily guarded locations such as Saigon, Cholon (the big Chinese section of Saigon), and the Imperial City of Hue. Fighting was fierce and brought by television into American living rooms.

In Saigon, 1,000 NLF troops fought 11,000 combined American and South Vietnamese forces to a standstill, and it took three weeks to kill or expel the NLF forces.[8]

Hue was quickly occupied and a coalition municipal government formed of those who had been active in the Buddhist struggle of 1966 against Nguyen Cao Ky and the invading NLF and North Vietnamese forces. NLF soldiers marched through the city distributing leaflets. Citizens fed and welcomed them. For almost a month the NLF flag flew over the citadel until the U.S. Marines bombed and strafed from the air. Fighting house to house, the joint Marine and ARVN forces finally ejected or killed the Vietcong occupiers.[9]

The destruction of Hue was massive: 9,776 houses of a total of 17,134 were destroyed and 3,169 more badly damaged.[10]

The NLF had been charged not only to destroy the government in Hue but also to set up a revolutionary administration. There were lists of persons at all levels who were to be executed, including the local police and civil servants. Lower-level civil servants were to be reeducated, more senior ones executed.

Sympathetic American observers acknowledge there were executions, especially at the start of the takeover, but that many civilians were killed in the bombardment and fighting in the taking of the city. These same observers seem equally convinced that the executioners were NLF, not North Vietnamese forces.

The aftermath of the Hue siege brought sordid discoveries of shallow graves holding many civilians who had been specifically fingered by the NLF, hands bound and executed for at least purportedly working for the government. The U.S. military estimates that 2,800 individuals found in graves and 5,700 civilians in Hue were massacred during the communist occupation.[11]

The fear of reprisals following a communist victory in the South led regime supporters to fear a bloodbath if North Vietnam and the Vietcong won the war. These fears, in part, motivated hundreds of thousands of "boat people" to flee the South. While the dark events in Hue remain murky, the massacres left an indelible mark on the communities connected with the United States or South Vietnamese government.

One document captured and provided by Don Oberdorfer outlined Hanoi's plans and hopes: "Use very strong military attacks in coordination with the uprisings of the local population to take over towns and cities. Troops should flood the lowlands in the Mekong Delta. They should move toward liberating the capital city [Saigon], take power and try to rally enemy brigades and regiments to our side one by one. Propaganda should be broadly disseminated among the population in general, and leaflets should be used to reach enemy officers and enlisted personnel. The above approach should be fully understood by cadre and troops; however, our brothers should not say that this order comes from the Party and Bac Ho [Uncle Ho], but say it comes from the Front. Also do not specify times for implementation."[12]

Except for Hue, the United States and ARVN quickly retook cities and towns around the country. Tet elicited a mixed reaction locally. The destruction of Hue, Ben Tre, Cholon, My Tho, and Vinh Long "to save them" left a bitter aftertaste for many. However, to many Vietnamese, the strength of the NLF forces, their surprise, the widespread nature of the attacks, and the fact that so many had been killed in the uprising elevated the prestige of the NLF.[13]

In early March, the U.S. commander reported that some 2,000 Americans and 4,000 South Vietnamese soldiers were killed during the Tet Offensive. Westmoreland's intelligence officials claimed that 50,000 of the 67,000 estimated Vietcong insurgents were killed. A prominent communist told Stanley Karnow in early 1981, "We lost our best people, recalling that Vietcong military units composed mostly of indigenous southerners had borne the brunt of the fighting and suffered the heaviest casualties."[14]

Over the next year, the MACV's Phoenix Program, inspired by the CIA, in which individual Vietcong were targeted, captured, and usually killed, devastated the surviving communist political organization. As a result, Northerners moved South to replace the dead Southerners, rebuilt the communist apparatus, and remained to pursue the war to its conclusion. In the process they antagonized Southerners, who regarded the Hanoi-trained Northern communist cadres as "rigid and doctrinaire." Karnow's communist interlocutor said, "They behaved as if they had conquered us."[15]

General Vo Nguyen Giap wrote an assessment in which he conceded that the struggle was deadlocked—at least on the battlefield. The communists lacked the strength to match America's superior firepower, while the U.S. forces were too dispersed in protecting their bases and other installations to pursue the Vietcong and North Vietnamese units.

In Giap's estimation, according to Karnow, "Stalemate favored the guerrillas. The United States could not escalate the conflict without committing additional soldiers and materiel, and could not boost its investment without reducing both its global defense responsibilities and its domestic economic and social programs. Thus," Giap concluded, "the United States was overextended—its resources strained by 'a little war that had grown into a big war.' "[16]

Giap's long-range strategy was to bleed the Americans until they agreed to a settlement that satisfied Hanoi. Communists were willing to endure terrible casualties during the Tet campaign, as throughout the war. The Tet Offensive was not conceived as a decisive operation, but one episode in a protracted war that might last "five, ten, twenty years."

As Ho Chi Minh had warned the French a generation before, "You can kill ten of my men for every one I kill of yours. But, even at those odds, you will lose and I will win."[17] This morbid logic held true during the American War.

As Karnow explained, "Giap's grand design stemmed from his perception that the United States and South Vietnamese clients were inextricably interdependent. Although the 'puppets' relied completely on the Americans for their survival, they nevertheless played a vital role in defending the U.S. facilities, fulfilling police functions, managing pacification projects, and performing other static duties. The veneer of sovereignty cloaked a neocolonial relationship." But Giap believed that the alliance was basically unstable and would eventually disintegrate as the United States pressured the South Vietnamese to prosecute the war more effectively. Latent anti-American sentiment could also be exploited. One of the Communist goals in "Tet" was to drive a wedge between the South Vietnamese and Americans. "This led to the mistaken expectation that South Vietnam was ripe for revolution and that the weary government soldiers, dislocated peasants, frustrated religious factions, fractious youths, and other unhappy elements of the Southern population would rise in opposition to the Saigon regime and the Americans."[18]

Despite their hopes for uprising and revolution, the communists realized even if Southerners would not rise up, overthrow the government, demand a neutralist government that included the Vietcong, and throw out the Americans, the offensive would advance the communists' basic objectives against the weary Americans.

There was one more element in Hanoi's strategy: a diplomatic initiative to raise doubts in Saigon about the reliability of the Americans.

On December 31, 1967, North Vietnam's foreign minister, Nguyen Duy Trinh, issued a new offer, which omitted earlier conditions. Trinh announced that communists "will" open discussions with the United States once it halted air strikes against North Vietnam.[19]

But the communists also blundered. Communist sources admitted they had been "guilty of many errors and shortcomings." Their deficiencies included failure to inspire the South Vietnamese population to rebel and an inability to lure South Vietnamese soldiers to rally to the uprising. Despite their enormous sacrifices, they still faced a long struggle. Official reports expressed alarm at the loss of morale and erosion of confidence in communist leadership and victory.

A senior North Vietnamese general in the South, Tran Van Tra, in a military history published in Hanoi in 1982, commented that the offensive had been misconceived from the start. "During Tet of 1968," he wrote, "we did not correctly evaluate the specific balance of forces between ourselves and the enemy, did not realize that the enemy still had considerable capabilities and that our capabilities were limited." The communists had set objectives "that were beyond our actual strength," founded "in part on an illusion based on our subjective desires." Thus, he added, "[w]e suffered large losses in materiel and manpower, especially cadres at various echelons, which clearly weakened us. We were unable to retain the gains we had made and had to overcome a myriad of difficulties in 1969 and 1970 so that the revolution could stand firm in the storm."[20]

Karnow recalled with great surprise the comments of communist cadres with whom he spoke in 1982 who had "bad memories of Tet" and "openly expressed disappointment with the outcome." Duong Quynh Hoa, at the time a secret Vietcong operative in Saigon, joined the Vietcong in the invasion of the capital. She denounced the offensive as a "grievous miscalculation" by Hanoi, since it had "wantonly squandered the southern insurgent movement." A North Vietnamese captain, Tran Dinh Thong, remembered feeling "depressed and worried about the future," and he blamed the planners for having "incorrectly" surveyed the situation beforehand.[21]

General Tran Van Tra did not call the offensive a resounding triumph. He explained to Karnow: "In all honesty, we did not attain our main objective, which was to spur uprisings throughout the South. Still we inflicted heavy casualties on the Americans and their puppets, and that was a big gain for us." As for making an impact in the United States, contradicting General Giap and others, "It had not been our intention, but it turned out to be a fortunate result."[22]

There remains in Vietnam considerable controversy about Hanoi's intentions, expectations, and assessment of Tet. In his June 23, 2009, talk, University of Hanoi professor Pham Hong Tung provided his assessment of Tet to my Princeton Summer Seminar: "In a decisive Communist Party Politburo meeting in June 1967, Secretary General Le Duan led a decision to order a 'decisive shock attack' [before the U.S. presidential elections] on Saigon and other cities of South Vietnam. In a subsequent Politburo meeting in October, which neither Le Duan nor General Vo Nguyen Giap attended, an order for a 'maximum general attack to liberate the South' to 'gain a decisive victory or Party victory,' to 'try to capture (President) Nguyen Van Thieu, (Vice President) Nguyen Cao Ky, or (General) Westmoreland.'" The siege at Khe Sanh was conceived as a deceptive mission.[23] None of these objectives, as Dr. Tung laid out, was achieved.

The word "uprising," a key phrase in Vietnam-Marxist terminology, was not the word used in the orders but came to be expected by the most ambitious planners. To address this issue, the planners would have to consider the forces available. The difficulty of smuggling sufficient guns and weapons into the cities was also pertinent. If the event was a victory, that would be great, but if not, it could lead to disaffection among supporters, especially those in the South.[24]

In the event, General Giap did not call the Tet attack a "general uprising" but a "general military attack." But he reportedly "lost faith" in the results of the attack. There were differences of opinion within the leadership about Tet, and perceptions before and after Tet changed. The leaders did not contemplate the numbers of casualties. While U.S. forces concluded that some 40,000 Vietcong and cadre were killed, of the 67,000 total, Vietnam's Ministry of Defense uses these figures:[25]

Killed in action	44,824
Wounded in action	61,267
Missing in action	4,511
Captured	912
Ran away	10,899
Capitulated	415
Other	1,265
TOTAL	113,295

Adding to North Vietnamese and NLF losses, the decision to launch another round of attacks in the northern Mekong Delta resulted in the killing of most of those involved. It took at least two years for the NLF to recover, and in some places in the Mekong Delta recovery was much slower. In the meantime, PAVN reinforcements filled the gap and assumed even greater control over operations in the South.[26] Le Duan apparently concluded in the late Sixties that the spirit of '45 had to be recreated to inspire uprising.

In another wrinkle, Chairman Ho Chi Minh was sick in bed from early 1969 and wrote to the Politburo that he should prepare to go South. Some guess that Ho Chi Minh thought he was going to die and wanted to do so fighting for reunification.[27] Ho Chi Minh died on September 2, 1969.

However much the Tet Offensive cost the communist cause and failed to achieve its stated objectives, the impact on morale in the United States was such that many have come to see Tet as a key inflection point leading toward communist victory. This was the first American war to be covered by television. Easy access to battles, generals, and local attacks was common and regularly reported, and there was great interest in the United States The Tet Offensive, however, stunned the nation, and the media led the way in displaying the battles and the breadth of the attacks. Leading television channels provided huge coverage. Many recalled the assessment General Westmoreland's gave to Congress in October 1967 of "light at the end of the tunnel," the hollowness of his understanding, and the shock of Tet following in its wake. Some hawks joined Westmoreland and called for stepped-up retaliation. But most focused their shock and ire on President Johnson, and his public approval quickly plummeted. Tet was followed by the point-blank shootings of a handcuffed young Vietcong on February 1, 1968, on the streets of Saigon by the chief of national police, Brigadier Nguyen Ngoc Loan.[28] This event riveted Americans on the moral horrors of the war and our Vietnamese allies who were conducting it.[29]

After the war, in an angry tirade against the U.S. media, General Westmoreland alleged "voluminous, lurid, and distorted newspaper and particularly TV reports of the Tet attacks had transformed a devastating Communist military defeat in Vietnam into a psychological victory for the enemy."

Westmoreland acknowledged he had not anticipated the scope of the offensive, but he had put his forces on "maximum alert," unlike President Thieu, who had allowed liberal leave policies for the South Vietnamese forces. South Vietnamese officials were angry at the lack of preparedness, but there was also a feeling that the Vietcong and North Vietnamese were guilty of duplicity because they had attacked during the holiday of Tet. Others felt a sense of foreboding at the scope of the attacks throughout the country.[30]

Ambassador Bui Diem in Washington feared the effect the offensive would have on American public opinion. He was concerned that Americans would accept the judgment of Hanoi of a great victory, when in fact the ARVN had fought bravely, well, and had not been defeated. Bui Diem commented, "Although the enemy had billed Tet as a 'general offensive and uprising,' there had not been a single uprising. Whatever claim the revolution might have had of controlling the South Vietnamese people's hearts had been revealed as baseless. Whatever hopes they had had for precipitating mutineers within the South Vietnamese army had evaporated. On the contrary, ARVN had shown itself capable of quick retaliation and effective fighting."[31]

Nguyen Cao Ky, the aggressive South Vietnamese prime minister, found another "irony." "In a way," he said, "Tet was a victory for us—or would have been had we struck back. The great tragedy of Tet is that though the Americans never recovered from the blow, the North Vietnamese losses were so great that I believe we might have been able to inflict serious blows had we been allowed to go to an immediate counterattack."[32]

In fact, the Vietcong and North Vietnamese suffered continuing and very serious losses following Tet ,and the counterattacks and Phoenix program took their toll over the next year.

While both sides declared victory to write history, considering the number of deaths (especially of NLF guerrillas and cadres during Tet and the follow-up attacks), it certainly was a defeat. But in hindsight, judging from the world's reaction to Tet, most Vietnamese concluded that the offensive was a key turning point toward victory for Hanoi in 1975.

13

American Military Strategy

Although many Americans prefer to overlook the painful national experience of the Vietnam War, the historical debate continues, with some arguing that defeat was not inevitable, that the United States was on track to win militarily but lost it politically when media and popular pressures forced the United States to withdraw. Since this is a crucial issue, let us examine it in greater detail.

The Kennedy Perspective

President Kennedy initially saw the Vietnam challenge as one battle in the larger East-West, anticommunist struggle. He believed the United States must not lose territory to the communists, especially in the wake of the Bay of Pigs, his confrontation in Vienna with Khrushchev, and the Cuban Missile Crisis. However, pragmatically, he did not see the loss of South Vietnam itself as a vital strategic issue and was, in my judgment, prepared to compromise, as he had on Laos.

Kennedy correctly viewed Vietnam as a new kind of struggle that required a new kind of response. This perception led him to resist calls for combat forces (initially and thereafter; in 1961 his military advisors called for dispatching 200,000 troops to Vietnam) and focus on counterinsurgency as the key to dealing with the challenge. With Magsaysay's success, American support in the Philippines, and British success in Malaysia, he was fascinated with the concept of counterinsurgency and ordered the establishment of the Green Berets as the instrument for dealing with such a challenge.

In the wake of the apocalyptic brinksmanship of the Cuban Missile Crisis, the counterinsurgency approach was a way to de-intensify war and move away from the "mutual assured destruction" strategy adopted by Eisenhower.

For these reasons, the notion of Kennedy's willingness to withdraw support from Ngo Dinh Diem and withdraw American advisors from Vietnam after the 1964 elections was plausible. Whether this position would have been sustained in the face of near collapse in 1964–65 is an unanswerable historic question.

Johnson's Approach

President Johnson was driven by a different set of perceptions. He was determined not to be the first American president to lose a war, and he deeply feared that a loss would allow the right wing to lambast his policies, jettison his Great Society goals, and take power in America. He tailored his response to Vietnam based on those fears, even though he reportedly told his aide Kenneth O'Donnell and Senator Richard Russell, Democrat of Georgia, that the situation in Vietnam was, in effect, hopeless. He told Senator Russell, "I don't believe that the American people ever want me to run [abandon Vietnam]. If I lose it, I think they'll say I've lost it. At the same time, I don't want to commit us to a war. And I'm in a hell of a shape."[1]

Immediately after taking control, Johnson sent a message to Saigon assuring the generals that America would maintain its support for the Saigon regime. Early in 1964, only months after assuming the presidency, the Johnson administration began plotting escalation. In the spring of 1964, Johnson was determined to expand support for South Vietnam, even as the fortunes of the Government of South Vietnam declined. There was little reflection in the new Johnson administration on the Army's suitability for the conflict in Vietnam, according to U.S. Army Major Andrew F. Krepinevich, Jr., who retired as a colonel and provides an excellent assessment of the role of the army in his *The Army and Vietnam*.[2] Even with an eye on the 1964 elections against Barry Goldwater, which dictated extreme caution, the Johnson administration prepared and approved in June 1964 a Congressional resolution that would allow significant expansion of the struggle in Vietnam: the Gulf of Tonkin Resolution. His caution was designed to paint Goldwater as a dangerous warmonger and himself as a man of peace. Johnson's campaign ad of the little girl with daisies threatened by a mushroom cloud encapsulated his intended and electorally successful stance.

Fatefully, Johnson found his man in General William Westmoreland, who replaced the perpetually optimistic General Harkins as commander of U.S. Military Assistance Command Vietnam (COMUSMACV) in June 1964. This reflected the belief of the JCS that the impending struggle would rely upon traditional military operations. As an indication of the JCS's greater influence in Vietnam, the JCS chairman, General Maxwell Taylor, a very close friend of President Kennedy, replaced civilian statesman Henry Cabot Lodge as ambassador to Saigon.

Although he recognized the political and social dimensions of the conflict, Ambassador Taylor later said he "viewed it unlikely that they could ever establish that solid political and military base which we all wanted in South Vietnam before taking military action against the North."[3] Taylor believed military action against the North was a prerequisite for success in Vietnam. In 1961 he favored introduction of U.S. forces as a hedge and use of American airpower. In Karnow's view, Taylor regarded "the insurgency as a military problem amenable to a military solution resting in the application of military power against the Democratic Republic of Vietnam (DRV)."[4] Taylor's search for a military solution accorded with the thinking of JCS and other close Johnson advisors.[5]

Near unanimous Congressional approval of the Tonkin Gulf Resolution granted great authority to the president to shape his military response to the conflict in Southeast Asia. The resolution authorized the president "to take all necessary measures to repel any armed attack against the forces of the United States and to prevent further aggression," a virtual carte blanche, especially for policymakers who were less attuned to the political realities of the Vietnamese insurgents. In discussions with the NSC in November 1964, Ambassador Taylor described the Vietcong's ability to replenish its forces as a "mystery." But MACV acknowledged that only 15 percent of the Vietcong forces were infiltrated in 1964; the remainder were local.

In NSC meetings on November 28 and 30, 1964, the NSC approved a two-pronged approach. In Phase I, over the first 30 days pressure would increase gradually on North Vietnam, while the United States attempted to strengthen the GVN. Phase II would involve air strikes, code-named Rolling Thunder, against North Vietnam.[6]

The U.S. Army judged that by late 1964 the insurgency would enter Phase III: insurgent operations of a quasi-conventional warfare that reflected the U.S. Army's preference for conventional warfare. The Army at that point identified North Vietnam as the source of aggression against South Vietnam. One year after Kennedy's assassination, the emphasis was no longer on "nation-building." It had become "nation-saving."[7] In fact, the U.S. Army emphasis had never been "on nation-building," which only in 1966–67 became the mission of MACV/CORDS.

Special Forces

The U.S. Special Forces had a history beginning near the end of World War II, growing from the work of OSS, which, ironically, had worked to support Ho Chi Minh from 1943 until October 1945, when the United States ended support for the Vietminh The regular Army disparaged the quasi-military Special Forces designed to conduct commando–style operations, raids, reconnaissance, and organize and lead the *maquis* behind the lines in a general war. The Army managed to kill the proposals to establish special forces promoted in 1945 by OSS chief William Donovan. Between 1945 and 1950 the Army dabbled superficially in unconventional warfare, but not counterinsurgency. The JCS and Army opposed the establishment of a guerrilla warfare school and managed to push the nation's special forces into the newly formed CIA, formerly OSS.[8]

During the Korean War, the U.S. Air Force formed "Wolfpacks" of Koreans to conduct raids against the North, but the Army managed eventually to merge them into conventional units.

Finally, in March 1952, the Army chief of staff authorized formation of the Tenth Special Forces Group as part of the new Psychological Warfare Center at Fort Bragg, North Carolina. Nonetheless, the Army was reluctant to use the Special Forces in Korea and used them only in unconventional warfare, not counterinsurgency—a position the Army also took in Vietnam.[9]

The counterinsurgency role emerged only after John Kennedy became president. He was convinced of the utility of Special Counter-Insurgency Forces, which he had established. The Army naturally honored the new president's desires, but they contorted their use, turning them toward Soviet conventional forces in Europe rather than insurgents in Asia. Moreover, Major Krepinevich concludes, "As the percentage of Special Forces in Vietnam relative to advisory and support groups diminished, so would their role in Army counterinsurgency plans. With the introduction of large numbers of helicopters, the perception of air mobility as a technical-tactical solution gained increasing currency."[10]

Training also revealed the scant interest of the Army in counterinsurgency. Backup brigades received just two days of area orientation but a year and six weeks of counterinsurgency training, with the culminating exercise featuring a battalion-sized exercise requiring offensive action to destroy a hostile enemy force. In effect, Special Forces were tangentially used in counterinsurgency and instead were employed to be a front behind which conventional European training and operations could be pursued. As Major Krepinevich's saw it, "In the final analysis, airmobile forces served not to enhance counterinsurgency operations but as a 'technological fix' that helped the Army avoid them."[11]

According to Krepinevich, the Army remained convinced the essence of the conflict was military, not political. Politics would take a back seat while the Army inflicted sufficient damage on the insurgents to force them to the peace table. Once it became clear, by 1964, that the communists were gaining strength, the Army's primary concern was the deployment of forces to execute the same strategy at which the ARVN had been failing for years. However, now it would include greater resources, increased intensity, and introduction of U.S. military forces on the ground.

Although the army thus would have alternatives regarding its approach to counterinsurgency, the service's hierarchy gave them short shrift. The army was interested in waging the war it had prepared for, and while there was great frustration over the limits imposed on horizontal (geographical) escalation of the war, the civilian leadership gave the commander in the field his traditional freedom to escalate vertically—that is, to escalate the level of violence with South Vietnam if the level remained beneath the nuclear threshold.[12]

The Army was trained and committed to impose the Korea model on its approach to Vietnam. U.S. combat forces were introduced in the spring of 1965, initially in Danang and Phu Bai. Westmoreland proposed them as protective forces for the U.S. military enclaves, but he intended to use them as offensive forces against the Vietcong. With scarce justification, Westmoreland contended that the insurgents were entering the initial stages of Mao's Phase Three, the stage of conventional battles, and therefore must be countered by U.S. combat forces.

In June, Westmoreland paid lip service to the notion of counterinsurgency but in fact was intent on pursuing conventional warfare. On June 12, Westmoreland noted:

> There is no doubt whatsoever that the insurgency in South Vietnam must eventually be defeated among the people in the hamlets and towns; however, to defeat the insurgency among the people, they must be provided security of two kinds:
>
> (1) Security of the country as a whole from large, well-organized and equipped forces, including those who may come from outside the country;
> (2) Security from the guerrilla, the assassin, the terrorist, the informer.
>
> MACV is convinced that U.S. troops could contribute heavily in the first category of security. Therefore, the MACV concept was to employ U.S. forces against the hardcore DRV/VC forces in search-and-destroy operations and thus permit the concentration of (South) Vietnamese troops in heavily populated areas along the coast, around Saigon and the Delta.[13]

As Westmoreland's requests for U.S. forces jumped from 45,000 to 100,000, 200,000, 506,000, and in his final proposal, which was rejected, jumped to 706,000, his core strategy did not change. Offensive search-and-destroy operations were his game, bolstered by massive bombing, which destroyed substantial areas of South Vietnam and, unintentionally, enlisted recruits for the Vietcong. Counterinsurgency was at best a distracting side note.

The corollary to General Westmoreland's strategy of attrition in the South was the bombing of the North. Long advocated by General Westmoreland and Ambassador Taylor and the JCS, a Vietcong attack on a U.S. base at Pleiku in the highlands precipitated the start of the bombing campaign Rolling Thunder on February 11, 1965. Hitting the North would be directed at the aggressors, reduce the Vietcong "sanctuary," and save American lives by striking from the air.[14] As U.S. combat forces were steadily escalated in the South, the bombing campaign was structured to steadily turn up the heat and destruction in North Vietnam, though calibrated to avoid inducing the Chinese or Soviets into entering the war to rescue North Vietnam. Initially, the United States spared the port of Haiphong to avoid striking Soviet ships, and bombing was prohibited near the Chinese border, where Chinese antiaircraft and engineers took over from North Vietnamese to free them to fight in the South.

Among his top governmental advisors, only the undersecretary of state, George Ball, saw things differently, focusing on the political and social dimensions of the insurgency war. In a memo to the president on June 18, 1965, Ball wrote: "Ever since 1961—the beginning of our deep involvement in South Vietnam—we have met successive disappointments. We have tended to underestimate the strength and staying power of the enemy. We have tended to overestimate the effectiveness of our sophisticated weapons under jungle conditions. We have watched the progressive loss of territory to Vietcong control. We have been unable to bring about the creation of a stable political base in Saigon. This is no one's fault. It is in the nature of the struggle."[15]

The strategy of attrition was modeled on the doctrine and force structure designed for conventional contingences in Europe and used in Korea, where the critical difference was that the South Korean government had already mercilessly and successfully eliminated the Communist Peoples' councils and communists in the South in 1947–48. Faced with an invading army of conventional North Korean troops, there was little faith in counterinsurgency, even among many civilian leaders.

Firepower and strategic mobility promised success and minimized U.S. casualties. With 184,000 troops, including a South Korean division, allied U.S. forces engaged the North Vietnamese in the Ia Drang Valley November 10–14, 1965, resulting in savage, bloody fighting that left 1,200 North Vietnamese killed to only 200 U.S. losses. Westmoreland regarded the Ia Drang victory as validation of his assessment and strategy.[16]

Based on their history in participating in insurgency conflict, the Marines had a different concept of counterinsurgency, stressing the aim of social, economic, and political development in a small war, coupled with tolerance, sympathy, and kindness in the relationship with the mass population. This meant conceptually protecting the villagers, who may or may have not needed protection, and deploying small units in the villages themselves to defend the people. Such a plan called for increasing the number of night patrols, destruction of the insurgent infrastructure, and sharing responsibility for security with the popular forces (PF) of the village in Combined Action Platoons (CAP), with Marines partnering with Popular Forces as a force multiplier to defend villages. Though this approach better suited local conditions and reduced U.S. casualties, the absence of language-training and failure at higher levels to link individual village efforts together into "oil spots" detracted from their overall success. Nonetheless, U.S. casualties were lower than in search-and-destroy operations. In later stages, as the United States deployed Marines in search-and-destroy operations, their effectiveness diminished.[17]

The CAPs were employed to protect the city and surrounding villages near Danang and the DMZ, even as the Marines' large units were operating independently in the same areas.

Overall, the Army overwhelmingly opted for mid–intensity conflict, big–unit operations, and minimization of U.S. casualties through heavy firepower. Moreover, the short tour for soldiers and officers, emphasis on enemy body counts, and field commanders' "attrition" strategy to kill Vietcong all proved counterproductive from a counterinsurgency standpoint. Pacification—the "Other War"—was left for ARVN. Pacification was too slow a process for the quick victory Westmoreland sought. Moreover, the U.S. Army was never in one place long enough to know the terrain or people. It was far easier to rely on logistical and technological elements of strategy—sensors, ground radars, firepower on call, helicopter gunships, herbicides, and defoliants—all of which gave the Army the opportunity to wage "counterinsurgency, America-style."[18]

Pacification and RUFF-PUFFs

The U.S. Army did lead efforts at pacification, intelligence gathering, and destruction of the insurgent infrastructure, but they were a sideshow, channeled through the civilian-led Civil Operations and Revolutionary Development Support (CORDS) program and the Special Forces. The CORDS program, initiated in mid-1967, was the massive advisory effort, a mix of civilians and military that worked with provincial and district governments across a wide range of activities. Some of the activities are mentioned above, but these also included building infrastructure to gain the support of the population for the government.

The CORDS training of the RUFF-PUFFS (regional and popular forces) in joint patrols was much more effective at pacification than ARVN, but these were regarded as far secondary to the main mission of the military—search-and-destroy and attrition.

The Tet Offensive, January 31, 1968

I have discussed the Tet Offensive elsewhere, but let us look at it from the military perspective. For the first time, the Tet Offensive brought the Vietcong and NLF out of their lairs into open, pitched battles, where American firepower devastated them. Almost two-thirds of the NLF infrastructure was destroyed in the Tet Offensive. While Tet was costly to the NLF militarily, it demonstrated the widespread influence of the Vietcong throughout South Vietnam, smashing Westmoreland's rosy report late in 1967 of "light at the end of the tunnel." In addition, pacification was dealt a devastating setback, since Tet revealed the depth of influence the NLF enjoyed throughout South Vietnam.

In the aftermath of Tet, Westmoreland did not reevaluate his strategy. He thought more of the same would do the trick, as he had anticipated in his escalation of forces over the previous three years. He was relieved from duty in September 1968 and his replacement, General Creighton Abrams, agreed to cut back on search-and-destroy operations, although they continued to be the main thrust of the Army's efforts. There was also renewed interest in pacification for a time, but Nixon's election in the fall of 1968 produced a new ball game to focus on: "Vietnamization" of the conflict. Vietnamization entailed slowly withdrawing U.S. troops while seeking a negotiated settlement with Hanoi, and ended resources for pacification.

The Victorious Interpretation of the Vietnam War

General Westmoreland, South Vietnamese Prime Minister Nguyen Cao Ky, and others have claimed the Vietnam War was won or could have been won in 1968 or in 1972–73 by escalating of the number of U.S. forces immediately by 200,000 and intensifying the bombing of the North. I find these claims specious.

Alternatively, an invasion of North Vietnam was thought to raise the probability of China's and/or the Soviets' entering the war to save North Vietnam. Considering the challenge the United States faced in a southern guerilla war, the proposition of a full conflict throughout the North and South, backed by strong foreign enemies, was too much to contemplate. An invasion of North Vietnam would have brought global condemnation, and an increasingly war-weary American public would not have supported such actions.

Others proposed alternative strategies for fighting the war. Colonel Harry G. Summers, in his seminal *On Strategy: A Critical Analysis of the Vietnam War*, to significant applause proposed establishing a defensive line across Vietnam and into Laos.[19] Summers's book, written in the early 1980s, has since been promoted in the Army and is still widely regarded in senior Army circles as the most incisive analysis of the conflict in Vietnam. The incursion strategy is a revisionist version of the El Paso Plan proposed by Westmoreland. Summers's proposal called for a joint U.S.-ARVN-ROK (South Korean) incursion across the Laotian panhandle from the DMZ to Savannakhet on the Thai border to hermetically seal South Vietnam from infiltration from North Vietnam. The plan called for eight divisions (five U.S., two ROK, and one ARVN), with a total cost of some 160,000 men, an enormous military burden that would have subjected the troops to constant harassment and attack, as indeed the forces deployed for the "McNamara line" on the DMZ suffered.

Summers claims that, with the South sealed, the ARVN could have managed over time to destroy the insurgents. This claim flies in the face of the fact that the Vietcong almost took over South Vietnam in 1964 before the PAVN forces entered in December 1964. In the meantime, they had expanded throughout South Vietnam, were almost destroyed during Tet, but again had rebuilt their strength by 1970.

Major Krepinevich expresses serious doubts regarding Summers's proposal because of the enormous cost of the defense forces, which he estimates would require 18,000 engineers in addition to the combat forces. He suspected the ROK would have been unwilling to participate in such a static operation. Even if they could muster the forces, Krepinevich questioned the impact. He noted that northern infiltration was a minor factor in the conflict, which, until Tet, was driven by Vietcong forces with South Vietnamese popular support. If the ARVN did not fare well under that challenge, he questioned whether a sealed defense line in Indochina would alter the balance of the conflict.[20]

ARVN, with U.S. encouragement, attempted the ill-fated Lang Son 719 operation in 1971. The operation was a limited-objective offensive campaign conducted in the southeastern portion of Laos between February 8 and March 25, 1971. The United States provided logistical, aerial, and artillery support to the operation but its ground forces were prohibited by law from entering Laos. The objective of the campaign was the disruption of a possible future offensive by the North Vietnamese using the Ho Chi Minh Trail.

By launching an attack against PAVN's long-established logistical system, the American and South Vietnamese high commands hoped to address several matters. A quick victory in Laos would bolster the morale and confidence of the ARVN, which was high in the wake of the successful Cambodian campaign of 1970. It would also serve as proof that ARVN could defend South Vietnam as U.S. ground combat forces withdrew. As it turned out, Lang Son 719 was a disaster for ARVN, decimating some of its best units and destroying confidence built over the previous three years.

In another popular book on the Vietnam War, *Unheralded Victory: The Defeat of the Vietcong and the North Vietnamese Army, 1961–1973,* American-born Australian writer Mark Woodruff claims the United States defeated the Vietcong and the North Vietnamese but failed because a media and elitist antiwar minority weakened resolve among civilian leaders and miscast the results as failure.

Woodruff correctly points out that the United States prevented the Vietcong from taking over South Vietnam in 1964 and militarily the Vietcong suffered a devastating defeat during the Tet Offensive. He argues that the bombing campaign successfully turned back the Vietnamese spring offensive in 1972 and brought the North Vietnamese back to the negotiating table. However, Woodruff asserts that the U.S. media and political leadership, cowed by public opinion, lost the opportunity to continue to pursue the war to a successful end. In his foreword to the book, Marine Corps General James J. Jones notes, "His [Woodruff's] thesis is simple: While the American political base at home was never solid enough to wage a protracted war in Southeast Asia, the war effort in theater was far from the quixotic venture to which many have relegated it in hindsight. Within the constraints imposed by the political environment of the day, the conflict was fought with a high degree of professionalism and competence."

Despite accurately describing military developments, Woodruff draws false conclusions because he ignores the political nature of the conflict. His convoluted arguments about victory in 1964 are misleading. Yes, American military intervention brought South Vietnam back from the brink. But Woodruff overlooks the reasons why a small force of Vietcong, with minimal assistance from Hanoi at that point, nearly overran the country in 1964. Woodruff's approval of the military intervention ignores the fact that American assistance was designed to bolster the anti-communist capacity of the GVN and the ARVN, a program that conspicuously failed.

Woodruff's championing of massive aerial bombardment to force Hanoi's hand ignores both the human costs of such large-scale bombing as well as the counterproductive nature of bombing and collective punishment in a politically oriented war. Woodruff's logic is the same as the infamous remark that the United States "had to destroy Ben Tre to save it." The broader claim, made by Westmoreland and Nguyen Cao Ky, that if we had continued the battle at full force (and with 206,000 additional troops), after the devastation of the NFL forces during and after Tet, we could have "won" the war. This was highly unlikely in my view.

We had Americanized, militarized, and radicalized the struggle in Vietnam and attempted to ram a conventional military conflict onto a political struggle. As we won battle after battle (U.S. forces never lost a significant battle), the political structure of South Vietnam was eaten away by guerrilla war and political decay.

The U.S. Army fought the war it wanted and had trained to fight, but that was not the war that was underway in a revolutionary environment. The real war was a civil war we transformed into a war against American occupation, against which the Vietcong and North Vietnamese seized initiative as the "patriots," playing on a familiar and timeless motif in Vietnamese history: the indomitable will and understanding that by not losing, Vietnam would win. The Vietnamese communists prepared to fight to the end to retake their country and reunite Vietnam.

American troops fought bravely and valiantly, but their leaders, civilian and military, misled the country and misdirected the military in directions that applied a conventional war to a revolutionary environment. The American people, the elite and common folks, realized after Tet the claims of imminent victory were meaningless and demanded an end to the carnage.

Had political will not demanded its end, and had we followed General Westmoreland's "attrition strategy" to the end, we could have killed a million or more Vietnamese and tens of thousands of young Americans would have died in vain. It would have cost America and Vietnam proportionately more, but, in the end, I doubt the results would have been very different.

Had we bombed North Vietnam back to the Stone Age, as General Curtis Lemay advocated, or invaded the North, we would have risked intervention by China and the Soviets and have become mired in an enlarged quagmire at best and a major war at worst.

I discussed in Chapter 8 what I thought at the time and subsequently my views on what would have been a more apt approach to the conflict in South Vietnam, namely that we should not have Americanized and militarized what was a political conflict, a civil war we turned into a struggle against foreign military occupation. This is the mistaken judgment in Summers's and Woodruff's analyses, and the crucial fault of our political and military leadership in dealing with the Vietnam conflict not as a political conflict, despite obeisance to this interpretation, but as a military confrontation against a profoundly committed nationalist movement that had struggled for thirty years to eject foreign occupiers. Their claims prevailed.

There was also a moral dimension to this equation. Ambassador Bui Diem in his book, *In the Jaws of History,* highlighted the moral horrors of the war: "It was a paradox: Although the Vietcong and North Vietnamese were conducting what they called a people's war, which by its nature drew the civilian population into the carnage, blame for the massive destruction and the consequent uprooting of the rural population all devolved on the Americans and the South Vietnamese (administration). It was a burden we would carry for the rest of the war."[21]

14

The American Fighting Man

I worked closely with many of the U.S. servicemen in the mid-Sixties, just before the United States launched CORDS in June 1967 to integrate civilian and military advisory organizations. My contacts with the military advisors were frequent, and my impression of the men was very favorable. They were remarkably intelligent, very hardworking, and devoted to their cause. I was proud of them and became friends with many. But I acknowledge that I did not work with the ordinary foot soldiers or Marines who withstood the worst of the combat experience; I worked with the "advisors" to the South Vietnamese government.

Because I was familiar with the advisory soldiers, I could readily see how difficult the lives of the combat forces must have been — the physical challenges and the proximity to grave physical harm or death were ever-present. They bore these challenges with customary American fortitude, good humor, and a heroic dedication to one another.

I was also not in Vietnam in the early Seventies, when morale and spirit broke down for many. Spirits were high during my tours in 1965–67, and I did not experience the disillusionment that set in later, when "fragging lifers" and use of drugs became all too common.

Of the three million young Americans who served in Vietnam, a large portion were stationed in Saigon or other cities with desk, logistics, or other administrative duties and did not go into combat. Pilots and other Air Force personnel were stationed on bases and after bombing runs frequently returned to their well-kept bases with clubs, beer, and movies at night.

Except for naval personnel in the swift boats in the Mekong Delta, most sailors were onboard ships and, therefore, not subject to personal combat. There were also thousands of provincial and district advisors who worked with Vietnamese officials and were comfortably situated in relative safety.

Even for the Army foot soldiers and Marines, there was great variety depending upon which part of the country they were stationed in. American "grunts," as they called themselves, could slog in muddy paddy fields in the Mekong Delta. They battled leeches and mines as often as tangling with snipers as they trudged day after day through water, drenched by rain and sweat in monsoon season.

In the Highlands, soldiers were much more likely to engage with large units of Vietcong or North Vietnamese. In the coastal towns near bases, firefights and mines were common as soldiers patrolled base perimeters. Many spent long, lonely nights manning artillery on mountaintops, often subjected to bombardment by mortars or direct-armed attack. Vietcong guerrillas sometimes overran small detachments of Special Forces and Montagnard mercenaries.

Draftees were subject to a single, one-year tour; most were counting the time remaining from the moment they arrived. At the start the United States did not send them as units, so they arrived and were assigned to units in which they knew no one, and many felt very lonely. A feeling of alienation in a sea of hostility where few—if any, some thought—Vietnamese could be trusted compounded their loneliness. Survival became their main motive, especially in a war with no front lines and in which it was unsafe virtually everywhere.

A survey taken by the Veterans Administration in the Eighties revealed that most felt they had been in combat but, in fact, only a minority had clashed with North Vietnamese units, Vietcong irregulars, or had run into mines or booby traps. But 76 percent had been on the receiving end of mortar or rocket attacks, and 56 percent had seen fellow Americans killed or wounded.[1]

In some ways, Karnow reports, the Americans were no less ideological than the Vietnamese they fought. Presidents Kennedy and Johnson exhorted the troops to join the fight to halt the spread of global communism. All knew that the United States had never been defeated in a war, and they were inspired by popular folk heroes, such as Audie Murphy and John Wayne. They might imagine themselves as dashing heroes who bravely destroyed the enemy and came home to heroic welcomes by their beautiful girlfriends.[2]

The same VA poll found that 71 percent were "glad" to have gone to Vietnam, 74 percent "enjoyed" their tours, and 66 percent were willing to serve again. But as the war dragged on, increasingly soldiers became disillusioned; 82 percent asserted that "political leaders in Washington would not let them win." They viewed the war as tragic but almost universally claimed the effort was noble.

Despite their mistrust of the Vietnamese, I witnessed many GIs befriending and helping Vietnamese, reflecting the good side of most Americans. They were especially friendly to Vietnamese children, handing them candy or playing with them. I often saw American advisory soldiers visiting villages with a retinue of small children in tow.

Karnow quotes one Marine, however, describing his concerns:

You never knew who was the enemy and who was the friend. They all looked alike. They all dressed alike. They were all Vietnamese. Here's a woman of twenty-two or twenty-three. She is pregnant, and she tells an interrogator that her husband works in Danang and isn't a Vietcong. But she watches your men walk down a trail and get killed or wounded by a booby trap. She knows the booby trap is there, but she doesn't warn them. Maybe she planted it herself. The enemy was all around you.[3]

Soon after the Marines in I Corps landed in Danang in March 1965, they embarked on "cordon and search missions." In theory, the Marines would surround a group of hamlets, distribute food, and dispense medical care to the inhabitants as they searched for Vietcong cadres.

In practice, however, the Marines would often go through a village before dawn and roust everybody out of bed, kicking down doors and dragging villagers out if they moved too slowly. All huts had underground bunkers to protect the villagers from bombing and shelling, but the Marines viewed the bunkers as Vietcong hiding places and destroyed the structures.

If extra rice was lying around, Marines might confiscate it to prevent it from reaching the Vietcong. Marines herded villagers into a pen to spend the day in the heat or rain. A Vietnamese police officer, a Marine interrogator, and an interpreter interrogated selected villagers to discover the whereabouts of the Vietcong. If any chosen failed to have an appropriate identification card or were uncooperative, they might be beaten, tortured, hauled off to jail, or even worse. If such Vietnamese were not pro-Vietcong at the start of this experience, one Marine told Karnow, "they sure as hell were by the time we left."[4]

Scenarios of violence and alienation unfolded with alarming regularity. Upon receiving fire from an area or information that raised suspicions, U.S. forces would storm into villages, tear them up, burn the huts, and terrorize the inhabitants. Frequently the Vietcong had taken refuge. Many villages were "cleaned out" several times. Repeatedly, soldiers or Marines would occupy a village and, as soon as they left, the Vietcong would return and reconstitute the village.[5]

The monotony, especially in the Mekong Delta, of trudging through rice paddies or heavily forested areas was overwhelming. To many, the rain and insects were almost worse than the enemy. Drenched in sweat, packing 50- to 70-pound backpacks, the men waded through flooded paddies, stopping from time to time to pick leeches out of their boots. Such days seemed endless.[6]

Another described to Karnow a desire for a fight to end the monotony:

> When you made contact with the enemy, you went from the most horrible boredom to the most intense excitement I've ever known in my life. You couldn't remain detached. Someone was trying to kill you and you were trying to kill someone, and it was like every thrill hitting you at once. When I didn't feel safe, there was a distinct beauty to it—a sense of exultation, the bullets cracking around your head and the tracers flying so close that they would blind you for a moment.[7]

South Vietnamese ambassador to Washington Bui Diem wrote of the GIs in his book *In the Jaws of History:*

South Vietnam's army had become a close witness of the American style of waging war. Vietnamese soldiers, no less than Vietnamese civilians, looked with amazement on the logistical miracle that sprang into being to serve the GIs. They saw the vast military stores (PXs) with their dazzling array of goods aimed at easing the hardship of American soldiers who were fighting ten-thousand miles from home. They saw the endless stream of military supplies funneled into the American units—though not, they noted, into their own.

They knew the Americans were spending vast sums on bombs and shells, which they used with such prodigality. They were, on the one hand, resentful. On the other, they were already acquiring the idea that this was the correct way to fight a war. It was a style to which they would become habituated in a short time, and that would prove disastrous when the Americans eventually withdrew their support.

Beyond that, with General Westmoreland's search-and-destroy strategy moving into high gear by the spring of 1966, the American-inspired pattern of warfare began to create serious problems in the countryside. The U.S. army rule of thumb for engagement was expend shells, not men.

Among other things, this meant "softening-up" bombardments by artillery or naval gunfire, B-52s, or other air strikes preceded every operation. I witnessed these operations frequently from my rooftop in Bien Hoa in 1965–66. One consequence was that the element of surprise was lost and huge operations often turned up only a few enemy snipers and the remnants of bases. More important, the lavish use of firepower also resulted in horrible casualties for the villagers and peasants in areas where the operations took place.[8]

Bui Diem also noted: "One of the guerrillas' main tactics was to conceal themselves among the peasants who lived in the countryside. Knowing the American habit of responding to contact with overwhelming firepower, they often deliberately provoked shelling and air strikes on villages to foment hatred of the GIs."

After Tet in January 1968, U.S. bombing increased in the Mekong Delta, for example, and many towns were destroyed as the United States attempted to eradicate the Vietcong in the wake of the Tet Offensive.[9]

War Literature

Literature from the time allows readers to hear the anguish of monotony, of meaninglessness that pervaded the fabric of soldiers' lives. Samuel Becket in *Waiting for Godot* captured these sentiments in the intellectually equivalent islands of meaninglessness.

Tim O'Brien in his first book, *If I Die in a Combat Zone, Box Me Up and Ship Me Home,* captured the meaninglessness:

> After a few months, it began to seem crazy, but you didn't dare to draw conclusions that might point in terrifying directions. Maybe we Americans weren't the guys in white hats, riding white horses. Maybe we shouldn't be in Vietnam. Maybe I'd gotten my ass out in these bushes for nothing. Still, it never occurred to me to lay down my rifle and quit. Instead, you develop a survival mentality. You stop thinking about what you are doing, and you count days. I knew that I was in Vietnam for three hundred and ninety-five days, and if I was still alive at the end of the three hundred and ninety-five days, I'd go home and forget the whole thing. That's the way you operated.[10]

O'Brien, in his *The Things They Carried,* conveys lyrically the same drumbeat of nothingness, the loss of soul, and the seeming senselessness and dehumanization of war:

They carried diseases, among them malaria and dysentery. They carried lice and ringworm and leeches and paddy algae and various rots and molds. They carried the land itself—Vietnam, the place, the soil—a powdery orange-red dust that covered their boots and fatigues and faces. They carried the sky. The whole atmosphere, they carried it, the humidity, the monsoons, the stink of fungus and decay, all of it. They carried gravity. They moved like mules. By daylight they took sniper fire, at night they were mortared, but it was not battle, it was just the endless march, village to village, without purpose, nothing won or lost. They marched for the sake of the march. They plodded along slowly, dumbly, leaning forward against the heat, unthinking, all blood and bone, simple grunts, soldiering with their legs, toiling up the hills and down into the paddies and across the rivers and up again and down, just humping, one step and then the next and then another, but no volition, no will, because it was automatic, it was anatomy, and the war was entirely a matter of posture and carriage, the hump was everything, a kind of inertia, a kind of emptiness, a dullness of desire and intellect and conscience and hope and human sensibility. Their principles were in their feet. Their calculations were biological. They had no sense of strategy or mission.

They searched the villages without knowing what to look for, not caring, kicking over jars of rice, frisking children and old men, blowing tunnels, sometimes setting fires and sometimes not, then forming up and moving on to the next village, then other villages, where it would always be the same. They carried their own lives. The pressures were enormous. In the heat of the early afternoon, they would remove their helmets and flak jackets, walking bare, which was dangerous but which helped ease the strain.[11]

In The Things They Carried, O'Brien conveys lyrically the same drumbeat of nothingness, the loss of soul, and the seeming senselessness and dehumanization of war:

They carried diseases, among them malaria and dysentery. They carried lice and ringworm and leeches and paddy algae and various rots and molds. They carried the land itself—Vietnam, the place, the soil—a powdery orange-red dust that covered their boots and fatigues and faces. They carried the sky. The whole atmosphere, they carried it, the humidity, the monsoons, the stink of fungus and decay, all of it. They carried gravity. They moved like mules. By daylight they took sniper fire, at night they were mortared, but it was not battle, it was just the endless march, village to village, without purpose, nothing won or lost. They marched for the sake of the march. They plodded along slowly, dumbly, leaning forward against the heat, unthinking, all blood and bone, simple grunts, soldiering with their legs, toiling up the hills and down into the paddies and across the rivers and up again and down, just humping, one step and then the next and then another, but no volition, no will, because it was automatic, it was anatomy, and the war was entirely a matter of posture and carriage, the hump was everything, a kind of inertia, a kind of emptiness, a dullness of desire and intellect and conscience and hope and human sensibility. Their principles were in their feet. Their calculations were biological. They had no sense of strategy or mission.

They searched the villages without knowing what to look for, not caring, kicking over jars of rice, frisking children and old men, blowing tunnels, sometimes setting fires and sometimes not, then forming up and moving on to the next village, then other villages, where it would always be the same. They carried their own lives. The pressures were enormous. In the heat of the early afternoon, they would remove their helmets and flak jackets, walking bare, which was dangerous but which helped ease the strain.[11]

O'Brien also captures America's emotional detachment from the world, as if marooned beyond Earth, and the rash, vindictive rage against the Vietnamese guerrillas when a comrade is senselessly killed. Lieutenant Jimmy Cross takes the burden upon himself for his comrade's death, merging his remorse with the hopelessness of his unrequited love of a girlfriend named Martha. Lieutenant Cross floats hopelessly beyond the real world, America, and the reality of hellish Vietnam.[12]

He plumbs the depths of despair in judging the reasons the soldiers find themselves in war—not for the noble reasons often cited but driven by shame to kill and perhaps be killed, the pinnacle of absurdity.[13] He captures this same absurdity in the plight of another young man who tries to escape the draft by fleeing to Canada, but the same capitulation to submit because of embarrassment traps him.[14]

Tim O'Brien also expresses anger, directed at American leaders who got us into this senseless war and the military leaders who had no effective means for managing the war: "There should be a law, I thought, if you support a war, if you think it's worth the price, that's fine, but you have to put your own precious fluids on the line . . . help spill the blood."[15]

Glorifying War

James Webb, in stark contrast to O'Brien, may have written the best traditional war book on Vietnam of any American, *Fields of Fire*. He portrays the lives of the grunts, their sense of absurdity, but also their humor and a certain nobility in their embrace of war.

> A simple yes [to an offer to Lieutenant Hodges to remain in Okinawa, not return to combat in Vietnam] and the war would be over.

> But so would everything else, and for the first time, he confronted that truth. Yes, Major, thank you, sir, and the rest of his life would be anticlimax. There was nothing on the other side. What does a man do when his war is over, wondered Hodges, except keep fighting it? All expectancies then lived, and if not fulfilled, well, at least confronted.

> The bald, red hills with their sandbag bunkers, the banter and frolic of dirt-covered grunts, the fearful intensity of contact. It was too deep inside him, and he had not yet done

enough to be free of it. He suddenly felt superior to the Major, a creature apart, capable of absorbing combat's horror without asking for quarter. Down South (in Vietnam) his men were on patrol, or digging new perimeters, or dying, and he was nothing if he did not share that misery.

He stared deep in the Major's face, enjoying the one moment of nobility that his months of terror had allowed. "Thanks, Major. But I didn't come halfway around the world to referee basketball games."[16]

War's fatal attraction has long been a staple in film and literature. Audie Murphy and John Wayne personified the noble warrior fighting for God and country. Jim Webb, American author and politician, shared a belief in the transcendent nobility of purpose in the commitment to defend one's country. Here is one enlisted man's revelatory explanation of such emotions.

He [Snake] watched the mountains, and the almost quaint repetitions of paddy and tree line that led to them, and acknowledged that he could do this forever. He sensed that, beyond the terror that was today, there was a fullness that no other thing in the remainder of his life would equal. That, beyond doubt, the rest of his life would be spent remembering those agonizing months, revering their fullness. That, yes, he was now twenty—well, almost twenty—and what would have always been the greatest, the most important experience of his life, had almost passed. If he were to go back now—when he did go back—there was nothing, not a thing that would parallel the sense of urgency and authority and—need. Of being a part of something. And of being needed and being *good.*

Extend? Hell yeah. I'll extend until this goddamn thing is over.

He sensed that it was all here, everything, and there was none of it there. All of life's compelling throbs, condensed and honed each time a bullet flew: the pain, the brother-love, the sacrifice. Nobility discovered by those who'd never even contemplated sacrifice, never felt an emotion worth their own blood on some else's altar. The heart-rending deaths. The successes. All here. None there, back in the bowels of the World. Except for the pain, and even that a numbed, daily pain, steady, like blue funk, not the sharp pain of an agonizing moment, capable of being purged, vindicated, replaced by a beautiful, lilting memory: Baby Cakes was a Number One dude, you know? He'da died for me. And I killed 'em back for him.[17]

15

The Aftermath of the Tet Offensive

Journalist Don Oberdorfer encapsulated exquisitely the experience of Tet: "It would be an exaggeration to maintain that the Tet Offensive alone turned a great nation around, deposed a President and brought sweeping changes in military policy. Tet was the final ingredient in a process involving many other elements—the fortunes of war, tides of public and political opinion, trends in the nature and technology of news gathering and transmission, personalities, errors, and accidents of history. It was also a psychological fact, providing the public and its leaders with a rationale for abandoning earlier positions and commitments and changing their minds about the war."[1]

The stunning attacks, occurring simultaneously across the country, proved the communist forces enjoyed far more popular support than previously thought and were a larger military threat than U.S. officials had claimed. The attacks suggested one of two lessons: The United States needed to introduce ever-larger forces to cope with the strong and growing threat, or the United States would not win the war at a price they were prepared to pay. Both conclusions were unacceptable to Johnson.

Local forces undertook the brunt of the attack, which also posed a dilemma. Tet presented a startling reality—the NLF and Vietcong forces were so strong that a nationwide offensive had been possible. To those willing to review the recent past, the Americans were perceived as the hapless heirs to French colonialism, now caught in a hopeless anti-colonialist struggle they could not win.

On the other hand, the heavy casualties among the Vietcong attackers meant huge numbers of their political and military cadres had been wiped out, leaving some to conclude this was the time to press harder and destroy remaining elements. Although thrown off-stride, the Americans had not been pushed into the sea, as advertised, and were already rapidly mopping up the Vietcong.

As noted, General Westmoreland and Nguyen Cao Ky concluded that the Vietcong and Northerners had suffered terrible defeats and the offensive was now with the American and South Vietnamese forces, who should press their new advantage.

U.S. bombings shifted from the North to the South, primarily the Mekong Delta, where U.S. aircraft bombed the towns under siege by the Vietcong, destroying the Vietcong but also wreaking destruction on towns and villages. Attendant alienation from the United States and GVN was obvious. ARVN troops added to the misery by plundering the towns and villages as the Vietcong retreated.

The American press in Vietnam accepted the U.S. military judgment that Hanoi and the NLF had suffered a serious military defeat, especially the NLF, but the media did not accept Tet as a great victory for the United States as Westmoreland claimed.

Reaction in the United States

The breadth of the attacks stunned the State Department, even those who worked on Vietnam. Before the offensive, we had not been sanguine about Westmoreland's optimistic assessments of the conflict, and we put little stock in his description of Tet as a victory for Americans and South Vietnamese, but we were shocked at the capabilities demonstrated by the attacks. Although I did not accept Westmoreland's rosy assessments, the extent of Vietcong capability throughout the South surprised me. Those of us who had been assigned to the provinces were more realistic about the strength of the Vietcong than officials who had spent most of their time in Saigon. We knew families contained sons in the ARVN and others in the Vietcong, thus splitting their loyalties. But we thought most of the peasants would prefer to live alone in their traditional villages and not be bothered by the political conflict that surrounded them.

The political world was agog and the government thrown into

disarray. The American people could not fathom how this could have happened after the repeated assurances that there was "light at the end of the tunnel" and the Vietcong were suffering terrible defeats.

Oberdorfer reported that Dean Acheson summarized the views of the "wise men" convened to advise the president on the war just prior to the president's crucial speech to the nation on March 31, 1968. Acheson concluded that "the predominant view was that American objectives could not be achieved with the time and resources available, and therefore the policies would have to be changed." Acheson, who as a senior advisor to Presidents Kennedy and Johnson had strongly supported escalation and bombing of the North, now told the president that "the bombing was more damaging to support for the war at home than it was militarily beneficial abroad and should be stopped immediately," Oberdorfer wrote.[2]

Henry Kissinger, who was just months away from being plucked from academia into the new Nixon administration, recalled in his book *Diplomacy:* "Tet was recognized as a major communist defeat. Superior American firepower wiped out almost the entire guerrilla infrastructure. Nevertheless, the Tet Offensive turned into a major psychological victory for Hanoi. American leaders, including leading 'hawks' Dean Acheson, John McCloy, McGeorge Bundy, and Douglas Dillion, advised that escalation be ended and the liquidation of the war begun. American leaders had had enough."[3]

Many drew the conclusion that these attacks, which penetrated all the way into the embassy grounds, could not have taken place without the cooperation of the South Vietnamese people. This forced a reevaluation of the American assumption that they were supporting a regional democracy against foreign communist aggression.

The crushing of the Tet Offensive deepened the crisis in American public consciousness. Particularly, the *AP* photo of the shooting in the head of a young unarmed, bound Vietcong on a Saigon street by the National Police Chief General Nguyen Ngoc Loan shocked America. What were we fighting for? Are these our allies?

Dean Rusk, viewing the photo on television, angrily asked "which side the *AP* photographer was on"—a remark that put the U.S. government morally in the same bottomless pit as General

Loan.[4] Walter Cronkite, probably the most respected man in America as a nonpartisan observer, in an unusual personal statement on February 27, 1968, said, "To say that we are closer to victory today is to believe, in the face of evidence, the optimists who have been wrong in the past." In his February 27, 1968, report after a visit to Vietnam, Cronkite wrote, "It is increasingly clear to this reporter that the only rational way out then will be to negotiate, not as victors but as honorable people who lived up to their pledge to defend democracy, and did the best they could."[5] If Cronkite was the steady barometer of American moderates, he had just tripped an important marker. President Johnson, according to Oberdorfer, commented, "Cronkite was it"—there was no stopping the tide against the war.

Gallup polls reflected the change. In November 1967, when Westmoreland had made his optimistic remarks, 50 percent of Americans thought the United States was "making progress." After Tet the number dropped to 26 percent.

Congressional Reaction

On March 10, 1968, the *New York Times* reported Westmoreland had proposed to Johnson an increase of 206,000 troops. The report was incendiary in the Washington climate.[6] Such an increase would acknowledge that the Tet Offensive had been a major communist victory. To President Johnson, it would also necessitate calling up the Reserves. General Westmoreland insisted that the results of Tet had been a major military defeat for the communists, so why would the military require 206,000 more troops?[7]

Johnson believed military and embassy claims that the communists had been "defanged," but the attack on the embassy belied these assertions, and Johnson finally accepted them. He ordered Westmoreland to provide daily briefings to reassure the public the situation was under control.

There were calls from the Pentagon to step up bombing of the North. President Thieu hoped for such measures amid fears in the administration and the U.S. embassy in Saigon of a serious morale breakdown in the Saigon government. Congress and the Johnson administration were aghast and sought alternatives. Influential figures were in an uproar.

In an open Senate Foreign Relations Committee hearing called by Senator William Fulbright on March 11, senators pressed Rusk hard on the *New York Times* report.. Rusk avoided a direct response regarding military or diplomatic considerations, but Fulbright issued a stern warning: Congress had to clear any escalation of the war *first.*[8] Even conservative Senator John Stennis (Democrat of Mississippi) said he was "absolutely opposed" to sending more troops.[9]

Public support for the war had been dwindling for over a year due to mounting casualties, rising taxes, and a suspicion that there was no end in sight. After a brief rallying round the flag, support continued to slip.

By 1967 a plurality thought the United States had made a mistake in committing U.S. combat troops to Vietnam. But this perception camouflaged two different reactions to the reason for the mistake: on the one hand was opposition to the war itself, while others criticized Johnson for not pursuing the war vigorously enough.

In November 1967, 44 percent favored withdrawal, but 55 percent favored a tougher policy. Johnson's popularity started at 80 percent but fell to 40 percent by 1967 because of his economic and social policies, as well as the war. After Tet, support for him fell to 26 percent of Americans. As Karnow saw it, Johnson's credibility was gone.[10]

More important, Karnow concluded, was that influential voices had forsaken the president—media commentators, business executives, educators, clergymen, and elites. The administration no longer controlled the media narrative crucial to any war effort.

The voices decided after Tet not only that the effort was futile, but it was also causing national anguish, diminished external support, and loss of faith in the United States.

Frustrated by the deteriorating situation in Vietnam and slackening public support for the war effort, Rusk took an intemperate swipe at the media. He thundered at a press briefing: "Whose side are you on? Now, I'm Secretary of State of the United States, and I'm on our side. None of your papers or broadcasting apparatuses is worth a damn unless the United States succeeds. They are trivial compared to that question. So, I don't know why people have to be probing for the things that one can bitch about, when there are two-thousand stories on the same day about things that are more constructive."[11]

The Ethical Dimension

Karnow reports comments by Johnson speechwriter Harry McPherson that caught the ethical dimensions of the war. McPherson said, "I watched the invasion of the American embassy compound and the terrible sight of General Loan killing the Vietcong captive. You got the sense of the awfulness, the endlessness of the war—and, though it sounds naïve, the unethical quality of the war in which a prisoner is shot at point-blank range. I was fed up with the optimism that seemed to flow without stopping from Saigon."[12]

Meanwhile, the military leadership was slow to grasp the new reality of public opinion. The JCS's chairman, Earle Wheeler, cabled Westmoreland that Johnson was "not prepared to accept defeat" and "if you need more troops, ask for them." Westmoreland, though privately profoundly shaken, dutifully asked for 206,000 more troops. He believed "only additional troops would allow for the U.S. to take advantage of the new ball game."[13] This could only be accomplished by mobilizing the reserves, a step Johnson was loath to take, in part because he had so often refused to take the step before.

Westmoreland fashioned a new analysis: The United States had been preparing for a prolonged struggle, but now it was obvious that the communists had changed their strategy and were seeking a quick victory."[14]

Back in Washington, JCS Chief Wheeler discounted Westmoreland's optimism and described Tet as a "near thing, risking collapse" of the U.S. position.

Carver, Dupuy, and Habib's Assessment

Following General Wheeler's return from Vietnam with his own pessimistic assessment, State's Philip Habib, CIA's George Carver, and General Dupuy from the Pentagon briefed President Johnson.[15]

Despite the pessimistic views he heard, including that the situation in Vietnam could not be brought to a satisfactory status before public support had evaporated, Johnson was so impressed with the briefing that he had it presented to the "wise men's group" with whom he regularly consulted on the war.

Clark Clifford, a wealthy patrician lawyer who had been a regular advisor to several presidents, including President Johnson, replaced McNamara as secretary of defense on March 1, 1968. Clifford had firmly supported Johnson's war policies but began to have doubts in late 1967.

After Tet, the advice of Pentagon figures such as Paul Warnke and the briefing by the Habib-Carver-Dupuy group completed Clifford's evolution and brought him to the point of opposing continuing the war.

Financial realities also diminished Washington's appetite for escalation. Treasury Secretary Henry Fowler outlined the financial measures necessary for continued escalation of the war and warned of severe economic and financial difficulties in simultaneously pursuing the war in Indochina and the goals of the Great Society. Raising taxes represented an acknowledgement of policy failure and risked undermining the dollar as the world's reserve currency.

Pentagon Review

In the wake of Tet, Robert McNamara resigned and Johnson ordered the new defense secretary, Clark Clifford, to complete a total review, by March 1, 1968, of Vietnam policy and its implications for the United States and Vietnam.

The draft, assembled and inspired by Paul Warnke, described a grim scene: The communists could match any number of U.S. troops fielded and the escalation advocated by Westmoreland and Wheeler promised "no early end of the conflict."[16]

The strategy would entail substantial costs in Vietnam and especially in the United States, leading to the subordination of economic
and social expenditures to military outlays. Without reducing either military or social expenditure, the United States, in Warnke's
report, "would run great risks of provoking a domestic crisis of un-
precedented proportions." Moreover, the report concluded, a large
influx of additional military forces into Vietnam would encourage
the Saigon regime to believe "that the U.S. will continue to fight its
war while it engages in backroom politics and permits widespread
corruption." Warnke advocated pulling back U.S. forces to defend
populated areas on the coasts and training and equipping the Vietnamese army as a more effective force. Warnke's assessment appalled many in the military. Westmoreland was at the time advocating more vigorous actions, including U.S. incursions into Laos.
Admiral Robert Sharpe urged more intensive bombing of North
Vietnam. "Toughness [is] the only policy that Communists understand," Sharpe reportedly asserted.[17]

That his military advisors could not answer critical questions,
such as how long the war would last, dismayed Clifford. How
many troops would be necessary? Would 200,000 more troops be
sufficient? What was the plan to win the war? The military brass
could offer few answers apart from their intentions to "wear out
the Communists through attrition." And no one, not even the most
fervent supporters of the war, had any idea when the enemy might
be "worn down."

"By early March, Clifford was convinced 'all we are doing is
wasting our treasure and lives of our men out there in the jungles.'
Clifford sent his recommendations to the president on March 4."
They were not as alarmist as Warnke's had been but urged him not
to focus only on the troop numbers, but to focus on the wider picture. Clifford's thoughts set the agenda for the spring.[18]

Just as the Clifford report was released, Westmoreland's request for 206,000 additional troops surfaced publicly, setting the
scene for a major policy debate. Johnson's reaction was cautious; he
was more inclined to listen to the military commanders in the field
than to Pentagon civilians.

Rusk approached the president with an alternative to escalation: Curtail the bombing and undertake a major peace initiative.

If it did not work, then Johnson could reconsider the troop-level question.

Clifford and Warnke argued against Rusk's initiative because they doubted Hanoi would accept the terms and, in that case, the Pentagon would argue for escalation.

Several prominent senators, led by Senate Majority Leader Mike Mansfield, argued forcefully against escalation. On March 6, Johnson met with Senators Mansfield, Fulbright, Sparkman, Aiken, and Hickenlooper for a conversation centered on Westmoreland's request for additional troops. Mansfield declared, characteristically, "It is my intention to uphold the hand of the president as much as I can do in this particular matter, and at the same time stick to my own convictions."

Mansfield handed Johnson a memo—his 19th—urging him to resist calls for an increase of troops. He continued: "That does not mean that we have to get out of Vietnam. It does mean that we should concentrate and consolidate the already great commitment we have there. It means the adoption of a patient strategy—less destructive of the country and less voracious in the consumption of our resources for purposes of negotiating a decent settlement of the conflict."

Mansfield alone credited Johnson's motives and efforts to find a negotiated solution as being in good faith. Mansfield felt Johnson "has not gone as far as I would like; but he has done his best in a difficult situation." Nonetheless, "we are in the wrong place, and we are fighting the wrong kind of war."[19]

The New Hampshire Primary

On March 12, Johnson suffered humiliation when he barely out-polled the antiwar Senator Eugene McCarthy in the New Hampshire primary, with McCarthy receiving only 300 fewer votes than the powerful president.

Four days later, Bobby Kennedy threw his hat into the presidential ring. The Tet Offensive, according to his brother Ted Kennedy, removed Robert's last reservations. In a speech about his book, *To Seek a Newer World*, brother Ted said, "Robert Kennedy excoriated all of the war's facets, from muddled U.S. policies to the corruption of the South Vietnamese regime."[20]

The "wise men"—Dean Acheson, Arthur Goldberg, George Ball, McGeorge Bundy, Henry Cabot Lodge, Abe Fortas, Maxwell Taylor, General Omar Bradley, diplomat Robert Murphy, and, of course Dean Rusk, Clark Clifford, Walt Rostow, and JCS Earle Wheeler—met for dinner and a briefing at the State Department on March 25. Outspoken Philip Habib, a deputy assistant secretary of state, described the corruption and ineptitude that riddled the South Vietnamese government and army and said that it "might take five to ten years to achieve any real progress." The group was stupefied. Acheson, the most prestigious person there, "bluntly set the tone: 'The administration had to find a way out of the war.' "[21]

Johnson met for lunch with the "wise men" the next day. All favored disengagement except Bradley, Murphy, Fortas, and Taylor. Acheson summed up the discussion, declaring "You know damned well this what we are trying to do—to force the enemy to sue for peace. It won't happen—at least not in the time frame the American people will permit. . . . [A]s long as we continue to bomb, to alienate ourselves from the civilized world."[22]

Henry Cabot Lodge recommended ending "search–and-destroy operations and use of American troops to shield the South Vietnamese society to develop as well as the North Vietnamese society had been able to do"—an interesting proposal from the ambassador who had sanctioned the buildup in the first place.

Johnson was furious. He called in two of the three government briefers to brief him (Habib had left town). In his memoirs, Johnson wrote that the "wise men" had swayed him. He felt America had collapsed on the home front rather than on the battlefield. Swayed by the reaction of the "wise men," but also by the aroused voice of the American people, Johnson made his decision.

President Johnson invited Majority Leader Mansfield to the White House on March 27, 1968, to discuss Vietnam, including the president's anticipated speech slated for March 31. Mansfield told Gregory Allen Olsen for his book *Mansfield and Vietnam:* "I went down to the White House, very reluctantly, after mutual friends repeatedly urged me to go to see the president and talk with him about Vietnam. I didn't think it would do any good." The president offered the existing draft for his March 31 speech and invited comment.

After reading it, Mansfield recalled: "I told him that it would be a mistake to make the speech because it offered no hope to the people and it only indicated a further involvement. He did mention the possibility of ending the bombing north of the twentieth parallel. He asked my opinion about sending forty thousand more troops. I said, 'No, we've got to get out, should not have been there in the first place.' I urged him as strongly as I knew how to bring this tragic war to end because it was an area which was not and never had been vital to our security. I spent three and a half hours there that night with Johnson; and as I finally got to the door, he said, 'Mike, I wish my leader would support me.' Well, I was not his leader, I was the Senate's leader. 'But,' he said, 'I want you to know I appreciate your honesty in telling me how you feel about it.'"[23]

President Johnson Withdraws from the Presidential Race

On March 31, the president opened his televised speech with these words: "My fellow citizens: Tonight, I want to speak to you on the prospects for peace in Vietnam and Southeast Asia."

His final words startled the world. Johnson announced, "I have concluded that I should not permit the presidency to become involved in the partisan divisions that are developing in this political year. I shall not seek, and I will not accept, the nomination for another term as your president."[24]

Johnson also ordered the cessation of bombing over 90 percent of North Vietnam, continuing only in the area just north of the DMZ.

Five days later, North Vietnam agreed to send officials to begin peace talks.

Averell Harriman represented the United States, and Xuan Thuy, a second-ranked communist veteran, represented North Vietnam. The conference opened in Paris on May 1, 1968, with high expectations on both sides. Impasse developed within a few weeks as each side repeated demands. The United States insisted on the withdrawal of the North Vietnamese forces inside South Vietnam;

North Vietnam rejected the demand and insisted on shuffling the Saigon regime to include Vietcong representatives.

The talks would drag on for five years, during which time more Americans would be killed in Vietnam than had died there previously. By the end of March 1968, more than 24,000 Americans had been killed in the Vietnam theater since 1955; a total of 58,220 would die in the Vietnam War by 1973. Political turmoil in the United States was as fierce as it had been in a century.

On the last day of March, Martin Luther King preached in the National Cathedral in Washington, predicting that failure to bring hope to the "ghetto" would further exacerbate racial tensions in the coming summer. Joining the plight of the poor with the Vietnam War, King said:

> I want to say one other challenge that we face is simply that we must find an alternative to war and bloodshed. Anyone who feels, and there are still a lot of people who feel that way, that war can solve the social problems facing mankind is sleeping through a great revolution. President Kennedy said on one occasion, "Mankind must put an end to war or war will put an end to mankind." The world must hear this. I pray God that America will hear this before it is too late, because today we're fighting a war.
>
> I am convinced that it is one of the most unjust wars that have ever been fought in the history of the world. Our involvement in the war in Vietnam has torn up the Geneva Accords. It has strengthened the military-industrial complex; it has strengthened the forces of reaction in our nation. It has put us against the self-determination of a vast majority of the Vietnamese people, and put us in the position of protecting a corrupt regime that is stacked against the poor.[25]

King was assassinated at a Memphis hotel four days later and protests exploded throughout the nation, fusing the war, race relations, and lack of opportunity in the United States.

Robert Kennedy was assassinated two months later at a Los Angeles hotel, bringing despair to many Americans who saw the nation and its hopes as out of their control. During my tenth re-union at Princeton University I watched the train carrying Robert Kennedy's body move through Princeton Junction and wept—feeling a sense of hopelessness only similar to what I had felt when President Kennedy was assassinated.

Post-Johnson: The Presidential Race

Vice President Hubert Humphrey was nominated to be the Democratic candidate for president in a tumultuous convention in Chicago. Riots broke out as police clumsily attempted to bring order to chaos surrounding the convention. Wrath against the war and the murders of Martin Luther King and Robert Kennedy exploded at the convention.

Despite his personal views, Vice President Humphrey held closely to the Johnson administration's line on Vietnam. Without a strong stance to electrify voters, his campaign was faltering, to the horror of many Democrats who had a deep distaste for Richard Nixon.

Concerned Democrats urged dramatic action to salvage Humphrey's candidacy. Johnson reluctantly agreed to a complete cessation of bombing of the North, implicitly linked to a halt of rocket attacks on Southern cities, respect for the DMZ, and, in addition, participation of the Saigon regime and the NLF in the peace talks. With this hope of peace, Humphrey's poll deficit shrunk from 8 percent to 2 percent, seemingly because Nixon's "secret plan" for peace was not convincing.[26]

Working through Henry Kissinger, Nixon's campaign publicly supported the peace moves. Privately, however, according to information obtained from intelligence telephone taps between the Vietnamese embassy in Washington and Saigon and through Anna Chennault, General Claire Chennault's widow, Nixon urged South Vietnam's President Thieu to feign support for the moves but actually to abort or cripple a deal to resume negotiations with Hanoi. In a speech to the National Assembly in Saigon on November 1, Thieu stated he would never sit down with the Vietcong. The talks and the peace initiative collapsed. The purported Nixon perfidy outraged William Bundy.[27]

Despite pleas by Rusk and Harriman for Johnson to persevere, the president chose instead to press for the end of direct and indirect aggression by North Vietnam against the South. A separate South Vietnamese state remained Johnson's goal. The talks remained stalemated.

16

Mr. Nixon's War

Richard Nixon worked his way to the top as a fervent anticommunist, secretive and deceitful, aloof, withdrawn from the public, and with few friends. Yet he was also a brilliant if sometimes erratic strategist brought down for subverting his office by commissioning a series of felonies he refused to acknowledge.[1]

Vietnam was the center of his presidential agenda. His promise of a "secret plan" to end the war was a chimera, and his handling of the war contributed to his downfall with Watergate.

In the spring of 1968, while he was working for presidential candidate Governor Nelson Rockefeller, Henry Kissinger telephoned me one night at my basement apartment near Dupont Circle in Washington to ask for my thoughts on Vietnam. I followed the line of the assessment we FSOs had presented to Eugene Rostow the previous year: The United States had Americanized and militarized the conflict, radicalizing Vietnamese society by its overwhelming presence, policies, and strategy.[2]

I said we should turn the war back over to the Vietnamese and provide support. I suggested several ways to achieve this and offered to send him a paper reflecting my views, which I did. I never knew whether he was looking for ideas or people for a potential staff, but Kissinger never called me back or offered me a job. The idea of Vietnamization, embedded in my comments, may have found its way into Kissinger's playbook as he advised President Nixon.

In the year Nixon assumed the presidency, Congress passed a law that prohibited funds for the introduction of American ground troops into Thailand or Laos but left Nixon in control of activities in Vietnam, Laos, and Cambodia. Nixon took advantage of these loopholes to bomb and invade Cambodia and bomb Laos.[3]

Nixon's Approach to War: The Madman Theory

Nixon told delegates at the Republican National Convention that the best way to win a war was to expand it. Eisenhower had ended the Korean War by threatening the Chinese and North Koreans that he would not stand for a war of attrition, suggesting he would expand the combat zone. Within a matter of months, the Chinese and North Koreans negotiated.[4]

"It's all a poker game," Nixon was reported to have said.[5] Since Nixon had observed Johnson's seemingly futile escalations, he explicitly did not expect military victory in Vietnam, but he was known to say that he, like Lyndon Johnson, was not going to be the "first American president to lose a war."

Voicing his strategy, Nixon said to his chief of staff, Bob Haldeman, "I call it the madman theory, Bob. I want the North Vietnamese to believe I've reached the point where I might do anything to stop the war. We'll slip the word in to them: 'For God's sake, you know Nixon is obsessed about Communists. We can't restrain him when he's angry—and he has his hand on the nuclear button—Ho Chi Minh himself will be in Paris in two days begging for peace.' "[6]

In March 1969 Nixon decided to send a message to the NLF and PAVN that they had no sanctuary by agreeing to the military's request to conduct B-52 raids on Vietnamese base camps in Cambodia, a complex of tunnels and underground camps misleadingly compared to the Pentagon. While some of the base camps were destroyed, some remnants fought fiercely while most simply moved further into Cambodia or deeper into their bunkers. To avoid an outcry, Nixon kept the raids on this neutral country secret from Congress and American people.[7]

Neither Ho Chi Minh nor his successors got Nixon's message. Ho Chi Minh himself, after a prolonged illness, died at the age of 79; officials announced his death on September 3, 1969. Doctrinaire Marxist-Leninist Le Duan, who had already been in charge as Ho Chi Minh's health declined, replaced Ho.

President Ho Chi Minh had written with conviction a last will and testament the previous May asserting his confidence in "total victory," although he doubted he would live to see it. "Our compatriots in the North and the South shall be reunited under the same roof. We, a small nation, will have earned the unique honor of defeating, through a heroic struggle, two big imperialisms—France and America—and making a great contribution to the national liberation movement." He asked for "no grand funerals" upon his death and "no waste of people's time and money." He ended by writing, "To the whole people, the whole Party, to my nephews and nieces, the youth and children, I leave my boundless love."[8]

Omitted from the published version was his insistence on cremation, with his ashes buried on mountains in the three regions of Vietnam without tombstone or statue. Leaders ignored his wishes and erected the huge Mausoleum at Ba Dinh Square in his honor, where his body, embalmed by the Russians, still lies, like the frozen Lenin in Moscow and Mao in Beijing.

A Soviet and Chinese Angle?

Nixon also toyed with the notion of trying to engage the Soviet Union and even the Chinese to press North Vietnam to acquiesce in a reasonable ending of the war.

On the night Johnson resigned, Nixon had intended to deliver a speech in which he opened the door to Soviet diplomats. He would argue, "If the Soviets were disposed to see the war ended and a compromise settlement negotiated, they have the means to move Ho Chi Minh to the conference table."[9]

Nixon reasoned that the Soviets' massive aid program to Vietnam, a country well outside the USSR's immediate orbit, was costly. Moreover, their support for North Vietnam endangered détente with the United States, in which General Secretary Leonid Brezhnev placed great stock. Access to U.S. technology and arms-control goals weighed importantly in Brezhnev's eyes, but he could not count on U.S. assistance unless he recognized the "linkage" to reduce tensions in Berlin, the Middle East, and Vietnam.[10]

According to Henry Kissinger's special assistant, Winston

Lord, "Kissinger and Nixon believed that Russia and China could be helpful in at least isolating North Vietnam psychologically, if not in terms of military aid. They felt that improving U.S. relations with Russia and China might help pressure Hanoi to negotiate. Also, Russia and China might have a greater stake in improving their bilateral relations with the United States, rather than standing by their so-called friends and allies in Hanoi. But Nixon always put more emphasis and hopes in Russia's help than Kissinger did. He was more inclined to tie other elements of our dealings with Moscow to Vietnam than was Kissinger."[11]

Any effort on behalf of the United States, however, would risk Vietnamese condemnation of a sellout and cost the Soviet Union, which competed with the Chinese in supporting the world struggle against global imperialism. This, of course, was not a concern of the United States.

Regarding the Chinese, despite being a strong supporter of Chiang Kai-shek, Nixon had contemplated eventual rapprochement with China. He had written in the October 1967 edition of *Foreign Affairs* that the West could no longer leave China "forever outside the family of nations." In 1970, Nixon, as the reports of Sino-Soviet tensions emerged, wondered if China might not need a counterweight against the Soviets and therefore be interested in rapprochement with Washington. In this context, he thought China might be willing to nudge the Vietnamese toward a settlement.[12]

Kissinger and Vietnam

The perfect instrument for Nixon's strategic goals was Henry Kissinger, the Harvard professor—brilliant, witty, abrasive, duplicitous, Machiavellian, and well connected in American and international political and academic circles. Nixon named Kissinger his national security advisor.[13]

Disdainful of the State Department and profoundly interested in foreign policy, Nixon intended to direct foreign policy from the White House. Kissinger avidly agreed and worked assiduously to exclude State, the Pentagon, and the CIA from sensitive foreign-policy issues. Throughout the Nixon administration Kissinger operated as a plenipotentiary of American diplomacy.

In an article on Vietnam in *Foreign Affairs* that appeared in January 1969, just as he and Nixon took office, Kissinger argued that Westmoreland's strategy of attrition was futile. The communists could easily sustain larger forces than the Americans and would therefore "win" as long as they did not "lose." He also dismissed the military losses to the communists at Tet. In Kissinger's opinion, the impact of Tet lay principally in the limits it placed on American flexibility because public opinion made inevitable the necessity of a diplomatic solution. The question was how to reach a settlement.[14]

Kissinger shared President Johnson's view that military and political issues should be handled separately. America and North Vietnam would deal with military issues and the Vietnamese themselves would resolve the political issues. Because of the complexity of political issues, he argued that America's decisions must consider our allies' views and goals, but allies should not be allowed a veto. He was also aware that North Vietnam might be intransigent on certain issues, and Kissinger therefore insisted on maintaining an American presence in South Vietnam to retain leverage vis-à-vis North Vietnam.[15]

Nixon and Kissinger wanted an "honorable" end to the war for the sake of America's global prestige and did not oppose serious military pressure on Hanoi. However, there were differences, at least of nuance, in certain areas. Kissinger thought there might be limits on the amount of pressure the United States could bring to bear on Moscow because it could endanger broader diplomatic goals, e.g., arms control and détente.

On the ultimate settlement, Nixon worried about the history of "who lost China," and did not want the public accusing him of "losing Vietnam"; Kissinger wanted to achieve a "decent interval" and a reasonable chance for the South Vietnam regime to survive. Kissinger never publicly explained the phrase "decent interval," but Ken Hughes, on C-SPAN, in a symposium July 22–23, 2011, at the University of Virginia, made the following statement: "We want a decent interval." Kissinger scribbled in the margins of his thick briefing book, as historian Jeffrey Kimball later discovered, "You have our assurance."[16]

"It's a strange phrase, nearly forgotten, but 'decent interval' meant something in the latter days of Vietnam," Kimball writes, "when our leaders groped for a way to get out of the war without admitting they couldn't find a way to win it." As Daniel Ellsberg wrote a few months before Kissinger's secret trip to China, "During 1968, Henry Kissinger frequently said in private talks that the appropriate goal of U.S. policy was 'a decent interval'—two to three years—between the withdrawal of U.S. troops and a Communist takeover in Vietnam."

"This interval, it was argued at the time, would protect the nation's credibility from the humiliation of defeat," Karnow later explained. "But a transcript prepared by Kissinger's own aides of his first meeting with Chinese Premier Zhou Enlai reveals how willing Nixon was to sacrifice America's credibility abroad to preserve his political credibility at home." As Kissinger explained it, "the president would agree to complete withdrawal of American troops in return for Hanoi's release of American prisoners of war and a ceasefire ('say eighteen months or some period') under international supervision, as long as the political settlement was left to the Vietnamese people to decide."[17]

Kissinger undertook a massive survey of opinions within the government as to the prospects for South Vietnam. The responses varied from comparative optimism from the Pentagon to pessimism from most civilians, and the estimates of time it would take to achieve a semblance of peace varied from eight to thirteen years. In Kissinger's judgment, this lack of consensus permitted the White House to choose its own course. [18]

Target Cambodia

Lacking clear military options within the borders of Vietnam, Kissinger and Nixon eyed Cambodia.

Prince Sihanouk barely managed independence from France in 1954, after which he leaned on the United States. When the United States shifted its weight toward Vietnam and Thailand, Cambodia's historical enemies, Sihanouk began looking toward China. Expecting Vietnam to win its war with the United States, he negotiated use of Cambodia's eastern flank with Vietnam in exchange for Hanoi's promise not to support the Khmer Rouge.[19]

Sihanouk's strategy faltered in late 1967 when China retreated into isolation as Mao's Cultural Revolution intensified and North Vietnamese and NLF forces, preparing for the Tet Offensive, built up their presence in Cambodia. Sihanouk lost leverage over his Vietnamese neighbors and some degree of control over the east of his country.

Thus, Sihanouk shifted yet again. He invited First Lady Jacqueline Kennedy for a high-profile visit to Angkor Wat. He revealed to the *Washington Post* in late December 1967 "a formula to discourage the Vietnamese communists, tether more grandiose plots by Westmoreland, and minimize encroachments on Cambodian territory. Sihanouk stated he would grant the United States the 'right of hot pursuit' against the North Vietnamese and Vietcong in Cambodia" so long as they did not harm Cambodians.[20]

He also had suggested President Johnson send a special envoy to Cambodia to discuss the situation, mentioning specifically Senator Mike Mansfield, as "a just and courageous man whom we consider a friend."[21]

President Johnson instead sent Chester Bowles, U.S. ambassador to India, to whom Sihanouk repeated the same message he had to the *Washington Post*. Johnson, however, was reluctant to expand the war and did not take a follow-up. However, covert teams of U.S. Special Forces and local mercenaries continued to cross the border for intelligence-gathering.[22]

Within a week of Nixon's inauguration, chairman of the JCS Earle Wheeler, with the backing of the vice chief of staff of the Army, General Creighton Abrams, who would replace Westmoreland, appealed again for U.S. military action against the Vietnamese communists in Cambodia. Abrams calculated that the communists had moved 40,000 troops into Cambodia as backup for the Tet Offensive.[23]

Abrams recommended a quick raid by B-52s to destroy COSVN in its Cambodian sanctuaries, falsely contending that there were no Cambodians living in the area.

Nixon hesitated, but in late February ordered the bombing of Cambodia. Kissinger, Secretary of State William Rogers, and Secretary of Defense Melvin Laird were all concerned that this impulsive action could harm ongoing U.S.–Vietnam peace feelers and arouse harsh criticism from Congress, the media, and the public. Nixon insisted the only way to get the communists to negotiate was to take actions to get their attention and ordered the bombing in March 1970.[24]

The "quick duration" bombings in fact lasted fourteen months and emulated Eisenhower's "threat" regarding Korea. Nixon would have preferred resumption of strategic bombing of North Vietnam but feared it would disrupt ongoing peace talks, which were in fact not making progress in Paris. Over a fourteen-month period, the United States conducted 3,630 B-52 raids in Cambodia, releasing 110,000 tons of bombs. The bombings devastated much of eastern Cambodia.

The United States conducted the operation in total secrecy, calculated to avoid protests from Sihanouk of bombing a neutral country that the United States professed to recognize, which could cause an international uproar.

Sihanouk kept silent because he welcomed the threat to Vietnamese positions and did not wish to give a public pretext to the Vietnamese to attack him openly. Later Sihanouk even supplied intelligence on Vietnamese locations to the United States. The Vietnamese kept quiet, since complaint would acknowledge their presence in neutral Cambodia.[25]

Secrecy averted the renewed outburst of public protest of war during Nixon's honeymoon period. The administration informed only a few sympathetic members of Congress, the military, and government at-large.[26]

In May, however, *New York Times* reporter William Beecher broke the news of the bombing campaign. It aroused no public outcry, but Nixon and Kissinger were furious and initiated wiretaps on administration officials to determine who had leaked the news—with the aim "to destroy them." Thus began the initial string of Watergate offenses that eventually led to Nixon's downfall.[27]

When officially acknowledged in 1973, the clandestine bombing campaign prompted a clamor for Nixon's impeachment. In Senate testimony, several distinguished lawyers, including Johnson's attorney general, Nicholas Katzenbach, agreed that Nixon had exceeded his constitutional prerogatives and supported legislation to curb the president's ability to wage war. This resulted in passage of the War Powers Act.

Meanwhile, the Cambodian bombings, like all military escalation before it, did little to deter the North Vietnamese.

Playing the Soviet Angle

Even while escalating the war in Cambodia, Kissinger put out diplomatic feelers. In March 1969, he dispatched former deputy defense secretary Cyrus Vance to Moscow to open preliminary discussions with the Soviets on control of strategic weapons, making the "linkages" clear—Soviet help in ending the Vietnam War would facilitate arms-control agreements.[28]

Vance also arranged, through Soviet auspices, a meeting with an influential North Vietnamese to stress Nixon's eagerness for a settlement in Vietnam.

In organizing Vance's mission, Kissinger warned longtime Soviet ambassador to Washington Anatoly Dobrynin that the United States would intensify the war if they could not create a Vietnam settlement, thus driving home Nixon's "linkages."

At that stage, the Soviets refused to accept the Vietnam "linkage," fearful that pressure from Moscow would lead the Vietnamese to tilt toward China, with whom the USSR was by now locked in intense rivalry.

Ambassador Winston Lord assessed the pressures on Vietnam as perhaps stronger than they appeared, even though Russian and Chinese leaders had a stake in the development of our bilateral relationship. Nixon thought the Russians and Chinese would lean on Hanoi to make a reasonable deal with the United States, as they could move ahead with their bilateral ties with the United States, and this would cause unease in Hanoi.[29]

Vietnamization

While attempting to play the communist powers against one another, Nixon and Kissinger's Vietnam strategy settled on an approach called "Vietnamization." This process would allow the United States to pull its combat troops out of Vietnam by transferring responsibility for the war to the South Vietnamese. In tandem, the United States would negotiate secretly with North Vietnam, circumventing the South Vietnamese, who were extremely fearful that any agreement would undermine their position in the South.[30] As this process developed, Nixon also hoped to gain the quick release of the roughly 400 U.S. POWs held by Hanoi to assuage opinion in America.

Nixon's underlying aim was to get the United States out of Vietnam without obvious defeat on his watch. This two-pronged approach seems inherently contradictory, as U.S. troop withdrawals would inevitably cost Washington its leverage. Bombing and invasion of Cambodia were also elements of this strategy aimed at reducing pressure on the South Vietnamese as the United States withdrew. Why would Hanoi be conciliatory if the United States was leaving anyway? The North Vietnamese could wait indefinitely, and time was on their side. South Vietnam nearly collapsed in 1964 until Johnson sent in U.S. combat forces. It seemed foreordained this would happen again.

Ambassador Lord recalled: "The basic strategy that was devised during the early months of the first Nixon term in 1969 involved two threads. One key element was the Vietnamization of the war. That meant turning over to the South Vietnamese the major responsibility for their own defense. It was a Nixon/Kissinger strategy, but it had the strong support of Secretary of Defense Laird, Secretary of State Rogers, and others. For several reasons, they concluded that we should begin Vietnamization or de-Americanization of the war, but at a pace that was bearable. We had spent a lot of time and effort, as well as American blood and treasure, in helping the South Vietnamese.[31]

Ambassador Lord further remembered:

First, Nixon and Kissinger felt that it was time for the South Vietnamese to assume more of the burden in terms of justice and American domestic support. Secondly, they felt that, if this process were accomplished gradually, it was doable. We would strengthen the South Vietnamese through the provision of training and military aid. Gradually, American troop withdrawals, military assistance, and training would make it possible for the South Vietnamese to assume more of the burden. Third, this process would show the American people that there would be an end, at some point, to our involvement and that we were at least heading in the direction of ending our involvement in an honorable way.

The other track was simultaneously to try to negotiate an end to the conflict and by applying military pressure, if necessary, to show Hanoi that they couldn't win and that negotiations were in their interests. We sought to couple that effort, as we went on, with Russian and Chinese help. We also believed that by making progress on the negotiations, Hanoi would see that it was in their interest to bring the war to an end. This was a version of the carrot and the stick, as it were. I did not become aware of the serious aspect of the secret negotiations with North Vietnam until I became a Special Assistant to National Security Adviser Henry Kissinger in February 1970.[32]

In Lord's analysis, "The problem with this two-track approach, which Kissinger himself acknowledged, was that there was some tension and contradiction in it. We were reducing our involvement and Vietnamization meant that we would be pulling our troops out. So why shouldn't Hanoi just wait until the Americans had sufficiently withdrawn so that the South Vietnamese were on their own and sufficiently weak so that North Vietnam could win, anyway?"

"The analytical response was that the withdrawals would be fast enough to maintain U.S. domestic support but slow enough to allow the South Vietnamese time to adjust and take on the North Vietnamese. Therefore, we would hope that North Vietnam would calculate that American domestic support would not collapse. Ending the draft reduced militant opposition to the war in the United States; large demonstrations ended when the danger of the draft ended."

"This became a more and more decisive consideration when Congress began reducing the aid we had promised to supply the South Vietnamese, and the growing demonstrations against American actions and policies. These events certainly fed Hanoi's intransigent stance in the negotiations."[33]

Reflecting on the complexities of the negotiations, Secretary Lord noted: "One miscalculation might have concerned how able South Vietnam was to handle this struggle, largely on its own. Another misjudgment might have concerned the willingness of Hanoi to negotiate seriously. The North Vietnamese were revolutionaries who did not like to negotiate and compromise. They wanted to win everything. In addition, Hanoi may have concluded that American domestic support for the war was fading fast, mitigated by ending the draft."[34]

Nixon envisioned removal of more than 500,000 American troops from Vietnam, but at the same time he promised the government of South Vietnam to strengthen the South Vietnamese army with advisors, equipment, and a shield of B-52s and other aircraft to prevent a communist takeover. By assuring South Vietnamese security, he would not be the "first American President to lose a war."

Nixon spelled out his thoughts to reporters in Guam in July 1969. In his remarks, the United States would provide military and economic assistance, but the South Vietnamese and other Asian allies would also have to provide the manpower to defend their security against communism. Later dubbed "The Nixon Doctrine," this was not a formula for the United States to get out of Asia but assurance that America could, on a stable basis, remain in Asia and play a responsible role.[35]

Most Americans were willing to give Nixon a chance to prove his policies, but Congress was less patient—Democratic senators Mike Mansfield, Ted Kennedy, and William Fulbright, as well as Republicans Hugh Scott of Pennsylvania, Jacob Javits of New York, and Chuck Percy of Illinois all urged prompt reduction of U.S. forces in Vietnam and argued that Nixon's pace was too slow.

Nixon's public remarks were a rehash of Johnson's call for mutual troop withdrawals, but he added a call for total pullout within a year. Kissinger again told Dobrynin that the petulant Nixon would escalate the war if the Soviets did not produce a settlement.[36]

Hanoi did not play along with Nixon's formula, nor did Moscow.

In mid-June 1969, after a meeting with President Thieu on an isolated atoll in the Pacific to avoid demonstrations, Nixon announced a withdrawal of 25,000 troops, later 40,000 more, and another withdrawal subsequently in 1969. Throughout this process, Defense Secretary Melvin Laird consistently called for more dramatic reductions. While Kissinger publicly stressed the desire to move quickly to remove the troops, privately he counseled Nixon against it, since it cost the United States leverage.[37]

While Nixon's public ratings remained high in the fall of 1969, with a 71 percent approval rating, Congress still chafed under Nixon's slow pace of action in Vietnam. By October 1969, a new wave of antiwar protests emerged, led by Coretta Scott King, Martin Luther King's widow, and this time dominated by older, middle-class Americans. These protesters organized a "moratorium" in which 250,000 protestors marched in Washington. Similar marches took place in New York, Boston, Miami, and Detroit.[38]

Another moratorium two weeks later was larger than the original, as Americans began to learn of uncomfortable moral questions involved in the war. The "Phoenix" program, which involved assassination teams to eliminate Vietcong, became a rallying point for opponents of the war. Some labeled it "mass murder" and called it inefficient, corrupt, and abusive. Reports emerged that a Special Forces team allegedly summarily executed a suspected Vietcong spy. At the same time, the U.S. Army indicted Lt. William Calley and Sgt. David Mitchell for the massacre of civilians in the coastal town of My Lai, Quang Ngai Province, in the aftermath of the 1968 Tet Offensive.[39]

The war became "Nixon's War." However, 30,000 Americans had already been killed when Nixon became president. Within his first year as president, another 10,000 were killed.

Yet the communist forces were not without their own difficulties. By early 1970, following the devastation of the NLF and Vietcong forces during and after Tet and by the Phoenix program to eliminate Vietcong infrastructure, the Vietcong had regained some strength, but still about two-thirds of the estimated 125,000 communist regulars in the South were in fact North Vietnamese.[40] Morale among southern cadres reflected their losses, and the arrival of North Vietnamese "masters" worsened the situation. Sentiments were compounded by the relentless bombing devastating the countryside.[41]

Against a backdrop of low morale, the knowledge of Nixon's withdrawals of 65,000 to 100,000 troops in 1969 and another 150,000 by the end of 1970 gave the communists some respite.

Cambodia, Again

By the spring of 1970, Nixon decided on another wild gamble in Cambodia.

Karnow describes conditions in Cambodia as follows: "Prince Sihanouk's charisma was fading because, in part, he had not been able to improve Cambodia's economy. Although peasants continued to deify him, middle-class Khmers felt alienated and were envious of the American-stoked economies of Saigon and Bangkok."[42]

The "ragtag" Cambodian army was disaffected. Sihanouk's neutralism had deprived the military of generous American support, which earlier had allowed many, including General Lon Nol, to profit from U.S. weapons and other supplies shipped to the Vietnamese and Vietcong. But as Cambodia's relations with North Vietnam deteriorated, Cambodian military and government officials overwhelmingly longed to reestablish the lucrative American link.[44]

Early in 1969, after Sihanouk allowed the secret American bombing of Vietnamese bases, the North Vietnamese began arming and training the Khmer Rouge. To pressure Sihanouk, the Vietnamese infiltrated 12,000 Khmer Rouge soldiers back into Cambodia. Sihanouk thought he could rid Cambodia of Vietnamese through diplomacy, but this supposition was erroneous.[43]

In March 1970 Prime Minister Lon Nol and a cousin, Deputy Prime Minister Sirik Matak, stirred public emotions to create turmoil as a prelude to a coup and encouraged Cambodians to sack the North Vietnamese legation and demand the departure of the North Vietnamese from Cambodia. Cambodians went on a rampage, killing resident Vietnamese and destroying their property. Whatever the truth, Lon Nol and his coterie thought CIA agents were encouraging a coup. Rather than rush home when these rumors surfaced, Sihanouk left Paris and went to Moscow to get Soviet help in ejecting the North Vietnamese. The Soviets, however, greeted Sihanouk with the news that he had been overthrown. Sihanouk, thereafter, went to Beijing.[44]

Tempestuously, Sihanouk suddenly announced formation of a coalition with the Khmer Rouge![45]

Immediately after the coup, Lon Nol renounced "intrusive forces and declared strict neutrality," Karnow recounts. The Lon Nol government quickly reversed the edict and indicated it would cooperate with U.S. forces, stating that the United States could perform as they wished. However, this was a short-range prospect, since the chaotic situation, coupled with the U.S. invasion and bombing of eastern Cambodia, added fuel to the Khmer Rouge appeal to the suffering peasants.[46]

Chaos broke out in Cambodia. Cambodians attacked both Cambodians and Vietnamese; the North Vietnamese army and the Khmer Rouge pushed the Cambodian army back into the interior. In response to the rapidly deteriorating situation in Cambodia, the United States sent ground forces in secretly and illicitly to accompany South Vietnamese forces across the Cambodian border without informing Lon Nol. Nixon had secretly decided to support Lon Nol a month before the coup. He wanted a more pliable and cooperative government in Phnom Penh, seeing Sihanouk as too mercurial. Frustration over press leaks of the U.S. bombing of Laos, rejection by the Senate of two Nixon Supreme Court nominees, and the return by Kissinger from a futile first round of talks with Vietnamese Politburo member Le Duc Tho might also have contributed to Nixon's impetuous decision.[47]

With the Khmer Rouge rapidly closing in on Phnom Penh, the U.S. position was precarious. American military commanders argued another large U.S. troop withdrawal from Vietnam could jeopardize their position in Vietnam unless they eliminated the enemy bases in Cambodia.[48]

Nixon again thought a spectacular drive against the Vietnamese units in Cambodia might lead the Vietnamese to negotiate, but he decided to move in that direction gradually and deceptively—by beginning secret talks with the Vietnamese in Paris. He immediately ordered augmenting the Cambodian government and military.

Reflecting an ongoing concern, there was a belief among congressional and even some intra-administration opposition that

Nixon was contemplating "going beyond Constitutional prerogatives," a concern that later led in part to Nixon's downfall. Nixon's decision to send American forces into Cambodia without informing Lon Nol led several members of Kissinger's staff to threaten to quit in protest.[49]

Nixon announced his decision with pomposity: "If, when the chips are down, the world's most powerful nation acts like a pitiful, helpless giant, the forces of totalitarianism and anarchy will threaten free nations and free institutions throughout the world." He said he had spurned all political considerations. He would follow his conscience and would prefer to be a one-term president rather than a two-term president at the cost of making American a second-rate power. A force of 20,000 American troops was attacking as Nixon spoke.[50]

Despite expecting to wipe out the "Vietcong Pentagon," U.S. forces found no COSVN, only scattered tunnels, huts, and bunkers abandoned in anticipation of an invasion. Nixon trumpeted a great victory, citing quantities of ammunition and secret documents captured, but, aside from temporary relief in Saigon and virtually the whole southern part of the country, there were few long-term consequences in Vietnam. Leading opinion-makers and the Eastern press attacked the incursion, but the "silent majority" supported Nixon.[51]

Nixon railed against opponents. Ohio Governor James Rhodes ordered the National Guard to contain student demonstrations at Kent State; the National Guard killed four students, and pandemonium ensued. At Jackson State College in Jackson, Mississippi, an African American university, on May 14, 1970, city and state police confronted a group of students protesting against the Vietnam War, specifically the United States invasion of Cambodia. Shortly after midnight, the police opened fire, killing two students and injuring twelve. In the wake of these events, more than 400 universities and colleges shut down. Roughly 100,000 protesters marched on Washington, encircling the White House and government buildings.[52]

In the meantime, pressure mounted to announce a deadline for withdrawal of all U.S. forces from Vietnam. Nixon appointed a Republican commission, led by former Pennsylvania Governor William Scranton, to look at the cause of unrest in the universities.

According to Karnow, Scranton's commission concluded that the war was splitting the nation and "nothing was more important than an end of the war."

Nixon's pit bull, Vice President Spiro Agnew, called opponents of the war "radic-libs" or "radical liberals" and accused even Scranton's commission of "neutralism," a word that was anathema to Americans in 1970.[53]

Nixon authorized illegal surveillance of domestic critics and famously commented, "When the President does it, that means that it is not illegal."[54]

Nixon's Retreat

The Cambodian incursion reminded America that, despite some troop withdrawals, the war not only continued but expanded into Cambodia and Laos.

To reduce political opposition to the war, Nixon ended all student and occupational deferments in 1971 and ended the draft itself in 1973. Demonstrations suddenly all but ceased. In Vietnam, morale deteriorated among the American troops. Discontented U.S. soldiers initiated "fragging" — tossing a grenade at conscripts and much-resented "lifers," long-serving soldiers. "Fraggings" increased rapidly, averaging two a week. Between 1969 and 1973 there were at least 788 fraggings, a symptom of deep divisions within the military.

A Marine colonel wrote vividly of conditions in an article for the *Armed Forces Journal*, describing the "collapse" of the military: "Individual units avoid or refuse combat, murder their officials and noncommissioned officers, are drug-ridden and dispirited if not mutinous."[55]

To make matters worse, even after dispirited soldiers left the bombing, fire, napalm, and psychological trauma, they often returned home to a hostile reception from the antiwar public.

Veterans groups expanded and became increasingly vehement in their denunciations of the war. By 1971, veterans, many without arms and legs, participated in demonstrations. The massacre at My Lai and the trial of Lieutenant William Calley fueled extraordinary discontent. Racism and dehumanization characterized many of the attacks.[56]

On April 24, 1971, 500,000 demonstrators arrived in Washington to protest the war; for days thereafter, antiwar and welfare activists joined forces to lobby Congress, emphasizing the link between the war and poverty in the United States.[57] Despite the participation of both groups, there was disagreement over whether the antiwar and poverty movements should join forces. In fact, they did, including the National Peace Action Coalition (NPAC), dominated by the Socialist Workers Party, and the People's Coalition for Peace and Justice (PCPJ), a far more inclusive group led by faith organizations, pacifists, organizations of people of color, and the labor movement. Martin Luther King decisively advanced this joint effort. Early on, King spoke out strongly against American involvement in the Vietnam War, making his position public in an address, "Beyond Vietnam," on April 4, 1967, at New York's Riverside Church. His involvement in the antiwar movement reduced his ability to influence national racial policies and made him a target of further FBI investigations.[58]

In March 1971, Daniel Ellsberg, a former Marine and Pentagon staff aide, then working for the Rand Corporation, gave *The New York Times* a body of work collected by the Pentagon about the war, which became known as the "Pentagon Papers." Ellsberg contended that they provided ample grounds for convicting President Nixon and others of war crimes. The papers, published in part by *The New York Times*, detailed much of the government's behind-the-scenes decision-making and chronicled a pervasive breakdown of democratic government. After a court stay, the papers were released on June 13, 1971, and included alleged incriminating actions by the Kennedy, Johnson, and Nixon administrations.[59]

The impact in Washington was electric. The vision of a breakdown of government flickered. The government had lost its authority and engaged in dishonest, duplicitous, and illegal behavior.

17

Peace Negotiations and the Paris Accords

Henry Kissinger had never negotiated with a seasoned revolution-ary like Le Duc Tho, who was trying to end a war regarded by the Vietnamese as an existential issue. Thus, negotiating with Tho was very different from Kissinger's normalization talks with Chinese revolutionaries. Tho was a founder of the ICP, a charter member of the Vietminh, a longtime inmate of French colonialist jails, and a jungle fighter who ran operations in South Vietnam through the long war.[1]

Tho subjected Kissinger to endless haggling over details, stood firm and determined in defending core North Vietnamese demands developed over fifty years of negotiations, and presented a vision of independence stretching over 1,000 years.

Tho and Kissinger conducted secret talks while formal talks were held elsewhere in Paris. Both men were devoted to secrecy, in-trigue, and duplicity. Kissinger preferred these offline talks, which allowed him to avoid the Washington bureaucracy, negotiate as he and Nixon pleased, and cut out the secretaries of State and Defense. Kissinger commanded complete control of information flowing to the outside world and corralled his small negotiating team to avoid undesired leaks.

Kissinger and Nixon had assured President Thieu that he would have to accept any agreement reached. Nonetheless, while Thieu was informed, Kissinger maintained considerable leeway in negotiations. While Thieu had the most to lose and was dependent on U.S. financial and military support for his survival, Kissinger held the dominant hand.[2]

Just as Kissinger was happy to sideline President Thieu, Tho was pleased to negotiate without having the NLF directly involved. Tho hoped to drive a wedge between the United States and Thieu but had to be mindful of violating the trust of the NLF. Tho also had to consult closely with Ho Chi Minh at every step of the way until Ho died in 1969.

Critically, Kissinger was under tremendous domestic pressure to achieve a settlement, while Tho had faced far less domestic pressure to forge an early settlement.

Tho initially insisted on the resolution of political and military issues simultaneously, and an armistice had to be linked to replacement of the existing regime in Saigon by a coalition that included the NLF. No American president could agree to this proposition. Thus, the talks continued for two years with this quandary unresolved.

In the 1954 Geneva Talks, the major powers, including the Soviet Union and China, had insisted that Hanoi accept an agreement without final resolution of the political questions, which were to be settled in an election two years hence. After fifteen years of war and no free elections, Hanoi was unwilling to accept any such conclusion in its talks with the Americans.

In some ways, Nixon's negotiating situation was more complicated than Lyndon Johnson's because Nixon had expanded the war into Cambodia, and North Vietnam had by that time tightened its grip on Laos.[3]

Nixon, thus, had assumed responsibility for all of Indochina rather than just South Vietnam. At the same time, Nixon committed to a steady withdrawal of U.S. forces, reducing his capabilities in Indochina while he was losing leverage over North Vietnam.[4]

Peace Negotiations

From the start, the issue of "mutual withdrawal" from South Vietnam of both North Vietnamese and U.S. forces was a key U.S. demand in the negotiations with Hanoi. This followed the formula President Johnson had employed. Nixon also insisted on the return of some 400 American POWs.[5]

In a speech in Guam in July 1969, Nixon suggested a "ceasefire" but did not mention a mutual withdrawal of forces. But Kissinger continued to publicly insist on mutual withdrawal.[6]

Kissinger tried to handle the key question of a continuing North Vietnamese military presence in the South by proposing to forego an announcement of North Vietnamese troop withdrawals but with a commitment to withdrawal.[7]

Tho, like his colleague in the public talks, rejected this idea. He insisted Vietnamese forces were defending sacred Vietnamese territory and could not in any way be equated with American "aggressor" forces. In Kissinger's proposal, however, Tho detected a "softening" of Kissinger's position. Tho suspected this might imply the United States would eventually drop its insistence on the withdrawal of North Vietnamese forces, although this was not Kissinger's stated position at the time.[8]

In 1969, the NLF joined other groups to form the Provisional Revolutionary Government (PRG) and issued a new proposal.[9] The PRG Thirteen-Point Proposal called for the withdrawal of all American forces, formation of a coalition government of equality, democracy, and mutual respect composed of the PRG, GVN, and "neutralist elements" but excluding Nguyen Van Thieu. The proposal also assured democratic freedom of speech, the press, assembly, belief, and step-by-step reunification. The United States publicly ignored these proposals, but ultimately, apart from the removal of President Thieu, accepted a very similar settlement in 1972.

However, in a televised speech on October 7, 1970, which was billed as the most comprehensive statement yet on the war, Nixon elaborated on actual and projected American troop withdrawals and included a mention of a "standstill ceasefire." According to Karnow, Kissinger intimated to his aides that the phrase was "actually a disguised concession of major proportions, intended to convey that the United States had scrapped the mutual withdrawal requirement and that their forces could remain in place only if they dropped their demand that Thieu be jettisoned." Le Duc Tho rejected the proposal and continued to insist on Thieu ceding power to a coalition. However, Nixon backtracked to reporters on a plane trip the next day, saying that his proposal was based on previously stated "principles" that included mutual withdrawals.[10]

Thieu, along with Kissinger, rejected this proposal. For Thieu this would mean acceptance of a continuing North Vietnamese military presence in the South. The North Vietnamese suspected the proposal was another camouflaged suggestion that the United States would be willing to allow North Vietnamese forces to remain in the South. Nixon's conciliatory speech may have been designed to placate congressional and public calls for faster troop withdrawals, but two years later it became the U.S. position. Nixon's backtracking placated President Thieu, for whom Northern troops remaining in the South was anathema.[11]

Lam Son 719: Test of Vietnamization

In the first major experiment with "Vietnamization," there would be a major buildup of South Vietnamese men, material, and supplies in 1971. To this end, the United States conceived of a South Vietnamese incursion on February 7, 1971, labeled Lam Son 719, into Laos to stop the North Vietnamese buildup via the Ho Chi Minh Trail. After massive bombardment by U.S. planes, the South Vietnamese attacked across the border but were repelled, suffering a humiliating defeat and retreat. This was a severe blow to the goal of Vietnamization, raising serious questions about the ability of the South Vietnamese military to maintain control should U.S. forces fully withdraw.[12]

Still, Nixon proudly proclaimed in a televised speech on April 7, 1971, that Vietnamization had proven its success in Lam Son 719 near the Laotian town of Tchepone, even though it had been a disaster for South Vietnamese forces. North Vietnamese forces smashed ARVN forces, and only massive U.S. bombing rescued the South Vietnamese. That ARVN had been willing to take on the attack without U.S. ground forces after the massive U.S. bombing was the only positive indicator regarding the success or failure of Vietnamization. For his part, Kissinger privately questioned the success of Vietnamization, blaming poor U.S. planning, faulty South Vietnamese execution, and what he termed "warped Nixon leadership." The display of military ineptitude also shook ARVN and government leaders as a harbinger of things to come.[13]

Ten to fifteen years of training by the United States for conventional warfare had ill-prepared the South Vietnamese forces for the kind of battle they faced, whether conventional or insurgent. They also represented a regime that rewarded fidelity rather than competence, an ominous reality. Constantly fearful of a *coup d'état*, President Thieu valued loyalty to his regime over military prowess.[14]

U.S. criticism also struck raw nerves among the South Vietnamese, whose irritation and concern resulted in skittish behavior and anti-American incidents. This also reflected a lowered respect for American soldiers, a draftee force suffering low morale and drug problems. By 1970 the U.S. command in Saigon reported that 65,000 American soldiers, out of roughly 335,000, were using drugs.[15]

Negotiations Resume

Kissinger resumed his discussions with Le Duc Tho in Paris in May 1971. The talks dragged on for another year, with the principal focus on the disposition of the Saigon regime.[16]

In the summer of 1971, the possibility of peace flickered briefly. In June Hanoi and the PRG responded favorably to a major shift of the negotiating stance of the United States—Kissinger offered to set a specific date for the complete withdrawal of U.S. troops in return for a ceasefire and the return of all U.S. POWs. For the first time, the United States dropped its demand for "reciprocal withdrawal" —North Vietnamese troops in the South were not mentioned.[17]

Hanoi and the PRG shifted slightly in response, no longer demanding the removal of South Vietnamese president Nguyen Van Thieu before serious negotiations could begin but insisting that the United States stop supporting Thieu's regime. In the upcoming presidential elections in South Vietnam, the United States could refrain from interfering and Thieu could be defeated by a candidate, presumably a "neutralist," who was prepared to negotiate a political settlement. Fair elections in Saigon in September 1971 could fulfill Nixon's expressed hope for peace with honor. While it was doubtful a candidate favorable to the NLF could win a fair election, the NLF seems to have thought this was a possibility that could lead to a U.S. withdrawal.[18]

In August 1971, Hanoi and the PRG published a "seven point" peace proposal based on Kissinger's latest offer. Hanoi spelled out steps for the organization of a coalition government in Saigon, the withdrawal of U.S. troops, and the return of U.S. POWs.[19]

Embarrassed by publication of the negotiations, Kissinger obfuscated and said Hanoi was demanding the "overthrow" of Thieu as a precondition, an obviously dishonorable move. At the time, many Americans believed Hanoi was merely demanding fair elections in September because they thought Thieu would lose.

A three-way race seemed likely: President Thieu would run for reelection, challenged by his ebullient vice president, Nguyen Cao Ky, and Duong Van Minh, one of the leading generals who had overthrown Diem. Duong Van Minh, or "Big Minh," was thought to be a "neutralist" who might negotiate a settlement with the North. Many thought if Thieu and Ky split the vote, Minh might win.

Neither Nguyen Cao Ky nor Big Minh enjoyed much popular support, and Minh's previous attempt at governing had been a disaster. Stanley Karnow reported that the U.S. Embassy and CIA provided ample funds for President Thieu to make sure people knew whom to vote for and, eventually, to persuade Ky to withdraw from the race. Promising a fair election, the U.S. Embassy urged Minh not to withdraw when he saw what was happening, since a single-candidate race would be a farce. With all the levers of power, the secret police, huge amounts of money, and CIA help, Thieu won.[20]

If the American negotiators felt pressure from domestic U.S. politics, their North Vietnamese counterparts feared increasing international isolation, even from the Soviet Union and China. Nixon again threw out the notion of a standstill ceasefire, whereby all troops would cease fire while the international community negotiated a settlement. Reinforcing this proposition, Nixon in two major speeches on January 25, 1972, and May 8, 1972, failed to mention mutual withdrawal, again hinting the United States might abandon this position.

Karnow faults both Kissinger and Tho for not taking advantage of this softened shift. In Karnow's view, Kissinger should have utilized the shift to aggressively promote a settlement rather than allow it to slowly become the U.S. position without concessions from the North Vietnamese. Similarly, Tho could have pressed Kissinger and prompted an earlier settlement. Both seemed content to let the war continue.[21]

Nixon Seeks Soviet and Chinese Help

With the promising period of bilateral peace negotiations dashed by electoral chicanery, Nixon made another attempt to engage the Soviet Union and China and break the impasse. Ironically, the United States had entered the war to prevent the expansion of Soviet and Chinese power into Southeast Asia. Now, to avoid a humiliating defeat in Southeast Asia, Nixon was engaging these same powers in the region's affairs.

Nixon dreamed of extraordinarily bold steps to transform the world. The president who had built his reputation as an anticommunist fighter and had once condemned Americans who had "lost China" began the extraordinary step of normalizing U.S. relations with China, then still deep in the throes of the Cultural Revolution. The irony of Nixon's bringing about rapprochement with China was too exquisite to ignore. But just as it took Lyndon Johnson, a Southerner, to pass the Civil Rights Act, it took a well-known red-baiter to bury the hatchet with Maoist China.

Nixon began publicly advocating a rapprochement with China as early as his *Foreign Affairs* article in 1967.[22]

Nixon reasoned that rapprochement with China would exacerbate the Sino-Soviet split. A visit to both would raise concerns in each about advantages due to a strengthened U.S. connection. Nixon harbored hope that Beijing might be willing to help end the Vietnam War. The rewards would certainly assure Nixon's reelection, and he could parade as a "man of peace."

During Kissinger's secret visits to Beijing in 1971 to prepare for the Nixon visit, Kissinger repeatedly attempted to engage China's help in ending the Vietnam War. China agreed that the Vietnam War was more urgent to resolve than the Taiwan issue, a matter of momentous importance to China. Mao commented that China could wait fifty years to resolve the Taiwan issue, but the Chinese were eager to resolve the Vietnam War, a position, of course, that

Beijing had not taken as recently as 1968, when it was calling for prolonged struggle in Vietnam. Hanoi agreed to negotiations with the United States in April 1968. China had stepped up aid in 1971 to sustain its rivalry in Vietnam with the Soviet Union.[23]

The Chinese seemed prepared to discuss a settlement with Vietnam but were not prepared to pressure Hanoi to capitulate. Beijing asked Vietnam if officials should discuss the situation there during Nixon's visit to China. Fearing another sellout, as in 1954, Hanoi was extremely resistant to a U.S.-China discussion, fearing it would undermine Vietnam's position.

Nonetheless, Kissinger made clear U.S. concerns about another Vietnamese offensive in 1972, informing the Chinese that any offensive would be met with fierce retaliation.

Thus, both sides maintained "principled positions" in support of their respective allies, even as they acted pragmatically, as typical of Chinese diplomats.

During Kissinger's secret visit to Beijing and his more open visit to Moscow to lay the groundwork for Nixon's visits to China and the USSR, Kissinger did not press either country hard on the Vietnam questions, fearing this would undermine larger geostrategic goals with both nations.

Kissinger claims in his memoirs—disingenuously in my view—that the "standstill ceasefire" had already supplanted mutual withdrawal. In Kissinger's view, he may have dropped the demand for mutual withdrawal, but if he had, he gained no concessions from the Vietnamese for doing so. I conclude he wanted to recast his caving on this basic earlier demand.

The North Vietnamese again read this as at least a hint that Kissinger would drop the demand for mutual withdrawal, key to a solution from the Vietnamese side.[24]

This set the stage for the intense negotiations that followed over the summer of 1972, as both Hanoi and Washington saw the U.S. elections as providing impetus to conclude the talks. Nixon believed his reelection prospects were directly tied to concluding peace with Vietnam, while Hanoi saw the election as an opportunity to pressure Washington to drop key demands.[25]

Nixon to China

Hanoi's greatest fear had increasingly been the possibility of rapprochement between the United States and China, as well as continued thawing of U.S. relations with Brezhnev's Soviet Union. Both Beijing and Moscow were showing clear signs of interest in improved relations with Washington. Nixon's visit evoked the nightmare of China's "sellout" in Geneva in 1954, a move some estimated would force Hanoi into another decade of fighting with the United States to reunify Vietnam. Hanoi feared China was negotiating behind its back. Beijing had urged Hanoi to defer the question of Thieu's status to secure a quick withdrawal of U.S. forces from Vietnam. The Chinese position suggested to Hanoi that Beijing was again fostering delay in reunification.

Mao pointed to the similarity of their objectives and China's dream of conquering Taiwan. But this suggested that just as Taiwan would not soon reunite with China, in China's view Hanoi could delay resolving Vietnam. Hanoi saw the "fix" in the Shanghai communiqué language. Nixon promised to reduce the military presence on Taiwan "as tension in the area diminishes"—a clear indication to Hanoi that China was using withdrawal from Taiwan in pursuit of peace in Vietnam. Suspicious of Beijing's motives, Vietnamese officials acknowledged that the fight in Vietnam could become very difficult in the face of a Sino-American understanding at Hanoi's expense.[26]

In conjunction with Hanoi's plans for its spring offensive in 1972, China had increased its aid to Vietnam in late 1971 to keep pace with the heavy equipment, including tanks and other armored vehicles, that Moscow was providing.

Fearful of jeopardizing his trip to China, Nixon threatened serious retaliation against Hanoi but applied no pressure on China to curb the Vietnamese. In contrast, he sent word to Leonid Brezhnev that his visit might be jeopardized if the Soviets allowed the North Vietnamese to undertake actions "designed to humiliate us." Brezhnev was vague and unresponsive, probably because he had almost no leverage over Hanoi's plans.[27]

The 1972 Spring Offensive

At the end of March 1972, 200,000 North Vietnamese infantry and tanks smashed across the DMZ into Quang Tri's border in a move that was as bold as Nixon's trip to China. By routing the South Vietnamese defenses, Hanoi boldly announced Vietnamization was a failure. As it had during the Tet Offensive, Hanoi hoped this offensive might topple the Saigon regime. The entire province of Quang Tri was under North Vietnamese control, and the road to Hue was open as South Vietnamese fled, abandoning their weapons and equipment.[28]

ARVN forces moved from Quang Ngai to Hue. ARVN, airborne, and Marine divisions moved north from the Saigon area to Quang Tri. These forces and B-52s stopped the invasion. In the Mekong Delta, the NLF resumed its aggression and shook the ARVN forces. If the North Vietnamese had not hesitated, they might also have taken Kontum in the highlands. Such an action could have led to the collapse of ARVN forces in central Vietnam and paved the way for a battle for Saigon itself. The North Vietnamese could have seized Hue, but they did not try.

U.S. air power finally turned the tide. Three-hundred B-52 strikes around Kontum saved the city. As the B-52s were available, the North Vietnamese were unable to move troops for an effective ground assault. The United States smothered the Mekong Delta with bombs and obliterated the provincial capital of Quang Tri.

Twenty-five thousand ARVN troops were lost, but perhaps 100,000 North Vietnamese were killed. One million more South Vietnamese became refugees.[29]

ARVN and the United States quickly reversed the results of the offensive, but Hanoi had made its point—Vietnamization had failed. This was the principal point Hanoi wished to make in preparation for what it expected to be final negotiations before the fall U.S. presidential elections, but it might have been partially directed at U.S.-China negotiations on normalization. While the Chinese had the capacity for leverage, they did not use it.

The massive U.S. bombing during the spring offensive was designed to reassure a nervous South Vietnamese President Thieu of U.S. retaliation should the North Vietnamese attack after a U.S.

pullout. It also demonstrated to the communists that they would be subjected to fearsome retaliation should they violate a peace agreement. Many observers believed the bombing was intended to push Hanoi to negotiate seriously a ceasefire and subsequent withdrawal of the last U.S. troops. All of these purposes may have been true.[30]

. . . and to Moscow

During his preparatory visits to Moscow, Kissinger repeated previous positions, but in his official trip he added that North Vietnam must withdraw the troops that had invaded the South for the present offensive.[31]

Many historians regarded Kissinger's "demand" as another major American "concession in disguise." By demanding the withdrawal of recently introduced troops, Kissinger was tacitly agreeing that the ones that had been in the South prior to the recent offensive could remain, thereby dropping the mutual withdrawal that had been a central piece of U.S. demands from the start.[32]

Nixon's spring summit in Moscow focused on the cosmic issue of nuclear weapons, of utmost importance to both countries. Nonetheless, Nixon made clear that he would forego the Moscow summit if Brezhnev did not persuade Hanoi to accept peace. Kissinger by then had abandoned such "linkage" in his negotiations with Moscow, but he was obliged to try to convince Brezhnev to help regarding Nixon's obsession, Vietnam.

Kissinger feared a collapse of the summit would alter the balance of international power by costing the leverage the United States gained against China through an effective U.S.-USSR relationship. Moreover, he doubted that Moscow had much influence in Hanoi, despite the massive military and financial support Hanoi received from Moscow, much of which was provided merely to keep up with China.[33]

These conditions set the stage for the intense negotiations that followed over the summer, as both Hanoi and Washington saw the U.S. elections as providing impetus to conclude the talks. Nixon believed his reelection prospects strongly hinged on concluding peace with Vietnam, a weakness Hanoi used to pressure Washington to drop key demands.[34]

Negotiations Resume

Following Nixon's visits in 1972 to Beijing and Moscow, where the Vietnamese feared their communist supporters might betray their "lofty internationalist duties" for their own narrow interests, Hanoi recalculated its position and decided to press ahead with negotiations.[35]

Negotiations resumed in October 1972 in response to Kissinger's dropping mutual withdrawal and picking up again the notion of a "standstill ceasefire." In response, North Vietnamese negotiators dropped the demand for President Thieu's resignation. This became Kissinger's position in late 1972—a willingness to accept North Vietnamese troops in the South in exchange for not forcing Thieu out.

Ambassador Lord, in his oral history, supports Kissinger's thesis that an agreement was impossible earlier, saying, "almost from the beginning of the negotiations [in 1969] the American position was that we were prepared to resolve the military portion of this agreement. This was foreshadowed very concretely in a Presidential speech in November 1969, and particularly in May 1971, when we secretly indicated that we were willing not to insist on a North Vietnamese withdrawal."[36]

North Vietnam had failed to defeat the Americans militarily, although they had defeated a South Vietnamese incursion into Laos and had strengthened their position in the Mekong Delta and in Quang Tri on the DMZ.

Hanoi Settles

Hanoi had several options. The Vietnamese could resume guerrilla warfare and fight on, but Nixon was increasingly frustrated, belligerent, and considered potentially dangerous. Nixon had expanded the war to Cambodia and Laos and shown willingness to heavily bomb North Vietnam, but not to invade it.

Alternatively, Hanoi could concede on the removal of Thieu, after which the Americans could go home and the struggle would continue. The early judgment that Lam Son 719 and Quang Tri demonstrated the military weakness of the South Vietnamese in contrast to the prowess and determination of the North and Viet- cong continued to highlight the dilemma the United States faced in its negotiations. In Hanoi's view, North Vietnam and the Vietcong had the upper hand. Vietnamization was failing, and the United States seemed willing to make concessions with regard to North Vietnamese troops remaining in place. Nixon's reelection hopes lay just ahead and could convince him to compromise to get the war behind him before the election. South Vietnam appeared weak po- litically and militarily and would be unable to withstand a total as- sault, if it came to that. This combination bolstered those in Hanoi arguing for a settlement.[37]

Hanoi decided to compromise because it judged that the Unit- ed States was now willing to allow North Vietnamese forces to re- main in the South, the key to Hanoi's ultimate victory. Le Duc Tho returned to Paris in August 1972 with slightly diluted positions. He appeared for the first time to moderate his previous insistence on the linkage of military and political issues and hinted that he would no longer insist upon Thieu's removal.[38]

In a public speech in Hanoi in August 1972, Premier Phan Van Dong did not mention Thieu. Intelligence reports in the South told cadres to prepare for a settlement by expanding their territorial reach as widely as possible.[39]

Ambassador Lord concluded that the upcoming U.S. elections created "the basic dilemma underlying most of the secret negotia- tions throughout the period from 1970–72. It was not until the fall of 1972 that Hanoi realized, despite their hopes the United States would elect a more pliable Senator McGovern, President Nixon was the likely victor. Hanoi realized it was going to have to deal with Nixon, a mad man in the White House who would no longer have to worry about being reelected. Therefore, Hanoi had an in- centive for negotiating seriously, and in October 1972, they finally dropped their political demands and were prepared to settle for an agreement that they could have had a couple of years earlier."[40]

With these conclusions in mind, Tho introduced on October 8, 1972, a nine-point proposal with a simple and realistic formula: The United States and North Vietnam would arrange a ceasefire, followed by a full American troop withdrawal, prisoner exchange, and other military resolutions.[41]

Political problems were left to the opposing Vietnamese sides, which would form an interim body, a "Council on National Reconciliation," composed of the Saigon government, the NLF, and "neutralist" representatives. The council would supervise eventual national elections and achieve permanent peace. Meanwhile, the government and communist forces would remain separate military forces in distinct areas. Except for the temporary division at the DMZ, the political process was like that produced in the Geneva Accords of 1954, but this time there would be no foreign presence or arrangements beyond Hanoi's control.

Ambassador Lord describes the breakthrough as follows: "We went over to Paris for this meeting in October 1972, and were given a present by Le Duc Tho. It incorporated the unilateral withdrawal of U.S. forces and the release of our prisoners, on the military side. The language of the proposal was specific in this respect. The North Vietnamese proposal also included a ceasefire in place and international supervision of the agreement. The North Vietnamese had moved away from their insistence on a coalition government. There still was some tough negotiating, but they used some new language. They proposed a national reconciliation arrangement, but, in effect, they would leave President Thieu in power in Saigon. So, the North Vietnamese dropped the political demands that they had stuck with for years."[42]

"We received this North Vietnamese proposal at the opening session. Kissinger called for a break in the meeting. I still remember walking with him on a Sunday afternoon in a garden, somewhere in the Paris suburbs. We said to each other: 'This is it. We've done it.' We knew that we had a lot of tough slogging ahead with the North Vietnamese. Then, of course, we had to get South Vietnamese agreement. However, the North Vietnamese had dropped their political demands and were willing to have a military settlement only, even though there was a lot of fudgy language about it."[43]

The favorable element of the proposal was that it would foster early U.S. withdrawal, but the political and military arrangements for the Thieu regime were vague and risky. On the political side, nothing guaranteed the establishment of the Council on National Reconciliation or the emergence of a long-term democratic settlement. On the military side, the communists would be left in a superior position, with the North Vietnamese main forces remaining in the South.[44] Kissinger acknowledged he had failed after four years of negotiating to obtain the withdrawal of the North Vietnamese forces: "We had long since passed that threshold," he said. He instead obtained a promise that North Vietnamese troops would not be resupplied.[45]

Despite the proposal's flaws, Kissinger was elated. All his staff was not. Senior aide John Negroponte argued that the communists' offer was badly flawed. By leaving the enemy forces intact, it left the situation "basically unresolved." Kissinger wrathfully countered Negroponte: "What do you want to do? Stay there forever?"[46]

Prior to the ceasefire date, the United States also agreed to rush 2 billion dollars' worth of material in six weeks to bolster South Vietnam. To circumvent another clause of the agreement, the United States secretly transferred ownership of its military bases to the South Vietnamese. Just as the North Vietnamese had instructed the NLF, Kissinger sent word via Ambassador Ellsworth Bunker to Thieu to seize as much territory as quickly as possible—particularly in the area around Saigon.[47]

Nixon vacillated about Thieu. In the summer 1972, he sent Alexander Haig to Saigon to assure Thieu "under no circumstances would South Vietnam's security be traded away," as reported by Karnow. But in October, with "peace possibly at hand," Nixon told Kissinger, "the tail can't wag the dog." On October 21, the text was completed, Nixon agreed to the provisions, and Kissinger was to fly to Hanoi to sign the agreement at the end of October.

Phan Van Dong gave an interview to *Newsweek*'s Arnaud de Borchgrave in which he labeled Thieu "*passé*." The premier envisioned the Council of Reconciliation as a coalition of "transition." This enraged Thieu.[48]

Thieu Balks

Kissinger had a tumultuous meeting with Thieu in late October 1972. Kissinger argued that he saw no alternative to the agreement he had reached with Le Duc Tho and told Thieu the communists would suffer the "most serious consequences" if they violated the agreement. Thieu accused Kissinger of paving the way for the communists to take power in Saigon, objected strenuously to allowing the North Vietnamese to remain in the South, and insisted the DMZ be an international border, all of which in effect wiped out the key provisions of the agreement. Ambassador Lord, who participated in the meeting, recalled that Thieu, weeping, charged that "[h]aving fought a war to defend South Vietnam's independence, the United States was now denying its legitimacy."[49]

Lord recounted: "On the way to Saigon Kissinger and I were relatively optimistic about this meeting with President Thieu, although we knew that he would huff and puff. We thought that he would accept the agreement, because we had eliminated the political elements of a settlement, the call for his resignation, for a coalition government, etc. John Negroponte was very skeptical about Thieu's reaction, more pessimistic. Among other factors was the fact that North Vietnamese troops would remain in South Vietnam.

"Although we had been following this approach since at least May 1971. Negroponte felt that Thieu would have a real problem with the agreement, primarily with the United States withdrawing its forces and the North Vietnamese remaining in South Vietnam.

"In the meeting with President Thieu, at which we would receive his response, we were blasted. Thieu was very upset with the agreement, across the board. He picked out all kinds of other language which he thought was weak, in terms of international supervision, supplies, the amount of aid, or whatever. He complained about everything, but above all he objected to the continued presence of North Vietnamese troops in South Vietnam.

"Secondly, Thieu said, in effect, that we had misled him. He said that this agreement went way beyond what we had been reporting to him and what he thought was in store for him. Thirdly, in negotiating this agreement, we had been negotiating the fate of South Vietnam. Now, he said, you come to me, a couple of weeks before your elections, and expect me to accept this agreement, which will seal the fate of my country and my countrymen in a couple of days. He said that the agreement was wrong in terms of principle and also wrong in terms of perception, with the Americans ramming this agreement down my throat and not taking into account the fate of the South Vietnamese people."[50]

Kissinger, also enraged, reported to Nixon that Thieu "verged on insanity." According to Karnow, Nixon cabled Thieu threatening to cut off all American assistance to South Vietnam. Thieu's intransigence, wrote Nixon, "would have the most serious effect on my ability to continue to support you." Nixon threatened to sign a separate deal with North Vietnam. Thieu remained adamant, and Kissinger departed within 24 hours without securing Thieu's signature.[51]

Nixon then backtracked again, fearing that scuttling Thieu would lead to a communist takeover. Kissinger worried that the impasse endangered the agreement he had reached with Le Duc Tho.

Thieu publicly denounced the draft agreement and ordered his forces "to wipe out the communist forces quickly and mercilessly," as reported by Karnow.[52]

Ambassador Lord remembers the ensuing exchanges: "So we went back to Washington, but within a day or two there was a press release out of Hanoi, lambasting the United States, President Nixon, and Kissinger. The statement said that the United States had agreed to a deal with Hanoi and now, under the pretense that it couldn't tell their lackeys in Saigon what to do, the United States was now reneging on the arrangements we had made. Hanoi said that we had broken a solemn agreement with Hanoi and also an agreement for Kissinger to visit Hanoi. They then proceeded to publish the entire agreement that we had reached with them on about October 25, 1972, perhaps 10 days before the [U.S.] election."[53]

Karnow writes, "For all of these reasons Kissinger used the phrase: 'Peace is at hand.' What he meant by that is that we didn't have it yet, but this is real progress. To Hanoi, we stick by the essential agreement. We weren't going to bow out of the agreement, but we had to renegotiate some of it. To Saigon he said, in effect, that we appreciate your objections up to a point, but you're going to have to live with this deal.

"To the press, on October 24, 1972, Kissinger said, "We believe that peace is at hand. We believe that an agreement is in sight."[54]

"President Nixon was also sending a message to the Saigon government," Ambassador Lord recalled. "He was determined, as Kissinger was, to stick to the original agreement, essentially, as well as to try to get some changes in it. So, Nixon was saying in effect to Saigon: 'If you buy this agreement, we'll stand behind you. I'm bombing the hell out of Hanoi right now. We can anticipate some disagreements once we conclude the agreement. I'm showing you that I'm willing to bomb Hanoi and North Vietnam. So, if you sign this agreement, you can count on my enforcing it.' So, the bombing of North Vietnam was not only a signal to North Vietnam to be reasonable but also to South Vietnam to be similarly reasonable and to sign off on the agreement."[55]

After his landslide reelection, Nixon gave Thieu his "absolute assurances that he would take swift and severe retaliatory action" should North Vietnam violate the agreement, according to Karnow. Nixon contradicted Kissinger and let it be known that there would be a delay while some differences were worked out. He directed Kissinger to present Thieu's 69 proposed amendments to Le Duc Tho. To Kissinger, this was "preposterous!"[56]

Kissinger and Le Duc Tho both hardened their positions in resumed talks in early December. Kissinger recommended to Nixon renewed, intensified bombings or to break the talks until January. In one of his wild swings, Nixon demanded that North Vietnam undertake serious negotiations within 72 hours, or else. He ordered the chairman of the JCS to prepare massive bombings on all targets including railroads, power plants, and radio transmitters in Hanoi, and docks and shipyards in Haiphong, including many targets that had previously been off-limits.[57]

On December 18, Nixon's "Christmas bombing" featured 3,000 sorties by B-52s and other aircraft, dropping over 40,000 tons over eleven days in the heavily populated corridor between Hanoi and Haiphong.

Popular reaction in the United States was muted, since most of the troops were back in America, but the *New York Times* called it "Stone Age barbarity" and the *Washington Post* labeled it "savage and senseless." The world was horrified.

The Vietnamese shot down 26 aircraft, including 15 B-52s; 93 pilots and crew were lost and 31 captured.[58]

Kissinger and Tho resumed their talks on January 8, 1973, and completed the revisions in one day. Nixon sent an ultimatum to Thieu: "You must decide now whether you desire to continue our alliance or whether you want me to seek a settlement with the enemy which serves U.S. interests alone." Thieu capitulated.[59]

Ambassador Lord reflected: "In effect, the letters [to President Thieu] were a combination of reassurance, persuasion, and threat. These letters later became controversial, because Congress felt President Nixon had promised in them to respond with further bombing to a renewal of North Vietnamese aggression, without consulting Congress. In effect, some members of Congress felt that Nixon had made some secret commitments."[60] President Thieu showed the letters to the press.

As for speculation about Kissinger's seeking a decent interval, as of the signing of the agreement on January 27, 1973, Ambassador Lord said: "I can tell you that Kissinger, President Nixon, and I felt that the agreement on Vietnam could work, and there was no thought of a decent interval. People like John Negroponte and Al Haig were more skeptical of it but were not violently against the agreement. No one was sure that it would last, but all thought that it might work, especially if the United States were firm about compliance. So, I want to make clear that there was no thinking about a decent interval going on here to work out a cynical deal which Kissinger and his associates didn't think would hold up."[61]

The arrangements left 150,000 North Vietnamese forces in the South. The Paris Agreement created a Four-Party Military Commission (U.S. DRV, PRG, GVN), a Two-Party Military Commission (GVN & PRG), an International Commission of Control and Supervision to control and supervise the implementation of the accords, and the National Council on Reconciliation and Concord to arrange elections and the future of South Vietnam. These various commissions were not established and did not carry out their responsibilities.

In a gesture to Saigon, North Vietnamese forces would not be resupplied. Approximately 2 billion dollars of military equipment were supplied to South Vietnam before the agreement went into effect.

The accords called for all U.S. and other foreign forces to withdraw within 60 days and their bases to be destroyed. However, the United States transferred ownership of all its bases to the government of South Vietnam, so no bases were destroyed.[62] Both sides would repatriate all POWs within 60 days.

A North Vietnamese Assessment

The DRV ambassador, Nguyen Khac Huynh, former ambassador to Mozambique, participated as senior foreign-ministry advisor to the DRV delegation throughout the Paris Peace Talks; he gave his assessment of the talks to my Princeton Global Summer Seminar in 2009.[63]

Ambassador Huynh saw that the American delegation was hampered in its efforts because the American people no longer supported the war after Tet. As a result, the United States had to use diplomacy to overcome major difficulties to gain American support. President Lyndon Johnson had laid out the basis for the talks, which President Nixon then inherited.

Secretary Kissinger was a very capable negotiator, very able, according to Ambassador Huynh. The other U.S. negotiators were experienced, highly trained diplomats. U.S. diplomacy was based on strength.

Weakness on the the Vietnamese side, exhausted by years of fighting, hampered the nation. Vietnam's diplomacy needed the support of the international community, particularly from the Soviet Union and China, but also from sympathetic countries such as Yugoslavia and India, which tried to help.

In the wake of heavy fighting since 1963, the question was where the negotiations would begin. As the aggressor, the United States had no basis for negotiations. The United States sent troops to invade Vietnam. How could Vietnam negotiate in such a situation? By 1967, Huynh said, it was evident the United States could not win a military victory, so Washington decided to try to obtain victory through negotiations. After Tet in 1968, the United States' strategy was in serious trouble.

The negotiations were inevitably lengthy because neither side could win a decisive military victory that would force the hand of the other. On the battlefield, the United States depended on the imbalance in forces. Negotiations were intended to achieve victory through diplomatic finesse.

U.S. Goals

In Huynh's view, the United States attempted to end North Vietnamese support of the NLF through the removal of PAVN forces from the South.

Second, the United States insisted on keeping Nguyen Van Thieu in power in the South to fight for public support there against the North Vietnamese.

Third, the United States was determined to secure the release of the POWs, especially the pilots who had been shot down.

Fourth, the United States wanted to secure a decent interval for the Thieu regime to try to withstand the forces of the North and the NLF.

But in the beginning a top objective was to remove all PAVN forces from the South and de-link political and military issues.

North Vietnamese and NLF Goals

A major goal of Vietnam was to avoid the pitfalls of the Geneva Conference, which kept the country divided and, therefore, laid the basis for renewed foreign intervention.

Thus, Vietnam wanted a political settlement as well as a military agreement, a position that the combined DRV and NLF delegations held to strenuously in early negotiations.

The top North Vietnam and NLF goal was the withdrawal of all U.S. forces.

To gain acceptance of two entities in the South politically and militarily, the government of Vietnam and the PRG—as the NLF and Vietcong became—insisted U.S. forces must withdraw without conditions. North Vietnam had the right to defend the nation in any part of the country and therefore to station its forces anywhere needed to this end. The Vietnamese would determine the political government of the South. This was not the business of the United States.

The North advocated the formation of a coalition government including the PRG, SVN, and neutralist elements.

The United States withdrew 400,000 troops between 1968 and

October 1971, and in October 1971 hinted an end of its insistence both sides should withdraw—a fundamental North Vietnamese objective in the negotiations.

Vietnam committed to withdraw its forces from Laos (which in my view, it never did). Commitment by Vietnam to assist Cambodia in restoring peace satisfied the Cambodian aspect of this issue, even though the commitment (from my perspective) went unrealized until 1991.

October 1972

U.S. positions finally began to shift in talks in October 1972 with pressure mounting for an agreement before the 1972 U.S. elections. Kissinger was in a hurry at this point, whereas the North Vietnamese had no domestic pressures for a quick solution.

After three years of talks, the United States finally realized that, even with 1 million U.S. allies, ARVN forces could not win; diplomats had to try to win for them.

In summary, the negotiations began on May 13, 1968, with only one issue decided: The United States had ended bombardment of the North. From 1969 to 1972, the United States tried to gain the support of the American people for withdrawal of U.S. forces, according to Huynh. From 1972, when neither side could win the war, the fighting had to continue. The real negotiations did not begin until that point and took five to seven months to complete. The remaining time was spent trying to gain international and domestic support.

Ambassador Huynh's assessment tracks closely to reality of the negotiations, as I understand them. He authoritatively states formal DRV positions, and his comments on the plight of the Americans are respectful and even sympathetic, reflecting the very difficult position in which the United States and Secretary Kissinger found themselves. The American political crisis stemming from Watergate and the North Vietnamese military invasion of the South in 1975 also fatally crippled the United States' ability to carry out its commitments to President Thieu and South Vietnam.

The United States accepted a settlement very close to the terms proposed by the PRG and NLF in 1969 and 1970, respectively, except President Thieu ultimately could remain as head of the government of South Vietnam. However, the communists were left in a superior military position with the 150,000 North Vietnamese troops that remained in the South. The Council on National Reconciliation was never formed. Finally, Hanoi made the decision to take over the South by force, which it accomplished in April 1975.

Secretary Lord's Rebuttal

Secretary Lord refutes the thesis that a settlement was obtainable in 1969 or 1970.[64] In his oral history, Lord takes this on:

> There is one other retrospective theory that I want to shoot down. I'll make this clear as we go through the chronology. That is, the proposition that the deal we made with the North Vietnamese in 1973, negotiated at the end of 1972, could have been achieved much earlier through a unilateral U.S. withdrawal, and not what we negotiated, which involved withdrawal of American forces, a ceasefire, return of prisoners, and international supervision of the agreement reached. There are some revisionists who claim that, if we had just offered a unilateral withdrawal at some time in the period from 1969 to 1971, we could have had an end to the war at that time.

> This view is absolutely wrong, and I will show why it is. In fact, beginning on May 31, 1971, we offered such an arrangement in the secret talks. The basic problem was that Hanoi's stipulation for an agreement to end the war was that there would have to be a military and a political settlement at the same time. Nixon and Kissinger said, and I agreed, that we would only agree to a military settlement. The political future of Vietnam would have to be worked out by the Vietnamese themselves. More concretely, Hanoi's position was that the United States should get out of Vietnam unilaterally. However, as we left, we would have to overthrow

the South Vietnamese government under President Thieu and help to install a coalition government in South Vietnam. Then we would get our prisoners back. That was their consistent position in the negotiations until October 1972.

At another point, Secretary Lord makes this point again: "I mention this because it was consistent with earlier positions and demonstrates again that the January 1973 settlement could have been reached earlier if Hanoi had been reasonable. For example, the Presidential Statement of November 1969 that called for a ceasefire in place. You could interpret this to mean that the North Vietnamese were remaining at least temporarily in South Vietnam. So, the record will show, especially from 1971 on, that we couldn't have reached the final deal of January 1973 any sooner than we did, contrary to critics' assertions. These critics have been totally irresponsible on this point. The historical record is irrefutable on this point."

In author's view, Ambassador Lord's explanation tracks with the record, and I have enormous respect for his judgment and wisdom. Nonetheless, I believe we should have tried much harder to negotiate a settlement built upon the PRG 1969 proposal. A U.S. proposal for unilateral departure, leaving 150,000 PAVN troops in South Vietnam and President Thieu in place, would have been a tempting offer to make to Le Duc Tho in 1970. I realize the case that Ambassador Lord constructs argues forcefully against my suggestion, but I have the gnawing feeling an earlier settlement might have been achieved. If the U.S. position had changed from mutual withdrawal, as Nixon announced in October 1970 and then backed away from, to allow North Vietnamese forces to remain in the South, why did we not use that fundamental shift as leverage to obtain concessions from Hanoi regarding political issues? Moreover, Kissinger told Zhou Enlai in July 1971 that "the president would agree to complete, unilateral withdrawal of American troops in return for Hanoi's release of American prisoners of war and a ceasefire ('say eighteen months or some period'), under international supervision, as long as the political settlement was left to the Vietnamese people to decide." The Chinese must have passed this on to the Vietnamese, so why did we not make this offer to Le Duc Tho in 1971, or earlier, as well? Instead, for two years we hinted at the change, as

Ambassador Huynh states Hanoi understood, without gaining any advantage from the change which we finally made expressly only in late 1972. Though unexpressed, was this handling designed to give President Thieu and South Vietnam time to adjust?[65]

18

North Vietnamese and Vietcong Strategy

Most American commentators focus on why South Vietnam or the United States lost the American War in Vietnam and pay little attention to why the Vietcong and Hanoi prevailed.

As Marc Jason Gilbert points out in *Why the North Won the Vietnam War*, "Unfortunately, Hanoi could win the guerrilla war merely by not losing to Saigon's less adept forces, and it possessed the political will, human resources, and battlefield strategy to win the war of attrition." Handicapped by the political influences in the United States, America's traditional anti-imperialism instincts, the fear of bringing the Soviet Union, China, or both into the war, and the inability to persuade his South Vietnamese allies to undertake needed reform, Johnson was in no position to win a war of attrition. Hanoi refused to play into Westmoreland's traditional military strategy.[1]

Gilbert sums up his conclusions in sweeping language, which I perceive as accurate: "America's leadership had a limited vision of the nature of the war that helped obscure fatal policy errors, variously attributed to an arrogance of power, to obsessive anti-communism, to the nightmare of appeasement, to an imperial presidency, to a 'can-do mentality,' and to an overly bureaucratic war-making machine."[2]

The Vietminh enjoyed widespread support against the French and subsequently in South Vietnam, especially in the Mekong Delta, Quang Ngai, and Binh Dinh in central Vietnam. Even though Diem's ruthless policies devastated them from 1956 to 1959, the brutal Vietcong exploited popular discontent with the South Vietnamese regime and its American backers. Resentment was profound, and the wily Vietcong obtained a ready audience for dissidence. They eschewed talk of communism or the policies in their political creed and built instead on popular resentment toward the government. They promised an overthrow of their oppressors, return of local government, ending the destruction of war and bombing, ridding the country of the new "occupiers," distribution of land to peasants, justice, and an end to corruption. The Vietcong barely, if ever, mentioned building a Marxist utopia and stressed its efforts to overthrow the unpopular regime and rid the country of foreign "occupiers." This was a winning message.

The appeal of the NLF only grew as the war was Americanized. Westmoreland's attrition strategy, reliance on massive bombing campaigns by air, as well as the search and destroy strategy on the ground, destroyed the spirit and livelihood of peasants. The prominent role of Americans also emasculated the GVN and ARVN in the eyes of South Vietnamese, including peasants.

The Vietcong built on these resentments, constantly recruiting local dissidents for the NLF and utilizing highly visible guerrilla attacks against ARVN and the U.S. forces, then melting into the jungles and villages. The consequent counterattacks resulted in the devastation of the villages, which further corroborated the Vietcong's message.

The Vietcong also lived in an ambivalent environment in the villages, where peasants wished to avoid trouble. Passive acceptance of the Vietcong presence became the norm, especially since within almost every family there were Vietcong and GVN supporters and sympathizers, even among the ostensible GVN supporters, who frequently favored the guerrillas' message.[3]

The great test was Tet, when Hanoi directed the NLF to mount a general uprising in keeping with Mao Zedong's guerrilla-warfare doctrine. In seeming secrecy, the NLF prepared and carried out the offensive under the noses of the ARVN and U.S. forces. Although there were intelligence reports predicting attacks, the depth and breadth of the attacks were unforeseen and a devastating psychological blow against the Americans.[4]

Though the communist leadership considered Tet to be a military failure, it turned out to be the single biggest propaganda victory of the struggle.

North Vietnamese Strategy

Under Ho Chi Minh and General Giap, the Vietminh developed a finely honed, flexible, and inspired guerrilla force during the eight-year war against the French, which ended decisively in 1954 at Dien Bien Phu. After the communists seized control of China, the Vietnamese studied Mao's guerrilla-warfare techniques. The Chinese advised the Vietnamese at Dien Bien Phu on tactics, and they enjoyed direct access to Chinese weapons, financial support, and sanctuary in China.

To the charges of resentment against a repressive and inept government, the communists could then paint the South Vietnamese government as puppets of an occupying force, an unforgivable slur in such an ancient, proud land. The steady expansion of the U.S. role in military and political affairs emasculated the South Vietnamese government and military, as a succession of military coup leaders took over. Even after September 1965, the stable Thieu-Ky regime suffered from the public-relations burden of accepting massive foreign military and economic support.

Hanoi's and the Vietcong's strategy was based on the siren call of liberating the country from colonialist occupiers, equating Americans with the French and rejecting the government as their puppets.

Militarily, the communists only had to survive to win, and their guerrilla mode of warfare, evading the ever-enlarging U.S. military forces' attacks, hit and run tactics, refusal to engage directly the Americans, and chipping away at the ARVN forces and administration, all proved effective in making sure the reduced Vietcong who survived Tet could continue their efforts. Ironically, the Tet Offensive was both the closest the Vietcong came to being wiped out and its most dramatic gesture of continued visibility and relevance.

While the North Vietnamese restrained their presence in South Vietnam until late 1964, when Hanoi first introduced one division into the South, they increasingly began to play a role, especially in the highlands. They were the backup forces for Tet, but after the devastation of the Vietcong forces during and after Tet, PAVN endured most of the struggle. The Spring Offensive in 1972 and the takeover of Saigon and the South in 1975 were principally the work of North Vietnamese.

From serious support during the First Indochina War and early during the struggle against the Americans, Chinese political, military, and financial support and aid was crucial. Chinese funds supported the NLF from 1960. The secret agreement with Hanoi in 1965 provided up to 100,000 Chinese engineers to rebuild roads and bridges; antiaircraft units and MIG-17s; and defense along the Vietnamese-China border. The agreement allowed Hanoi to leave Northern Vietnam to Chinese defense and permitted Hanoi to send its forces to fight in the South. The concern about China's entering the war also served as a restraint on U.S. military activities in the North. Without Chinese aid, the struggle would have been much longer and more difficult.

So, too, the vacuum in Laos allowed Vietnam to use, with near impunity, the Ho Chi Minh Trail through Laos to supply the NLF and its own forces in the South. Similarly, Sihanouk's periodic willingness to ignore Hanoi's use of eastern Cambodian corridors for resupply, rest for forces in adjacent southern Vietnam, and to supply its forces in the South, was important.

If the Vietnamese communists carefully worked to portray themselves as "David," the United States carelessly presented itself as "Goliath." The U.S. bombing campaign brought around much the rest of the world, including Europeans, who saw the destructive bombings in the South and North as an indictment of American policies and moral standing. Hanoi did not ignore public opinion in the United States itself, drawing on Ho Chi Minh's mantra, "the American people are not bad, but the American government is."[5]

Ho Chi Minh and Giap understood, if American civilian and military leaders did not, that a combination of patience and the ability to simply deny victory to the Americans (while killing them in sufficient numbers) over a long-enough period would itself produce victory. In the end, American political resolve to continue fighting crumbled, not because of critical military reversals but rather because of U.S. intolerance of the prolonged and bloody military stalemate. The U.S. military, nonetheless, could have fought in Vietnam more effectively. While it could not have been expected to change its style of warfare, it could have fought with more discerning tactics and strategy. In so doing, it likely would not have changed the Vietnam War's outcome, but it could have increased the price of victory for Hanoi."[6]

All these factors were elements of a successful war, but they were glued together by the iron-willed determination of Hanoi's leadership to reunite the country. Until his decline in health a couple of years before his death in 1969, Ho Chi Minh's uncanny ability to rouse the South and North to mobilize to fight the United States and their South Vietnamese clients was the most important component of their success. Ho Chi Minh achieved this remarkable support because of the simplicity of using nationalism to energize the Vietnamese, despite the odds and dreadful costs. Ho Chi Minh's gentle, familial leadership was the preferred style of Vietnam traditionally. Even after his death, Ho Chi Minh's name remained the banner in fighting for victory in the South.[7]

19

The Aftermath of the 1973 Paris Accords

When the 1973 Peace Accords were signed in January, I was one of 40 FSOs sent as U.S. forces departed to report on military (including Vietcong and NVA compliance with the Paris Accords), political, economic, psychological, and social developments in the wake of the accords. All these FSOs had previously served in Vietnam and spoke Vietnamese.

Along with one colleague, I was sent in February 1973 to the Mekong Delta town of My Tho in Dinh Tuong Province. Our job was to report on developments in the Dinh Tuong, Kien Phong, and Kien Tuong provinces, all sensitive border provinces providing access to North Vietnamese and Vietcong for infiltration or retreat via Cambodia.

As a condition for undertaking what was a risky and disruptive return to Vietnam, the FSOs had insisted that we not report through the embassy, which notoriously edited negative reporting to agree with the judgments of the ambassador and the U.S. military leaders in Vietnam. Secretary of State Kissinger rose to the occasion and agreed to our demands, which were presented by FSOs stationed in Washington. We reported directly and unedited to Washington through four U.S. consulate generals in the four corps into which Vietnam was divided administratively and militarily.

I was excited to return to Vietnam at such a historic moment, despite the risky prospects. Since all American military forces were departing within a few weeks, we would travel around provinces to report where the Vietcong and PAVN had significant presence. We were uncertain how the GVN military and police forces would protect us, especially in the wake of the Paris Accords, which displeased the Thieu government. The assignment was disruptive, in my case, since I was in my last six months working as a political officer at the U.S. Embassy in Taipei in the wake of Nixon's visit to Beijing, which was seen as a grave threat to Taiwan's future. Nonetheless, I was eager to participate at this critical moment in Vietnam.

My Tho was a pretty town on the Mekong River with a famous French seafood restaurant, La Plage, overlooking the river. While the town was safe, there were parts of the province not far away that were contested and known to be dominated and even administered by the Vietcong.

Dinh Tuong Province, of which My Tho was the provincial seat, was home to the Ninth ARVN division, one of the strongest units in the army and so counted upon by the Thieu regime should there be a coup attempt in Saigon. My Tho was also the native home of President Thieu's wife. The town was the center of commerce in the area with rice, fish, and rich resources. Chinese merchants, as was frequently the case in Mekong Delta markets, dominated commerce, including the rice trade.

By comparison to the pleasant safety of My Tho, Kien Tuong and Kien Phong provinces were the "Wild West," much farther from the grip of the central government and its forces. The Vietcong administered parts of all three provinces, and the Ho Chi Minh Trail led straight into Kien Tuong and Kien Phong provinces on the border with Cambodia. Significant PAVN forces were stationed in these two provinces and, because of the Paris Accords, Vietcong and PAVN forces were stationed in protected sectors.

FSO Herb Cochran and I shared a house, with no staff, where we composed our reports and sent them to the consulate general in Can Tho. We had no minders and operated completely on our own. We both spoke Vietnamese and had no problem navigating the provincial and local government offices, where we were warmly received. Similarly, I visited many villages to talk with local officials, schoolteachers, and villagers, and most were warm and happy to talk. I did notice that villagers in contested zones were more aloof and not eager to talk with me. I traveled widely, alone in an International Scout, to the riskier provinces, as well as traveling regularly around Dinh Tuong Province, including, in the daytime, to towns that were very much on the fence in both the ideological and political contests.

My only previous acquaintance with Dinh Tuong was a taxi ride in early 1967 with a close Vietnamese friend from Saigon for a weekend in My Tho. During the ride, the taxi had been stopped at what looked suspiciously like a Vietcong black-pajama checkpoint, but nothing untoward came of it, despite their eyeing me tucked in the backseat of the vintage black Citroen in which we rode.

Thus, I knew no one in My Tho or Dinh Tuong Province when I arrived in February 1973, but I was excited and happy to be in the forefront of reporting what happened when, as stipulated in the Paris Accords, American forces said, "Goodbye, good luck," boarded helicopters, and left me alone at the heliport of My Tho as they flew away to America. It was an exhilarating moment.

Surprise in Dinh Tuong

I had to figure out how to accomplish my objectives and provide meaningful information for Washington to evaluate the results of the agreement, just concluded, ending the Vietnam War. I was particularly surprised with the situation in Dinh Tuong in 1973. When I had left Vietnam six years earlier in 1967, the South Vietnamese government was in a precarious military position, the administration was weak, and popular support was ambivalent.

The government in 1973 was the biggest surprise—it was functioning effectively. The province chief of Dinh Tuong, a lieutenant colonel in ARVN, and his service chiefs were confident in taking the initiative of governing. The province chief frequently traveled around the countryside, and when I accompanied him his confidence and command impressed me.

I worked more closely with the civilian deputy province chief for administration, Nong, who was friendly and invariably receptive. In the province chief's daily morning staff meeting, which I was welcome to attend, he provided instructions to the various service chiefs on aspects of provincial governing—education, health, the economy, security, finance, and the construction of schools and medical facilities. I found him to be effective, responsive to my suggestions, but taking the initiative impressively in deciding, devising, and directing the service chiefs in carrying out their responsibilities. The province chief welcomed discussion, listened to his subordinates, and entertained their suggestions. He held separate meetings with his military advisors, which I did not attend. However, I chatted with military officers and soldiers and asked pointed questions, which they tried to answer. I felt I was dealing with an effective government because it was running the province quite well.

I also worked closely and had lunch with the Dinh Tuong Province's police chief, who was extremely well informed and connected. Much of my best information on the state of security in the province came from the police chief

Traveling to the villages, I could talk with anyone I wished, so I spent time checking schools, health facilities, the economy, and security. I met the local officials and military. I usually had an entourage of tiny children holding my hands, laughing, and calling out their friends to join us on my wanderings.

I also called on the military commanders. On a military level the Ninth Division's performance was impressive: It appeared very much in command, confident, forward-looking, and kept the communist forces on the defensive. Rather than being on the ropes, the Ninth Division was, in fact, gradually pushing the Vietcong and North Vietnamese forces back toward the Cambodian border. This violated the provisions calling for a freeze in military positions by both sides.

This encouraging initial assessment remained during my five-month stay in My Tho. We were dealing with a very different government and military than I remembered from 1967.

There was one discordant note in my assessment. I wrote a long airgram to Washington pointing out that, despite the effective functioning of the government, one figure stood out for his authority and actions—the chief of police from the Interior Ministry. He seemed to occupy a very special place in the province.

Over time I surmised that the police chief was the channel to and from President Thieu and his wife, especially the latter. I concluded he was also the conduit for funds from the province to the president's wife, who was widely thought to be corrupt.

This convinced me, in retrospect, despite the appearance of effectiveness, that corruption was a significant feature of the regime and likely to continue to deepen from 1973, when I left Vietnam, until the collapse in 1975. Even in a secure province, corruption was a fundamental weakness of the Thieu regime.[1]

After my assignment to My Tho, I wrote an assessment of the military equation in the three provinces from which I was reporting. My information came from Ninth Division commanders and officers; the province, district, and village chiefs; and local regional and popular commanders. I derived my conclusions about the Vietcong and NVA proselytizing and intentions from what I heard and perceived in these conversations.

20

Perspective on Soviet and Chinese Roles in Vietnam

Following his assumption of power in Vietnam in September 1945, Ho Chi Minh sent a letter to Moscow seeking to establish relations, but like the United States, Moscow did not respond. Moscow did not recognize the Democratic Republic of Vietnam until January 30, 1950, following Beijing; but Moscow was an indifferent observer from 1954 to 1964.[1]

Throughout this period, Moscow had several competing goals in Vietnam. The Soviets did not want to disturb relations with the United States, particularly as U.S.-Soviet relations moved toward détente. Initially, the USSR did not wish to provide military assistance to Vietnam because it preferred a negotiated settlement of issues. At the same time, it wanted to make Vietnam a reliable member of the Comecon bloc.[2]

Despite serving as co-convener with the UK at the 1954 Geneva Conference, the USSR had few direct interests in Indochina. The USSR enjoyed friendly relations with communist China after Mao seized power in 1949. Moscow supported the communists in the Korean War but relied on China to carry out the war effort. In the 1950s, Moscow saw remote Indochina as a backwater, left within Beijing's sphere of influence, and an unlikely agent for the world revolution Soviet international proletarianism advocated. However, the USSR played a significant role in devising the settlement in Geneva and pressed the Vietnamese to accept less than they wanted to end the struggle against the French, even though Ho Chi Minh had lived and served the Comintern in Moscow for five years. Moreover, Moscow had supported reliable pro-Soviet Vietnamese apparatchiks in the 1930s and saw Ho Chi Minh as a nationalist, more interested in independence for Vietnam than in the international proletarian revolution.

Moscow remained much more focused on its Western neighbors, consolidating its control over Eastern Europe, and then expanding its influence further into Western Europe, the Middle East, Latin America, and Africa.

Despite sponsoring the conference, the Soviet Union exercised no role in post-Geneva Indochina. Neither the British nor the Soviets raised an outcry when Vietnam did not hold the 1956 elections, despite their roles as overseers of the Geneva Conference outcome.[3]

After denouncing Stalin at the 1956 twentieth Communist Party Conference, Khrushchev undertook the policy of "peaceful coexistence" and détente with the United States. As part of this policy, Moscow abetted the status quo in Vietnam, preferring a peaceful resolution of Vietnam's problems rather than an armed struggle. Moscow also underestimated the strength of revolutionary forces in South Vietnam and the potential influence that Vietnam's experience might contribute to global proletarian revolution.[4]

The USSR provided little economic and military aid to North Vietnam in the late 1950s, since Moscow's priorities lay elsewhere. This aloofness continued until Moscow began to envisage a more robust role in the "Third World" in the early 1960s. After the Bay of Pigs invasion in 1961, Moscow began a new relationship with Cuba, an island hitherto firmly in the American sphere. Moscow decided to pursue a much more activist role, directly opposing American hegemony around the world. This was exacerbated by the growing difficulties between China and the Soviet Union in the 1960s and Moscow's efforts to remain the principal advocate and supporter of global revolution in its competition with China. Through its more robust foreign policy, Moscow attempted to counter Beijing's drive to label the USSR as revisionist and reactionary. In this context, Moscow added Vietnam to its circle of global interests.

As Ilya V. Gaiduk observed in *The Soviet Union and the Vietnam War*, it had become clear to Moscow as early as 1959 that Vietnam intended to use military force to reunite the country and "save" the South from the "domination of American imperialists" and their accomplices. In the early 1960s, as the U.S. buildup grew from a small advisory to a more prominent and vocal role of support for South Vietnam, Moscow began to step up its aid to Hanoi.[5]

As mentioned earlier, the NLF, established on December 20, 1960, inspired by communists and supplied by North Vietnam, provided the mechanism for achieving "liberation." Following the Lao Dong Party's Ninth Plenum in December 1963, the North Vietnamese prepared a paper for a meeting between Le Duan and the Soviets in Moscow that voiced strong determination to prepare a general uprising in the South by forming "powerful armed units throughout South Vietnam." Despite pressure from Le Duan, the Soviets remained cautious in Vietnam. In a 1964 speech surveying the world's problems, General Secretary Nikita Khrushchev mentioned Vietnam, along with Korea and Germany, saying, "It was necessary to avoid the use of force, to allow the peoples of those countries [including Vietnam] to resolve questions of unification peacefully."[6]

As the Sino-Soviet split became more apparent, China deepened its role in 1962–64, as Vietnam was increasingly viewed in the context of the Sino-Soviet rivalry. Moscow aimed to be seen as more vigorous than China in its support for Third World proletarianism and anti-imperialism. The Soviet leaders postured as promoters of peace as opposed to warmongering revolutionaries. China, in contrast, did not promote its image as a peaceful force but emphasized its revolutionary character. Thus, in response to the American military buildup and increased role in Vietnam, Moscow and Beijing rushed to outdo one another in supporting the revolutionary regime in Hanoi, both for its intrinsic advantage and to counter the other.[7]

The Soviet Union also attempted to pry Vietnam away from China. Khrushchev made clear Moscow's general support, but he also made clear that the close cooperation sought by General Secretary Le Duan was not available so long as Hanoi maintained its revolutionary (pro-Chinese) positions. The Soviets thereafter provided propaganda support but not the arms and other supplies Hanoi sought.[8]

Because it was walking a fine line between obligatory pro-communist support and diplomatic caution, the Soviet leadership hoped the conflict in Vietnam would not escalate. In the 1964 U.S. election Moscow preferred Lyndon Johnson over the hawkish Barry Goldwater, but events after the elections, especially the Gulf of

Tonkin incident, disappointed Moscow's hopes for a moderated conflict.[9]

As the conflict escalated in the mid-1960s, Beijing and Hanoi concluded new agreements on arms supply. Not to be outdone by its communist rival, Moscow also constructed economic and military supply agreements with Hanoi. They hoped closer relations with Vietnam would improve ties with Thailand, Malaysia, and the Philippines to woo them away from American influence. So, despite its ideological differences with Hanoi, Vietnam's strong nationalist streak, links to rival China, and Moscow's strong desire to pursue détente with Washington, Moscow carefully increased its aid to Hanoi.[10]

Washington's Perspective

Washington valued the Sino-Soviet split, and its abiding concern was of a rapprochement between the Soviet Union and China. Consequently, as Washington attempted to strengthen relations with both Moscow and Beijing, it had to be careful not to let the simmering conflict in Vietnam unite the two communist powers.

Several possibilities were envisaged:

If the United States failed to take strong action to counter the perceived "China threat" to Southeast Asia, Moscow might conclude that a restoration of the Sino-Soviet Alliance was desirable. Secretary of State Dean Rusk promoted the notion that any stunning Chinese success in Southeast Asia or along the Indian border could trigger such a development. This was a stretched variation of Eisenhower's domino theory.

Others, including Senate Majority Leader Mike Mansfield, took a different tack. With the Korean experience fresh in mind, they worried that a vigorous U.S. military action against North Vietnam, including bombing near the Chinese border, could trigger China's full-fledged entry into the Vietnamese conflict. Some also believed a harsh attack on North Vietnam might lead China and the Soviet Union to reunite in efforts to support Vietnam against the United States.

However, most in Washington concluded the Soviet Union was

not enthusiastic about the military conflict in Indochina and was not willing to jeopardize relations with the United States for the sake of a country in Southeast Asia that had not been important to Moscow historically.

These conclusions were questioned when Soviet Premier Alexei Kosygin visited Hanoi in February 1965 to consolidate Soviet-Vietnamese relations. A North Vietnamese attack on the U.S. base in the highlands during the meeting could have been coincidental. Nonetheless, the attack on Pleiku was used by Washington to justify the bombings that began against North Vietnam—ignoring the damage they could cause to U.S.-Soviet relations. During Kosygin's visit, with rivalry with China very much in mind, Moscow took a more positive interest in Vietnam as a demonstration of support for international proletarianism and world revolution. At the same time, Kosygin was careful not to ignore Moscow's commitments to the West regarding détente and favoring peaceful resolution of Vietnam's problems.[11]

Despite the unfortunate timing of the Pleiku attack in the wake of Kosygin's visit, the Soviets increased material and financial support for North Vietnam and by 1968 exceeded the support China was providing Hanoi. General Secretary Brezhnev raised the Cold War temperature by denouncing American imperialism for its "assault on the independence and integrity of a socialist country" and proposed sending Soviet volunteers to Vietnam, a possibility he continued to raise for some time. In fact, at one time in the late 1960s, there were 1,165 Soviet experts in Vietnam, including pilots and advisors on advanced weaponry, but these were crack military experts, not "volunteers."[12]

Brezhnev's mention of volunteers received a mixed blessing in Hanoi, because, if Hanoi accepted Soviet volunteers, how could it turn down other Eastern European and Chinese volunteers, which would complicate and undermine Hanoi's goal of its own sacred fight for independence. Vietnam had a long history of Chinese and European troops who overstayed their welcome, and Hanoi therefore was cautious about accepting foreign ground troops.

General Secretary Le Duan reciprocated Kosygin's visit by traveling to Moscow in May 1965. During his visit, Moscow agreed to provide modern weapons to Vietnam—fifteen MIG-15/17s, 100 armored personnel carriers equipped with antiaircraft guns, and IL-28 light bombers, all shipped by rail through China. Supplies later expanded to include surface-to-air missiles, rockets, and antiaircraft guns, designed to assist North Vietnam in its defense against American bombing. Moscow also sent Vietnam industrial and telecommunications equipment, medical supplies, machine tools, iron ore, and nonferrous metals. Some 2,600 Vietnamese were sent to the USSR for training in the air force and in air defense.[13] By 1967 Soviet aid amounted to the equivalent of $618 million (in U.S. currency) of a total of $1.5 billion (U.S.) provided by all East European socialist countries to aid North Vietnam.[14] (Unless otherwise specified, all dollar signs [$] in this text denote U.S. currency.) The following year, the Soviets boosted their share of aid to over half. Moscow also voiced full support for Phan Van Dong's "Four Point" proposal for resolution of the conflict. While this support was welcomed in Hanoi, the Vietnamese were anxious not to become too close to Moscow and rarely kept the Soviets closely informed about their plans, especially military ones.

Soviets' Role in Peace Efforts

Despite concerns, Washington, paradoxically, welcomed a Soviet role in Indochina as a counter to Chinese influence. President Johnson sought to use Moscow to cajole Hanoi into a peace settlement, but his efforts were, it seems to the author, clumsy and confused. Military and diplomatic efforts were frequently at odds, undermining peace feelers at crucial junctures. Moreover, despite their distaste for the Indochina conflict, the Soviets were extremely careful not to press the Vietnamese too hard for fear this would drive Hanoi further into Chinese arms.

In addition, despite the Vietnamese theoretical commitment to pursue political and military goals espoused by Moscow and Beijing, the urge to struggle for national goals dominated their strategy. Above all, Hanoi wanted a military victory over the United States, a position encouraged by the Chinese. Nonetheless, Soviet leaders regularly encouraged Hanoi to look at the possibilities for a negotiated settlement.

Washington remained torn between those who advocated intensified bombings and those who supported a more vigorous diplomatic effort. The 37-day bombing pause that started in December 1965, undertaken in consultation with the Soviets, was the first. It led to nothing.

There was another Soviet display of activity in late 1966, when a Polish diplomat and representative to the International Control Commission (ICC), Janusz Lewandowski, inserted himself as an envoy to North Vietnam to try to encourage negotiations with the United States. Washington assumed the Soviets were behind the Pole's activities, but Moscow did not want the Vietnamese to perceive heavy pressure from the Soviets. Thus, Moscow camouflaged its role from Hanoi. A new U.S. bombing campaign near Hanoi scuttled these hopes.

In February 1967 the United States attempted a new initiative, tagged "Sunflower." An American diplomat approached the Vietnamese in Warsaw at the same time U.K. Prime Minister Harold Wilson encouraged an extension of a 1967 bombing pause during Kosygin's visit to the UK. Wilson conveyed a proposal for mutual restraint by Hanoi and Washington in their troop replacement. Warsaw conveyed a much tougher message to the Vietnamese with the demand that all North Vietnamese forces poised to go south halt. Despite knowing Hanoi did not favor negotiations at that point, the Soviets nonetheless pressed Hanoi for an opportunity to open talks. As reported by Karnow, Phan Van Dong's reply arrived late in the middle of the summit: "Stop the bombing and the North Vietnamese would immediately go the negotiating table." Fearful of being dragged around at a negotiating table as the French had been, Johnson wanted results in advance to which the Vietnamese could not agree. The proposal led nowhere. Wilson was aghast that Johnson had spoiled the first serious opportunity to engage Kosygin and the Soviets in efforts to end the war. Johnson resumed the bombing. A promising opportunity ineptly mishandled embarrassed Kosygin.[15]

A visit by Kosygin to a special UN General Assembly meeting on the Middle East in June 1967 provided the first opportunity for President Johnson to meet Kosygin, and the "Glassboro, New Jersey" summit was organized for a full exchange for the first time between the two. The talks on Vietnam were perfunctory. We now know the Vietnamese were preparing for the Tet Offensive of February 1968 and therefore had little interest in negotiations.

It was the Tet Offensive and Johnson's announcement that he would not run for reelection that led to the start of the Paris Talks in the spring of 1968. Soviet pressure on Vietnam played little, if any, role in Johnson's decision.

Nixon "Links" Advances with Soviets to Vietnam War

As mentioned, Nixon framed the Vietnam War as one of the critical 'linkages" that could unlock improved relations with the Soviets, who shared the desire for strategic-arms talks and improved economic ties. The commencement of peace talks in Paris relieved Soviet fears that the Vietnam War might spread and lead to a wholesale U.S.-Soviet confrontation. The talks were an assurance that conflict would be contained.

With Nixon, the Soviets steadfastly resisted any attempt to have them mediate between the United States and Vietnam but were willing to play a limited role of messenger between the two. This lesser role was dictated by Soviet preoccupation in 1968 with threat of the "Prague Spring." Just as talks began, reform attempts in Prague challenged Soviet hold over crucial Czechoslovakia and threatened Poland, East Germany, and indeed the whole Soviet Empire. Soviet attention turned to this existential crisis at the expense of conflict in distant Indochina. The outbreak of military hostilities between China and the Soviet Union on the Ussuri River in the spring of 1969 further clouded the Soviet role regarding Vietnam.

Rumors in 1971 of secret talks between Washington and Beijing and the deterioration of Sino-Soviet relations raised the stakes for all three players. When Nixon decided to "play the China card" and visit Beijing, Nixon and Kissinger were eager to exacerbate tensions between Moscow and Beijing but were careful not to go as far as to produce a counter-reaction that might lead to reconciliation. Luckily for the United States, Brezhnev's principal goal was to strengthen U.S.-Soviet relations, and he was especially eager for Nixon to visit Moscow in 1972. When the China trip was announced for February, this only strengthened Brezhnev's determination to have the Nixon visit take place later in June. Nixon's gamble of playing the USSR and China against each other worked in the Sino-Soviet context, leading to improved leverage with both countries.

Despite Kissinger's insistence on Moscow's help on the Vietnam front, there was little Moscow could do, for example, regarding Hanoi's 1972 "Spring Offensive." For the first time, North Vietnamese regulars overtly crossed the DMZ en masse, occupied Quang Tri Province, and threatened Hue and Loc Ninh near Saigon. These moves raised profound questions about Nixon's Vietnamization plan and led to massive retaliation on the eve of Nixon's visit to Moscow in June. Washington accused Moscow of colluding in the offensive, which was not true, of course, but it put Moscow on the defensive—to the pleasure of Nixon and Kissinger. Moscow denied a role and accused the Chinese and Vietnamese of conspiring to damage the Nixon-Brezhnev summit.

During the 1973–75 period, Moscow did, however, urge Vietnam to honor the Paris Peace Accords by holding back on new military offensives. General Secretary Brezhnev made these points to Le Duan in July 1973, as did Premier Kosygin to Premier Phan Van Dong the same year. Professor Pham Quang Minh (University of Social Sciences and Humanities, VNU) told the Princeton seminar students that in early April 1975 the Soviet ambassador to Vietnam urged Phan Van Dong to end its military operations in South Vietnam.[16]

Nonetheless, after reunification in April 1975, the Soviet Union wished to strengthen its ties with Vietnam. As Vietnam's relations with China deteriorated in the late 1970s, Moscow stepped up its efforts to strengthen relations with Vietnam. As Vietnam prepared to invade Cambodia in late 1979, Moscow concluded a Treaty of Friendship with Vietnam that included security commitments to Vietnam. Under pressure from Cambodia and China, Hanoi finally, after resisting for years, agreed to join Comecon, the Warsaw Pact's economic bloc.

China's Role

China's role was much more involved from the start of the Indochina wars, as it had a much deeper history with its southern neighbor—2,000 years of troubled history between Vietnam and China and repeated efforts on China's part to absorb Vietnam until the nineteenth century. In the contemporary era, China's deep fear of American forces surrounding its border, and rivalry with the Soviet Union for leadership of the Communist movement, especially as the Sino-Soviet split deepened, further complicated Sino-Vietnamese relations. Finally, concern that Vietnam might independently dominate the former Indochina (present-day Cambodia and Laos) and domestic developments during a turbulent period of China's history all contributed to the role China pursued in the conflict between America and Vietnam.

From the first decades of the twentieth century, similar anti-imperial and modernizing struggles linked Vietnam and China. These ties were personal as well as political. Ho Chi Minh and his Vietminh movement lived and had been nurtured in China for several years before returning to Vietnam at Bac Po in 1941. Ho Chi Minh had gotten to know many of the Chinese leaders, including Zhou Enlai. In the late 1940s, during Mao's struggle with the Kuomintang, despite the Vietnamese struggle with the French, Ho Chi Minh reciprocated and allowed the Chinese communists to cross into Vietnam for refuge.

China was also intimately involved in the Vietminh struggle against the French, particularly from 1950 to 1954. The Chinese provided weapons (rifles, pistols, machine guns, mortars, artillery, and bazookas), sustenance, and a significant number of advisors to help train and advise the Vietnamese in developing their soldiers and battle plans against the French. After Mao took power in 1949, China would serve as a rear base, which was of critical importance to the outcome of the Vietnamese struggle against the French.

Chinese generals helped plan the border operations, countering the Navarre Plan in 1953–54, and contributing to the counteroffensive that led to the siege of Dien Bien Phu. Some Chinese military advice led to failure, such as encouraging General Vo Nguyen Giap to attack French strongholds in the Red River Delta, which led to massive Vietminh losses. The mass frontal assault, tried initially at Dien Bien Phu, was similarly costly.

On the political front, Mao's peasant-centric communism was more influential than Stalin's industrial-proletariat strain of Marxism. The Chinese promoted and helped devise the 1953 land-reform program similar to Mao's programs in China. While the distribution of land was successful, the class struggle—pitting rich and middle-class property owners against the peasants—was at variance with Ho Chi Minh's united-front tactics. In the 1940s, Ho's tactic successfully brought together a broad base of shopkeepers, petit bourgeoisie, intellectuals, and farmers of all classes in the fight for independence. Land-reform policies, conversely, stirred animosities that would take years to overcome. Truong Chinh, who directed the land reform, was fired because of the class-struggle emphasis he adopted from the Chinese. He nevertheless remained a member of the Politburo. Ho Chi Minh and General Giap both publicly expressed regret with the excesses of Vietnam's land reform.

Zhou Enlai played a major role at the Geneva Conference in 1954, the first international outing of the new Communist Chinese government. Zhou skillfully avoided turning the conflict into an international issue, as had happened in Korea. Because of the Korean War and the need to concentrate on Chinese economic recovery, Zhou helped settle nettlesome issues that ousted the French, prevented further war, and kept the United States from intervening in Vietnam in support of the French, another major Chinese goal at Geneva. Keeping the United States away from Chinese borders has been a historic goal of Beijing. The United States did, of course, intervene in support of the nascent South Vietnamese government.

Zhou also managed to separate Laos and Cambodia from Vietnam's sphere of influence, in the face of Vietnamese determination to supervise the futures of those two young states. A larger Indochina might have threatened China's interests. Vietnam agreed to withdraw its forces from Laos, although it never withdrew. Through these provisions, Zhou undercut Vietnam's goal of an Indochina Federation. Zhou's contention that neither Laos nor Cambodia was ripe for revolution and "revolution cannot be exported" also undermined Vietnamese goals.[17]

Zhou, with Soviet and French aid, prevailed on Vietnam to accept the critical provision for a temporary separation of the two Vietnams at the 17th parallel, a repatriation of soldiers and civilians to either zone, and national elections in 1956. Hanoi never forgave the Chinese for betraying its reunification goals at the Geneva Conference. This created a new and permanent suspicion about Chinese-communist goals vis-à-vis Vietnam. There were also residual complaints about China's patronizing attitude and chauvinistic Han superiority over Vietnam, while the Chinese found the Vietnamese stubborn, unwilling to admit mistakes, or change course.

The moderate results at Geneva were in keeping with Zhou's "Five Principles of Co-Existence," which became China's mantra as long as Zhou dominated China's foreign policy.[18]

Consolidation and Reunification, 1954–61

Following the Geneva Conference, Ho Chi Minh had two primary requirements: rebuilding the ravaged Vietnamese economy and reunifying the country. The Chinese prepared to provide considerable assistance in economic recovery, repairing irrigation facilities, recovering farmland, preventing famine, and building transportation and telecommunications systems. Vietnam looked to China as the model for many social, economic, and political reforms. However, Stalin and Mao pressed land reform upon Vietnam; but Hanoi chose to follow the Chinese rather than the Soviet model. In contrast to Moscow's urging of peaceful coexistence, Beijing urged Hanoi to undertake and prepare for a long struggle. Because of China's own economic difficulties, Mao softened his material support in 1954–56 for communist insurgencies. But Mao did not lessen his ideological support in the long term for revolution. Moderation was a temporary expediency.

The uprisings in Poland and Hungary in 1956 also gave pause as to the best course for Vietnam to follow, and those events must have perplexed Ho Chi Minh. Preoccupied with the uprisings in Eastern Europe, Moscow focused on its backyard. Those events did not distract China from its interests in Vietnam, but Beijing was nonetheless engrossed in its "Great Leap Forward."

With domestic turmoil abating, Zhou Enlai declared that North Vietnam remained the base for reunification and urged the North to develop its economic and political institutions to provide strength for the struggle and eventual success. China in the mid-Fifties urged North Vietnam to concentrate on building socialism at home and leave the southern question for later. But by 1960 the Chinese agreed with Hanoi—armed struggle would be required for reunification, and Beijing would support that struggle but insisted on the pursuit of political and armed struggle in tandem.[19]

Accordingly, in December 1960, Hanoi established the NLF as the public and political face of the Vietcong in the South. Beijing immediately recognized the NLF and began to provide financial support to the organization.

In July 1960, the Soviets abruptly withdrew their economic assistance teams from China, and the Sino-Soviet rift that had been building became apparent. The North Vietnamese were dismayed and for some time attempted to play the role of peacemaker to overcome the rift. Their efforts came to naught.

Distancing China from the Soviet orbit, Mao identified China with the underdeveloped world of Asia (including Vietnam), Latin America, and Africa. Mao's "Third World Theory" thus emerged.[20]

Geneva Conference on Laos

The 1962 Geneva Conference reestablished the "neutral" status of Laos and displayed one interesting aspect of Vietnam's relations with China—Chinese jealousy over Vietnam's strong ties with the Communist Pathet Lao. This reflected China's continuing concern about a dominant Vietnamese role in Laos and Cambodia, despite China's support for Vietnam. Indochina under Vietnam's aegis might take all three countries away from the Chinese orbit and could form a small but significant block to the expansion of Chinese influence into Southeast Asia. China would subsequently attempt to leapfrog Vietnam through its influence with the anti-Vietnamese Khmer Rouge.[21]

China provided more explicit assurances to Vietnam in 1963, promising to serve as Vietnam's "rear" if war with the United States broke out. These assurances were made at about the same time the Buddhist crisis erupted in South Vietnam. The assassination of Ngo Dinh Diem in November, and the ineffectual military regimes that followed, further heartened the NLF, Hanoi, and Beijing. It was at this stage that Mao assented to the increased North Vietnamese dispatch of a few companies, and even battalions, to the South, while China continued to advocate guerrilla warfare.[22] As relations with the Soviets deteriorated and the situation in the South became perilous, Hanoi continued to argue for deployment of North Vietnamese main forces to the South.[23]

In 1961–63, China's clear support for Vietnam, in contrast to lukewarm support from Moscow, led Hanoi to lean toward the Chinese side in the Sino-Soviet rift, though not universally. Le Duan and Le Duc Tho took the lead in this tilt, while Giap resisted. For this reason, General Vo Nguyen Giap was shunted aside, and several of his close friends were also purged. The pro-Soviet Vietnamese faction nevertheless supported many of China's diplomatic objectives. In line with Hanoi's tilt to China, Hanoi opposed the U.S.-Soviet Partial Nuclear Test Ban Treaty in line with Beijing's insistence that socialist countries not be denied nuclear options. Beijing was preparing for its 1964 nuclear test.[24]

While Hanoi followed Beijing's international call for revolution, domestic industrial policies in Vietnam followed Soviet models in building state socialism. This meant Hanoi after 1960 followed more orderly procedures, investing in infrastructure and state-owned enterprises, building agricultural facilities and production and regulated industries. Hanoi had been consolidating this Soviet pattern of bureaucratic administration and hierarchy. Vietnam emphasized bureaucratic management and shunned the Maoist model of popular mobilization and mass movements. Hanoi pursued parallel policies adopted by Liu Shaochi and Deng Xiaoping in the wake of the Great Leap Forward in 1958–63. Liu and Deng did not adhere to the Maoist idea of "uninterrupted revolution."[25]

After the Tonkin Gulf incidents in August 1964, Mao told Hanoi if the United States invaded North Vietnam, China would send troops as "volunteers" to support Vietnam, as it had done for North Korea during the Korean War. China increased its own military defenses in South China, sent fifteen MIG-15s and MIG-17s to Vietnam, and agreed to train Vietnamese pilots and build new airfields in Vietnam.[26]

As mentioned, North Vietnam sent its first division to the South in December 1964.

China's Aid

While Soviet aid surpassed China's by 1968, Beijing continued to supply major assistance to North Vietnam. Beijing was the chief supplier of hard currency (dollars) to the NLF, in addition to sizeable supplies of food and arms. More important, in a secret 1965 agreement between Hanoi and Beijing, China agreed to send military units to the northern provinces of Vietnam. The force was to reach from 60,000 to 100,000 by 1967, consisting of railway and conventional engineer units and other military-support units. There were also regular troops responsible for anti-aircraft defense of the North Vietnamese provinces and three aircraft regiments of MIG-17 jet fighters to defend North Vietnamese territory against American airplanes.[27]

On June 8, 1965, Zhou Enlai (through President Julius Nyerere of Tanzania and Foreign Minister Chen Yi on May 31) sent the message to the UK *chargé* in Beijing, "China will not provoke war with the U.S., but if the U.S. bombs China, that would mean war, and there would be no limits to war. The United States got the message and stayed clear of the Vietnamese-China border. The United States made very clear its intentions in talks in Warsaw that it had no plans either to destroy North Vietnam or to invade the PRC."[28] The total number of troops China sent to Vietnam between June 1965 and March 1968 was 320,000, including engineers and advisory personnel. At the peak in 1967, China had 170,000 soldiers in the DRV. They operated antiaircraft guns, built and repaired roads, bridges, and rail lines, and constructed factories. This allowed PAVN to send far more troops to South Vietnam. When the Chinese forces withdrew in August 1973, 100 Chinese soldiers had died and 4,200 had been wounded.[29]

By late 1964, the Chinese agreed to Hanoi's proposal to send North Vietnamese forces to South Vietnam to enter the conflict. The fact that Chinese troops were necessary to defend sacred Vietnamese territory was intrinsically contradictory, and, to Hanoi, their presence also represented a long-term danger to Vietnam's independence. This danger was thought to be mitigated because Hanoi and Beijing were ideologically very close, sharing views about the nature of revolutionary struggle and the national-liberation struggles in Southeast Asia. They also shared views of the broader international struggle between communism and capitalism and were less sympathetic to coexistence at this point than the Soviets.

Nonetheless, reports surfaced in 1965 that Hanoi had become suspicious of Beijing's long-term intentions in Southeast Asia. Ho Chi Minh attempted to balance its relations with Beijing and Moscow and not become overly allied with either. The Cultural Revolution Mao instigated in 1966 fed directly into growing wariness about China, particularly when Beijing encouraged similar pandemonium in Vietnam. The Soviets also used problems with a shipment of military support materials to Vietnam to urge the Vietnamese to raise this issue with the Chinese, in part to create friction between the two.[30]

Arguing against Hanoi's plans for Tet, China did not share the hopes of some in Hanoi that a "general uprising" would succeed in achieving the withdrawal of U.S. forces. Beijing continued to advocate a protracted guerrilla struggle in the rural south rather than a frontal assault on the cities.[31]

In response to U.S. escalation of the war over the coming months, and until it peaked in 1968, China continued to increase its aid and support for Vietnam. The Chinese, through 1968, urged the Vietnamese to keep up the protracted struggle for victory. China's opposition to negotiations with the United States stemmed from China's international position calling for continuous revolution against "imperialism and revisionism." Mao wanted the Vietnam War to continue to tie down and weaken the United States, so the United States would not have military forces to deploy elsewhere. Moreover, he hoped victory in Vietnam would be a brilliant example of national-liberation movements globally.[32]

As outlined, the Soviets occasionally were involved in efforts to start U.S.-Vietnam talks. Hanoi finally agreed to start talks in 1968, despite firm opposition from Beijing. Should the United States, with Soviet connivance, succeed in finding peace in Vietnam, it might lead to Mao's strategic nightmare—U.S.-Soviet collusion to dominate the world. In 1969–70, China withdrew its advisors, and support dropped markedly in response to Hanoi's decision to begin peace negotiations with the United States.

China Relents on Negotiations

By late 1968, China began to relent on Vietnam's negotiations with the United States. China became more concerned about the threat from the Soviet Union and the possibility of a Soviet attack against China. The Soviets' smashing of the Prague Spring and the announcement of the "Brezhnev Doctrine" — that the Soviet Union reserved the right to intervene in any socialist country where socialism was threatened—coupled with talk of "taking out" the Chinese nuclear facilities at Lop Nor significantly raised fears in Beijing and focused attention on the threat from the north.[33]

At the same time, by 1968 Washington had made it clear the United States would be withdrawing from Vietnam and thereby reducing the influence and threat of the United States on China's southern border. With Sino-Soviet tensions running high, Beijing preferred a gradual American retreat to leave the United States strong so Washington could continue to be an effective counterbalance to the Soviet enemy.

Thus, even China, the most ideological of the great powers of the time, shifted its policies toward Vietnam to fit the evolving equation of superpower politics.

Nixon Goes to China

At the time of Nixon's visit to China, Hanoi reminded Beijing of its mistake at the Geneva Conference in 1954 when China forced Vietnam to accept the continued, if supposedly temporary, division of Vietnam. Hanoi resisted China's proposal to discuss Vietnam with Nixon.

During Nixon's visit, Beijing insisted that China would continue to support Vietnam fully, despite rapprochement between China and the United States. China followed the promise to the letter and showed Hanoi the transcript of the discussion to prove it. The desirability of a successful peace agreement before the U.S. elections in the fall of 1972 was apparent in Hanoi, as elsewhere. Beijing's concessions to Washington on the central question of Taiwan during Nixon's visit heightened Vietnamese fears that China was again prone to sell out. If Mao was willing to cede territory in China, he was not likely to remain steadfast regarding the territory of Vietnam.[34]

However, China saw Vietnam's victory in 1975 as vindication of the efforts of the millions of Vietnamese who had fought to achieve victory over the Americans and now deserved better lives. Vietnam's success represented the beginning of the collapse of Western imperialism and the rise of Marxism-Leninism. America's arrogance in the face of the indomitable determination of the Vietnamese people led to its defeat. The Chinese believed that America had underestimated the impact of their loss and reached the wrong conclusions. China saw America's defeat as integral to the decline of America and its dominant influence in the world.[35]

But while 1975 brought a brief period of celebration and solidarity, relations between Vietnam and China quickly degenerated to their lowest point in centuries. In subsequent years, Vietnam's fears of Chinese intentions in Cambodia and Vietnam's invasion and subsequent occupation of Cambodia in December 1978 led in February 1979 to the "lesson" China hoped to teach its unruly southern neighbor. Relations were only normalized in 1991, when China successfully demanded that Vietnam's deputy prime minister, Nguyen Co Thach, who was thought by the Chinese to be too "pro-American," be replaced.

Nguyen Co Thach was placed under house arrest until August 1995, exactly the time I arrived to open the U.S. Embassy in Hanoi. Nguyen Co Thach had worked assiduously since 1977 to normalize relations with the United States and, of course, almost achieved that goal in October 1978. My reading of Thach's motives, based on my meetings with him, was that he was acutely aware of the historic dangers of the giant China and thought closer relations with the United States would serve as a barrier to China's ambitions in Southeast Asia.

Moreover, he was aware of the key role the United States played in the international economy, particularly in the international financial institutions. Since Vietnam's moribund economy vitally needed international support to rescue it, normal relations with the United States would be crucial to achieving international economic access. Relations with the United States would foster access to the international economy, including specifically from the principal non-Chinese economies of Asia, such as Japan and South Korea. Despite the Chinese shunting Thach aside, this was exactly the path Hanoi chose so successfully to follow.

21

Postwar Vietnam and Cambodia

I was assigned to the embassy in Bangkok in the summer of 1977 as deputy political counselor. Since 1975 all Americans had been evacuated from Vietnam and Cambodia, so the Bangkok embassy served as the most pertinent American listening post into the communist regimes of Vietnam and Cambodia. Thus, I was also assigned to serve as the "Indochina watcher." My principal responsibility was to interview refugees from Vietnam, Cambodia, and Laos to understand what was happening in the three countries, especially Vietnam and Cambodia, where the United States had no relations or representatives. I interviewed hundreds of refugees on the Cambodian-Thai border—those fleeing Pol Pot, those fleeing the Vietnamese after their occupation of Cambodia in 1979, and hundreds of Vietnamese boat people in the refugee camps in Thailand and Malaysia who fled because of conditions in Vietnam. I learned a great deal about what was happening and had happened in Vietnam after the takeover of the South in 1975.

From the refugees I learned of a Vietnam that was victorious in war but severely strained under the weight of the devastation of the war and its own economic mismanagement. From the neo-Stalinist model adopted from 1957 until 1976, the communist party's objectives were spelled out at a plenum meeting in 1974, putting forth a five-year plan (1976–80) that did not consider the rapid collapse of the South in 1975. Under review, as Adam Fforde reports, Hanoi decided to proceed along the same lines in both zones of Vietnam.[1] The broad objectives were to promote "three revolutions: production, ideology and culture, and science and technology."

Extra energy was to be devoted to science and technology out of the belief that industry and commerce in Vietnam were burdened by primitive technology characterized by small-scale and labor-intensive techniques.

Emphasis was on heavy industry—coal, iron, machinery, hydroelectric power, and improvement of the transportation and communications sectors. But plans for agriculture were equally ambitious, calling for annual increases of 8 percent, achieved through improved irrigation, fertilizer, higher yields, increased croplands, and planting subsidiary crops in collectives to be established throughout the South and which already existed in the North. The South pursued many of these objectives, especially in the early Seventies, but, after the dislocations of 1975–78, needed a new push.

Following the takeover of South Vietnam in 1975, under the direction of Nguyen Van Linh, a southerner who, despite the Plenum decisions described above, took a comparatively moderate approach and reduced the fear of southerners somewhat of North Vietnamese and Communist domination. Pro-NLF southerners were relieved by Nguyen Van Linh's comparative moderation.

In southern economic policy, Hanoi at first went slowly, stating that only "bourgeois compradors, speculators, and hoarders would be subject to punishment, William Duiker reports."[2]

No changes were announced for the agricultural sector "as long as South Vietnamese worked for the nation, they need have no fear," wrote William Duiker, quoting announcements by the new Vietnamese government.[3] Land reform under the South Vietnamese government and the Vietcong, both of which had already distributed most land to the tillers, deprived the communists of clear political advantage on the issue at this juncture.[4]

Debate on "Socialist Transformation"

Following the takeover or "liberation" of the South, serious, complex debate emerged in Vietnam about consolidation of victory—how to revive the national economy while building a socialist society in a hitherto capitalist South full of (usually Chinese) entrepreneurs, comprador classes, and former regime officials. Vietnamese leaders also had to decide how to deal with the murderous and xenophobic regime that emerged on Vietnam's southwestern border in Cambodia.[5]

There was considerable interplay among these policy challenges, but I will attempt to disaggregate them into the economic, human, and Cambodian challenges. Nonetheless, they are in some instances so intertwined that this will almost be impossible.

There was from the start a vigorous debate between those, such as Secretary General Le Duan and senior party official Do Muoi, who thought the north and south should be reunited quickly and a "socialist transformation" undertaken at the same time. There was also special concern about securing control of the southern economy from moneylenders, warehouse owners, big businessmen, and manufacturers and distributors. This involved mostly ethnic Chinese from Cholon and the other bigger towns of the south, particularly in the Mekong Delta—My Tho, Bac Lieu, Soc Trang, and Can Tho—and the anti-Chinese implications incensed China.

Reunification intentions were announced in July 1976 to the surprise of the NLF, PRG, and foreign countries who thought the notion of a separate state in South Vietnam, at least for a time, was likely. Several countries had even opened embassies in Saigon. The government hastily renamed Saigon "Ho Chi Minh City." Mme Nguyen Thi Binh, who was foreign minister of the PRG government at the Paris Peace Talks and vice president of Vietnam from 1992 until 2002, told the Princeton Seminar in 2007 that, from her point of view, "the sooner reunification took place the better;" but she acknowledged "all Southerners did not agree."[6] Indeed, most did not.

By late 1975, opinion in the Politburo began to shift in more doctrinaire directions. Nguyen Van Linh continued to urge proceeding slowly. But, in a summer 1977 speech, hardliner Secretary General Le Duan called for socialist consolidation. Editorials in the government newspaper, *Nhan Dan*, embraced the cause. By August the Politburo decided to proceed simultaneously with complete reunification and socialist transformation. The leadership shifted to reflect the hardline positions, with the comparatively moderate Nguyen Van Linh replaced by his deputy, Do Muoi, who was committed to early reunification and socialist transformation. By early 1978, Do Muoi moved ahead with both.[7]

From the Vietnamese "boat people" I interviewed in Thailand and Malaysia, I heard a great deal about socialist transformation. To initiate socialist transformation, in February 1978, youth shock troops invaded Cholon, the huge Chinese section of Saigon, and seized warehouses and goods; owners were reimbursed, but at greatly depressed prices. Protests broke out in Cholon to oppose these unpopular policies, but the participants were arrested.

In March 1978, Vietnam nationalized all remaining large-scale commercial and industrial enterprises, leaving only small-scale family business in private hands. "Youth shock troops" raided businesses to confiscate supplies and worked to prevent former owners from evading new regulations. The March raids were more efficient and netted larger numbers of capitalists; it effectively wiped out the big merchant classes, mostly ethnic Chinese, in South Vietnam. The goal of "Socialist Transformation" was the elimination of enterprise and the exertion of state control of the economic system. As a result, business stagnated. Inflation set in. Goods were scarce. Industrial production rapidly declined.

The government offered compensation worth only a fraction of the value of the goods. Some 30,000 businesses were taken over, leading to disruption in production and distribution. Secretary General Le Duan was intrigued by Soviet *agrogorods*, which clustered 30,000 to 40,000 people in agricultural–industrial communities, especially moving the population from north to southwest along the Cambodian border.[8] Many were former ARVN soldiers.

Collectivization of agriculture in the South began simultaneously with the elimination of private enterprise in the cities. At first, farmers formed joint work-exchange teams and collectively set production goals, purchased seeds, fertilizer, and equipment from government agencies, but initially retained ownership of their land and draft animals.

Through the remainder of the 1970s, the farmers were increasingly cajoled or forced into collectives, or New Economic Zones (NEZs). Resistance was frequently passive, such as refusal to meet production goals. In protest, farmers fed their rice as *basede*, a rice wine, to pigs and then ate the fatted pigs rather than surrender the rice or pigs to government quotas. The NEZs were more like prisons, and starvation was common. Politically, life in the cities was not productive and was regarded as corrupt. People were sent to the NEZs to work and live.

Agriculture was hit in 1978–80 by a combination of bad weather and new collectivization policies. As peasants lacked incentive to produce and some communities passively resisted the new regime, production plummeted. Hunger became widespread in the South.

The economic results of these events were not as desired —production of rice, for example, plummeted from 13 million metric tons in the South to 11 million tons, 5 million tons short of the targeted goals for 1977–78. By the early 1980s only 3,000 of an approximately 13,000 agricultural collectives in the South had not collapsed.[9]

Industrial production also fell—South Vietnam became a drag on the national economy rather than providing the bounty anticipated.[10]

Hundreds of thousands sought to flee and boarded small boats, trying to escape to Thailand and Malaysia, where I interviewed hundreds from 1967 to 1990. Of the estimated 1.5 to 2 million who sought to flee, the United States accepted 543,000 refugees (988,000 refugees and immigrants by 2000); Britain accepted more than 19,000; France accepted 128,000; Australia 238,000; and Canada 192,000. Many ethnic Chinese fled to Hong Kong and China.[10a]

Financial Difficulties

Hanoi's plans quickly ran into trouble. To seamlessly transition to a socialist economy, Hanoi had counted on large sums of foreign assistance, which did not materialize. The Soviet Union kept aid at previous levels. Because of growing tensions, China reduced its aid and, when Vietnam joined the Soviets' Council for Mutual Economic Assistance (CEMA) in 1979, China withdrew its economic advisors and ended all remaining economic assistance.

The $4.7 billion promised by Nixon, of course, was a dead letter. Of the Western nations, only France and Sweden provided significant aid.[11]

After Vietnam's occupation of Cambodia in 1979, even though U.S.-Vietnam trade was minimal, the United States ordered an embargo on trade with Vietnam and denied Hanoi access to the International Monetary Fund (IMF), World Bank, and Asia Development Bank. Other countries, such as Japan, moved glacially to increase economic exchanges with Vietnam. Despite passage of a liberal investment law, private foreign investment was scarce, reflecting concern about a risky economy and questionable business practices.

The transition from a wartime to peacetime economy also produced problems. Wartime managers were not necessarily those needed for business or commerce, and many of the qualified commercial classes had fled, been pushed from the country, or were undesirable in the new socialist economy.

In the South, the rigid new rules were disregarded and hoarding was common, since farmers did not accept the low prices offered by the government for their rice and other food commodities.

While marginal economic reform began in 1979, real changes did not start until 1986 with *Doi Moi*, after Ho Chi Minh's Stalinist successor Le Duan died and was replaced by the same Nguyen Van Linh who had overseen the flexible Socialist Transformation program in the South after 1975. Fundamental reform further accelerated in 1989, as the Soviet Union collapsed and Tiananmen Square frightened Hanoi as well as Beijing. American discussions with Hanoi of POW/MIAs and a road to normalization took place against this evolving economic change.

Cambodia: The Khmer Rouge

Conditions in Cambodia under the Khmer Rouge were devastatingly worse than in beleaguered Vietnam. In 1975, the Khmer Rouge emptied Phnom Penh of the bulk of its population, driving people out of the cities of Cambodia. The Khmer Rouge used an ancient Khmer name, "Angkor," as the conceptualized ruler of the Khmer Rouge revolution. In "Angkor's" name, they murdered, tortured, and terrorized their own people and unleashed a radical social-reform process to create a living hell for all Khmers. The refugees from the cities found that "Angkor" had followed them into the countryside as they sought to return to their original rural homes to survive. Urban dwellers, teachers, capitalists, shopkeepers, intellectuals, those with any connection with foreign nations, and those who wore glasses were killed under the orders of "Angkor." Farmers worked as slaves of "Angkor." Any sign of deviation from orders, questioning, or independence could result in death. On the border I heard Khmer refugees from every corner of Cambodia recount countless times that mothers, fathers, brothers, sisters, and other relatives had been killed by Khmer Rouge cadres or taken to "Angkor" with poles and beaten to death for minor deviations.

The Khmer Rouge sought to turn Cambodia back into utopian agrarian collectives. Industry was shut down. Cities became ghost towns.

As we now know, probably two million of some seven million Cambodians died from executions, disease, or being worked to death.

"Angkor," it turned out, was the small group of Khmer intellectuals who studied together at the Sorbonne in Paris and took back to Cambodia their idealistic notions of creating a utopian agricultural society. We know their names—Pol Pot, Nuon Chea, Ieng Sary, Son Sen, Khieu Samphan, and Ieng Thirith—but the Khmer whom they drove from the cities and those who operated the vast killing fields only heard of them as "Angkor."

The Vietnamese Invasion

After the Vietnamese invasion and occupation of Cambodia in December 1978, Khmer continued to flee across the border, fearful of what life might be like under Vietnamese occupation. But many others felt the yoke of the Khmer Rouge rising. By February 1979, I heard from Khmer refugees on the Thai border that Khmer were trying to return to their homes and find their families. A certain amount of chaos had set in. Many were farmers, and they frequently said that they were preoccupied with searching for loved ones and homes and had not planted crops. Staying primarily on the border, I increasingly heard that farmers were not planting crops. This phenomenon deepened in March.

The embassy sent cables to Washington reporting on this finding and began suggesting that this meant severe food shortages were likely. In early April, Assistant Secretary Richard Holbrooke sent a cable to our superb ambassador, Morton Abramowitz, asking if the reports were reliable. The ambassador responded, "Dick, the reports are being written by your good friend, Desaix, and they are, of course, absolutely reliable." With that message, Holbrooke mobilized Washington. USAID, working with the Thais, amassed huge quantities of food, medicine, tents, and tarpaulins to care for the Khmer who emerged on the border. When a throng of 200,000 Khmer crossed the border en masse in June in huge clouds of dust, the administration was ready and responded immediately and effectively, undoubtedly saving thousands of lives.

22

Early Efforts for Normalization

The Vietnam War and Watergate scandal made the American people fervently hope for honesty in government, and Jimmy Carter seemed like just the man, in part because he had vowed to never tell a lie.

As a candidate, Carter had focused especially on foreign policy in Latin America, the Middle East, and China, but, in a bold and controversial move, the newly inaugurated President Carter extended a full and unconditional pardon to nearly 10,000 men who evaded the Vietnam War draft.

Even before the smoke had cleared from Saigon, the POW and MIA issue entered U.S. domestic politics and came to impede efforts to normalize the relationship with Vietnam. During the 1976 presidential election campaign, President Gerald Ford insisted that accounting for the missing from the war be done prior to normalizing relations with Hanoi, effectively precluding any chance of early movement.

Although candidate Carter refused to apologize to Vietnam for the war, he sought reconciliation with Vietnam. His election as president opened a window for sidestepping the POW barrier to reconciliation. On December 17, 1976, just weeks before Carter's inauguration, the House Select Committee on Missing Persons, led by Congressman Sonny Montgomery, released a report concluding that "No Americans are being held alive as prisoners in Indochina or elsewhere as a result of the war in Indochina," and that "a total accounting by the Indochinese governments is not possible and should not be expected."[1]

The debunking of the POW charges against Vietnam ostensibly

provided opportunities for Carter's foreign-affairs team. Secretary of State Cyrus Vance and Assistant Secretary for East Asia Richard Holbrooke, who headed President Carter's Asian foreign-policy team, believed it was in the national interest to normalize relations with Vietnam. Reflecting the priorities of the Carter administration, the president dispatched a distinguished delegation led by Leonard Woodcock, president of the United Auto Workers (UAW), to Hanoi to seek resolution of the POW/MIA question. The Woodcock delegation, including Senate Majority Leader Mike Mansfield, UN Ambassador Charles Yost, Congressman Sonny Montgomery, and human-rights activist Marian Edelman, arrived at Gia Lam Airport March 17, 1977, less than two years after the fall of South Vietnam in 1975.

In an initial standoff, Vice Foreign Minister Phan Hien called for reparations as the *quid pro quo* for accounting for the MIAs. Woodcock urged Hanoi to accommodate the humanitarian request for accounting without conditions. During a break, however, Woodcock conveyed the notion of delinking of aid and accounting in a way that led Phan Hien in the next session to discuss MIAs, normalization, and economic assistance as separate but closely related issues. While the Woodcock mission departed without striking a grand bargain, a conceptual breakthrough began to emerge when Woodcock pledged to promote humanitarian assistance to Vietnam and the Vietnamese produced twelve sets of MIA remains as a token of good faith. From a deep winter in relations and just two years after the fall of Saigon, U.S.-Vietnamese relations appeared to be starting on a positive trajectory.[2]

To sweeten the atmosphere at the next round between East Asia Assistant Secretary Richard Holbrooke and Vice Minister Phan Hien in Paris May 3–4, 1977, the president authorized a waiver for $5 million in private humanitarian aid to Vietnam, despite the trade embargo. Holbrooke tried to convince Hien that indirect aid after normalization might be possible. But, ignoring the massive violation of the Paris Accords Vietnam committed in 1975, Hien insisted the United States deliver the $3.5 billion in grant aid plus $1.5 billion in commodity aid that Nixon had promised in a letter to Premier Phan Van Dong dated February 1, 1973.[3]

To bolster his claim to billions in aid, Phan Van Dong released the secret letter from Nixon containing a promise to provide $4.7 billion of assistance.[4] Reaction to the letter was harsh and swift. Congress passed a binding amendment to prohibit the administration from negotiating reparations, aid, or any other form of payment to Vietnam. The bill, passed by a 266 to 131 majority, ended any flexibility in the U.S. negotiation stance and, therefore, any chance of early movement.

A third Holbrooke-Hien meeting in December 1977 produced no solution to the aid question, but Hien proposed a Phase A and Phase B approach, whereby normalization would occur first and aid would be provided later. After delays and uproar from the trial of an American for spying, and despite several hints of new flexibility from Hanoi, no new meeting was scheduled.

An independent visit in the summer of 1978 by a delegation led again by Congressman Sonny Montgomery, in which the Vietnamese returned fifteen more sets of MIA remains, raised optimism in Hanoi that a settlement was possible.[5]

When Holbrooke met Vice Foreign Minister Nguyen Co Thach on September 22, 1978, in Paris, Thach continued to press for aid as part of normalization. Holbrooke broke off the talks two times, but in the third session Thach agreed to normalization without conditions. Holbrooke was jubilant. Their deputies would iron out the details, and the Vietnamese foreign minister would sign the normalization at the UN in early October 1978.[6]

Americans then stalled, citing the impending congressional elections as an excuse. Carter's own team, led by National Security Advisor Zbignew Brzezinski and Leonard Woodcock, who had since been appointed ambassador to China, urged Carter to postpone normalization to avoid offending the Chinese during the ongoing negotiations to move to full normalization.

Holbrooke's deputy, Robert Oakley, negotiating in New York with Thach's lieutenant, Tran Quang Co, raised three issues that, he said, required Hanoi's response before normalization could move forward: (1) the question of the large number of boat people escaping from Vietnam; (2) Vietnam's intentions regarding Cambodia, where the Vietnamese appeared poised to attack the Khmer Rouge regime, then a Chinese ally; and (3) Vietnam's intentions vis-à-vis the Soviet Union. These justifiable reasons for not proceeding were

voiced, but the overarching reason—China's and Brzezinski's opposition—was not.[7]

The massive Vietnamese invasion of Cambodia in December
1978 halted the path to normalization. In September 1979, Bob Oakley told me that on October 10, 1978, while he and Holbrooke read
the morning intelligence reports together, Holbrooke exclaimed,
"My God, they are going to invade Cambodia." Oakley raised this
with Tran Quang Co in New York, who denied it, but Oakley then
raised it with Co's deputy, Le Mai, pointing out that an invasion
would be a disaster and take ten years for Vietnam to overcome.
Oakley asked if there was not another way to deal with the Cambodian problem, such as working through the UN.

Le Mai, who was vice minister when I went to Hanoi in 1995
and extremely helpful to me in opening and running the embassy, acknowledged Oakley's first point—an invasion of Cambodia
would be a disaster, but regarding an alternative, he said, "That's
the only way they know how to deal with it."[8]

I was unsurprised when Vietnam continued to show signs of
mounting a full-scale invasion in late 1978.

Vietnam's Invasion of Cambodia

As "Indochina Watcher" in the U.S. Embassy in Bangkok since the
summer of 1977, I reported extensively on the initial incursion by
Vietnam into Cambodia in December 1977. I noticed in the U.S.
government's Foreign Broadcast Information Service (FBIS) radio
reports that fighting was breaking out among Khmer Rouge groups
in the northeast provinces of Cambodia, Mondolkiri, and Ratanaki-
ri. I reported by telegram that Khmer refugees on the Thai border
told me Vietnam was recruiting Khmer Rouge dissidents in those
same provinces and taking them back to Vietnam to train for an
invasion. Vietnamese forces crossed the Cambodian border in December 1977, punishing the Khmer, and then retreating back across
the border.

After that incursion in the summer of 1978, I reported that Vietnamese refugees I interviewed in the Thai-Malaysia refugee camps
knew trains were shipping heavy weapons and Soviet military

equipment from the North to the Cambodian border in Tay Ninh Province. In addition, the Vietnamese military was building up its forces across the border in 1978. FBIS also reported increasingly vitriolic propaganda from Vietnam and Cambodia. The Cambodians were threatening to retake territory lost to Vietnam in the eighteenth century all the way to Saigon. The Vietnamese I interviewed were reporting myriad Cambodian attacks across the border, the killing of soldiers and peasants in Vietnam, beheadings in which the heads were mounted on posts, vitriolic verbal exchanges, and southern movement of Soviet military material in Vietnam.

I sent numerous telegrams to Washington weaving all these items together into a fabric of preparation for another invasion, confident both Holbrooke and Oakley were reading them. They were, of course, receiving a variety of reports, including from the Intelligence and Research Bureau (INR) of the State Department and the CIA, who were undoubtedly reading the same FBIS reports. However, I was the sole firsthand reporter with direct reports from Khmer and Vietnamese refugees. Considering my conclusions and reports, the fact that the United States seemed to be moving steadily toward normalization with Vietnam was surprising to me.

The signs had been evident since the summer. I foresaw mounting, telltale indications that an invasion was highly likely. Most significantly, the continuing Vietnamese buildup on the Cambodian border, shipping of military supplies south, and threatening vituperations across the border, as well as the arrogant provocations from the Cambodian side, indicated that a second Vietnamese invasion was probable.

For months, the State Department (meaning Holbrooke, Oakley, and INR) asked that my telegrams reporting on developments in Vietnam and Cambodia be repeated to all East Asian posts and, as appropriate, provided to friendly governments in ASEAN, Japan, South Korea, Australia, New Zealand, and Thailand. From this, I assumed they all were reading my reports.

As I understood their position, Holbrooke and Oakley concluded that the hope for early normalization with the United States would serve as a brake on an invasion of Cambodia and Hanoi's steady movement toward the Soviet Union. This assessment persuaded Holbrooke and Oakley to discount what I foresaw—that a full-scale invasion was imminent and not likely to be halted by the U.S.-Vietnam talks. I raised this with Holbrooke and Oakley subsequently, and they argued that normalization was a powerful goal in Hanoi and it could have forestalled these developments. I remained skeptical, given the developments I tracked from Khmer refugees on the Thai border and Vietnamese refugees in the Malaysian boat-people camps regarding invasion.

These differing assessments of the likelihood of a second invasion of Cambodia by Vietnam resulted from our having different sources. My information came principally from Cambodian and Vietnamese refugees, not usually a terribly accurate source of intelligence. However, in this case they provided tidbits that I thought indicated a pattern of preparations for a second invasion. Holbrooke and Oakley engaged with Vietnamese who were dealing with people close to the decision-makers in Hanoi, and those Vietnamese were anxious to conclude the agreement with the United States, particularly Foreign Minister Nguyen Co Thach. During my own meeting in 1996 with Thach, he told me he had opposed the occupation of Cambodia. Thach probably himself hoped normalization with the United States might deter the Politburo in Hanoi from what Thach's lieutenant, Le Mai, foresaw as a "disaster."

Other issues notwithstanding, Vietnam concluded a security treaty with the Soviet Union in November 1978, and the subsequent invasion and occupation of Cambodia in December ended any movement toward normalization.

The invasion resurrected discussion of the Pol Pot regime and whether the United States or the international community had failed to react to the horrendous genocidal regime in Phnom Penh. After its anguished experience in Vietnam, the United States was exhausted and in no mood to reengage in Southeast Asia. I had reported from the Thai-Cambodian border over the past year and a half, based on interviews with hundreds of Cambodian refugees, of the pervasive Khmer Rouge atrocities against the Cambodian people after the Khmer Rouge takeover of Phnom Penh on April 17, 1975. Although there were fervent calls from American human-rights advocates for U.S. intervention against the Khmer Rouge, the Ford administration and Congress were adamantly opposed to a U.S. unilateral or multilateral effort to oust the despicable Pol Pot regime.

Not inconsequentially, the modern nation-state had its origins in Europe in the Peace of Westphalia of 1648 and developed in several grand transformations into the current form at the end of World War II. As enshrined in the UN Charter, Article 2, a stable international order has been based on the sovereignty of nation-states and the inviolability of national borders, an understanding that prohibits one nation from invading another.[10]

In keeping with the UN Charter, the focus of U.S. efforts in Cambodia was denying legitimacy to the puppet Khmer Rouge Heng Samrin that Vietnam installed in Phnom Penh after it overthrew the Pol Pot regime. Although the approach was widely criticized in the United States and elsewhere as protecting the Democratic Kampuchea regime, the United States judged it was essential to avoid acceptance of a fait accompli, the Heng Samrin regime, implanted by another state, Vietnam. We worked with ASEAN, China, France, and Japan on a solution that would end Vietnam's occupation of Cambodia while avoiding the return to power of the Khmer Rouge. This position paralleled the widespread condemnation of the Soviet invasion and occupation of Afghanistan on December 24, 1978. The two invasions prodded an international consensus of firmness in dealing with both invasions.

Vietnam, Laos, and Kampuchea: Reagan Administration Tests the Waters

Richard Holbrooke, assistant secretary of state for East Asia and Pacific Affairs, and his deputy, Robert Oakley, rewarded me for my reporting on Indochina, by making me country director for the three Indochinese countries in the summer of 1980.

The efforts by Secretary of State Cyrus Vance and Holbrooke to achieve normalization with Vietnam were aborted by Vietnam's Treaty of Friendship with the Soviet Union, the joining of the Soviet Comecon, and Vietnam's invasion and occupation of Cambodia in December 1978–January 1979. In the fall of 1980, Ronald Reagan was elected president.

Surprisingly to me, the Reagan administration decided to test Hanoi's willingness to end Vietnam's occupation of Cambodia as a step toward normalization with the United States. Initially, it was thought the deputy assistant secretary, John Negroponte, would conduct a meeting with the Vietnamese. Then the administration decided one step down was a preferable level. Thus, as the country director for Vietnamese, Laotian, and Cambodian affairs—the next level down—I was the obvious choice to conduct the test.

The Vietnamese Ministry of Foreign Affairs' North American Affairs director, Tran Quang Co (with whom East Asia deputy assistant secretary Robert Oakley had worked in 1977), and I met in New York in January 1981. We met first in a neutral room at the UN building, after which I invited Mr. Co and his associates to lunch at a nearby restaurant. Co spoke English and French, as well as Vietnamese, of course; he was urbane, cultivated, and friendly, but firm. He spoke with obvious authority. I explained to Co that the United States was prepared to move toward normalization of relations with Vietnam if Hanoi agreed to withdraw from Cambodia

Mr. Co contended that Vietnamese forces were in Cambodia at the request of the Cambodian government of Heng Samrin, whom the Vietnamese had installed during the 1978–79 invasion. Politely but firmly, Mr. Co steadfastly defended Vietnam's actions, stating that the occupation of Cambodia was in response to calls from the legitimate government of Cambodia for Vietnam's support of it. This was an issue between two sovereign countries, he insisted, and the United States had no role in the matter. In Vietnam's view, those who called for Vietnam's withdrawal were in effect supporting the return of Pol Pot and the Khmer Rouge to power. The United States should recognize the "new realities" in Cambodia. Vietnam was prepared to undertake discussions on normalization, but it could not accept U.S. demands for withdrawal from Cambodia. This was not an appropriate matter for U.S. involvement. Co was a polished diplomat, thoroughly conversant in every aspect of the issues, but not confrontational, despite the firmness of his responses.

Over the lunch I hosted at a small French restaurant, we went round and round, back and forth across this wide gulf. There was no flexibility in Hanoi's or Washington's stance regarding Cambodia and, therefore, no prospect for moving to normalize relations. In keeping with the administration's desire to keep the meeting low-key to avoid a firestorm of criticism from the right wing in

Congress, there had been no publicity about our meeting, and it remained secret.

The impasse surprised neither the administration nor me, but I was pleased we had at least made the effort and that the focus had been exclusively on Vietnam's withdrawal from Cambodia, despite residual animosity in the United States toward the Vietnamese regime. The Vietnamese position on Cambodia proved intractable, and thus our relations remained frozen.

When I opened the embassy in Hanoi in 1995, Tran Quang Co was vice minister of foreign affairs, a solid friend of U.S.-Vietnam relations, and extremely helpful to me.

UN Conference on Kampuchea

As mentioned, the Vietnamese occupation had occurred at the same time that Soviet military forces invaded and occupied Afghanistan, and the parallel stiffened Western resistance to Vietnam's actions. We turned to efforts to resolve the Cambodian issue as the path to normalization with all of Indochina. The United States worked assiduously to prevent the return of the government of Pol Pot to power, to hold internationally supervised elections, and establish a neutral Cambodia. To these ends, we agreed to work for a Conference on Kampuchea (Cambodia's official name in the UN). The United States and ASEAN, especially Singapore and Indonesia, saw the issue in very similar terms. We also worked closely with China, with which we shared a common objective—getting Vietnam out of Cambodia. Singapore's representative, Kishore Mahbubani, and I were close personal friends, and we found ourselves very much on the same track, so cooperation was easy and effective. The question of the seat at the UN, occupied by Pol Pot's Democratic Kampuchea, was very difficult. China approached it from the point of view of its own national interest. The United States detested the murderous Pol Pot regime but decided legally to deny the UN seat to the Vietnamese puppet Heng Samrin if we were ever to realize the departure of Vietnam from Cambodia. ASEAN agreed. Tactically, we were with China on this, but the administration was pilloried for taking this position.

A chief sticking point was the refusal by the coalition of countries, including the U.S., to recognize the Heng Samrin government installed by Vietnam. While Vietnam contended that the Heng Samrin government should occupy the Cambodian seat in the UN, the coalition insisted that the seat could not be passed to a foreign-imposed government in Phnom Penh. This meant that the government of Democratic Kampuchea (Pol Pot's Khmer Rouge government) should continue to occupy the UN seat until internationally supervised elections were held. The firm adherence of the Reagan administration to this position raised outcries in the United States and elsewhere that the U.S. and its coalition were supporting China's policy of support for the murderous Pol Pot government. I felt strongly that the U.S. position was correct. My strong conviction was grounded in the belief that invasions of other countries were unacceptable, and any regime imposed as the consequence of such an invasion should not be accepted. This was an essential component of a civilized world. At the same time, after having interviewed hundreds of Khmer escaping to Thailand from the Khmer Rouge regime in Cambodia, there were few more horrified than I by the Pol Pot regime. This did not change my abhorrence of foreign invasions.

In 1981 ASEAN, strongly supported by the United States and others, successfully pushed for a multilateral solution to the Cambodian problem. These efforts resulted in the Conference on Kampuchea, convened by the UN General Assembly, led by the special representative of the UN secretary general for Cambodia, Rafeeuddin Ahmed, and held in June 1981 at the UN in New York. John Negroponte, deputy assistant secretary of State for East Asia and Pacific Affairs, and I attended the conference and worked closely with ASEAN, Japan, China, the UK, and France to devise a settlement along the lines described above. Three Cambodian factions, which opposed the Heng Samrin government in Phnom Penh, participated in the conference: the United National Front for an Independent, Neutral, Peaceful and Cooperative Cambodia (FUNCINPEC), led by Prince Norodom Sihanouk; the Khmer People's Liberation Front (KPNLF), led by Nationalist Son Sann; and the Government of Democratic Kampuchea (Pol Pot), led by DPRK Foreign Minister Ieng Sary, one of the very small group of Khmer later charged with genocide by the UN.

The Heng Samrin regime was not invited. We worked with the other delegations to draft the proposed plan, which would require the withdrawal of all foreign forces from Cambodia, self-determination through UN-supervised elections by the Cambodian people, measures to ensure that the Khmer Rouge would not return to power, and the diplomatic neutrality of Cambodia. These "measures" were not spelled out but would include UN peacekeeping forces.

Negroponte carefully avoided being photographed with Ieng Sary, did not shake his hand, or even meet him by chance; nor did I.[11]

I worked closely with Kishore Mahbubani, a senior diplomat from Singapore, drafting the conclusions as we reached agreement along the lines described above. Vietnam and Heng Samrin denounced the proposal, but it remained on the table and served as the template for the ultimate settlement of the Cambodian impasse in 1991.

POWs and MIAs

Throughout the Eighties, political pressure was also growing in the United States on the POW/MIA issue. Progress was painfully slow in the early years, but the United States emphatically supported full accounting of the POW/MIAs. The U.S. government team worked closely with the National League of Families of Missing Americans, led by Ann Mills-Griffiths. The POW issue was most salient on the political front. There were near-constant rumors in the Eighties of POW sightings, rumors that inspired frequent criticism, especially from right-wing senators and congressmen. The companion MIA issue required intensive searches in Vietnam for the remains of the missing.

Initially, Vietnam doled out remains during congressional and other visits, which led to suspicions that the Vietnamese were selling the remains. But during a visit by General John Vesey to Hanoi in March 1986, Vietnam returned seventy sets of remains thought to be those of missing Americans, undoubtedly signaling a desire to improve relations with the United States. General Vesey had succeeded in 1986 in convincing the Vietnamese to permit U.S. search teams to operate throughout the country. This was a major development in getting this issue under control, even though the process continues today.

Subsequently, Congress passed a resolution urging normalization with Vietnam under three conditions: (1) liberalization of Vietnam's economy; (2) Vietnam's withdrawal from Cambodia; and (3) "emptying the warehouse," i.e., returning the alleged 400 sets of remains in a Hanoi warehouse, as a Vietnamese mortician reported. Conservative politicians and the League of Families seized on the report as proof of Vietnam's duplicity on the subject.

This was a story that never went away, despite serious doubts about charges that the Vietnamese held large numbers of MIA remains. When I went to Hanoi, I was to make accounting for the POW/MIAs my top priority. After appeals to the Vietnamese government, Vice Foreign Minister Le Mai told me emphatically, and I believed correctly, that there were no remains stored in a warehouse in Hanoi.

The George H. W. Bush Administration's Initiative

Upon assuming office in January 1989, George H.W. Bush's administration undertook a new, comprehensive approach to Vietnam. Under the leadership of East Asia Assistant Secretary Richard Solomon, the United States developed a policy that outlined a road map for normalization of U.S.-Vietnam relations. Working closely with other "UN Perm Five" nations (France, the UK, China, and the Soviet Union), Solomon developed a Cambodia "peace plan" that was, in effect, a detailed elaboration of the draft plan for implementation of the Kampuchea Conference of 1981. But Cambodia was not the only issue of concern in Washington.

Assistant Secretary Richard Solomon, in his oral history for the Association for Diplomatic Studies and Training (ADST), described the process:

> The issue for the United States was how far we should go with the Vietnamese towards normalization in the absence of fully resolving the POW/MIA set of issues. Therein lay tremendous bureaucratic fights, and the League of Families

[of Vietnam Veterans], led by Ann Mills-Griffiths, was determined to resist the expansion of our dealings with the Vietnamese towards normalization unless, in her view, they came clean with the return of 400 or more remains. The United States (Solomon) ended up creating a detailed field investigation and accounting process based on efforts led by former General John Vesey, who was the president's personal representative on POW/MIA accounting.

By the summer of 1990, the Permanent Five had agreed on a mechanism for settling the Cambodia issue, so the question had become whether as we moved to settle the issue, and as the Vietnamese withdrew their forces from Cambodia, would we concurrently move to normalization with the Vietnamese. After big internal struggles on the POW/MIA issue, we (Secretary Solomon) negotiated with the Vietnamese what became known as the "road map" for normalizing relations. The "road map" included some very specific benchmarks of performance that we expected of the Vietnamese in terms of POW/MIA accounting, in response to which we would lift the trade embargo and otherwise move forward to dismantle elements of our confrontation with the Vietnamese that had grown out of the Vietnam War.[12]

Building trust among all parties was essential, and Secretary Solomon worked assiduously to achieve it. Distrust on the Vietnamese side was obvious but expected, and Solomon eventually disarmed their mistrust. He and his team also worked diligently and succeeded in gaining the trust of the POW/MIA community.[13]

An initial effort by the Perm Five to bring together all Cambodian factions in 1990 failed because Hanoi urged Phnom Penh not to attend.

After consulting at Secretary of State James Baker's Wyoming ranch on July 29, 1990, with Soviet Foreign Minister Shevardnadze, without telling any other capitals (including ASEAN), Secretary Baker unexpectedly told the press that the United States was prepared to meet "all Khmer sides" except the Khmer Rouge. This broke the stalemate. The Vietnamese prepared to negotiate with the Perm Five based on this breakthrough.

By August 1990 the Perm Five, plus co-chairs of the Paris Conference, Indonesia and ASEAN, all agreed on the "peace plan," though at that point, Vietnam and Cambodia (then run by Hun Sen, another ex-Khmer Rouge commander friendly to Vietnam) still held off.

Vietnam's withdrawal from Cambodia in 1989 occurred against the backdrop of a quickly shifting geopolitical landscape favoring normalization. The Tiananmen crackdown seriously isolated China, which took steps in September 1990 to improve relations with Vietnam after Hanoi had withdrawn from Cambodia. Hanoi welcomed a thaw in relations with China because the USSR, Vietnam's leading benefactor, was retrenching and would soon disintegrate. The rebalancing of Vietnam's ties to the great powers encouraged its withdrawal from Cambodia, which in turn unlocked the "road map" to normalization with the United States. Vietnamese Deputy Prime Minister and Foreign Minister Nguyen Co Thach made a final effort to normalize U.S.-Vietnam relations by returning 25 more sets of remains. Thach visited Washington in October 1990 as a reward.

In a secret summit in Chengdu, China, in September 1990, Vietnam and China began normalization talks; they officially re-normalized ties in November 1991. The Communist Party Ideological Tsar, Dao Duy Tung, the fourth-highest official in the Politburo and a highly conservative figure in Hanoi's leadership—with whom I had a significant meeting on U.S.-Vietnam relations after I opened the embassy in 1995—represented Vietnam in Chengdu.[14]

Solomon finally presented the "road map" to Vietnam's UN ambassador in March 1991. Shortly thereafter, General John Vesey, who would become intimately involved in working for normalization with State Deputy Assistant Secretary for East Asia Ken Quinn, visited Hanoi to explain the road map. Thach angrily retorted that the road map had quietly raised the bar, delaying normalization. He described the road map as "too Chinese," a diplomatic sleight-of-hand brought about by pro-Chinese influences.

The next day, Thach asked Vesey to tell Secretary James Baker he had submitted his resignation. The Chinese had insisted at the Chengdu Summit that firing Thach be part of the package for normalization.

In fact, because of the Sino-Vietnamese understanding, Thach, whom the Chinese regarded as "pro-American," was removed and placed under house arrest until 1995. At the celebration of independence on September 7, 1995, shortly after my arrival to open the embassy, I met and chatted with Thach at the reception. Thach's house arrest had been lifted.

The Paris Conference on Cambodia convened in June 1991, for the first time bringing all of the Cambodian and international players together. They reached final agreement in October 1991.

The Agreements on a Comprehensive Political Settlement of the Cambodia Conflict were signed in Paris on October 23, 1991, at the final meeting of the Paris Conference on Cambodia. The principal elements were that an enduring peace could only be achieved through a comprehensive political settlement, including the verified withdrawal of foreign forces and a ceasefire and cessation of outside military assistance. The goal should be self-determination for the Cambodian people through free, fair, and democratic elections. All accepted an enhanced UN role in the resolution of the Cambodian problem. The United Nations Transitional Authority in Cambodia (UNTAC) would supervise implementation of the agreement.

Hanoi tacitly accepted the agreement in 1992, which in turn led the United States to lift its opposition to Vietnam's access to the World Bank and IMF.

President Bush's loss in the 1992 elections delayed normalization, but the ground had been laid for the incoming Clinton administration eventually to normalize relations with Vietnam, aided by John McCain and John Kerry, two prominent Vietnam veterans in the Senate, and the meticulous work done by Secretary Solomon on the roadmap.

23

The Road to Normalization

Following the Bush administration, Ambassador Winston Lord became assistant secretary of state for East Asia and Pacific Affairs in the Clinton administration. With highly distinguished service in the Department of Defense and the National Security Council, as national security advisor to Henry Kissinger, director of policy planning at State, and ambassador to China, Ambassador Lord was intimately familiar with American foreign policy at top levels, particularly as related to China, Russia, and Vietnam. As Kissinger's special assistant, he participated in the secret talks in Paris on normalization and composed most of the papers on the subject.

Based on his contact with the revolutionary North Vietnamese in the 1970s, Ambassador Lord formed a very negative attitude toward the Vietnamese communists, their uncompromising negotiating stance, inflexibility, and duplicitous nature.

Nonetheless, when he became assistant secretary 20 years later, one of his goals was to work toward normalization of U.S.–Vietnam relations. He expressed this in his oral history prepared by ADST.[1]

Lord wrote:

> I had a sense that Vietnam was an important country. It was important to try to heal the wounds left by the Vietnam War in our society. Moving ahead in relations was our best bet to get more information on our missing-in-action. Vietnam was also potentially important from the economic point of view. It obviously was also important in geopolitical terms. It has a large and dynamic population. Given the traditional Vietnamese antagonism toward China, it was also useful

in dealing with China, with which we wanted better relations, to improve our relations with some of China's historical enemies. This was just to remind the Chinese of the
balance-of-power considerations applicable in this situation, whether it involved India, Vietnam, Russia, or Japan.
Having good relations with those countries is helpful when
we deal with China. So, for these reasons I felt that it was
important to try to move ahead with Vietnam, even though
I had this distrust of them.[2]

In his oral history, Ambassador Lord described his specific
goals with Vietnam. Accounting for the MIAs was the top priority:

We had some potential economic interests with Vietnam,
both now, and greater potential in the future, given the large
population of Vietnam, the spirit of entrepreneurship of the
people, and the possibility of finding oil and other resources off the Vietnamese coast. I remember that the American
oil industry was interested in getting into Vietnam. In fact,
some American oil companies had held oil-prospecting permits issued by the former Saigon government. There could
be considerable trade and investment prospects in Vietnam
at some point.[3]

There was also the general question of our influence in
Southeast Asia, both in terms of Vietnam itself and when it
became a member of ASEAN. This affected both our bilateral ties with Vietnam as well and when Vietnam became
a member of ASEAN. This affected both our bilateral ties
with Vietnam as well as when Vietnam became a member
of ASEAN. Also, Vietnam would be a balance to China in a
modest way, with all the advantages that provided.

It was also in our general interest to build a Pacific community, including our former adversaries, whether it was
China or Vietnam, and try to maintain U.S. influence in the
area. Finally, moving ahead on normalizing relations with
Vietnam would have benefits in our own society, healing

the wounds that still existed from that war and trying to put it behind us. So, for these reasons we wanted to move ahead, and it was important that we do so.[4]

I, too, had noticed the U.S. business interest in normalization, especially—but not limited to—the petroleum companies. This was a useful counterweight to the political opposition from conservatives. On the Policy Planning Staff in 1994–95, I wrote policy recommendations advocating normalization of relations with Vietnam, virtually along the lines advocated by Ambassador Lord.

Ambassador Lord also noted that it was generally agreed within the administration that we should try to move forward to achieve our goals with Vietnam at a steady pace, with one huge exception—the White House.

Despite not wishing to criticize friends whom he respected, in his oral history Lord commented: "National Security Advisor Tony Lake in particular, whom I admire and with whom I worked on many issues, was the single, biggest brake on the policy of normalization of relations. Toward the end of this 1993–1995 period, I (the author) think Tony Lake had become more positive on relations[5] with Vietnam. By then both he and the President could see that there was modest political damage, and indeed some benefit, from moving ahead."

This is particularly interesting in view of Tony Lake's visit to Vietnam in July 1996, when Lake seemed to enjoy an epiphany in his attitude toward Vietnam and which I described during my report on my time in Hanoi as *chargé d'affaires*.[6]

From my perspective, the White House was reluctant to move forward for political reasons, such as the fervent opposition from conservatives in the House of Representatives, but also from Senate Majority Leader Bob Dole and Senator Robert Smith of New Hampshire. These elements, in league with the POW/MIA constituencies, had to be weighed against the geopolitical and other reasons Ambassador Lord pointed to when deciding whether to proceed before the presidential election in 1996. The president, I would surmise, felt particularly vulnerable because he had not served in the military in Vietnam. I ran into these constituencies directly—Senator Jesse Helms refused to see me before I left for Hanoi. The same

House members tried to prevent me from returning to Hanoi in 1996. At the same time, Ann Mills-Griffiths pleasantly introduced me at a reception to Majority Leader and 1996 Republican presidential candidate Robert Dole as the person destined to be the first ambassador to Hanoi. A leading opponent of normalization, Senator Dole grimaced but shook my hand without speaking. In my view, President Clinton always had the political impact very much in mind when considering politically risky moves.

Some veterans were inveterately opposed to normalization with Vietnam. Other important veterans—led by John McCain and John Kerry, former senators Bob Kerrey and Chuck Robb, the Vietnam Vets, and thousands of former servicemen—believed that reconciliation with this country that had caused us such anguish was necessary in itself but also to heal the wounds caused by the war.[7]

Ambassador Lord singled out Hershel Gober, also a Vietnam veteran and deputy director of the Veterans Administration (VA), who obviously had a clear interest in the Vietnam issue and turned out to be very important in this regard. Gober led a delegation to Vietnam in May 1995 and, because of his links with Vietnam veterans and the president, he had important influence in deciding whether to move forward at a more rapid pace, such as with military-to-military relations, a project that I eagerly advocated.[8] Gober also visited Hanoi after I was in place and strongly advocated strengthening relations with Vietnam.[9]

Responding to steady progress on MIAs and signs of broader progress in economic reform, President Clinton on February 3, 1994, lifted the trade embargo that had been put in effect when Vietnam invaded and occupied Cambodia in December 1978. In May 1994, the United States and Vietnam signed a consular agreement. On January 28, 1995, the United States and Vietnam signed agreements settling property claims and establishing liaison offices in each other's capitals, a move like the liaison offices the United States and China had set up in 1975.

During this critical period, I was principal deputy assistant secretary from 1989 to 1992, covering principally Japan, China, Korea, and Mongolia, but Secretary Solomon brought me into the discussions on strategy toward Vietnam. However, I was not the action deputy on Vietnam. I spent the year 1992–93 a diplomat-in-residence at Princeton and Rutgers universities, teaching and writing about East Asian political economies and strategic issues. In 1993–94 I served as the State Department coordinator for the APEC Leaders Meeting in Seattle, inaugurated by President Clinton in October, and following up on decisions made at the summit. In 1994–95, I was a senior Asia advisor on the Policy Planning staff, writing on a variety of East Asia policy issues, including a major piece urging rapid normalization of relations with Vietnam, stressing the strategic rationale and the benign impact normalization could have on the American psyche.

24

President Clinton Normalizes
U.S.-Vietnam Relations

President Clinton announced normalization of U.S.-Vietnam relations in a White House ceremony on July 11, 1995. Coming 30 years after President Johnson sent the first American troops to Vietnam, the announcement received widespread media coverage. President Clinton noted sustained progress on accounting for the missing-in-action, which had accelerated in the previous 17 months. Clinton singled out Democrats John Kerry, Robert Kerrey, and Chuck Robb and Republicans John McCain and Pete Peterson in the House as strong supporters of early normalization. He also noted strong support for normalization among Vietnam veterans.

In further comments, noted widely among Vietnam's leaders, President Clinton said: "I believe normalization and increased contact between Americans and Vietnamese will advance the cause of freedom in Vietnam, just as it did in Eastern Europe and the former Soviet Union. I strongly believe that engaging Vietnamese on a broad economic front of economic reform and the broad front of democratic reform will help to honor the sacrifice of those who fought for freedom's sake in Vietnam." Vietnam's leaders challenged me on these comments after I arrived in Vietnam.

Secretary of State Warren Christopher throughout was strongly supportive of normalization. Ambassador Lord commented, "Secretary Christopher has characterized his trip to Vietnam in 1995 as a very moving experience for him. He deserves a lot of credit for his effort in accomplishing this, working in cooperation with the White House, on this whole saga over a period of several years."[1]

A strong supporter of opening the embassy in Hanoi, Secretary Christopher did so on August 6, 1995. In his remarks, Secretary

Christopher announced that I, Desaix Anderson, would arrive shortly in Hanoi to run the new embassy as *chargé d'affaires.*

Secretary Christopher used his principal public speech in Vietnam to address legitimate U.S. concerns—e.g., POW/MIAs, human rights, et cetera. He reminded his audience of young Vietnamese foreign-service trainees that determining the fate of missing Americans remained Washington's primary concern and that continued progress on the issue would be the key to a closer relationship with Hanoi.

On human rights, he insisted on a formal government-to-government dialogue and appealed positively to Vietnamese self-interest, pointing out that economic growth is usually smoothest when accompanied by the rule of law and creative freedom. Directly addressing the young Vietnamese before him, he defined America's ideals of freedom and human rights with simple eloquence. "Each of you," he said, "ought to have the right to help shape your country's destiny, as well as your own."[2]

Commenting in his oral testimony on the opening of the embassy, Secretary Lord said: "We continued to try to flesh out that relationship with Vietnam. We had Desaix Anderson, a distinguished Foreign Service officer, initially serving in Hanoi as our first ambassador. Then Pete Peterson, a former POW, went to Hanoi to replace Anderson. We worked to get more information on repatriation and to move on trade and the MFN [Most Favored Nation] issue, discussed geopolitics, including China. We also talked to the Vietnamese about human rights. We had several dialogues on this issue while I was there. These were like the human-rights dialogues which we had with the Chinese."[3]

During a notable visit by Ambassador Lord to Hanoi in early 1996, Vietnamese Foreign Minister Nguyen Manh Cam and his ministry were pragmatic and relatively easy to deal with. "Interested in moving ahead with the Vietnamese-American relationship, in their own national interest, they wanted to be helpful on the MIA question," Lord commented.[4]

Ambassador Lord found the Vietnamese, especially in the foreign ministry and Prime Minister Vo Van Kiet, ready to deal pragmatically with U.S. representatives. He noted, "I had seen the same phenomenon in China, where, despite our mutual hostility and isolation for two decades, there was an immediate positive response to us. I got very little evidence of an adverse, emotional reaction to Americans."[5]

What Caused the Fundamental Change?

There were many advantages to Vietnam in normalizing relations with the United States, as Ambassador Lord has outlined above. But there were compelling reasons why opening to the United States was crucial to Vietnam's economy recovery.

In the early eighties, Vietnam's economy remained parlous. By the mid-Eighties, Vietnam faced an economic crisis—inflation rates between 400 and 700 percent, stagnant growth, and a dysfunctional economy. This contrasted dramatically with its neighbors outside Indochina.

Isolated from the Western and ASEAN neighbors because of its continuing occupation of Cambodia, the cost of maintaining 180,000 troops in Cambodia was staggering. At the same time, economic assistance from the Soviet Union was declining and then virtually ended.

In the process of "renovation," Vietnam began dismantling its centrally controlled command economy and building a "market economy with socialist orientation." This included:

- dismantling the forced collectivization of agriculture and turning management of the farms over to the farmers;
- opening Vietnam to foreign trade and investment;
- legalizing the private sector;
- initiating financial reform;
- gradually eliminating direct subsidies to state-owned enterprises (SOEs); and
- undertaking to make Vietnam a "nation ruled by law."

Hanoi also began withdrawing its troops from Cambodia in 1988, reduced PAVN from 1.2 million to 580,000 soldiers, reduced state-owned enterprises from 12,000 to 6,000, and fired 800,000 SOE workers.

Vietnam realized it must escape its communist moorings; dependence on the Soviet Union, the East Europeans, and China; and end its isolation from the contemporary world. This meant reaching out to establish meaningful relations with Japan, South Korea, Canada, Australia, Europe, and its neighbors. Hanoi realized that normalizing relations with the United States was crucial for economic reasons—to overcome, for example, resistance in Japan to genuinely committing to its economic relations with Vietnam, and, most important, to gain access to the international financial institutions, as well as the U.S. market for trade and investment. All of this was achieved in 1991–95. Pointedly, Hanoi saw relations with the United States as a counterweight to its Chinese neighbor.

Equivocation in Goals

However, Hanoi's longer goals were spelled out, as William Duiker points out,[6] in two documents, composed in late November 1990: "Draft Strategy for the Stabilization and Development of the Economy and Society in the Year 2000" and "Draft Platform to Build Socialism in the Transitional Period." Many viewed these documents as a departure from Hanoi's socialist doctrine.

Duiker saw these documents, in retrospect, not as outlining a transitional period to overcome existing difficulties but as a road whereby "the socialist system would ultimately triumph in its historic struggle with capitalism." A private sector would focus on the production of consumer goods, but the state sector would end the private-sector role and establish a socialist Vietnam. At the time, planners anticipated that this transition would last through two to three five-year plans.

Despite the lengthy period of transition, this contradiction would persist and become increasingly anachronistic as Vietnam engaged with the world. Engagement with the world seems also to have modified Hanoi's long-term plans.

Contradictions notwithstanding, the immediate results were very impressive:

- In the process, inflation dropped from 723 percent at one point in 1988 to double digits, and to 3.6 percent by the mid-1990s.
- Poverty was reduced from 90 to 12 percent.
- Trade and external investment increased and flourished.
- Reforms undertaken allowed Vietnam to move steadily away from the centrally controlled command economy and begin building a "market economy with socialist orientation."
- Agriculture was returned to the farmers.
- The private sector burgeoned.
- Vietnam indicated that it would become a nation "ruled by law."

These were phenomenal changes and bode well for Vietnam's future and its relations with the United States.

25

Reconciliation

In my view, the most gratifying experience a diplomat can enjoy is reconciliation with a former national enemy. Although the roots of reconciliation with Vietnam were many, my own career was threaded among them. I uniquely experienced the reward of all those efforts by opening the American Embassy in Hanoi, as *chargé d'affaires*, in August 1995, soon after the July 11, 1995, announcement by President Bill Clinton establishing diplomatic relations between the United States and the Socialist Republic of Vietnam. During Secretary Warren Christopher's August 7, 1995, visit to Hanoi, he announced that I would soon arrive in Hanoi to open and run the embassy.

Since I had served in South Vietnam from the mid-Sixties and, thereafter, in six different assignments in or on Vietnam, my name was frequently bruited about as the likely first ambassador to Vietnam as normalization loomed late in George H.W. Bush's presidency and President Bill Clinton's first term. I had become inured to the hope that I would get the call to become the first ambassador.

However, I did not know what to expect when, after a 23-year absence from the country, I boarded a plane on August 20, 1995, to the capital of a nation that had caused so much anguish in the United States. To say the least, we had not won the war with Vietnam; we had left in ignominy, with a thin pretense of a decent interval that was the prelude to collapse on April 30, 1975, of the structure we left behind in 1973. Twenty years lapsed as the United States sporadically attempted to normalize relations with Hanoi, a victor left impoverished and damaged by almost endless war for 30 years without virtually a penny of reparations.

I had served in Vietnam for the State Department in the US-AID program from 1965–67, handing out pigs, providing material to build schools and medical stations, and in early 1967 camping out with the Revolutionary Development Cadres in "zones contested" with the Vietcong to assess U.S. and GVN policies. In 1973 I returned to the Mekong Delta to report on what happened when the American forces left.

Nothing from my 33-year engagement in those six previous assignments in and on Vietnam prepared me for one facet of what I would face when I came to Hanoi to open and run the U.S. Embassy immediately after diplomatic relations were established.

As I flew across the Pacific to open the embassy, I pondered what reception I might receive. How would the Vietnamese government, Communist Party, and, most important, the Vietnamese people react to the arrival of the American, former enemy and "imperialist" presence in their midst?

I had hurried to Hanoi in late August 1995 to accompany former President George H.W. Bush on a visit to Vietnam sponsored by CitiBank. I had known and been favorably impressed by President and Mrs. Bush since they had stopped over in Tokyo in 1974 on his way to Beijing to serve as ambassador in the Liaison Office there. As the "China Watcher" in the Tokyo embassy, I was assigned as control officer for Ambassador and Mrs. Bush's transit through Japan. Subsequently, he occasionally asked that I send tennis balls or other items from Tokyo to Beijing. He once asked me to take care of his son George, who was passing through Tokyo for one night on the way to visit his parents in Beijing. I also frequently met the senior Bush as he rose to become vice president and then president of the United States. During his visit to Vietnam in 1995, he expressed strong public support for President Clinton's decision to normalize relations with Vietnam and for me to serve as the first representative.

As we traveled around Hanoi and the country for three days, the former president expressed astonishment at the warm reception he received at every turn. At a farewell dinner hosted by CitiBank representative Bradley LaLonde and attended by Vice Foreign Minister Tran Quang Co, President Bush rose to thank his Vietnamese and American hosts and commented on how amazed he was that he had heard no hostility but rather a warm welcome. How could an American be treated so hospitably? he asked.

Vice Minister Co responded that Vietnam was a small country, and, in its long history, it often had to fight to protect its existence. But after the wars were over, Vietnam could not afford to sustain hostility toward its former enemies and sought instead to make friends with them. This was a trait of the Vietnamese people. Sitting down, Minister Co cupped his hand and whispered to me, "And, never forget that it is also because it is in Vietnam's interest."

During my nearly two years in Hanoi as *chargé d'affaires*, as we sought to build a new relationship with Vietnam, never once did I sense hostility on the part of the thousands of Vietnamese I met. I heard suspicions about America's intentions from the more conservative elements of the Communist Party and security services, but the Vietnamese government and people greeted me with warmth, receptivity, and eagerness to learn about and from America. The great surprise was the responsive welcome I received as I wandered around Hanoi in shorts and visited every part of the country from August 1995 until May 1997. I would like to share my perspectives on Vietnam not as a war, but as the magical country I experienced.

Let us start with a basic fact: Contemporary Vietnam is vastly different from the common television images we have all shared since the Sixties; Vietnam is, instead, characterized now by its vibrancy, its youth, dynamism, and industriousness. Vietnam was trying to change every facet of the former socialist state into a contemporary nation with a market economy, engaged with the world. Despite this aura and the establishment of a functioning National Assembly, Vietnam remains dominated by the monopoly of power by the Communist Party and cadres. Ideology is gone, but controls remain.

A New Beginning with the United States

When President Clinton and the leaders of Vietnam established diplomatic relations in July 1995, they agreed to build a new relationship focused on the future.

Hanoi accepted as a humanitarian commitment the U.S.'s priority: accounting for missing Americans from the war. Hanoi had earlier accepted the other U.S. condition: withdrawal from Cambodia. Vietnamese leaders made clear to me that economic normalization was their top priority.

Since 1995, the United States and Vietnam have worked hard to build a new relationship, in the spirit of the leaders of both countries' commitment to work toward the future. A great deal of progress has been made in a relatively short period of time. I believe that we got the process off to an excellent start. Former Congressman and Ambassador Pete Peterson and ambassadors and friends Raymond Burghardt, Mike Marine, Mike Michalak, David Shear, and Ted Osius all worked hard and effectively to continue the construction of a strong U.S.-Vietnam relationship.

The U.S. government built on an impressive legacy established by American NGOs and a few brave senators like John McCain and John Kerry. NGOs such as the Mennonites, the Vietnam Vets, led by Chuck Searcy, and U.S.-Vietnam Trade Council President Virginia Foote made huge contributions to normalization.

Strategy for Reconciliation with Vietnam

When I was appointed to Hanoi, Secretary Christopher summoned me to his office to give me my instructions. He spoke pleasantries, so I finally asserted that I would pursue, as top priority, an accounting for the missing from the war. Christopher nodded agreement. Second, I would work firmly to promote human rights. I thought, however, the U.S. approach to human rights in China had been counterproductive, and I wished to avoid public confrontation with Vietnam on the subject. But I would promote human rights directly with the government and especially with young Vietnamese. Secretary Christopher concurred. Third, I planned to work to build a new, constructive relationship between the United States and Vietnam. Christopher answered, "Yes." Those were my basic instructions, and I never received others!

In a letter sent to me shortly after my arrival in Hanoi, former Secretary of State George Shultz noted the anomaly of my position: "Congratulations on the daunting challenge—but with *no resources!!*"

After arrival in late August 1995, we devised a strategy for developing the new relationship we sought with Vietnam. I was blessed with an excellent staff that had been in Hanoi since the establishment of the Liaison Office in January 1995—an excellent deputy, energetic and effective political and economic officers, and very competent administrative and consular officers. We identified three broad instruments in our strategy to advance the new relationship:

1. We would make strenuous efforts to meet as many Vietnamese as possible—the elite and common folks—so that we could understand their attitudes toward the United States and overcome any negative residual attitudes toward the United States from earlier history. We would expose Vietnamese to America's contemporary goals in Vietnam and to Americans themselves.
2. We would facilitate as many links as possible between American governmental and private institutions and the Vietnamese establishment to build the networks between our two societies that normally develop over many years but are the real basis of a relationship between two countries. In these connections, we would encourage reputable private American institutions, particularly American universities, to develop relationships in Vietnam. To advance this goal, Secretary for Health and Human Services Donna Shalala and the Centers for Disease Control (CDC) became great allies on health assistance.
3. In both governmental actions and encouraging the private sector, I decided that we should work hardest to contribute to Vietnam's health and education needs—which could most easily be sold to not a few congressional critics as the least politically sensitive kinds of assistance.

I was determined to get to know young Vietnamese, their attitudes toward America, toward their own futures, toward democracy, and the process of changing Vietnam's economy from a Marxist-Leninist to a market economy. Although they universally wanted Vietnam to become a democracy, and America was their ideal, they almost uniformly opposed U.S. pressure for human rights and political change. They would get there themselves at Vietnam's own pace, they told me.

I sought out revolutionary and other Vietnamese leaders to learn their perspectives. Talks with former Deputy Prime Minister Nguyen Co Thach and General Vo Nguyen Giap were intriguing in their historical perspectives, but my discussion with former Premier Phan Van Dong, the day before my departure, was the most fascinating of my career.[1]

The Leadership

I also observed the triumvirate at the top of the government and party—the president, the Communist Party secretary-general, and the prime minister. A pattern had developed to have one of the three from each of the three regions of the country: a southerner, a northerner, and one from central Vietnam. One slot always belonged to an individual from the military and security sector, one from the party, and one more suited to the government. During National Security Advisor Tony Lake's July 1996 visit I saw the three leaders in two days. It was an excellent opportunity to see them directly reacting to the same pitch on the Orderly Departure Program, a proposal that aimed to interview yet again any Vietnamese who might have had links to the United States.

Reformers

The southerner, Prime Minister Vo Van Kiet, was a reformer, friendly, open, and forthcoming to the extent that the Politburo would allow. Prime Minister Kiet was a veteran of the war against the French and later the Americans. He lost his first wife and two children in a U.S. bombing raid. He was prime minister of Vietnam from August 1991 to September 1997 and led Vietnam's return to the world arena after decades of war and isolation. He was a key Vietnamese political leader who led the *Doi Moi* economic reforms. In Tony Lake's 1996 meeting with him, Kiet was sympathetic to agreeing to the controversial Orderly Departure Program. The deputy prime ministers and foreign ministry tracked closely with the prime minister. Kiet had overruled the interior minister who opposed allowing me to rent a villa close to the Interior Ministry, fearing, I assume, that I would spy on the ministry or blast the ministry with some nefarious rays. After he stepped down as prime minister, Kiet continued to work for reform of the governmental and political system. He died on June 11, 2008.

Pragmatists

The party secretary-general, Do Muoi, was a stalwart Marxist-Leninist party bureaucrat from the north who had replaced moderate Nguyen Van Linh in 1976 to promote the quick "socialist transformation" in the South and reunification. He served as prime minister just prior to Kiet. Despite his Marxist-Leninist credentials, in 1966 I escorted visiting Senator John McCain to call on Do Muoi. He astounded Senator McCain and me by saying, "Look at this Mao suit I am wearing. In China it costs five dollars; in Vietnam it costs eight dollars." He then almost shouted, "WE HAVE GOT TO LEARN HOW TO COMPETE." An economist friend had been tutoring Do Muoi on the refinements of a market economy of *Doi Moi* that Vietnam had been pursuing since 1986, but I could not believe that he had been as effective as Do Muoi's words with McCain proved.

The party was not as doctrinaire as its elder leaders might be. I had developed a relationship with the party international-affairs department chief, Hong Ha, from a meeting at my home in Washington in early August 1995 shortly before I went to Hanoi to open the embassy. After normalization was announced, I invited a group of Vietnamese officials visiting from Hanoi for drinks at my Logan Circle residence in Northwest Washington. As the event was winding down, I received a telephone call from the Secret Service saying, "We have a communist from Vietnam who wants to visit your home. Is it okay?" I knew it was Hong Ha, so I said, "Yes," but asked how I would know when he arrived. "No worry, you will know," the Secret Service responded. Shortly afterward I heard sirens blaring into the night and several cars appeared in front of my home, from which Hong Ha and a couple of lieutenants emerged.

Hong Ha stayed two hours and with his friends finished off two bottles of cognac. I had a fast friend in the communist party when I arrived in Hanoi.

U.S. negotiators had swapped several properties in North and South Vietnam with the government of Vietnam. In the exchange, the United States received a French villa that was to be the ambassador's residence in Hanoi. The residence was built in 1903 in the style of the Hanoi Opera House, built at about the same time and modeled after the Garnier Opera House in Paris. I strongly urged the State Department to let me identify an American contractor in Hanoi to implement the prepared plans (as I had extensive experience remodeling Victorian homes in Washington). Washington turned me down. So I looked for a temporary residence for the chief of mission. In my initial meeting in Hanoi with Hong Ha at the Communist Party Headquarters on Ba Dinh Square, I mentioned that I was having trouble finding a place to stay. Hong Ha generously invited me to move into the Communist Party Headquarters. After expressing appreciation with a hearty laugh, I told him that I feared that my Uncle Jesse (Helms) would not approve.

The younger communist party officials in Hong Ha's department, in meetings with me and my political officers, asked how the Jinminto (LDP) in Japan, Kuomintang (KMT) in Taiwan, the Institutional Revolutionary Party (PRI) in Mexico, and Democratic Progressive Party (DPP) in Singapore had historically been able to retain power despite some openings to other political parties in their countries. The implications of their interest were important, since the Communist Party was obviously contemplating someday opening the political process in Vietnam, a thrilling thought. They sought to learn how to hold onto power with a facade of democracy and tame opposition.

A couple of months or so before the 1996 U.S. presidential election, the Communist Party International Department ask me to have the embassy's political officers brief them regularly on the U.S. elections and how they worked. I agreed with alacrity to brief them on the democratic process in America, and my officers followed through. Normally, embassy chiefs of mission invite the American community, Republicans and Democrats, to an "election watch." We decided to invite the young officers in the Communist

Party International Department also to attend and watch the 1996 election results in my residence. They were the first to arrive and last to leave and knew exactly for whom to cheer and whom to discredit, demonstrating that they were carefully studying the American political scene and process.

Conservatives

President Le Duc Anh, a former general and politician, was the representative of the military and security forces. These were the forces that were most suspicious of the United States, frequently favored closer relations with the Communist Party of China, and believed and spread the numerous conspiracy theories that floated around Hanoi. Over time, these elements would gradually fade into the background, but they still had influence in Hanoi during my stay.

But, in pursuing our agenda, we had to overcome considerable skepticism among conservative figures in the Communist Party, the Defense Ministry, and security services. Thus, one of my major responsibilities was to try to disabuse such figures of what they perceived as evil U.S. intentions. I was determined to reach out to the powerful conservative figures who harbored such suspicions and asked to call on Dao Duy Tung, number four in the Politburo, ideological tsar for the Communist Party, and a well-known hardliner.

After courtesies, I made general comments about the U.S.-Vietnam agreement by our leaders to look to the future and build a constructive relationship. I appreciated the Party's and the Vietnamese people's assistance with our top priority, accounting for the missing from the war. I outlined U.S. hopes to construct with Vietnam a broad-based relationship and noted several areas, such as health and education, where we had made beginnings. I also outlined Washington's strategic views regarding East Asia and the Pacific. After Mr. Tung expressed appreciation for these views, I noted that I had heard several accusations about America's activities and would like to discuss these directly with Mr. Tung so the Party would be aware of our intentions.

There were continuing rumors, I told Mr. Tung, that President

Clinton's remarks on July 6, 1995, on normalization of relations, were misinterpreted to indicate that the U.S. intended to try to overthrow Vietnam's political system. We had no such intention. The president's remarks were observations about changes that might take place as Vietnam opened its society to the rest of the world, but they did not reflect a policy attempting to change Vietnam's political system. His remarks were analytical, not a policy statement, and reflected expectations stemming from Vietnam's own *Doi Moi* policies. Similarly, Secretary Christopher's remarks on August 5, 1995, at the Institute of International Relations on individual dignity reflected Americans' welcome of increasing openness in Vietnam and respect for individuals' rights in Vietnamese society. The embassy and Americans would express long-held American views supporting the individual and democratic society, but we were not trying to impose these views on Vietnam.[2]

Rumors that the United States was supporting Vietnamese-American dissidents in Cambodia who were attempting to overthrow the Vietnamese government, as some U.S. congressional figures were publicly advocating, were similarly off the mark. U.S. laws forbid individuals or groups of Americans to use violence to overthrow the political systems of other countries. We publicly opposed such actions and would prosecute under U.S. law any American using violence for such ends. In this case, we had cooperated with the Cambodian government for the repatriation of any Americans who might be considering such efforts.

We were also aware that Vietnam regarded Radio Free Asia as provocative. I traced the origins of Radio Free Asia and pointed out that its charter calls for objective reporting on developments. Vietnamese authorities should call any violations to my attention and we would correct them.

I noted that a book circulating on "Peaceful Evolution," an import from the Chinese portraying U.S. plans to urge change designed to subversively undermine Vietnam's political system, was highly misleading. Americans support the change that Vietnam has undertaken through its own *Doi Moi* policies.

Mr. Tung welcomed my comments, ordered small glasses of Scotch, and then proposed a toast to friendly U.S.-Vietnam relations.

I learned reliably a few weeks later that Mr. Tung had been

pleased with our meeting and appreciated my efforts to deal directly with problem areas. He had the entire Politburo briefed in full on our conversation, after which the Politburo agreed that I could travel anywhere and see any party or government official in Vietnam I wished. This proved to be the rule during my tenure. No appointment request was ever denied. I spoke freely, particularly with young Vietnamese about democracy and open political systems and societies. I was able, for example, to address the student body of the large Can Tho University in the Mekong Delta without any clearance of the substance of my address or time.

Conversation with Former Deputy Prime Minister Nguyen Co Thach

I had a fascinating conversation at lunch on March 14, 1997, with former Foreign Minister and former Deputy Prime Minister Nguyen Co Thach. Thach had worked zealously with Richard Holbrooke to establish relations with the United States soon after the end of the war, and, as mentioned above, had been under house arrest from 1990 until 1995 to satisfy China's demands that he be punished for being "pro-American."

Regarding the invasion of Cambodia, Thach claimed that the attacks by Pol Pot with Chinese backing were the reason that Vietnam had to act strongly against Cambodia in the late Seventies. Pol Pot's forces had penetrated 100 kilometers into Vietnam's Tay Ninh Province and were threatening to attack Saigon. At times they were even claiming all of the former Khmer lands in southern Vietnam that had been lost to Vietnam over the years. It was essential to deliver a sharp blow to Phnom Penh to end these provocations. Even when Vietnam first invaded, it was known that a second and deeper invasion would be necessary to end the threat from Pol Pot and that all of Cambodia would have to be occupied to get rid of Pol Pot permanently. Vietnam's mistake, Thach said, was to remain in Cambodia until 1988. Thach had argued for deep strikes followed by rapid withdrawal. Other views had prevailed, which he regretted.

Asked if he was surprised by the widespread adverse reaction to Vietnam's attempt to get rid of the abhorred Pol Pot and the Khmer Rouge, Thach said that he was not surprised that there was a sharp reaction but was surprised that it was so universal. This he had not anticipated.

I noted that Vietnam's invasion of all of Cambodia up to the Thai border convinced many that Vietnam was trying to create by force the "Indochina Federation" called for in Ho Chi Minh's testament. Not so, said Thach. Hanoi had never intended to create a Federation or to absorb Cambodia and Laos, but rather hoped to build strong solidarity with Laos and Cambodia as fraternal countries in the same way that Vietnam and China had at times shared fraternal solidarity. The "Federation" charges were propaganda.

Thach commented somewhat disparagingly on Hanoi's decision to try to implant Heng Samrin as the leader of Cambodia. This was misguided, he said. The Cambodians had to choose their own leadership; Vietnam could not do it for them! I remarked that during my observation watch on the Thai border with Cambodia, I had been told by Khmer refugees that Khmer Rouge regimental commanders were defecting from Pol Pot and developing links with the Vietnamese in Rattanakiri and Mondolkiri Provinces in northeastern Cambodia.

I asked if the difficulties the "Hoa" people (ethnic Chinese) suffered in southern Vietnam during the "Socialist Transformation" of the south in late 1977 and early 1978 reflected concern about their being used by China as a fifth column; or were they, as wealthy traders and bankers in the south, the incidental targets of "Socialist Transformation?" The attempt to move to "Socialist Transformation" was too rapid, Thach said. Hanoi should have proceeded more slowly. The Chinese people in South Vietnam were not feared as a potential fifth column because they had their own differences with China. It had been a mistake to move so rapidly to socialize the economy because it fired up emotions among ethnic Vietnamese who were jealous of or disliked the Chinese residents. Emotions were incendiary. To arouse them was a mistake, and the leaders should have known it would lead to adverse consequences.

In contrast to Vietnam, China had decided to obtain financial support and credits from the United States and the West. The military strike "to teach Vietnam a lesson," was designed to demonstrate that the Soviet Union's little brother could be hit militarily despite the previously close relationship between China and Vietnam. Beijing wished to demonstrate its change of policy and orientation.

This was typical of China. Beijing had abandoned the Soviet Union in the early Sixties and turned Moscow from friend to foe. In the same fashion, during the Great Leap Forward and Cultural Revolution, Beijing had supported insurgencies in Southeast Asia to keep the West and its friends in Asia preoccupied and to divert attention from China's internal affairs. China will abandon a friend in a minute if it believes that its interests lie elsewhere.

For this reason, the United States had better stay alert vis-à-vis China. In 50 years China could replace the United States as the world's largest economy, and U.S. interests could be challenged. Thach returned to this notion several times during our conversation. China could not be trusted. China was not principled and was preeminently pragmatic.

I asked when Hanoi had decided to conclude a security alliance with the Soviet Union, which took place in November 1978. Only when the situation became grave, Thach responded, because of the attacks from China and Cambodia. Thach said that he had opposed abandoning the very successful policy of Ho Chi Minh to maintain equidistance between the two big communist powers and good relations with both. But the situation became so grave that, to protect itself from China and Pol Pot, Vietnam had no choice. China had opposed reunification of Vietnam in 1954. It constantly urged that Vietnam proceed slowly. Therefore, reunification created a danger from China for Vietnam.

I asked Thach if the U.S. policy of moving to support the French and not the Vietnamese in 1945–46 had made a major difference in the political and economic structure that developed in Vietnam. Was the U.S. posture at the time of the Geneva Accords significant to Vietnam's immediate future? Thach responded that there had been three periods of crisis for Vietnam: 1945–46, 1965–73, and 1978–79. Specifically, Thach said that 1945–46 was far more important than the period between 1946 and 1954. The United States' posture was not yet firm in 1945–46, nor was Vietnam's. In 1945, Vietnam's independence was under attack in the north by the Kuomintang, by the British in the south, and by the French as best as they could muster. Vietnam's independence was severely threatened. By the early Fifties, the United States had provided 80 percent of the funds for France's military efforts to reestablish control of Vietnam. At the Geneva Conference, Vietnam had its independence, the most important struggle. Vietnam had by then already established close relations with the Soviet Union and China. The die was cast.

U.S.-Vietnam Relations

I sought Thach's advice on handling the development of our relations in the future. Thach responded that we had made surprising progress over the year and a half after normalization, more than anyone had expected, and credited me for playing a major role in that progress. He had only one suggestion: We should provide humanitarian assistance to the people of Vietnam to soothe residual feelings about the tons of bombs that had been dumped on the Vietnamese people. We could also help tremendously with training, especially science and technology at the university level. This was vital to allow Vietnam to significantly speed its economic development.

I responded that over the past year and a half we had built a foundation for relations across the board—health, education, science, technology, energy, the environment, and even burgeoning military-to-military relations. I was somewhat surprised by the alacrity with which the Vietnamese military had wished to build relations. Regarding the other areas, we had emphasized the need for special U.S. contributions in health and education. We have encouraged U.S. companies to engage with Vietnam and provide training. We have encouraged U.S. universities to establish links with Vietnamese institutions to provide training. More than 20 have already done so, and another 20 are considering links. These are modest steps but in the right direction.

Thach also hoped for early conclusion of a trade agreement. Sharing his concern about the slowness, I said that it was due to our very different economic systems. U.S. requirements would, however, tally with requirements for Vietnam to enter the WTO.

I constantly pressed Washington to move on this, since it was crucial to moving forward in our economic relations, which I understand, as Thach had said, was vital to Vietnam's security interests.

Thach asked if I had met President Le Duc Anh, Party Secretary-General Do Muoi, and PM Vo Van Kiet. Yes, numerous times, I responded. I had already met other leaders, including Le Kha Phieu (who would replace Do Muoi) and Nguyen Tan Dung, who seemed close to PM Vo Van Kiet, for whom I had great respect. I told Thach that I had just enjoyed a good meeting with General Vo Nguyen Giap, which seemed to please Thach.

My meeting with Thach was quite remarkable. He was very candid, willing to address all the key issues, and, not surprisingly, strongly critical of China, which had demanded his house arrest for five years as the price for normalization of Vietnam-China relations in 1990. Thach also deeply regretted that the Cambodia problem and its consequences for Vietnam's relations with China and the Soviet Union had cost Thach his greatest diplomatic goal—normalization with the United States.

Constructing a New Relationship with Vietnam

While we tried to begin to build trust with skeptical Vietnamese, we went to work. The two countries soon began constructing ties and networks across the board, normal to most countries, and built over many years of relations and cooperation. Ties began in health, education, science and technology, agriculture, aviation, refugee issues, counter-narcotics, and HIV/AIDS; we began military-to-military exchanges; we engaged in dialogue in several channels on sensitive subjects such as human rights and religious freedom.

Of great, long-term significance was developing economic and commercial ties, Hanoi's top goal, but one that is also contributing to America's economy through exports.

Trade increased rapidly. After concluding a bilateral trade agreement in 2001, trade in goods increased from $451 million in 1995 to $54.624 billion in 2017. U.S. exports to Vietnam were worth $8.133 billion, and U.S. imports were $46.488 billion in 2017. In 2016, Vietnam was America's fastest-growing export market. U.S.

exports to Vietnam grew 77 percent between 2014 and 2016, the largest year-on-year increase of exports to any of the United States' top 50 export markets. However, possibly because of the withdrawal of the United States from the TPP (Trans-Pacific Partnership) negotiations, U.S. exports to Vietnam in 2017 declined from $10.0 billion to $8.133 billion; U.S. investment in Vietnam has grown significantly over the past seven years, to nearly $1.5 billion.

Despite serious problems—corruption, frustration with bureaucracy, lack of transparency, an erratic legal system, a weak financial structure, and a weak enforcement of contracts—the U.S. business community has widely believed that Vietnam is an important future market: Many U.S. companies are making money there, and there are now 700 companies and 1,500 representatives in the American Chamber of Commerce in Vietnam, compared to 400 companies when I left in 1997. U.S. businesses expect growing profits in the years ahead, and there is serious interest in shifting manufacturing business from China to Vietnam, as well as to other non-Chinese countries, such as Myanmar, because of hospitable environments and lower wages.

At the same time, there was steady progress on accounting for Americans missing from the war; Vietnam has stressed its "unilateral efforts" to complement excellent cooperation bilaterally. In 1973 there were 2,646 unaccounted-for Americans in Vietnam, and in August 2017 there remained 1,604 unaccounted-for there.

Annually, during my tenure in Hanoi, we expanded Fulbright scholarships for Vietnamese. Fulbright grants approximately 20 to 25 fully funded scholarships every year. There were 620 Fulbright scholars between 1992 and 2015. Since 1992, about 8,000 Vietnamese and American students have participated in the program. At the end of 2017, there were 31,389 Vietnamese studying in the United States, and Vietnam now ranks sixth among all countries sending students to study at U.S. institutions—mostly colleges and universities but also boarding and day schools. More than 25 annual international-visitor grants began during my tenure.[4] In 2018 there were 48 Fulbright scholars from Vietnam. Several dozen U.S. universities have established scholarships, programs, and other exchanges with strong U.S.-government encouragement to meet the universal desire in Vietnam to learn from the United States. My Princeton

Global Summer Seminar in Hanoi 2007–09 was part of my goal to encourage U.S. universities to engage with Vietnam.

In September 2001, we undertook cooperation on anti-terrorism; the Bush administration in 2004 added Vietnam as the 15th country to participate. The USAID/PEPFAR contribution decreased to $12,700,000 in FY2017, and the final contribution of $7,500,000 was made in FY2018.

Under the leadership of Senators John Kerry and John McCain, the U.S. devoted $160 million in funds that the Vietnamese government agreed to repay for debts incurred by the former government of South Vietnam to finance Vietnamese students' study in the United States.

In 2003, the two countries signed a counter-narcotics letter of agreement (amended in 2006), a civil aviation agreement, and a textile agreement. In January 2007, Congress approved Permanent Normal Trade Relations (PNTR) for Vietnam. A nuclear agreement was concluded in 2008 to convert Vietnam's nuclear reactor in Dalat from highly enriched uranium to low-enriched uranium, significantly reducing the risk of nuclear proliferation.

President Obama announced during his 2016 visit the establishment of the Fulbright University of Vietnam in Ho Chi Minh City, to accommodate 17,000 students in an open university, a first. The Fulbright University opened in 2018.

The United States also joined the Ford Foundation to provide funds, $9 million by 2010, for joint research on environmental contamination removal of dioxin (Agent Orange) in highly contaminated "hotspots" at Danang and Bien Hoa airports. Vietnam's Ministry of National Defense and USAID agreed in 2012 to clean up dioxin-contaminated soil and sediment at the airport left from the Vietnam War. The Bill and Melinda Gates Foundation and Atlantic Philanthropies also financed a $6 million laboratory that provides Vietnam with high-resolution dioxin-analysis capability. From 2008 to 2012, three USAID partners—the East Meets West Foundation, Save the Children, and Vietnam Assistance for the Handicapped—provided medical, rehabilitation, employment, and educational support for 11,000 people in Danang living with disabilities, regardless of cause.

The United States has provided, since 1993, more than $50 million in assistance with demining operations.

President Obama designated Vietnam as one of six "next tier" nations under his National Export Initiative, along with China, India, and Brazil.

A Comprehensive (Strategic) Partnership was launched by Presidents Obama and Truong Tan Sang in 2013.

Vietnam and the United States were negotiating with several other Asian and North and South American countries on the far-reaching Trans-Pacific Partnership (TPP). The Trump administration removed the United States from the TPP, but Vietnam and others continue to hope the United States will eventually adhere to it, especially since Hanoi had counted on the U.S. link to TPP as a strategic bulwark against China.

Former Premier Phan Van Dong Discusses History

The most fascinating conversation I had in my career occurred on May 6, 1997, the day before I departed Vietnam. It was with the former wartime premier, Phan Van Dong. He, along with General Vo Nguyen Giap, whom I also met, were the closest comrades of Ho Chi Minh.[5] The Foreign Ministry director for North American affairs, Nguyen Xuan Phong, and embassy officer Brian Dalton also attended the meeting and composed the report on my conversation with the Premier.

Phan Van Dong, the 92-year-old former revolutionary, foreign minister, and prime minister, was at the time one of three senior advisors to Secretary-General Do Muoi. The son of a Mandarin, Phan Van Dong had left school to join Ho Chi Minh in the jungles to bring independence to Vietnam. One of Ho Chi Minh's earliest comrades, Phan Van Dong was frequently compared to China's premier, Zhou Enlai, because of his background, intellect, charm, and conciliatory role. He represented Vietnam in the Paris Accord Negotiations, which also included Zhou.

Premier Dong lived in a spacious home in the gardens of the Presidential Palace and prime minister's offices. He received me in a large reception room, wearing an off-white-colored Mao suit. On one wall hung an exceptionally fine lacquered painting depicting cranes, the symbol of longevity, flocking in a gingko tree. The inscription on the painting commemorated Phan Van Dong's 90th birthday, a reminder that he was a participant in or witness to all the most significant events in Vietnam's modern history.

Premier Dong was alert and extremely engaged throughout our hour-long meeting, which I had to cut short for a farewell appointment with Prime Minister Kiet. Premier Dong appeared to be healthy, had excellent hearing, and stood to receive and bid me farewell as I arrived and departed.

Following his pointedly warm welcome, Phan Van Dong opened the conversation declaring his appreciation for my understanding of the history and people of Vietnam. "Your task of building a new relationship with Vietnam must have been very difficult," he commented.

I responded that, on the contrary, because of the government's and Vietnamese people's responsiveness and receptivity to building a new relationship with America, my task had been easy. I noted that President Clinton and Vietnam's leaders had agreed to look to the future and to build a new relationship between our two countries. Those were my instructions, and I found Vietnam eager to cooperate. The embassy and I had worked to meet as many Vietnamese people as possible to better understand the country and to increase interaction and exchanges with as many facets of Vietnamese society as possible. We tried to establish normal relationships with all elements of Vietnam's government and society, which are the basis of normal relationships between two countries but had not been the history between the United States and Vietnam. We had begun cooperative efforts on health, education, science and technology, and the measured normalization of military-to-military relations. The two nations had begun the process of building trust and mutual confidence, I commented, and we could now much more easily deal with sensitive issues than before.

I told Phan Van Dong that I believed there was a basis for building a strategic partnership between Vietnam and the United States. I thought that in recent years at least, the U.S. military presence in the Pacific had been a force for peace and stability in the region. Finally, I concluded by saying that I saw no contradictions in the national interests of our countries, which constituted a basis for a strategic partnership and a close relationship between Vietnam and the United States, which President Clinton sought. He wanted to see a strong and prosperous Vietnam, well integrated into regional and global institutions. The biggest challenge was to continue to build trust and normalize our economic relationship.

I asked if the premier wished to comment on anything I had said.

Premier Dong responded warmly to my comments, saying that he had nothing to recommend or add to the current course of development of relations. Dong commented that my task as the first U.S. representative had not been easy, but by overcoming difficulties posed from many directions, we had laid the first stones of the foundation for a new relationship. The premier reiterated his appreciation for my interest in Vietnam's history and people. He added that the officials and peoples of the two nations must hope for and trust in the development of cooperative and friendly relations.

With a meaningful laugh, Dong said that he knew somewhat the history of the United States. He was sorry that he never had the chance to visit the U.S. and doubted that it would now be possible. Because of the difficulties between the two countries, he knew the United States only through certain famous figures, such as Abraham Lincoln, Benjamin Franklin, and Franklin Roosevelt. He spoke of his high regard for the American people as represented by those figures.

He agreed that there were no conflicts between the national interests of the two countries and expressed gratitude for the chance to share his thoughts with me.

Anticipating my desire to ask questions, Dong invited me to pose any questions I wished, saying that he was ready for open conversation and had time to spare. With an inviting laugh, he said that he wanted to talk "as two friends, comfortable, without regard for diplomatic formalities."

Before posing questions, I noted the considerable mutual goodwill ready to be tapped in both countries, despite the suspicions of some. I commented that the majority of people in both countries wanted to advance our relations. The fact that we had been able to accomplish so much in the short time since normalization bore this out.

I then asked Phan Van Dong if, in 1945, the United States had not tilted toward France for its own security and strategic reasons, would Vietnam's economic and political institutions have developed differently. He demurred on second-guessing history, so I told him that I would pose the same question another way: When had he and Uncle Ho decided on the political and economic systems that would be instituted when the Vietminh took control of Vietnam?

Premier Dong laughed and said he believed that the desire for a political system similar to socialism had existed in Vietnam long before 1945. Only when Ho Chi Minh found the path was it possible to bring that desire to fruition.

I then asked Dong if at any time after 1956, when elections called for by the Geneva Accords were not carried out as stipulated, there would have been any possibility for a negotiated settlement of the conflict between North and South Vietnam.

Premier Dong stated that he had participated in the events of the 1950s and so he could answer the question definitively. Negotiations between North and South Vietnam were not possible between 1956 and 1963, Dong asserted confidently, because the family of Ngo Dinh Diem never sincerely wanted a peaceful negotiation. The Ngo family also was making active preparations for a military advance on North Vietnam—"*la marche vers le nord*," Dong said.

The premier told a story to illustrate his answer and shed light on other aspects of my questions. At one point, he said, when Ngo Dinh Diem and his brother were quarreling between themselves, Ngo Dinh Nhu communicated with Dong through the Polish representative to the International Control Commission, which monitored the Geneva Accords. Nhu suggested a "time out" in hostilities between North and South to set up relations between the two regions. "This was just a trick," Premier Dong stressed, "intended to allow time to address problems within the Ngo family."

After Diem and Nhu were assassinated, Dong continued, the North had a strong desire, both officially and informally, to set up relations between the two regions and to move toward elections as provided for by the Geneva Accords. Regrettably, Diem's successors, including Nguyen Van Thieu and Nguyen Cao Ky, never wanted such arrangements. "This was a fact," Dong emphasized.

I pursued this further, asking whether it would have made a difference if the United States had acted differently during that period. Dong said, "History is history," eliciting wry grins from the Vietnamese Foreign Ministry director for North American affairs. "One cannot guess how history might have evolved," Dong pointed out, "although historians and common people try to explore alternatives to how events actually happened. But in the history of U.S. relations with Vietnam, at long last," Dong allowed, "there was a chance to sit together and negotiate in Paris." "Some observers," he added, "wonder whether the fact that this negotiation eventually came about indicates that it would have been possible earlier. This is just a personal view of those observers and indicates the way that the observers wished events had turned out."

Still, Dong continued, in this way of thinking, he and some American scholars have come to the view that had President Kennedy lived and continued to work with Secretary of Defense McNamara, history would have been different.

I asked if the United States had miscalculated the degree of identity of interests between Vietnam and China and between Vietnam and the Soviet Union. As a result, did we fail to take advantage of areas of potential mutual interest between Vietnam and the United States?

Premier Dong responded, saying that the question was "very interesting" and his answer was "yes." Dong explained that the U.S. administration thought North Vietnam was heavily dependent on the two major socialist countries. He added, "Because of that perception, the U.S. thought it would be more effective to have the conflict resolved by dealing directly with China and the USSR, instead of with North Vietnam—even though we tried very hard to send signals we wanted to engage with top U.S. leaders for negotiations." Dong was emphatic about this last point.

I then asked whether, if the United States had worked directly with North Vietnam, history might have developed differently.

"Of course," Dong exclaimed with greater vigor than anything else he said during the hour's conversation. "It was very unfortunate that things did not go that way," he said.

Turning to Cambodia, I asked Premier Dong's judgment as to whether Vietnam's invasion and occupation of Cambodia had been a correct move or a mistake, or if the United States could have handled Cambodia differently.

Dong gave a pensive laugh and answered, "This is something I have thought about. That is a matter of great interest to me." I noted that his answer was very interesting, since the matter is one of importance. Dong replied, "That's right." I concluded that Dong had serious reservations about at least some important aspects of Vietnam's Cambodia policy in the late-Seventies and Eighties.

Looking at the broader strategic picture, I asked Premier Dong if Vietnam's long-term interests, moving into the twenty-first century, lay in close ties with China, Russia, ASEAN, Japan, or the United States.

Dong found the question "topical and forward looking." "The Vietnamese leadership," he said, "puts a lot of thought into identifying clearly Vietnam's geopolitical position and how Vietnam relates to Asia and the rest of the world." Moving his arms for the first time, broadly gesturing outward, Dong said, "It is hard to forecast, but in the near and foreseeable future, Vietnam would give priority to relations with whatever country with which Vietnam had no direct problems. In other words, Vietnam wishes to further relations with all countries that share an interest in developing constructive ties."

"Along that line," Dong said, "I am thinking about your country, the United States. And I want you to remember that, in this moment, I am not speaking as a diplomat."

Premier Dong reflected that these were historical events that might invite the question, "What might have been? But that question is hard to answer. History is history," he repeated, "and it is hard to rewrite the past. That said," he added, "Vietnamese since ancient times have wanted peace and a good life." Dong underlined this by quoting verbatim the lines from the United States Declaration of Independence that Ho Chi Minh had included in Vietnam's own Declaration of Independence on September 2, 1945. Dong said, "Vietnam continues to strive to accomplish those ideals."

I commented that the United States very much welcomed Vietnam's entry into ASEAN, a move of historic significance for the security of the region. I hoped that Vietnam saw the United States as a country with which it does not have problems, so there can be a partnership. There are people both in the United States and Vietnam who no doubt would be shocked by that prospect.

In closing, Phan Van Dong extended to me a warm welcome to pay a return visit to him whenever I next traveled to Vietnam, no matter in what capacity. He invited me to continue to communicate with him directly, through the Vietnamese ambassador in Washington, or via any channel I wished.

Afterwards Director Phong told me, "Phan Van Dong was delighted with the meeting and had commented that you were not like any other American he had ever met." Asked what that might mean, I got, in response, the same broad grin I had seen frequently during my conversation with Premier Phan Van Dong.

From this remarkable conversation, I concluded that Premier Dong recalled with sadness the American refusal to accept the Vietminh Revolution in 1945. Ho Chi Minh and Premier Dong had hoped for American support for Vietnam's independence and were deeply disappointed that America's lofty declarations supporting "self-determination" in 1919 and 1945 were slogans rather than actual policies. Instead, the U.S. support for France in 1945 had contributed to the 30 years of war Vietnam endured to regain its independence. He also obviously believed that, instead of trying to resolve Vietnam issues in Moscow or Beijing, if the United States had tried to work directly with Hanoi in 1945 and in 1963–64, both the Indochina War and the War with America might have been avoided.

Chairman Ho Chi Minh's, Premier Dong's, and often General Vo Nguyen Giap's more conciliatory approaches were characteristic throughout Vietnam's history. Unlike hardline Marxist–Leninists such as Secretary General Le Duan and Politburo member Truong Chinh, Chairman Ho and Premier Dong sought U.S. support in their early days and opposed the confrontational approaches on land reform of Truong Chinh in 1953–96.

Sadly, Phan Van Dong died on April 29, 2000, before I had the opportunity to return to Hanoi, so I had no chance to meet with him again.

My tenure as *chargé* in Hanoi to establish a new relationship between the United States and Vietnam after 50 years of animosity was an extraordinary experience, profoundly gratifying during a brief but important moment in history. The fact that former Premier Phan Van Dong validated our efforts justified my decision to follow President Kennedy's call to service.

26

Astonishing Results and the Legacies of the War

After 80 years as a colony of France, nearly 30 years of war, and then 20 years enmeshed in a Soviet-bloc economic system—some 130 years in all—Hanoi decided to join its neighborhood and the rest of the world.

In 1995, Vietnam joined ASEAN, concluded economic agreements with the European Union, and normalized relations with the United States. Vietnam joined the Asian-Pacific Economic Council (APEC) in November 1998 and the World Trade Organization (WTO) in 2006—indicating its intention to integrate fully into regional and global trading institutions, a dramatic change in orientation.

Vietnam's transformation is astonishing:

- GDP rose from $6.38 billion in 1989 to $187.68 billion in 2018. PPP (Purchasing Power Parity) rose from $6,171 in 2015 to $7,434 in 2018.)[1]
- The growth rate in 2018 was 7.18 percent, and the World Bank estimates that in recent years the average income of the bottom 40 percent grew at a rate of 4.5 percent, compared to the general population annual growth rate of 2 percent.
- Unemployment in 2017 was 2.2 percent. The poverty rate has dropped from 50 percent in 1990 to 6.9 percent in 2017.
- The World Bank reports that access to household infrastructure has improved dramatically. In 2016, 99 percent of the population used electricity as the main

source of lighting, up from 14 percent in 1993. In rural areas, in 2016, 77 percent of the population had access to sanitation facilities—compared to 36 percent in 1993. Rural access to clean water has also improved, up from 17 percent in 1993 to 70 percent in 2016. Access to these services in urban areas is above 95 percent.

Foreign Direct Investment (FDI) sources

- Top FDI investors are Japan, South Korea, Singapore, and, newly, China, as well as Malaysia, Taiwan, Hong Kong, the Seychelles, Switzerland, and the Netherlands. Although official statistics state that U.S. foreign direct investment in Vietnam ranks roughly eleventh, these figures do not reflect the fact that much U.S. investment goes to Vietnam via Singapore, the Seychelles, et cetera. Thus, U.S. investment is higher than statistics report. Major investments by Intel, Chevron, and GE are not carried as U.S. statistics, but they are contributing to Vietnam's infrastructure development. As of April 20, 2016, Vietnam had 803 valid U.S. investment projects, registered at more than $11.7 billion.
- Similar to previous years, Vietnam continues to attract the majority of its FDI from Asian countries. In 2017, there were 115 foreign investors in Vietnam, with Japan and South Korea alone accounting for almost half of the total FDI.

Japan's investment capital stood at $9.11 billion, accounting for 25.4 percent of the total FDI. Most of the investment was in two BOT (build-operate-transfer) thermo-power projects in Thanh Hoa and Khanh Hoa, accounting for $5.37 billion. South Korea's contribution stood at 23.7 percent with investments reaching $8.49 billion; Singapore invested $5.3 billion, accounting for 14.8 percent. This year, surprisingly, China emerges as the fourth-largest investor in Vietnam. It committed investments worth $2.17 billion.

- Manufacturing and processing continue to be a major attractor of FDI, with 2017 FDI reaching $15.87 billion, accounting for 44.2 percent of the total FDI. Power production and distribution ranked second, with $8.37 billion, accounting for 23.3 percent, followed by real estate at $3.05 billion, or 8.5 percent.
- Ho Chi Minh City continues to lead among all cities and provinces, followed by the northern province of Bac Ninh and the central province of Thanh Hoa. Other major FDI destinations include Nam Dinh, Binh Duong, Kien Giang, and Hanoi.
- The industry and construction sector grew the fastest at 8 percent, followed by services at 7.44 percent and agriculture, forestry, and fishery at 2.9 percent.
- Agriculture, forestry, and fishery: In this sector, the fishery sector grew the fastest at 5.54 percent, followed by forestry and agriculture at 5.14 percent and 2.07 percent, respectively.
- In the industrial and construction sector, the industry sector grew at 7.85 percent, higher than 2016's growth rate of 7.06 percent. Manufacturing, the major sector in the industry, grew 14.4 percent, its highest in seven years. Meanwhile, mining decreased 7.1 percent, mainly due to a reduction in crude-oil and coal output.
- One of the most attractive sectors for 2018 investors, the construction sector, continued its growth in 2017 at 8.7 percent. Within the services sector, the accommodation and catering services grew the fastest at 8.98 percent, much higher when compared to its 6.7 percent growth in 2016. Wholesale and retail sales grew 8.36 percent in 2017, driven by increases in urban population and income.
- Other sectors, such as the financial, banking, and insurance activities, witnessed the highest growth in the last seven years, at 8.14 percent, while real-estate business, another attractive sector for 2018 investors, grew 4.07 percent.[2]

Despite financing and other problems stemming from reform, Hanoi remains committed to universal health care and education and achieved a very high, 98 percent, enrollment rate for both boys and girls in primary schools in 2015, up from 77 percent in 1990.[3] Forty percent of children are enrolled in pre-primary schools, and some estimates put the percentage of students enrolled in secondary schools at 77 percent.[4] Between 2000 and 2013, the portion of college-age Vietnamese enrolled at universities rose from 10 to 25 percent; Vietnam currently has 234 universities.[5] Vietnamese are intelligent, industrious, disciplined, and quick learners, and eager to learn methods and skills required in the contemporary world—all studying English, computers, and business. The energy is palpable: 60 percent of Vietnam's population is under 30 years of age, and 85 percent are under 40. The death rate is 5.9 per 1,000 population (2016 estimate).

Reflections on America's Challenges

Americans must realize that we are working with a nation just emerging from more than 100 years of relative isolation and attempting to reconstruct itself along contemporary lines; the "new Vietnam" is very much a work in progress.

Many old habits from Vietnam's hard socialist design of the past persist, but they are changing steadily. Americans must be patient but encouraging, with some humility concerning the past coupled with pride in what America has to offer.

We must give Vietnam credit for its extraordinary cooperation on accounting for the missing; the decision to cooperate was an exceptional decision, especially since Vietnam itself has 300,000 missing from the war. That Vietnam has cooperated in excellent faith has been very evident.

We also need to take a more discerning view of the nature of Vietnamese society. It is no longer communist nor a dictatorship—it is, instead, an authoritarian nation under single-party direction slowly shedding its past and trying to move toward a very different future.

While human rights remain a subject of great interest to the United States, progress has been made in close tandem with the growth of Vietnam's economy. We should look at the broader scenario of where Vietnam is going and how we can encourage greater openness to help it get there. We should look to the long term with our broad interests in mind.

More than any other aspect of U.S. relations with Vietnam, economic normalization makes the United States a significant player in Vietnam's future. All U.S. goals, including human rights, are linked to the economic engagement that both countries seek. Implementation of the bilateral trade agreement concluded in July 2002, Hanoi's joining the WTO in 2006, and Vietnam's eagerness to participate in TPP point the way to enormous change in Vietnam's economic and social system.

The United States is helping to build the new Vietnam through economic exchanges, government programs, and help with Vietnam's legal system. Engagement is the contemporary and much more congenial form of nation-building.

Americans must realize, nonetheless, that Vietnam's future society will be shaped by economic growth, education, access to information through a free press, internet, extended interaction with the rest of the world, and, most important, by Vietnam's own history and culture.

Vietnam is increasingly open. The lives of ordinary Vietnamese are no longer oppressed or severely constrained. They can move about freely, live where they wish, meet with whom they choose, and, except for calling for a multiparty democracy or overthrow of the system, say almost anything they wish. While newspapers can criticize the government and frequently report on and criticize governmental corruption, the government advises the press of what it should publish.

Vietnam's Challenges

Despite these ongoing changes, Vietnam experiences challenges in reaching its policy goal of establishing a market economy and integrating into the regional and global trading institutions.

Further structural changes are needed:

1. The roughly 6,000 State-owned Enterprises (SOE's) and State Economic Groups (SEGs), which were meant to build Chaebol-like conglomerates like those in South Korea, were wisely judged to be an inefficient structure, and equitization began in the early Teens. The SEG's were essentially ended. The number of SOEs has fallen sharply, focusing more on key sectors. Vietnam missed the target of 632 SOE's by 2015, but plans now call for divestiture of 533 more companies by 2020 through direct sales or IPOs. Those eventually remaining will mainly operate in key areas, ensuring macro-balance for the economy: public interest, security, and defense. The rationalization will wisely continue in the 2020 to 2035 period, significantly improving the structure and profitably of Vietnam's economy.[6]

2. Vietnam should create a more genuinely level playing field for its multisector economy to make it more efficient and stimulate the private sector, which provides the most growth in jobs and is a major and innovative contributor to economic growth. The nonstate (collective, private, and household) and foreign sectors now represent 79.8 percent. The state sector has been reduced to 20.2 percent, a dramatic reduction. The state sector, however, still enjoys monopolies, subsidies, and special access to capital and resources; but this must be ended as required by the Trans-Pacific Partnership (TPP). Private enterprises contributed 65 percent of manufactured products and over 70 percent of non-oil exports in recent years.

3. Continue opening the trade, investment, and banking systems rapidly to require Vietnam's economy to learn how to compete, even if it is tough. Vietnam needs to look to the long term rather than protect the short term, to become competitive with its neighbors, within the nation itself, and also in the international arena.

4. Accelerate opening of the agriculture sector and liberalize the rice-export market. The latter could raise rural income for the 70 percent of Vietnamese who still live in rural areas. This would help deal with the growing and potentially risky rural-urban income gap.

5. An even greater challenge derives from climate change. The IMF concludes "that sea levels could rise one meter by the end of the century, which would cover 40 percent of the Mekong Delta (where half the rice is produced), 3 percent of coastal provinces, and 20 percent of Ho Chi Minh City, impacting directly 10–12 percent of the population and reducing GDP by 10 percent. In the Mekong Delta, rice, which is grown by 80 percent of Vietnamese farmers on 45 percent of the agricultural land, could see a reduction decrease by 9 million tons (13 percent) by 2050." According to the World Bank, in 1999 agriculture in the Mekong Delta accounted for 30 percent of Vietnam's GDP and more than 80 percent of its rice exports. However, without appropriate infrastructure, the Delta's many canals and irrigation networks were vulnerable to salt-water intrusion from the South China Sea during the dry season, threatening land arability and flooding during the rainy season, putting harvests in danger. Poor drinking-water supplies and inadequate rural transport also held down production levels and rural incomes. In fact, local farmers have been familiar with the salinity intrusion over the last many years. These agricultural problems will require enormous expenditures for infrastructure to try to protect against climate change and desalination.[7]

6. Accelerate reform of the financial system, making capital available for all businesses, not just the favored state-owned enterprises, for export credit and debt equity, as required by TPP regulations. Interest rates have been substantially decontrolled, but access to credit by the private sector is still inhibited.

7. Deal with the problems from which foreign and domestic businesses suffer. It is necessary to make the environment more hospitable, transparent, and objective, with clear avenues for just dispute resolution, curbing corruption, strengthening the weak legal framework, ensuring financial stability, adequate training and education opportunities, and overcoming detrimental bureaucratic decision-making. Vietnam needs to accelerate the refinement of its legal system. It is also important to enhance Vietnamese use of the internet and wireless networks, and to provide access to water.

8. While justified attention has been paid to rural poverty, the urban sector also has a fearsome list of needs. Although the slightly more than 10 million Vietnamese in three cities— Ho Chi Minh City, Hanoi, and Hai Phong—have recently been provided a clean fresh-water supply, there still remain housing shortages, environmental degradation, resettling the poor without decent homes, urban transportation, and city planning.

9. Finally, and most important, Vietnam's education system needs fundamental reform, a fact understood by the government. Vietnam is making efforts to strengthen the system from the bottom up in regular and vocational schools. The government is offering 10,000 government scholarships for overseas doctoral study between 2014 and 2020 (or 1,300 to 1,500 per year) to tertiary and research-institute staff. The so-called "911 Project," amended to become Project 599, will also offer scholarships to qualified nonacademic professionals committed to tertiary teaching careers. This ambitious project, together with the government's other scholarship and fellowship projects (including the Mekong 1000 projects), aims to produce highly skilled personnel capable of engaging in a contemporary-knowledge economy able to support Vietnam's continued socioeconomic development. This effort is crucial to Vietnam's economic competitiveness.[8]

10. Significantly, Vietnam will have the challenges and opportunities to deal with these issues in a multilateral context through economic ties with more than 220 economies, participating in and negotiating Free Trade Agreements such as TPP, and bilaterally with numerous countries in Asia, Europe, and the Americas. These organizational connections will press Vietnam to adjust the role of SOEs, procurement practices, the role of labor unions, and the protection of intellectual property rights.

To achieve Vietnam goverment's target of establishing a "basically industrialized and modernized economy" by 2020 with a per capita GDP of $3,000 and "an advanced economy with per capita GDP of $10,000" by 2050, Hanoi faces several basic challenges. Vietnam must industrialize under conditions of trade liberalization with huge restrictions on support measures (credit subvention, market protection). It must adjust to the impact of foreign supermarket chains on domestic retail trade. It must implement rigorous institution reform on transparency, regulation coherence, customs, and government procurement. Hanoi must ensure that banks and other financial institutions can cope with competition. To achieve these ambitious goals, Vietnam must "conduct fundamental reforms of its institutions, restructure its economy, and enhance science and technology research."

11. Finally, Hanoi needs, for its own sake, to accelerate openness and political reform. Vietnam must build a meritocratic society, develop democracy, and ensure human rights. In the assessment of one astute observer, "Political reform and institutional reform in Vietnam is clearly behind the economic reform and international integration. There is no counterbalance to State power at any levels; civil society is officially not allowed yet and only loyal mass organizations are authorized to operate. The press is strictly under control and surveillance. Transparency and openness are low and not efficient, accountability is not endorsed. The Constitution of Vietnam in 2013 has promulgated fundamental human rights, e.g., the freedom of expression, the freedom

of the press, the freedom of association, et cetera; but these rights have been not implemented and have to wait for various laws."

Vietnam unfortunately emulates Soviet and now Russian management of the media. Some papers, like *Tuoi Tre*, have been friskier than others, but a freer press would advance the invigoration of Vietnam's society. In recent years, the Vietnamese administration has increasingly suppressed freedom of the press while simultaneously becoming increasingly corrupt.

Local elections are common, and national elections for the National Assembly (NA) feature both party and "independent" candidates. The results in Assembly elections in 2016 demonstrated that voters opted for younger officials, with 71 candidates under 40 years of age securing seats in the National Assembly, a 9.1-percent increase over the last term. Over 60 percent of elected delegates have master's degrees or higher. There are 133 female delegates, accounting for 26.8 percent of the body.

The number of non-Party delegates for the 14th term is only 21 (4.2 percent of elected delegates), half the number of the 13th term, meaning 96 percent of NA delegates are Communist Party members. All candidates are carefully screened.

Rapid economic progress has, in effect, bought the party time, since most Vietnamese are enjoying increasing prosperity and are content to support government and party rule. However, a prolonged period of economic stagnation could change this equation.

There are those who long for a more open, democratic system. Open advocates for such are charged with treason and jailed, as the Saigon lawyer Le Cong Dinh was in 2009. Others share his views but are more discreet in their advocacy.

There is *sub rosa* discussion of resurrecting the 1946 Constitution of Vietnam (AKA Ho Chi Minh Constitution), which provided for free elections, free press, free assembly, workers' rights, and women's equality, among other liberal notions. That constitution was written when Ho Chi Minh was attempting to draw all elements into the fight for independence from France.[9]

Others advocate a reform movement within the Communist Party itself, resurrecting the Lao Dong (Labor) Party as a reformist component committed to reform and sworn to oppose corruption.

These ideas could be vehicles for promoting reform from within Vietnam's historic parameters, and, therefore, might be more acceptable than introducing a Western-style system outright.

Potential

With a fully normalized economic relationship, the complementary nature of the U.S. and Vietnam economies has led to a rapid expansion of our engagement; the United States is becoming a top investor in Vietnam's economic and human-resource development.

With 1.5 million Vietnamese-Americans, we can also count on growing human interaction, with education, science, technological, and intellectual exchanges in both directions. Opening the United Airlines link in November 2004 between San Francisco and Ho Chi Minh City facilitated interaction and reconciliation. The developing educational, cultural, and artistic exchanges between the United States and Vietnam are adding depth and richness to the relationship. Cultural exchanges are growing rapidly.

Finally, and most important, as I see it, there are no contradictions or conflicts between Vietnamese and U.S. national interests, both bilaterally and within ASEAN, and considerable commonality of strategic interests. The goal should be to build a strategic partnership between the United States and Vietnam. I was pleased to hear in a two-day conference in Hanoi in July 2010, during a 15th-anniversary commemoration of the establishment of U.S.-Vietnam relations, numerous speakers, both Vietnamese and American, talking about the U.S.-Vietnam strategic partnership and a military relationship.

The Legacies of the Vietnam War

As our legacy, I have concluded that the United States—despite noble intentions of defending what it treated as an international border and independent nation in South Vietnam, seeking to save the South Vietnamese people from takeover by the communists, and protecting Southeast Asia from communist domination—

intervened in a civil war. We Americanized and militarized the war, introduced politically destabilizing, revolutionary concepts into the Vietnamese political and social scene, wrecked the traditional economy with extraordinary dislocations, and assumed responsibility for running a war in a society of which we understood little. With reconciliation, the United States has embraced and supports Vietnam, very much for the betterment and strategic interests of both.

I had and have utmost respect for the several million American servicemen and women who fought in that bitter war. They risked and sacrificed their lives for a nation whose leaders took them into a battlefield they did not understand, and they deserve our profoundest gratitude.

To Vietnamese, the legacy is of a long, nationalist struggle against an America that was regarded as an extension of the long struggle with French colonialism. Vietnam's leaders, especially Ho Chi Minh, inspired Vietnamese to struggle despite the horrors of the war, its huge death toll, hundreds of thousands of Vietnamese soldiers still unaccounted for, a devastated economy, but, finally, sweet, proud victory by the Vietnamese people over the French and Americans, as Vietnam historically achieved over the Chinese. The victory was, ironically, in one of history's few wars in which the winner was left to struggle alone with the poverty and devastation the conflict left behind. At the end, a rigorously ideological system stymied the victory. Only finally in 1986, 11 years after the end of the war and reunification of the country, did the rigidities began to lift with the beginning of *Doi Moi*, and Vietnam could finally begin to define itself in the contemporary world.

Most Vietnamese would concur, I believe, that Marxist-Leninist economics and politics did not allow Vietnam to achieve its full potential. The entry into ASEAN in 1995 ended Vietnam's virtual isolation for the first time since France made colonies of Indochina 130 years ago. Vietnam finally joined the contemporary world economy. Because of the normalization of relations with the U.S. in 1995, the Bilateral Trade Agreement with the U.S. in 2002, Vietnam's entry into WTO in 2006, and eagerness to join the TPP, Vietnam is rapidly reforming its economy into a market economy. This transformation of the economy stemmed from an understanding that Vietnam could not thrive in the contemporary world in isolation.

Economic normalization notwithstanding, Hanoi still believes a Vietnamese-style democracy can be constructed that will be more appropriate to Vietnamese culture than the template multiparty democracy often promoted around the world.

In a discussion about democracy recently with a Vietnamese intellectual, my Vietnamese friend commented, "American notions of democracy and multiparty democracy are not natural to Vietnamese culture. Moreover, a multiparty political system was not the most urgent requirement of Vietnamese. Dealing with corruption is a much more important democratic goal. Empowering all the people is a democratic goal in Vietnam so that all have ability to contribute to society.

"Reducing poverty by 50 percent in a decade was a democratic goal of which Vietnam is justly proud. Local chiefs no longer tell people how to vote. About 9 percent of legislators (43 of 492 in 2014; 4.7 percent in 2016) in the National Assembly are non–party members. Both the government and legislature are seeking to increase this number. These are all seen as elements of a Vietnamese democratic system.

"Human rights as a concept has now moved to mainstream in Vietnam," my friend added, "but the concept does not have the same implications as in America or the West. To Vietnamese, it is more Jeffersonian in concept. "All men are created equal" is an important idea in the Vietnamese Constitution, borrowed from Jefferson. Vietnamese take seriously the idea of egalitarianism."

The Legacy of American and Vietnamese Engagement

The legacy of the Vietnam War also includes 2.5 million Americans who engaged with Vietnam in the war itself and the millions of Vietnamese who engaged with Americans because of the war or because they fled its aftermath for America.

More than 58,000 Americans lost their lives fighting in Vietnam. Hundreds of thousands of other Americans, 60 percent of whom were 19 to 20 years old, fought and then returned to the United States, where they were met with anger, disinterest, and even rejection as the war became perceived as a misbegotten or failed war, to be forgotten as quickly as possible. Happily, many Vietnam veterans have since paid return visits to Vietnam and, overwhelmingly, have been able to reconcile their roles of the past with the welcome and excitement of the currently vibrant Vietnam.

The 1.5 million Vietnamese who came to the United States as refugees have been a rich intellectual and cultural contribution to America. But many, especially older Vietnamese-Americans, remain even now disillusioned and beyond the redemption of reconciliation with the new Vietnam. In contrast, many young Vietnamese-Americans have visited the new Vietnam and found solace, peace, and engagement. This process of reconciliation is highly desirable and will, I believe, eventually reconcile most young Vietnamese-Americans with the new Vietnam.

We must also include in the legacy the 3 million Vietnamese soldiers and civilians who are estimated to have died during the war. Some 300,000 soldiers are still unaccounted for, compared to the few hundred Americans whose fates remain unknown. Part of the legacy of the war must be gratitude to Vietnam for its diligent help in the accounting for missing Americans, even though so many Vietnamese remain unaccounted for.

Finally, the legacy of Agent Orange affects hundreds of Vietnamese, former soldiers, and many children, in the common view of Vietnamese. I strongly believe that the United States has a moral obligation to try to help deal with this legacy. Fortunately, during the tenure of Ambassador Michael Michalak (2007–10), this process commenced and is now expanding.

Presidential Visits

At former U.S. Ambassador Ted Osius's invitation, I attended the 20th anniversary celebration of the establishment of diplomatic relations held in Hanoi on July 2, 2015. To my great delight, former President Bill Clinton was the principal speaker. He delivered a formidable speech to the 1,400 Vietnamese and foreign friends who attended. President Clinton asserted, "The normalization of relations with Vietnam was, for personal, political, and geostrategic reasons, one of the most important achievements of my career. It helped to heal the wounds of war, to build bonds of genuine friendship, and provide proof in an increasingly divided world that cooperation was far better than conflict."

Even more emphatically, President Barack Obama's May 2016 visit demonstrated the amazing progress in U.S.-Vietnam relations and outlined the benefits of a solid, comprehensive partnership. In his speech to the Vietnamese people, the president spoke of the ingredients for economic success in the twenty-first century: investment and trade under the rule of law without corruption, where people have the freedom to think for themselves and exchange ideas to innovate. He announced an agreement to dispatch the Peace Corps to Vietnam and to create a new Fulbright University Vietnam, Vietnam's first independent, nonprofit university. He emphasized his commitment to the TPP, which would afford Vietnam broader ties with more partners to advance human rights, with higher wages and safer working conditions.

Of great significance, the president described the lifting of the ban on defense sales, symbolizing the full normalization of U.S.-Vietnam relations, elevating security cooperation, and building trust between the American and Vietnamese militaries. Most pointedly the president said, "The 20th century has taught us all that international order upon which our mutual security depends is rooted in certain rules and norms. Nations are sovereign; no matter how large or small a nation may be, its sovereignty should be respected and its territory should not be violated. Big nations should not bully smaller ones. Disputes should be resolved peacefully."

His words evoked strong applause. Even more specifically, the president said that "in the South China Sea, where the U.S. is not a claimant, we would stand with partners in upholding core principles, like freedom of navigation and overflight, and lawful commerce that is not impeded, and the peaceful resolution of disputes through legal means, in accordance with international law." Without mentioning China, the president said that "as we go forward, the United States will continue to fly, sail, and operate wherever international law allows, and we will support the right of all countries to do the same," again evoking strong applause.

As the third element of our partnership, "addressing areas where our governments disagree," he spoke of the values laid out in the Universal Declaration of Human Rights, observing that the Vietnamese constitution declared that "citizens have the right to freedom of speech and freedom of the press, and have the right to access to information, the right to assembly, the right to association, and the right to demonstrate."

The president noted that Vietnam has made some progress regarding these rights. The TPP would further bolster this process through economic and labor reforms. While the people of Vietnam will decide the nation's future, he said, "As a friend of Vietnam, allow me to share my view—why I believe nations are more successful when universal rights are upheld."

President Obama ended his remarks with a quote from the epic Vietnamese poem *The Tale of Kieu*: "Please take from me this token of trust, so we can embark upon our 100-year journey together."

As I heard the president's eloquent words, I could not help but remember the agenda we envisaged and on which we embarked in 1995 when I opened the embassy, and my words to former Premier Phan Van Dong just before departing Hanoi in 1997—that there were no conflicts between Vietnam's and America's national interests, which meant that we should build a strategic partnership.

Epilogue

The Princeton Global Summer Seminar in Hanoi

Several years ago, Princeton University President Shirley Tilghman made clear to the university's faculty, including Michael Centeno, Director of the Princeton Institute of International and Regional Studies (PIIRS), that she found Princeton students too "isolated" from the contemporary world and thought efforts should be made to "globalize" their perspectives. As a member of the PIIRS Advisory Council, I suggested the possibility of a six-week, for-credit summer seminar for Princeton students on the Vietnam War, held in Hanoi. Professor Centeno and President Tilghman enthusiastically agreed.

I arranged the seminar with three professors of the University of Social Sciences and Humanities in Hanoi: International Studies Department Dean Pham Quang Minh, History Professor Pham Hong Tung, and Sociology Professor Do Thu Ha. This was the first such seminar anywhere for Princeton. Accentuating its uniqueness, we invited three Vietnam University students, chosen by the University professors and vetted by me, to participate in all activities of the seminar. We were at liberty to discuss freely any topic we wished. Our adventure, both academic and cultural, involved an intensive academic study of 2,000 years of Vietnamese history, during most of which Vietnamese were fighting to gain or regain their independence from China. I conducted the seminar for three summers in 2007–09.

Why undertake a retrospective on events that occurred 50 years ago and which have been dissected hundreds of times? Why is this history relevant today?

My desire to equip some of the next generation of leaders to navigate our country's increasingly complex security challenges motivated me to pursue an in-depth study and explore the lessons of the Vietnam War. As much as any experience I had with Vietnam, conceiving and conducting the Princeton Global Summer Seminar in Hanoi in 2007–09 allowed me to hear directly from Vietnamese in Hanoi their recollections about Vietnam's history and the war. I also benefited from the questions, comments, and analyses from the fresh minds of my students, themselves trying to discern the truth, free from the prejudices created by living through that epoch.

The structure of the seminar "America and Vietnam at War: Origins, Implications, and Consequences" was crucial. I conducted four seminars each week, Monday through Thursday and had a Vietnamese conduct a second seminar on the same subject each day, to provide at least three perspectives on the war—the U.S. government assessment, which I supplied; my own; and Vietnamese views on each subject. Heavy reading assignments bolstered their knowledge of Vietnam's history. In special informal afternoon sessions, I introduced the students to other interesting Vietnamese and former American soldiers living in or passing through Hanoi. Most important, the Princetonians would participate in community service every Thursday afternoon and spend weekends traveling to Ha Long Bay, Hue, Hoi An in central Vietnam, and Ho Chi Minh City, plus one weekend of community service in a village near Hanoi.

Exposing the students to several points of view allowed them to examine critical events and times in Vietnam's history and to decide for themselves where the truth, always a slippery concept through the lens of history, might lie.

The seminar also featured daily lessons in Vietnamese language. With six tones, Vietnamese is a difficult language, but my students were rewarded in the markets with better bargains and direct interactions with ordinary Vietnamese.

My goals in the seminar were to employ my extensive experiences to present an informed narrative to the students. Second, I aimed to use the historical events of the American role in Vietnam to illustrate the importance of studying history, its successes and mistakes, especially for the young generation that knows the history of the era only superficially. Third, I hoped to use insights into the Vietnam era and the American strategy, as presented by presidential decisions, to present a holistic view of the Vietnam War and, finally, the emergence of Vietnam from a Stalinist-Marxist-Leninist past striving to become a contemporary society with a market economy and, conceptually, an increasingly pluralistic social and political system.

The formula for the Princeton Global Summer seminar was magical. The students were entranced with historian Huu Ngoc's tracing of 3,000 years of Vietnamese culture and history in the Van Mieu Confucian Temple. The students also attained a serious understanding of the emergence of radicalism in Vietnamese society, explored the French Indochina War, the "American War," and U.S. presidential decision-making concerning the war. We examined junctures at which different decisions by U.S. presidents might have averted war or ended it earlier. We heard a discussion of Ho Chi Minh's role, led by an opposition National Assemblyman, discussion of the Paris Peace Talks by a senior Vietnamese participant, a Communist Party official's description of a strategy for building pro-Hanoi support in the United States, and a discussion of North Vietnam's military strategy during the Tet Offensive in 1968 by General Nguyen Dinh Uoc, a close confidant of General Vo Nguyen Giap at Dien Bien Phu and during the "American War."

The writer Bao Ninh, author of *The Sorrows of War*, enchanted the students by discussing his life and his antiwar novel, fighting for his soul as he fought in southern Vietnam. A seminar featuring a NLF operative's subversive activities in Saigon during the war and a perspective on the legacies of the war were spellbinding. The three Vietnamese University professors provided the historical narrative on which these specialists elaborated.

The Princetonians were deeply impressed with Vietnamese society and people. They loved the children, practiced tai chi at dawn on the shores of Hoan Kiem Lake in central Hanoi with young and old Vietnamese, and used their Vietnamese to order delicious specialties. Community service was highly meaningful to the students. Playing with Vietnamese children, who had been afflicted by Agent Orange through their fathers, at the Vietnam Friendship Association was deeply moving. Others delighted tiny children by teaching songs and dance at the cultural center.

The weekend community service in the village of Hoa Lo struck deep emotions in the students. We called on families with soldier-fathers afflicted by Agent Orange while fighting in the South, who then passed it on to their children, horribly damaged from birth. Many of the students described this as the epic event of the seminar—the extraordinary hospitality of former soldiers who had been shot point-blank in the head by American soldiers, themselves and their children devastatingly afflicted by Agent Orange, welcomed us into their homes, invited us to smoke "peace pipes," and without hostility responded to our pointed questions. Cleaning and whitewashing a Vietnamese military cemetery was a particularly poignant experience.

These Princetonians became among the best-informed Americans on the Vietnam War and could ably explore the nuances of events and U.S. presidential decisions. They easily spotted propaganda on the rare occasions when they heard it, but they just as expertly noted the similarities in cynical decision-making and the selling of wars in Vietnam and in Iraq. They marveled that one Vietnamese professor "sounded just like Stanley Karnow" and heard with surprise different Vietnamese with different interpretations, such as on the intentions and impact of the Tet Offensive. The reality of being in Vietnam itself significantly heightened their sensitivities and perceptions.

Since the seminar was conducted during the height of the Iraq and Afghanistan wars, it lent itself extraordinarily well to recognizing the challenges facing our leaders during those wars and in contemplating the handling of future crises, such as potentially with Iran. President Barack Obama faced dilemmas like those Presidents Kennedy and Johnson faced in Vietnam. Their experiences and the lessons that we either learned and ignored or did not learn should have instructed Presidents Bush and Obama in their decisions about wars that America contemplated or in which America was engaged or might face in future challenges. What happened in Vietnam was important, but even more important is what happens when one does not understand history or learn from experience.

During the initial seminars in 2007 and 2008, when the Iraq War was at its height, I purposefully did not mention Iraq very often, because I did not want my strong opposition to the war to turn the seminar into an anti-Iraq War obsession and risk tainting the atmosphere for an objective examination of the Vietnam War. As one 2007 student wrote in his blog, and I found out later, "Bringing up Vietnam is a cheap shot against Iraq. Certainly, there are ample parallels, but there are even more differences. The actors, motivations, circumstances, ideologies, and geopolitics are significantly different enough to make blanket comparisons between the two wars sound naïve and ignorant."

Nonetheless, I sensed that the students, including this one, were keenly aware of the almost endless succession of seeming parallels: concocting attacks on American ships in the Gulf of Tonkin and threatening mushroom clouds, the strong desire for congressional authorization, the fear that senators and presidents alike would be accused of "being soft on communism" or " soft on terrorism," for failing to support resolutions, escalations, or surges, the tarnishing of America's standing as a result of My Lai and Abu Ghraib, efforts to reform the local governments on America's model, and actual or real threats to take the war to neighboring countries to stop the flow of men and material. But the core point of this lengthy list is not that it is about Vietnam and Iraq, per se, but about America.

The parallels between Vietnam and Iraq are sparse. Vietnam was engaged in a civil war and Iraq was suffering from an invasion by a superpower. The parallels mentioned above were all on the American side, which suggests that American leaders may not have learned the lessons of the Vietnam War. More fundamentally, the similarities were that American leaders did not understand the nature of the conflicts into which they took the country. I often asked myself, "Did anyone ever tell President Johnson that Vietnam had fought for 2,000 years against Chinese efforts to take over Vietnam and was not going to be a Chinese surrogate?" As Deputy Prime Minister Nguyen Co Thach told me in 1997, explaining his personal opposition not to the overthrow of the Pol Pot regime but to the occupation by Vietnam of Cambodia: "One country cannot impose its political system on another."

At the behest of the students in my seminar in 2009, when the fury over the Iraq War had abated somewhat, at the final session of the seminar we discussed the wars. Although the Vietnam and Iraq Wars and the countries and circumstances themselves were quite different, the parallels seem overwhelming in Washington. U.S. leaders seem not to have learned or to have forgotten the lessons of history when contemplating the wars.

During lazy evenings floating on Ha Long Bay, the philosophical meaning of the experience easily slipped into conversations. The chance for thinking about great historical events a lifetime away but in the home of Ho Chi Minh and the Vietminh cast everything in a more engaging and exciting light. Discussions of the OSS and Deer Team work with Ho Chi Minh in 1943–45 made Archimedes Patti's reflections on his farewell dinner with Ho Chi Minh much more immediate. Many of the students spoke of a "life–changing experience" in describing their reactions to the seminar. One wrote, not atypically, "Living and learning amidst a foreign culture pushed me outside of my 'Western comfort zone,' fueled my respect for other cultures and lifestyles, and confirmed my passion for interacting with different kinds of people. The Hanoi seminar added a new dimension to my perceptions of humanity and the world. Learning about the war and evaluating the political and ethical activity of the United States and the Vietnamese, together with witnessing some of the lasting destructive impact of the war, offered insight into the often-complicated ethics of human action." One parent wrote, "What a gift! Thank you for creating and coordinating such a spectacular educational and cultural experience."

I felt that we probed a historical event in a more embracing manner than was the custom. As it had for the students, the experience gave me the opportunity to think more deeply about the events of the war and those surrounding the war.

Following seven assignments in or on Vietnam, this provided me the opportunity to genuinely consider all aspects of the war, and I reached very different conclusions that were not possible during the war. This crowning experience, probing together with my 41 students from 2007 to 2009, hearing their fresh and bright minds consider these crucial events, discussing those events in this environment, was among the most rewarding experiences of my life.

APPENDIX

Some Thoughts on the Situation in Vietnam[3]

This paper was composed near the end of 1966 by State Department Foreign Service officers who had been stationed in Vietnam as province or assistance provincial representatives, USAID since June 1965. They were Ray Reimer, Dac Lac Province; Steve Ledogar and Richard Brown, Quang Tri Province; Clay Nettles, Lam Dong Province; and Montagnard Officer Robert Meyers and Desaix Anderson, Bien Hoa 1965–66, Saigon Districts 6 & 8, June–December 1966, and Revolutionary Development Evaluator, 1967, until June. Several of these officers met in late 1966 or early 1967 with State Department Undersecretary for Political Affairs Eugene Rostow to discuss the ideas contained herein.

I.   SUMMARY—FACING THE FACTS

The basic danger facing the United States in its Vietnam effort is that of losing sight of the struggle's essential truth, that is, assistance from the North notwithstanding, that the war in South Vietnam remains a South Vietnamese political and civil war. Secretary McNamara has stated that it cannot be won in the North, bomb as we will. What he has not made clear is that it is equally sure that the war can never be won by force of arms alone in the South. Units of the North Vietnamese Army (NVA) were first sent South late in 1964 to give a speedy *coup de grace* to an already all-but-vanquished South Vietnamese state. Their disappearance would not remove the real danger to the state—that is, the Viet-Cong infrastructure, which is and, if present trends continue, will remain intact throughout South Viet-Nam.

To be sure, terrorism and other applications of brute force were and continue to be widely used by the "National Liberation Front" (NLF) in securing its position in South Vietnam. But banditry pure and simple (that is, violence without any popular roots or support) could not long exist in a state with a military and police structure as developed as that in South Vietnam today. The Vietcong were able to gain initial support and continue to flourish essentially because of grievances among the Vietnamese people. Vietcong terrorism is effective—there remains behind it a vision of a "just" society, affording equality of opportunity for the "masses." The GVN has not yet remedied these grievances, nor has it yet given the Vietnamese peasant or intellectual any vision to counter that of the Communists. The present Vietnamese governmental system, which both presidential and senatorial elections seem to have ratified, is essentially no more than a successor government to the colonial regime, with a privileged class of urban Vietnamese replacing the French in the hierarchy. Vietnamese governments continue to be unrepresentative and unresponsive, increasingly corrupt, and hopelessly bureaucratized. A paternalistic and very lethargic program of evolutionary change has of course been started, but at a pace which is unlikely to inspire and win the allegiance of the rural population.

We believe that the large turnout in the recent elections demonstrates that the South Vietnamese people still have hopes that their government may become worth believing in. We propose that these hopes, and the political situation arising from the elections, provide excellent ground for a program of fundamental reform, beginning now and dominating the coming months. Such a program of reform, accompanied by extensive efforts to promote reconciliation among the fragmented sections of Vietnamese society, can still lead to success in Vietnam. We do not believe this can happen overnight; it will still take several years of effort before these reforms achieve their goal of undermining and destroying the base of the Vietcong infrastructure. This effort will require American assistance and an American presence—civilian and military—until its successful completion. Belief in the military solution to the Vietnam conflict, which cannot but lead to frustration and eventually overwhelming impatience, seriously threatens our ability to maintain this presence for as long as is necessary. We ask that this belief be set aside, and that America concentrate its efforts in assisting the Vietnamese government and people fight the only war which can destroy the Communist threat to their country, that is, the political struggle against the Vietcong.

II.   THE VIETCONG INFRASTRUCTURE REMAINS

The present conflict in South Vietnam began as, and in essence remains, a civil war between the Government of Vietnam (GVN) and the Vietcong. Until late 1964, almost all insurgency in South Viet-Nam was carried out by the indigenous communist forces, the National Liberation Front (NLF), or the Vietcong. The original nucleus of the movement was composed of South Vietnamese communists, who either remained underground in the South after the Geneva Accords, or who went north at that time and returned south later. This leadership gathered around it, and continued to gather around it, a political and military force composed of communists and communist sympathizers, nationalists dissatisfied with the Diemist regime and its successors, Southern and Central Vietnamese opposed to a strong central government seemingly dominated by Northerners, and either dissidents, including young people who have simply given up on the stagnant South Vietnamese society. This essentially indigenous force has made steady gains in popular support throughout South Viet-Nam from 1957 on. It was this force, with only small outside assistance, which necessitated having some 23,300 U.S. military personnel in South Vietnam by the end of 1964.

During the last and most oppressive period of Diem's regime, and during the anarchic year and a half which followed the dictator's overthrow, the Vietcong took advantage of the weakening effects these political happenings inevitably had on the government's presence in the countryside to advance into a position where final victory seemed within its grasp. It was only then, towards the end of 1964—in order to give the crumbling South Vietnamese state its final blow—that this still essentially guerilla movement formed itself partially into battalion-sized units, was joined by units of the regular North Vietnamese Army (NVA), and converted from primary reliance on stolen arms and goods to externally furnished supplies. This entrance of the NVA into South Vietnam, and its initial successes in nearly cutting the South in two, gave rise to the dispatch of American combat troops to South Vietnam, and the beginning of the real escalation of the war. The North Vietnamese have answered this escalation in kind through the continued infiltration of NVA units into the South. This infiltration unfortunately has seemed to have substantiated the misleading and essentially propagandistic argument that the struggle in Vietnam is caused by "overt military aggression from the North." It is this error which more than anything else has diverted U.S. attention from the real war in the South to military actions against the North, its home territory and its expeditionary forces. Proponents of this misdirected emphasis overlook that it was the Vietcong forces alone which brought South Vietnam to near collapse in late 1964. They forget that even if all NVA troops left or were driven from the South—and the U.S. combat troops were likewise withdrawn—the GVN would be in not much better position than it was in 1964. Even if North Vietnam stopped sending all supplies to the Vietcong, the South Vietnamese insurgents would be no worse off in say 1960—considering the political gains they have made and the arsenal they have built up since then. It is a horrifying thought, but we suggest that even if the United States leveled Hanoi, and Peking too, we would wake up after the holocaust and find the NLF as much in control of the South Vietnamese countryside Vietcong's tactics. Nor do we suggest that the Vietnamese people are hopelessly enamored of the Vietcong as their only liberator. Given the choice, the majority of Vietnamese would like the Vietcong to disappear altogether, if that would end the war. But, the NLF isn't about to disappear—indeed, it still finds new people willing to join it. Until now, the essentially non-Vietcong majority has little it sees worth defending against the organized guerilla minority. If pressured in the slightest, the members of the majority yield to the minority. Few people defend themselves against the Vietcong, and we cannot hope to find enough policemen, in whatever uniform, to insulate them all. So, the Vietcong will remain until the people find reason to actively oppose them. In certain areas, as in some Catholic villages, and among the Hoa Hao in An Giang Province, where this motivation exists—due to religion rather than the GVN—the Vietcong are successfully withstood. It can be done; but how.

The level of participation in the last elections shows that the majority of the South Vietnamese people still have the hope that something will come of their government. But, although the people elected it, they are still far from believing that this government, and all its manifestations down to the province, district, and village levels, is really their government, and therefore worth defending. This identification between government and people has no historical basis in either the Mandarin or colonialist regimes—which administered, but felt no obligation to serve. Until now, South Vietnamese governments have deviated little from these patterns. This paper proposes ways to change this emphasis, to make the government essentially one of and for the people, and, therefore, worth fighting for. We propose that only when this happens will the "water" of the Vietcong "fish" dry up. Fail to destroy the Vietcong infrastructure in this way, and no military force in the world will succeed in Vietnam.

III.   SERIOUS SOCIAL AND ECONOMIC REFORMS ARE RE-
         QUIRED

As stated above, while the Vietcong proposes to the Vietnamese the possibility of a new society in which the inequities they have suffered will be removed, the South Vietnamese rulers have shown little evidence of a willingness to break the established order. Although three years of elementary schooling are now available to the majority of Vietnamese children, education beyond that level, a prerequisite for any kind of responsibility in the military or civil administration, remains what it has always been, a privilege for the few. What is needed is an expended system of full primary, secondary, and vocational education and a greatly enlarged scholarship program, based on need and merit and not on "connections." But education is only a prerequisite for social mobility, not its guarantee. Young Vietnamese must be able to see a future for themselves. Today it is not difficult to understand why so many young Vietnamese turn their backs on their stagnant society to "go with the swingers"—the Vietcong or the more ephemeral "Struggle Movement." The 13,000 young people who took part in the 1966 Sumner Youth Program demonstrated the Vietnamese youth can work for a useful cause. That political infighting among high GVN officials prevented the 1967 program from even getting started demonstrated how little the existing regime appreciates this fact. We propose that the primarily youth-oriented District_Six and Eight programs in Saigon be multiplied many times over throughout the country, so that as many Vietnamese young people as possible may take part in the building of their society.

Building a society is not only social programs, however, it is expanded political activity (discussed in the next section), and real economic development, to which little attention has been given in South Vietnam. South Vietnam has an essentially agricultural economy, traditionally based principally on the production of rubber and rice, and Vietnam has even become a net importer of rice. World market conditions are such that that it is unlikely that Vietnam could regain its position as a leading rubber exporter. Vietnam's natural advantages, however, would indicate the value of seeking its restoring its position as a net exporter of rice. We believe that a fundamental requirement for achieving this goal to assure an adequate return to the producer. At the same time, Vietnam's farmers must be freed from their dependence upon wholesalers and middle men for credit by the establishment of a truly adequate agricultural credit system. Cheap fertilizer, another prerequisite, should be made available by the completion of already-made plans for the construction of fertilizer plants in South Vietnam.

The Vietnamese are good farmers. Anyone who has visited a rural auto-repair shop would also be impressed with the ingenuity and ability of the Vietnamese as craftsmen. Today, these talents are being turned more and more to an artificial economy based on the American presence. Not enough is being done to maintain, let alone increase, a Vietnamese light industry capability, which would provide a soundly based system capable of surviving under more normal peacetime conditions. Young Vietnamese who have no future on the land and who do not want to be "parasites" have few places to go—and the Vietnamese economy has few prospects for the future. The continuation of the anti-inflation programs should ensure the existence of a sound base for economic development—but they should be a means, not an end. Studies show that interest in economic development has finally awakened; but plans and realities are not the same. Economic development cannot wait until victory. It is a vital precondition for success in Vietnam.

IV.   STEPS BEING TAKEN TO REFORM THE VIETNAMESE ADMINISTRATIVE AND POLITICAL. SYSTEMS MUST BE HASTENED AND EXPANDED

The dead hand of the traditional Vietnamese ministries now break-ing GVN revolutionary efforts must be lifted. On the national level, this means that the activist drive now provided in certain areas by such revolutionary organs as the Ministry of Revolutionary De-velopment (MORD) and the Special Commissariat for Highlander Affairs be extended to all civilian efforts. A strengthening of the present "Super Ministry" system, creating one large Revolutionary Development Super Ministry. Under its control would be the crit-ical Ministries of Education, Agriculture, Health, Economic Devel-opment, and the present Ministry of Revolutionary Development; alternatively, also discussed was creation of other action-oriented bodies having power to direct traditional ministries. Funding and other fiscal procedures, which now immobilize much of the GVN, should be radically simplified along the lines of the MORD's pres-ent procedures. General Thieu's announced plans for reforming the Vietnamese civil service are encouraging and should be strongly supported by the United States.

On the local level, local autonomy and initiative should be spurred wherever possible—in village, district, and province. This is not to diminish the necessity for a strong central leadership, but rather to build equally strong and motivated local partners for the central government. General Thieu's decree giving the province chiefs more power over the local ministry representatives (service chiefs) is a good step in this direction. Local governments, not Sai-gon ministries, should have the power of the purse on all but major projects. On the military side, the new organization for all Revo-lutionary Development support troops, with increased control by the province chiefs, should also help. The activities of the revolu-tionary Development and Truong Son cadre teams should be even more strongly supported, as they represent a real force for change.

Politically, we consider the election of a president to be over-emphasized at the expense of the senate and chamber of deputies elections. But, most important of all is the restoration of local self-government. After village self-government becomes a reality, plans for self-government on the district and provincial levels must be speedily implemented.

A promising scheme would guarantee local taxation prerogatives to hamlet and village governments. Funds from this source could be the local contribution to local development directed by the local elected governments. An imaginative provincial administration should inspire and encourage development not only of school and health systems but also of agricultural and other economic development schemes—ranging from irrigation systems to saw mills and brick kilns. The ready availability of additional funds and materials for the provincial governments would act as an incentive to locally initiated projects, and enable villagers to undertake needed projects beyond their own financial resources. This would, in effect, be an explanation of the self-help programs. which is one of the few proven successes in Vietnam to date.

The issue of corruption has perhaps not clearly been brought into focus. On the one hand, let us eliminate the "handclasp" symbol of U.S. commercial imports (items which have been paid for in full by their Vietnamese importers). This may turn more attention to real corruption, which continues to eat away at the Vietnamese social fabric at an ever-faster pace. While a degree of corruption is expected all over Southeast Asia, Vietnam has long passed the tolerance threshold of the average citizen. Sincere efforts by well-meaning individuals, even generals, will not solve this problem. To begin with, realistic salaries must be paid to civil servants; at the same time all office holders must be subject to the scrutiny of democratic institutions at all levels, through decentralization of political power. The Vietnamese army must be removed from the political administrative system at a far faster pace than is presently evident.

V.   A REFOCUSING OF AMERICAN ATTITUDES AND PRACTICES IS REQUIRED

In both military and civilian efforts in Vietnam, we must rid ourselves of the illusion of quantitative solutions. "Enough" personnel, and "enough" equipment, however they are defined in numerical terms, will *never* by themselves bring victory. There is already a surfeit of U.S. advisors, both military and civilian. On the civilian side, we propose rather than continue an endless inflation of the U.S. advisory team in Vietnam, a ruthless weeding out of "dead wood" should be instituted, aiming for a lean revolutionary civilian corps of no more than 1000, rather than the bloated 5,400 now planned. If, for humanitarian reasons, marginal personnel cannot be separated from service, let them gather dust in Upper Volta or the Maldive Islands, not Vietnam. Like their Vietnamese counterparts, technical advisors should be the servants of the revolutionary effort—not the authors of programs developed in a vacuum

On the military side, the need for rethinking is most urgent. To be sure, too weak a military force in Vietnam could be disastrous, as it nearly was in 1964. In 1967, however, the danger of our very presence in Vietnam lies in the opposite direction, in a grossly overemphasized and misdirected effort, functioning under its own logic and serving its own ends. The role of the military in Viet-Nam should be fundamentally reviewed—and traditional views of it should be decisively rejected. We cannot, for example, hope to destroy the enemy's total military capability, as in two World Wars. The United States does not propose to conquer the territory of North Vietnam. We trust it is not our goal to beat the Communists in a war of attrition. These are traditional military goals, and in Vietnam none of them is worth the price they would impose. What mission, then, is the military left with?

We believe the mission of the U.S. military in Vietnam is the essentially defensive one of neutralizing the enemy's military support to his political effort—that is to say, securing for us the base of operations for our real *offensive* effort—which must be revolutionary development. The base for revolutionary development is the people—not empty real estate. What is needed then is a military strategy fitted to aid in the South Vietnamese military and police apparatus in securing populated areas—all populated areas, not just coastal or defensive "enclaves"—for a period of time long enough for the social reforms to really take hold among the Vietnamese people and thereby weaken the popular appeal of the Vietcong and destroy their ultimate strength. Seen against this objective, our present military strategy is not only invalid, but it is extremely dangerous in that it promotes internal American trends which may force us to abandon our efforts in Vietnam before they can succeed.

The developing crescendo of increasing violence and death our present strategy has placed us in can be justified in American popular opinion only through the ever-increasing belief in a military solution. We cannot send division after division to South Vietnam, and lose plane after plane in the North, and expect the people to believe that "our boys," their lives and their deaths, play a secondary role in the struggle. If the American people look to the bombing of the North, or the attainment of 5 to 1 or even 10 to 1 kill ratios in fighting over wastelands in the south, as the way to win, they will be disappointed. As their hopes are frustrated again and again, as one "victory" on a barren hill-side follows another—leaving ever more American corpses behind—and still brings no such military solution, the people's patience will be exhausted. They will eventually demand either abject pullout from all of Southeast Asia, or a total nuclear war. The demand will come before revolutionary development has even a chance to succeed.

1. Because we believe that support of revolutionary development is the only valid role for the military, and because we believe that many more years will be necessary before the proposed reforms, and the continued gradual expansion of areas of government control which these reforms will hasten and solidify, but not supplant, can succeed in destroying the Vietcong infrastructure by depriving it of its popular support, we propose the following observations be considered:If our military purpose is what we have suggested and not to "destroy the enemy" per se, then there is no point in ground attacks against enemy defensive positions in unpopulated areas. We have noted our opposition to the "enclave" theory. Pacification should be conducted wherev-

er there are people—including the Central Highlands—and it should be adequately protected. While the best defense (of an area) is certainly a good offense (conducted around its periphery), we feel that the logic of this doctrine has been extended too far. We are not military men, but is seems to us that a combination of bombing and harassment patrols, with the possibility of immediate large-scale response if correspondingly large enemy units are encountered, would serve the purpose of keeping large Communist military units off balance and at a safe distance from areas being pacified. We do not believe the nature of the war justifies the sacrifice of hundreds of men in ground attacks against remote Communist positions in order to destroy even larger numbers of the enemy, prove once again that no place is safe for them, and then withdraw again. Even when such operations result in killing 500 or even 800 Communist soldiers at the cost of 100 KIA, they are but Pyrrhic victories. They represent needless losses of life, which only bring domestic patience a bit closer to the breaking point.

2. Bombing of "strategic" targets in North Vietnam, such as power plants, factories, oil depots, and cement plants, is unjustifiably expensive in terms of planes, men, and international and domestic public opinion. It does little to diminish the Communists' real strength in South Vietnam (they have never lost sight of the political nature of the struggle) and serves to divert attention—in our government and among the people—away from the only area in which the war can be won—among the people of South Vietnam.

3. Competition among the military services in publicizing their contributions to the total effort is positively harmful in that it distorts the nature of the struggle and, depending on the attitude of the individuals at whom the publicity is directed, either serves to further arouse foredoomed hopes of military victory or further increase abhorrence and rejection of the *entire* U.S. effort in Vietnam.

4. Another facet of the misdirected emphasis in the U.S. effort

in Vietnam is that Military Assistance Command Vietnam (MACV) has downgraded the role of the advisor in Vietnam to below that of the officer serving in the main force U.S. combat unit. We have for years berated ARVN for neglecting pacification support in favor of military operations often unrelated to the task, but producing good kill ratios and hence decorations and promotions. By subordinating the advisory to the combat role, we encourage exactly the same thing. As among the civilians, grossly over-expanded but mediocre MACV advisory teams should be replaced by lean teams of first-rate officers—officers who should, if they merit it, receive the highest honors and acclaim given for military service in Vietnam. Combat units too can and should perform an instructive role. The system of combining U.S. and ARVN or RF/PF units, as employed in I Corps, should be expanded to all Vietnam, so much the better. This paper suggests that it will.

VI.   THE IMPORTANCE OF BEING HONEST

It is absolutely essential that we start being honest with ourselves. "Accentuate the positive" reporting—standard operating procedure with the military and habitual with most civilians—must be replaced by the bare truth. Saigon cannot give Washington an honest evaluation if reports it receives from the field are themselves over edited and over cleared, and sometimes suppressed outright. There must be a prominent place in the internal U.S. reporting system for independent analysis and dissenting opinion. Statistics by the ream, which we now favor, remain a poor indicator of progress without sound evaluation.

VII.   WHAT ABOUT THE VIETCONG?

At the same time the above reforms are being carried out, we believe that extensive efforts should be made to develop contact with all dissident elements of the fragmented Vietnamese society, including the Vietcong. The Doan-Ket (unite) program, as it was originally conceived, is an example of this. Contacts with the

Vietcong need not, indeed should not be confined to contacts with the NLF leadership. Wherever there is a Vietcong commander who can be approached, on a village or district level particularly, contacts should be made. If they are willing to abandon military resistance to the GVN and continue their "reform" within the framework of that government, they should be given as large a role in their local areas—including a determining role—as their popular support merits. The GVN has had the courage to stretch out its hand to the Hoa Hao and the FULRO Montagnard rebels—let them do the same with the Vietcong.

Notes

Prologue

1. Stanley Karnow, *Vietnam: A History*, (New York: Viking Press, 1983), 547.
2. The term Việt Cong appeared in Saigon newspapers beginning in 1956, meaning Vietnamese Communists, and was used in the South until about 1977 when the country was reunified; Vietminh originated in 1935, lapsed and then reemerged in usage in 1941 and was used continuously by the Vietnamese communists.
3. Ton Nu Thi Ninh, "Princeton Global Summer Seminar Lecture" (Princeton Global Summer Seminar in Hanoi, Hanoi, July 9, 2009).
4. Robert S. McNamara and Brian VanDeMark, *In Retrospect: The Tragedy and Lessons of Vietnam* (New York: Vintage Books), 196, 39–41.
5. Karnow, *Vietnam: A History*, 253.
6. Keith Weller Taylor, *The Birth of Vietnam* (Berkeley: University of California Press, 1983), xvii–xxi.
7. Edward M. Kennedy, *True Compass: A Memoir* (New York: Twelve, 2011), 212–13.
8. Gregory Allen Olsen, *Mansfield and Vietnam: A Study in Rhetorical Adaptation* (East Lansing: Michigan State University Press), 87–112.
9. Karnow, *Vietnam: A History*, 268.
10. The Princeton Global Summer Seminar in Hanoi is discussed in some detail in the Epilogue.

Chapter 1

1. Huu Ngoc, "Three Thousand Years of Vietnamese History and Culture" (Princeton Global Summer Seminar in Hanoi, Van Mieu Confucian Temple, Hanoi June, 2007–09).
2. Ibid.
3. Keith Weller Taylor, *A History of the Vietnamese* (Cambridge: Cambridge University Press, 2014), 1–2.
4. Ibid., 12–13. Taylor also contends that Vietnam did not become genuinely independent until 1884.
5. Ibid., 19–21.
6. Ibid., 9–21.

7. Ibid., 29–37.

8. Taylor, *A History of the Vietnamese*, 17–59.

9. Ibid., 268–69.

10. Karnow, *Vietnam: A History*, 104–05.

11. Taylor, *A History of the Vietnamese*, 182–92.

12. Ibid., 158–60, 220–21.

13. Ibid., 321–338.

14. Karnow, *Vietnam: A History*, 61–65.

15. Ibid., 65.

16. Taylor, *A History of the Vietnamese*, 301–97.

17. Ibid., 398–404.

18. Karnow, *Vietnam: A History*, 110.

Chapter 2

1. Karnow, *Vietnam: A History*, 55–57.

2. Ibid., 56–65.

3. Ibid., 57–60.

4. Ibid., 65.

5. Ibid., 66–70.

6. Ibid., 71–80.

7. Ibid., 57, 63, 69–75.

8. Ibid., 80–88.

9. Taylor, *A History of the Vietnamese*, 446.

10. Ibid., 454–59.

11. Ibid., 446–55.

12. Ibid., 472–75.

13. Ibid., 475–77.

14. Ibid., 480–81.

15. Ibid., 480.

16. Ibid., 481–83.

Chapter 3

1. Hue-Tam Ho Tai, *Radicalism and the Origins of the Vietnamese Revolution* (Cambridge, MA: Harvard University Press, 1996), 22–24.

2. David G. Marr, *Vietnamese Tradition on Trial, 1920–1945* (CA: University of California Press, 1984), 1–13

3. Karnow, *Vietnam: A History*, 114–18.

4. Marr, *Vietnamese Tradition on Trial*, 3–4.

5. Ibid., 12–13

6. Ibid., 26–53.

7. Ibid., 26.

8. Ibid., 4–5.

9. Ibid., 5.

10. Ibid., 5–6.

11. Ibid., 5–6.

12. Ibid., 5–7.

13. Ibid., 7–12.

14. Ibid., 408.

15. https://en.wikipedia.org/wiki/Vietnamese_Famine_of_1945, January 4, 2011. "The exact number of deaths due to the 1944–1945 famine is unknown and is a matter of controversy. Various sources estimate between 400,000 to 2 million people starved in Northern Vietnam during this time. In May 1945 sources in Hanoi asked the Northern Provinces to report their casualties. Twenty provinces reported a total of 380,000 people starved to death, and 20,000 more died because of disease. In October a report from a French military official estimated half a million deaths. The French Governor-General Jean Decoux wrote in his memoires *A La Barre de l'Indochine* that about 1 million northerners starved to death. Ho Chi Minh in his Proclamation of Independence of the Democratic Republic of Vietnam on September 2, 1945 used a 2 million figure."

16. Marr, *Vietnamese Tradition on Trial*, 35–44.

17. Ibid., 39–41.

18. Ibid., 8–13.

19. Ibid., 9–10.

20. Ibid., 8–10.

21. Ibid., 9.

22. Ibid., 9–10.

23. Ibid., 9

24. Hue-Tam Ho Tai, *Radicalism and the Origins of the Vietnamese Revolution*, 57–67.

25. Marr, *Vietnamese Tradition on Trial*, 10–11.

26. Ibid., 11–13.

27. Ibid., 9–13.

Chapter 4

1. Marr, *Vietnamese Tradition on Trial*, 1–13.

2. Ho Tai, *Radicalism and the Origins of the Vietnamese Revolution*, 6.

3. Marr, *Vietnamese Traditions on Trial*, 12–13.

4. Ho Tai, *Radicalism and the Origins of the Vietnamese Revolution*, 224–25.

5. Ibid., 4, 57–58, 61–63.

6. Ibid., 4–6.

7. Ibid., 4.

8. Ibid., 16.

9. Ibid., 20–23.

10. Ibid., 22–23.

11. Ibid., 23.

12. Ibid., 184–86.

13. Ibid., 23–24.

14. Ibid., 25–26.

15. Ibid., 26.

16. Ibid., 26–28.

17. Ibid., 27.

18. Ibid., 27–28.

19. Ibid., 27–28.

20. Ibid., 28, 58–66.

21. Ibid., 29–30.

22. Ibid., 30, 36–42.

23. Ibid., 31–32.

24. Ibid., 32-34.

25. Ibid., 35–39.

26. Ibid., 140–41.

27. Ibid., 154–56.

28. Taylor, *A History of the Vietnamese*, 509.

29. Ho Tai, *Radicalism and the Origins of the Vietnamese Revolution*, 226.

30. Ibid., 4-5, 227–28.

31. Ibid., 4-5, 260–61.

32. Ibid., 226, 260.

33. Ibid., 226, 260–61.

34. Ibid., 260–63.

35. Ibid., 5, 262–63.

36. Ho Chi Minh is still referred to as "Bac Ho," my father's older brother.

37. Taylor, A History of the Vietnamese, 186–93

38. American College Dictionary, 1947–48th ed., 749. "Marxism: "System of Thought developed by Karl Marx, along with Engels, esp. the doctrine that the stat throughout history has been a device for the exploitation of the ages by a dominant class, that class struggle has been the main agency of historical change and that the capitalist state contained from the first the seeds of its own decay and will inevitably, after a transitional period, be succeeded by a socialist order and a classless society."

Chapter 5

1. Hue-Tam Ho Tai, *Radicalism and the Origins of the Vietnamese Revolution*, 67.
2. Ibid., 68–69.
3. Marilyn Blatt Young, *The Vietnam Wars, 1945–1990* (New York: Harper Perennial, 1991), 2–4.
4. Karnow, *Vietnam: A History*, 121–23.
5. Ibid., 122–23.
6. Hue-Tam Ho Tai, *Radicalism and the Origins of the Vietnamese Revolution*, 69–72.
7. Ibid., 69.
8. Ibid., 174–82.
9. Ibid., 175-78.
10. Taylor, *A History of the Vietnamese*, 509.
11. Ibid., 530.
12. Ibid., 530–31.
13. William J. Duiker, *Vietnam: Revolution in Transition* (Boulder, CO: Westview, 1995), 44–45.
14. Ibid.
15. Taylor, *A History of the Vietnamese*, 531–32.
16. Ibid., 532–33.
17. Duiker, *Vietnam: Revolution in Transition*, 44–45.
18. Ibid., 45.
19. Hue-Tam Ho Tai, *Radicalism and the Origins of the Vietnamese Revolution*, 256–57.

Chapter 6

1. Fredrik Logevall, *Embers of War: The Fall of an Empire and the Making of America's Vietnam* (New York: Random House Trade Paperbacks, 2014), 41.
2. Karnow, *Vietnam: A History*, 136–37.
3. Archimedes Patti, *Why Viet Nam?: Prelude to America's Albatross* (Berkeley: University of California Press, 1982), 51.
4. Memo: https://www.docsteach.org/documents/document/memorandum-roosevelt-secretary-hull;
   Text: Logevall, *Embers of War*, 41–62. Logevall, Embers of War, 46
5. Ibid., 41–46.
6. Karnow, *Vietnam: A History*, 136.
7. Logevall, *Embers of War*, 41–62.
8. Marr, *Vietnamese Tradition on Trial*, 262–70.

9. Logevall, *Embers of War*, 64–66.

10. Karnow, *Vietnam: A History*, 136–37.

11. Logevall, *Embers of War*, 139.

12. Karnow, *Vietnam: A History*, 138–39.

13. Ibid., 89.

14. Ibid., 106.

15. Patti, *Why Viet Nam?*, xvii–xx.

16. Karnow, *Vietnam: A History*, 138–40.

17. Patti, *Why Viet Nam?*, 53–55.

18. Ibid., 55–58.

19. Ibid., 58–60.

20. Karnow, *Vietnam: A History*, 141–42.

21. Ibid., 140.

22. Marr, *Vietnamese Traditions on Trial*, 322, 407–08.

23. Karnow, *Vietnam: A History*, 151–54.

24. Patti, *Why Viet Nam?*, 178–79.

25. Ibid., 155.

26. General Vo Nguyen Giap in meeting with Desaix Anderson, February 27 1997.

27. Marr, *Vietnamese Traditions on Trial*, 322, 549–52.

28. Patti, *Why Viet Nam?*, 348–49.

29. Ibid., 366–74. The remarkable report on Patti's farewell dinner with Ho Chi Minh

30. Ibid., 368–69.

31. Ibid., 372–73.

32. Ibid., 271–73.

33. Ibid., 374.

34. Karnow, *Vietnam: A History*, 146–47.

Chapter 7

1. Patti, *Why Viet Nam?*, 223–24, 250–53.

2. Karnow, *Vietnam: A History*, 151–52.

3. Ibid., 152.

4. Georges Thierry d'Argenlieu. https://en.wikipedia.org/wiki/Georges_Thierry_d%27Argenlieu (accessed November 3, 2019).

5. Karnow, *Vietnam: A History*, 145–46.

6. Ibid., 148–50.

7. Patti, *Why Viet Nam?*, 223–24, 250–53.

8. Karnow, *Vietnam: A History*, 152.

9. Ibid., 153–55.

10. Ibid., 153.

11. Logevall, *Embers of War,* 139.
12. Karnow, *Vietnam: A History*, 138–39.
13. Ibid., 153–54.
14., Logevall, *Embers of War*, 163.
15. Ibid., 63–65.
16. Ibid., 211.
17. Ibid., 205–11.
18. Ibid., 219.
19. Karnow, *Vietnam: A History*, 160.
20. Ibid., 175.
21. Logevall, *Embers of War*, 234.
22. Ibid., 226–28.
23. Karnow, *Vietnam: A History*, 176–77.
24. Ibid., 169–170.
25. Ibid., 177.
26. Taylor, *A History of the Vietnamese*, 548–51.
27. Karnow, *Vietnam: A History*, 181–90.
28. Bernard B. Fall, *Street Without Joy* (New York: Schocken Books, 1972), 36–40.
29. Logevall, *Embers of War*, 260–86.
30. Ibid., 153.
31. Ibid., 154–57.
32. Ibid., 138–39.
33. Taylor, *A History of the Vietnamese*, 558–59.
34. Karnow, *Vietnam: A History*, 153–54.
35. Logevall, *Embers of War*, 341, 466.
36. Karnow, *Vietnam: A History*, 158–59.
37. Logevall, *Embers of War*, 474–476.
38. Taylor, *A History of the Vietnamese*, 544–47, 556–59.
39. Karnow, *Vietnam: A History*, 160.
40. Logevall, *Embers of War*, 556–57.
41. Ibid., 226–28.
42. Ibid., 351.
43. Karnow, *Vietnam: A History*, 176–77.
44. Ibid., 169–170.
45. Ibid., 177.
46. Logevall, *Embers of War*, 584–85.
47. Taylor, *A History of the Vietnamese,* 560.
48. Fall, *Street Without Joy*, 36–40.
49. Logevall, *Embers of War*, 260–86.
50. Ibid., 320–22.

Chapter 8

1. Taylor, *A History of the Vietnamese*, 214.
2. Ibid., 561.
3. Karnow, *Vietnam: A History*, 224.
4. Ibid., 220–24.
5. Ibid., 220–21.
6. Ibid., 213–22.
7. Ibid., 223–24.
8. Ibid., 224–27.
9. Ibid., 227–37.
10. Ibid., 218–19.
11. Ibid., 222–23.
12. Taylor, *A History of the Vietnamese*, 225–26
13. Dinner Conversation with Professor Pham Hong Tung, University of Social Sciences and Humanities, VNU
14. Taylor, *A History of the Vietnamese*, 566–67.
15. Dinner Conversation with Professor Pham Hong Tung, University of Social Sciences and Humanities, VNU
16. Taylor, *A History of the Vietnamese*, 566–68.
17. Ibid., 571.
18. Le Duc Tho was later Henry Kissinger's counterpart in the secret negotiations in Paris.
19. Taylor, *A History of the Vietnamese*, 573
20. Ibid., 237
21. "Presentation in Princeton Global Summer Seminar" by unidentified friend of the author (lecture, Princeton Global Summer Seminar in Hanoi, VNU, Hanoi, July 15, 2009)
22. Ibid.

Chapter 9

1. The Independence Hall Association, "Ask Not What Your Country Can do for You," Orig. ed. s.v. "John F. Kennedy's Inaugural Address, January 20th, 1961," http://www.ushistory.org/documents/ask-not.htm (accessed November 10, 2018).
2. Karnow, *Vietnam: A History*, 247–50.
3. "Transcript of Broadcast on NBC's "Huntley-Brinkley Report," September 9, 1963. Online by Gerhard Peters and John T. Woolley, The American Presidency Project. http://insidethecoldwar.org/sites/default/files/documents/Kennedy%20Interview%2C%20September%209%2C%201961.pdf

4. *The Pentagon Papers*, written by Department of Defense personnel, attempted publishing by Daniel Ellsberg vol. 2 (Boston: Beacon Press, 1975), 818–19.

5. Kai Bird, *The Color of Truth: McGeorge Bundy and William Bundy, Brothers in Arms: A Biography* (New York: Simon & Schuster, 1998), 217.

6. Karnow, *Vietnam: A History*, 253.

7. University of Washington 100th Anniversary Speech, November 16, 1961 ed., s.v. President John Kennedy's Speech at 100th Anniversary, www.historylink.org/File/968.

8. Gordon M. Goldstein, *Lessons in Disaster: McGeorge Bundy and the Path to War in Vietnam* (New York: Times Books, 2009), 65.

9. Karnow, *Vietnam: A History*, 248.

10. Ibid., 247–48.

11. Ibid., 248.

12. Ibid., 250.

13. Bird, *The Color of Truth*, 256.

14. Karnow, *Vietnam: A History*, 251.

15. Ibid., 251–54.

16. Ibid., 252–53.

17. Ibid., 253.

18. Ibid., 258.

19. Ibid., 249.

20. Ibid., 358–59.

21. Goldstein, *Lessons in Disaster*, 63–64.

22. Ibid., 253.

23. Bird, *The Color of Truth*, 222–23.

24. Ibid., 223. This is based on "hitherto unpublished" Michael Forrestal's classified notes which represent the only contemporaneous documentary evidence that Kennedy "wished to reduce our involvement" in Vietnam.

25. Karnow, *Vietnam: A History*, 253.

26. Ibid., 253

27. Ibid., 253–54.

28. Ibid., 268.

29. Ibid., 253.

30. Ibid., 268.

31. Kennedy, *True Compass*, 212.

32. Bird, *The Color of Truth*, 258–59.

33. Ibid., 259.

34. Ibid., 260.

35. Karnow, *Vietnam: A History*, 259–62.

36. Ibid., 278–86.

37. Ibid., 278–79.
38. Ibid., 280.
39. Ibid., 281.
40. Ibid., 281.
41. Ibid., 281–311.
42. Ibid., 297–98.
43. Ibid., 295.
44. Bird, *The Color of Truth*, 262–63.
45. Karnow, *Vietnam: A History*, 311.

Chapter 10

1. Karnow, *Vietnam: A History*, 319–22.
2. Bird, *The Color of Truth*, 282.
3. Karnow, *Vietnam: A History*, 321.
4. Ibid., 323.
5. Ibid., 323–26.
6. Ibid., 324.
7. Ibid., 380–83.
8. Nguyen-cao-Kỳ, *How We Lost the Vietnam War* (New York: Cooper Square Press, 2002), 45–46.
9. Karnow, *Vietnam: A History*, 381–84.
10. Presidents George Bush I and II sought and achieved similar Congressional Resolutions before the Gulf and Iraq Wars.
11. Karnow, *Vietnam: A History*, 361–62.
12. Ibid., 362–63.
13. Ibid., 366–76.
14. Ibid., 369.
15. Ibid., 370–72.
16. Ibid., 418.
17. Bird, *The Color of Truth*, 296.
18. Karnow, *Vietnam: A History*, 395–97.
19. Ibid., 395–96.
20. Ibid., 395
21. Ibid., 413–15.
22. Ibid., 422–26.
23. Ibid., 341.
24. Ibid., 381.
25. Ibid., 397–98.
26. Ibid., 398–99.
27. Ibid., 399.
28. Ibid., 402–15.

29. Ibid., 403–04.
30. Ibid., 423.
31. Ibid., 405.
32. Ibid., 404–05.
33. Ibid., 404–06, 412.
34. Ibid., 412–13.
35. Ibid., 413.
36. Ibid., 413–14.
37. Ibid., 415.
38. Young, *The Vietnam Wars, 1945–1990*, 188.
39. Ibid., 453.
40. Karnow, *Vietnam: A History*, 424.
41. Ibid., 423.
42. Ibid., 424.
43. Bird, *The Color of Truth*, 330–40.
44. Diem Bui and David Chanoff, *In the Jaws of History* (Bloomington: Indiana University Press, 1999), 124–26.
45. Karnow, *Vietnam: A History*, 417
46. At a high-level White House meeting on April 1, 1965, President Johnson decided to give Westmoreland two more marine battalions as well as eighteen to twenty thousand logistical troops—since Americans never fight abroad without ample supplies of arms and ammunition, and vast quantities of beer, chocolate bars, shaving cream, and their favorite brands of cigarettes. The president also dictated an important tactical change Taylor, now resigned to having the marines in Vietnam, had insisted that they be restricted to defending U.S. bases and other installations along the coast. But Westmoreland, arguing that, "a good offense is the best defense," wanted them out patrolling the countryside Johnson backed Westmoreland. And the marines, as one of their commanders put it, would henceforth "start killing the Vietcong instead of just sitting on their ditty box."
47. Karnow, *Vietnam: A History*, 378–86.
48. Ibid., 386.
49. Ibid., 379–80, 504–06.
50. Bui and Chanoff, *In the Jaws of History*, 110–11.
51. Ibid., 112–13.
52. Ibid., 124.
53. Ibid., 133.
54. Ibid., 130.
55. Ibid., 130–34.
56. Ibid., 156–57.
57. Ibid., 158–59.

58. Karnow, *Vietnam: A History*, 444.

59. Ibid., 445–47.

60. Bui and Chanoff, *In the Jaws of History*, 189–90.

61. Ibid., 190.

62. Ibid., 190–92.

63. Karnow, *Vietnam: A History*, 438–44.

Chapter 11

1. FSO paper entitled: "Some Thoughts on the Situation in Vietnam: Facing the Facts," 1966.

The paper was composed near the end of 1966 by State Department Foreign Service Officers who had been stationed in Vietnam as · Province or Assistance Provincial Representatives, USAID, since June 1965. They were Ray Reimer, Dac Lac Province; Steve Ledogar and Richard Brown, Quang Tri Province; Clay Nettles, Lam Dong Province; Robert Meyers, Montagnard Officer; and Desaix Anderson, Bien Hoa 1965–66, Saigon Districts 6 and 8 June–December 1966, and Revolutionary Development Evaluator 1967 until June. Several of these officers met in early 1967 with State Department Under Secretary for Political Affairs Eugene Rostow to discuss the ideas contained herein. Full Text attached in the Appendix.

Chapter 12

1. Don Oberdorfer, *Tet!: The Turning Point in the Vietnam War* (Baltimore, MD: Johns Hopkins University Press, 2001), 3–8.

2. Ibid., 9–11.

3. Ibid., 7–8.

4. Ibid., 116.

5. Ibid., 51–54.

7. In fact, it may have been General Westmoreland who created the diversion in Khe Sanh.

8. Oberdorfer, *Tet!*, 141–51.

9. Ibid., 198–235.

10. Young, *The Vietnam Wars, 1945–1990*, 217.

11. Ibid.

12. Ibid., 207–08.

13. Ibid., 183–84.

14. Karnow, *Vietnam: A History*, 544–45.

15. Ibid., 601–03.

16. Ibid., 536.

17. Ibid., 169.

18. Ibid., 537.

19. Ibid., 538

20. Ibid., 544.

21. Ibid., 545.

22. Ibid., 544.

23. Pham Hong Tung, University of Social Sciences and Humanities, VNU, on "Tet" (Princeton Global Summer Seminar in Hanoi June 25, 2008).

24. Ibid.

25. Ibid.

26. Ibid.

27. Ibid. June 24, 2009.

28 Nguyen Ngoc Loan, chief of the national police of South Vietnam, raised his sidearm and shot Vietcong operative Nguyen Van Lem in the head, then walked over to the reporters and told them, "These guys kill a lot of our people, and I think Buddha will forgive me." Lem was reported to be the captain of a Vietcong "revenge squad" that had executed dozens of unarmed civilians, some that same morning.

29. Oberdorfer, *Tet!*, 161–65.

30. Karnow, *Vietnam: A History*, 544.

31. Bui and Chanoff, *In the Jaws of History*, 220–21.

32. Kỳ, *How We Lost the Vietnam War*, 163.

Chapter 13

1. Bird, *The Color of Truth*, 282.

2. Andrew F. Krepinevich, *The United States Army and Vietnam: Counterinsurgency Doctrine and the Army Concept of War* (Fort Bragg, NC: United States Army, John F. Kennedy Special Warfare Center, 1984), 93.

3. Maxwell D. Taylor, *Swords and Plowshares* (New York: Da Capo Press, 1990), 321.

4. Karnow, *Vietnam: A History*, 551–52.

5. Krepinevich, *The United States Army and Vietnam*, 95.

6. Ibid., 99, 142, 184.

7. Ibid., 99.

8. Ibid., 100–03.

9. Ibid., 44–45.

10. Ibid., 108.

11. Ibid., 118–27.

12. Ibid., 131.

13. *The Pentagon Papers*, Vol. 4, (Boston: Beacon Press, 1971), 606–09.

14. Krepinevich, *The United States Army and Vietnam*, 139.

15. Ibid., 155.

16. Ibid., 168–69.

17. Ibid., 172–77.

18. Ibid., 213–14.

19. Harry G. Summers, *On Strategy: A Critical Analysis of the Vietnam War* (New York: Presidio Press, 1995), 1–206.

20. Krepinevich, *The United States Army and Vietnam*, 139.

21. Bui and Chanoff, *In the Jaws of History*, 334–43.

Chapter 14

1. Public Health and Publications on Agent: https://www.publichealth. va.gov/exposures/agentorange/index.asp, (accessed November 3, 2019).

2. Karnow, *Vietnam: A History*, 465.

3. Ibid., 467.

4. Ibid., 467–68.

5. Ibid., 469.

6. Ibid., 470.

7. Ibid., 470

8. Bui and Chanoff, *In the Jaws of History*, 156–57, 168–69.

9. Ibid., 168–70.

10. Tim O'Brien, *If I Die in a Combat Zone* (London: Harper Perennial, 2006), 472.

11. Tim O'Brien, *The Things They Carried* (Boston: Houghton Mifflin Harcourt, 2009), 15.

12. Ibid., 16.

13. Ibid., 21.

14. Ibid., 59.

15. Ibid., 47.

16. James H. Webb, *Fields of Fire* (New York, NY: Bantam Books, 2001), 341.

17. Ibid., 355–56.

Chapter 15

1. Oberdorfer, *Tet!*, xvi.

2. Ibid., 308–11.

3. Henry Kissinger, *Diplomacy* (New York: Simon & Schuster Paperback, 2005), 670–71.

4. Karnow, *Vietnam: A History*, 166, 548.

5. https://www.vietnamwar50th.com/1968_tet_and_shifting_views/CBS-Evening-News-Anchor-Walter-Cronkite-Broadcasts-His--8220-Report-from-Vietnam-8221-/February 27, 1968

6. Ibid., 267–71.
7. Ibid., 271.
8. Ibid., 290–92.
9. Ibid., 556.
10. Ibid., 545–46.
11. Ibid., 548.
12. Ibid., 548–49.
13. Ibid., 549.
14. Ibid., 550.
15. Ibid., 561–62.
16. Ibid., 552–56.
17. Ibid., 554.
18. Ibid., 555–57.
19. Ibid., 556.
20. Kennedy, *True Compass*, 160–61.
21. Karnow, *Vietnam: A History*, 561–63.
22. Ibid., 562.
23. Olsen, *Mansfield and Vietnam*, 193.
24. Karnow, *Vietnam: A History*, 564–66.
25. "Remaining Awake Through a Great Revolution," ed. March 31, 1968 s.v. Martin Luther King's Speech, at National Cathedral, Washington, DC, March 31, 1968), American Rhetoric. https://kinginstitute.stanford.edu/king-papers/publications/knock.
26. Karnow, *Vietnam: A History*, 579–81.
27. Ibid., 585–86 and Bird, *The Color of Truth*, 371.

Chapter 16

1. Karnow, *Vietnam: A History*, 577–79.
2. Julian Zelizer, Project MUSE—Reflections: Rethinking the History of ... The American Project, February 19, 2007 ed.'s.v. "reassertion of congressional prerogatives" on foreign policy "On December 16, 1969, Congress finally used the power of the purse. In a closed floor session, Church and Cooper offered an amendment to a defense spending bill to prevent the further use of money in Laos or Thailand. The amendment received the support of 73 senators. Church called the amendment a 'reassertion of congressional prerogatives' on foreign policy. It survived the House-Senate conference committee, and Nixon signed the legislation." muse.jhu.edu/article/382920 9.
3. Karnow, *Vietnam: A History*, 582–83.
4. Young, *The Vietnam Wars, 1945–1990*, 237.
5. Karnow, *Vietnam: A History*, 582.
6. Ibid., 589–91.

7. Ho Chi Minh, *Ho Chi Minh: Selected Writings 1920–1969* (Hanoi: Foreign Languages Publishing House, 1973), 359–62.
8. Karnow, *Vietnam: A History*, 583; Ho Chi Minh's Last Will and Testament: https://www.hochiminh.org/Pages/1969_May_10.html
9. Ibid., 592–93.
10. "Winston Lord oral history interview conducted by Charles Stuart Kennedy and Nancy Bernkopf Tucker, 1998-4-28." *The Association for Diplomatic Studies and Training Foreign Affairs Oral History Collection.* https://www.adst.org/OH%20TOCs/Lord,%20Winston.pdf (accessed June 28, 2017), 192.
11. Richard Nixon, "Asia After Vietnam," *Foreign Affairs,* October 1967.
12. Karnow, *Vietnam: A History*, 582–83, 586–89.
13. Ibid., 588.
14. Ibid., 588–89.
15. "Understanding Richard Nixon and His Era: A Symposium," Understanding Richard Nixon's Vietnam Policy, https://www.c-span.org/video/?303693-4/understanding-richard-nixons-vietnam-policy. July 22, 2011, ed. s.v
16. "Winston Lord oral history interview, 174 and 228.
17. Karnow, *Vietnam: A History*, 589.
18. Ibid., 589–93.
19. Ibid., 589–90.
20. Ibid., 590.
21. Ibid., 590.
22. Ibid., 590–91.
23. Ibid., 591
24. Ibid., 592.
25. Ibid., 591–92.
26. Ibid., 592.
27. Ibid., 592–93.
28. "Winston Lord oral history interview, 192 and 228.
29. Karnow, *Vietnam: A History*, 593–95.
30. "Winston Lord oral history interview, 195–200.
31. Ibid., 193–94.
32. Ibid., 192–93.
33. Ibid., 193–94.
34. Karnow, *Vietnam: A History*, 594.
35. Ibid., 594
36. Ibid., 595.
37. Ibid., 598–99.
38. Ibid., 599-601
39. Ibid., 601.

40. Ibid., 601–02.
41. Ibid., 603–04.
42. Ibid., 604–05.
43. Ibid., 604.
44. Ibid., 604–05.
45. Ibid., 606.
46. Ibid., 603.
47. Ibid., 606.
48. Ibid., 607.
49. Ibid., 608.
50. Ibid., 609–10.
51. Ibid., 609.
52. Ibid., 611–12.
53. Ibid., 625–26.
54. Young, *The Vietnam Wars, 1945–1990*, 251.
55. Ibid., 256–57.
56. Karnow, *Vietnam: A History* Ibid., 600–01.
57. Young, *The Vietnam Wars*, 256–59.
58. Martin Luther King Jr. "Beyond Civil Rights," 1965–68 ed. s.v. Speeches by Martin Luther King, https://kinginstitute.stanford.edu/king-papers/documents/beyond-vietnam. January, 11, 1967, in New York Riverside Church.
59. Young, *The Vietnam Wars*, 559–61.

Chapter 17

1. Karnow, *Vietnam: A History*, 625–26.
2. Ibid., 624.
3. Ibid., 626–27.
4. Ibid., 625.
5. Ibid., 624–25.
6. Ibid., 626–27.
7. Ibid., 624–25.
8. Ibid., 625.
9. Marvin E. Gettleman, *Vietnam and America: A Documented History* (New York: Grove Press, 2000), 433–35.
10. Karnow, *Vietnam: A History*, 627–28.
11. Ibid., 628–29.
12. Ibid., 628-29.
13. Ibid., 629–31.
14. Ibid., 629–30.
15. Ibid., 631–32.

16. Ibid., 627–31.

17. Ibid., 635.

18. Ibid., 635–36.

19. Ibid., 647–48.

20. Ibid., 636.

21. Ibid., 628–29.

22. Richard Nixon, *Foreign Affairs*, "Asia after Vietnam" October 1967.

23. Karnow, *Vietnam: A History*, 638–39.

24. Ibid., 644–45.

25. Ibid., 647–48.

26. Ibid., 638–39.

27. Ibid., 639.

28. Ibid., 640–41.

29. Ibid., 641–43.

30. Ibid., 643

31. Ibid., 644–45.

32. Ibid., 646

33. Ibid., 644.

34. Ibid., 646–47.

35. Ibid., 638–39.

36. "Winston Lord oral history interview, 197.

37. Karnow, *Vietnam: A History*, 646–47.

38. Ibid., 648–49.

39. Ibid., 647.

40. "Winston Lord oral history interview, 198 and 244–45.

41. Karnow, *Vietnam: A History*, 648–49.

42. "Winston Lord oral history interview, 198 and 246.

43. Ibid., 247.

44. Karnow, *Vietnam: A History*, 648–50.

45. Ibid., 648.

46. Ibid., 647

47. Ibid., 648–49.

48. Ibid., 650.

49. "Winston Lord oral history interview, 252.

50. Ibid., 252

51. Karnow, *Vietnam: A History*, 650–51.

52. Ibid., 651.

53. "Winston Lord oral history interview, 254–57.

54. Karnow, *Vietnam: A History*, 651.

55. "Winston Lord oral history interview, 258.

56. Karnow, *Vietnam: A History*, 651.

57. Ibid., 652–54.

58. Ibid., 653.
59. Ibid., 654.
60. "Winston Lord oral history interview, 259.
61. Ibid., 260–63 & 266.
62. Gettleman, *Vietnam and America*, 472–87.
63. Nguyen Khac Huynh, "Presentation in Princeton Global Summer Seminar" (lecture, Princeton Global Summer Seminar in Hanoi, in Hanoi June 30, 2009).
64. "Winston Lord oral history interview, 260–262.
65. Ibid., 262.

Chapter 18

1. "Winston Lord oral history interview, 262.
2. Ibid., 172.
3. Marc Jason Gilbert, *Why the North Won the Vietnam War* (Basingstoke: Palgrave, 2002), 185–87.
4. Ibid., 188.
5. Andre Savaugeot, "Princeton Global Summer Seminar Lecture" (lecture, Princeton Global Summer Seminar in Hanoi, Hanoi, July 7, 2009).
6. Pham Hong Tung, "Tet" (Princeton Global Summer Seminar in Hanoi, University of Social Sciences and Humanities VNU, Hanoi, June 25, 2008).
7. Pham Van Chuong, Vice Chair, Vietnam Peace & Development Foundation; former Vice Chair, Communist Party External Relations Committee" (lecture, Princeton Global Summer Seminar in Hanoi, Hanoi, June 25, 2009).
8. Jeffrey Record, *The Wrong War: Why We Lost in Vietnam* (Annapolis, MD: Naval Institute Press, 1998), 133.

Chapter 19

1. Duong Trung Quoc, Secretary General, Vietnam Historical Studies Association Lecture (lecture, Princeton Global Summer Seminar in Hanoi, Hanoi, June 9, 2009).

Chapter 20

1. Pham Quang Minh, Dean of Faculty, International Relations Department, University of Social Sciences and Humanities, VNU, Lecture. (Princeton Global Summer Seminar in Hanoi, Hanoi, July 6, 2009).
2. Ibid.

3. Karnow, *Vietnam: A History*, 224.

4. Pham Quang Minh.

5. Nikita Khrushchev as quoted by Ilya V. Gaiduk, *The Soviet Union and the Vietnam War* (Chicago: Ivan R. Dee, 1996), 4–5.

6. Ibid., 4–7.

7. Ibid., 5–8.

8. Ibid., 8–10.

9. Ibid., 14–15.

10. Ibid., 16–19.

11. Pham Quang Minh.

12. Gaiduk, *The Soviet Union and the Vietnam War* (Chicago: Ivan R. Dee, 1996), 29–30, 37–42.

13. Ibid., 59–60.

14. Pham Quang Minh.

15. Karnow, *Vietnam: A History*, 495–96, and Young, *The Vietnam Wars, 1945–1990*, 180–81.

16. Pham Quang Minh.

17. "Record of the Second Meeting between Premier Zhou and Prime Minister U Nu," June 29, 1954, History and Public Policy Program Digital Archive, PRC FMA 203-00007-03, 46–57. Translated by Jeffrey Wang.

18. The principles were: mutual respect for territorial integrity, nonaggression, noninterference in each other's internal affairs, equality and mutual benefit, and peaceful coexistence.

19. Qiang Zhai, *China and the Vietnam Wars: 1950–1975* (Chapel Hill (etc.): The University of North Carolina Press, 2000), 83–89.

20. Ibid., 122–29.

21. Ibid., 108–09.

22. Ibid., 118–19.

23. Ibid., 128–29.

24. Ibid., 61–63.

25. Ibid., 122–29.

26. Ibid., 132–33.

27. Ibid., 132–37.

28. Ibid., 138–39.

29. Ibid., 134–37.

30. Ibid., 152–56.

31. Ibid., 178–79.

32. Ibid., 166–67.

33. Ibid., 168–70.

34. Ibid., 198–201.

35. Pham Quang Minh.

Chapter 21

1. Adam Fforde, *From Plan to Market: The Economic Transition in Vietnam and China Compared* (Canberra, A.C.T: Dept. of Economics, Research School of Pacific and Asian Studies, Australian National University, 1997), 12–13, 56–63.

2. Duiker, *Vietnam: Revolution in Transition*, 363–64.

3. Ibid., 134.

4. Ibid., 108–09.

5. Fforde, *From Plan to Market*, 128.

6. Binh, Nguyen Thi. "SRV Vice President Nguyen Thi Binh." (Princeton Global Summer Seminar in Hanoi, Hanoi, July 16, 2007).

7. Duiker, *Vietnam: Revolution in Transition*, 143.

8. Ibid., 134.

9. Ibid., 147–48.

10. Fforde, From Plan to Market, 204–09.

10a. Vietnamese Immigrants in the United States, Article by Elijah Alperin and Jeanne Batalova, September 8, 2018, on Refugees from Vietnam 1960 to 1995 ed.' s.v. https://www.migrationpolicy.org/article/vietnamese-immigrants-united-states-5 (accessed November 8, 2018).

11. Richard M. Nixon, *No More Vietnams* (New York: Arbor House, 1985), 487–88.

Chapter 22

1. Accounting meant that the fate of virtually every American MIA was resolved, whether through certainty of death through recovery of remains or other information that proved their death. Full accounting would thus mean that virtually every missing American should be accounted for—obviously unrealistic. Thus, the U.S. government has zealously continued to seek maximum accounting.

2. Desaix Anderson, *An American in Hanoi: Americas Reconciliation with Vietnam* (White Plains, NY: EastBridge, 2002), 132.

3. Gettleman, *Vietnam and America*.

4. Ibid., 487–88.

5. Former Representative G. V. (Sonny) Montgomery, a conservative Democrat from Mississippi who was a staunch voice for the military and the needs of veterans during his 30 years in Congress, died May 12, 2006, in his hometown, Meridian. He was 85.

6. Anderson, *An American in Hanoi*, 133–34.

7. Ibid.

8. Robert Oakley to author, September 1979.

10. UN Charter Article 2(4): All members shall refrain in their international relations from the threat or use of force against the territorial integrity or political independence of any state, or in any other manner inconsistent with the Purposes of the United Nations.

11. Ieng Sary, one of three surviving defendants in Cambodia's war tribunals, died in Phnom Penh March 14, 2013. Ieng Sary was Brother #3 in the murderous Khmer Rouge Regime and Pol Pot's brother-in-law.

12. "Richard H. Solomon oral history interview conducted by Charles Stewart Kennedy," *The Association for Diplomatic Studies and Training Foreign Affairs Oral History Collection.*
https://www.adst.org/OH%20TOCs/Solomon,%20Richard%20A.toc.pdf?_ga=2.191768169.252048613.1538158566-1561251255.1536867669 (accessed June 29, 2017), 59.

13. Ibid., 61–62.

14. Desaix Anderson, *An American in Hanoi: America's Reconciliation with Vietnam* (White Plains, NY: EastBridge, 2002), 24–25. A candid discussion on rumors about U.S. evil intentions in Vietnam were significantly dispelled in the Politburo by author's meeting in late 1995 with Communist Party Tsar Dao Duy Tung., 24–25

Chapter 23

1. "Winston Lord oral history interview, 698–720.
2. Ibid., 700.
3. Ibid., 706.
4. Ibid., 700.
5. Ibid., 696, 707.
6. Desaix Anderson, *An American in Hanoi*, 42–44, 52–61. NSA Anthony Lake proposed to the author, as *Chargé* in Hanoi, a visit to Vietnam to see constructive results., realized in July 1996, in which he met all top Vietnamese leaders with highly constructive results.
7. "Winston Lord oral history interview, 708–13.
8. Ibid., 711–12.
9. Desaix Anderson, *An American in Hanoi*, 33–34. During a 1996 visit Deputy Secretary Gober expressed condolences to PM Vo Van Kiet over the deaths of his wife and two children in a U.S. air attack during the war. The PM's poignant appreciation led him to link the sadness of his loss with an understanding of U.S. hopes to account for our missing., 33–34.

Chapter 24

1. "Winston Lord oral history interview, 706.

2. Secretary Warren Christopher's speech to Vietnam Foreign Ministry Diplomats; "Christopher, in Vietnam Speech Extols Freedom," in Hanoi, Vietnam, August 7, 1995, https://www.nytimes.com/1995/08/07/world/us-message-to-vietnamese-freedom-pays.html (accessed November 9, 2018).
3. "Winston Lord oral history interview, 698–720.
4. Ibid.
5. Ibid.
6. Duiker, *Vietnam: Revolution in Transition*, 154–55.

Chapter 25

1. Desaix Anderson, *An American in Hanoi*: The author reported extensively on conversations and activities of Minister Nguyen Co Thach, pp 12, 14, 28, 82, 97–101, 106 133, 137–39, 141; Normalization with the United States pp 97–101, 139–142; Invasion of Cambodia, pp 106–109, and General Vo Nguyen Giap, 12, 14–15, 104, 180–82, 191, 212, 267–69, 271: on Ho Chi Minh's respect for the United States; the war, future of U.S.-VN relations, Vietnam's national security pp 180–184; Author's conversation with Premier Phan Van Dong reported in full in this manuscript.
2. Ibid., 24–25, 34, 139.
3. U.S. Chamber of Commerce (AmCham) in Hanoi; www.uschamber.com/vietnam; weekly briefing.
4. Reports on state of Vietnamese economy in July 2017 from U.S. government sources;
   www.viet-studies.net/kinhte/Vietnam_IMF_July17.pdf; & World Bank: https://www.worldbank.org/en/news/press-release/2017/07/13/vietnam-economy-shows-fundamental-strength-with-stable-and-positive-medium-term-outlook.
5. Desaix Anderson, *An American in Hanoi*, 184–90.

Chapter 26

1. World Bank, "World Bank Willing to Support Vietnam's Economy," http://documents.worldbank.org/curated/en/536421528929689515/pdf/127168-WP-TakingStockENG-PUBLIC.pdf, June 27, 2018.
2. Foreign Direct Investment, "Vietnam: FDI Strategy for 2018–2023," https://www.vietnam-briefing.com/news/vietnam-fdi-strategy-2018-2023.html/, December 7, 2017.
3. World Bank, "Vietnam: Childhood Development," https://www.worldbank.org/en/results/2016/11/21/vietnam-more-young-children-are-ready-for-school, http://www.worldbank.org/en/topic/earlychildhooddevelopment (accessed November 17, 2018).

4. World Bank, https://data.worldbank.org/country/vietnam; https://www.worldbank.org/en/topic/education.
5. Teachers for Vietnam, "Education in Vietnam," https://www.world-bank.org/en/country/vietnam/overview (accessed November 15, 2018).
6 "Privatization of State-Owned Enterprise in Vietnam: Opportunities and Challenges," https://medium.com/@dataramatech/privatization-of-state-owned-en-terprises-in-vietnam-opportunities-and-challenges-5e418c69afec. July 26, 2017, (accessed November 15, 2018).
7. International Monetary Fund, "Vietnam IMF 3: Environment and Climate Change," https://www.imf.org/~/media/Files/Publications/CR/2017/cr17191.ashx, May 23, 2017, (accessed November 17, 2018).
8. "Strengthening Higher Education," http://www.eastasiaforum.org/2016/04/21/grading-vietnamshigh-er-education-reforms/ https://journals.sagepub.com/doi/full/10.11/17/1523422318803086 (accessed November 10, 2018).
9. The Vietnam Constitution of 1946, enacted November 9, 1946, now called "The Ho Chi Minh Constitution," http://vietnamlawmagazine.vn/the-1946-constitution-of-vietnam-4443.html, March 22, 2011, By Pham Diem State and Law Research Institute (accessed November 16, 2018).

Bibliography

Anderson, Desaix. *An American in Hanoi: America's Reconciliation with Vietnam*. White Plains, NY: EastBridge, 2002.

"Beyond Civil Rights." Beyond Civil Rights | The Martin Luther King Jr. Center for Nonviolent Social Change. Accessed June 28, 2017.

Binh, Nguyen Thi. "SRV Vice President Nguyen Thi Binh." Princeton Global Summer Seminar in Hanoi, Hanoi, July 16, 2007.

Bird, Kai. *The Color of Truth: McGeorge Bundy and William Bundy, Brothers in Arms: A Biography*. New York: Simon & Schuster, 1998.

Bui, Diem, and David Chanoff. *In the Jaws of History*. Bloomington: Indiana University Press, 1999.

Chuong, Pham Van. Vice Chair, Vietnam Peace & Development Foundation; former Vice Chair, Communist Party External Relations Committee." Lecture, Princeton Global Summer Seminar in Hanoi, Hanoi, June 25, 2009.

Duiker, William J. *Vietnam: Revolution in Transition*. Boulder, CO: Westview, 1995.

"Education in Vietnam." Teachers for Vietnam. Accessed June 29, 2017.

Encyclopædia Britannica. July 16, 2014. Accessed June 27, 2017.

Fall, Bernard B. *Street Without Joy*. New York: Schocken Books, 1972.

Fforde, Adam. *From Plan to Market: The Economic Transition in Vietnam and China Compared*. Canberra, A.C.T.?: Dept. of Economics, Research School of Pacific and Asian Studies, Australian National University, 1997.

Gaiduk, Ilya V. *The Soviet Union and the Vietnam War*. Chicago: Ivan R. Dee, 1996.

Gettleman, Marvin E. *Vietnam and America: A Documented History*. New York: Grove Press, 2000.

Gilbert, Marc Jason. *Why the North Won the Vietnam War*. Basingstoke: Palgrave, 2002.

Goldstein, Gordon M. *Lessons in Disaster: McGeorge Bundy and the Path to War in Vietnam*. New York: Times Books, 2009.

Huynh, Nguyen Khac. "Presentation in Princeton Global Summer Seminar." Lecture, Princeton Global Summer Seminar in Hanoi, Hanoi, June 30, 2009.

Karnow, Stanley. *Vietnam: A History*. 1st ed. New York: Viking Books, 1983.

Kennedy, Edward M. *True Compass: A Memoir*. New York: Twelve, 2011.

Kennedy, John Fitzgerald. *John F. Kennedy's Inaugural Address*. Project Gutenberg; NetLibrary, 2000.

Kennedy, John F. "Address in Seattle at the University of Washington's 100th Anniversary   Program.," November 16, 1961. Online by Gerhard Peters and John T. Woolley, *The American Presidency Project*.

Kennedy, John F. "Transcript of Broadcast on NBC's "Huntley-Brinkley Report.","September 9, 1963. Online by Gerhard Peters and John T. Woolley, *The American Presidency Project*.

Kissinger, Henry. *Diplomacy*. New York: Simon & Schuster Paperback, 2005.

Krepinevich, Andrew F. *The United States Army and Vietnam: Counterinsurgency Doctrine and the Army Concept of War*. Fort Bragg, NC: United States Army, John F. Kennedy Special Warfare Center, 1984.

Logevall, Fredrik. *Embers of War: The Fall of an Empire and the Making of Americas Vietnam*. New York: Random House Trade Paperbacks, 2014.

Lord, Winston. Interview by Charles Stewart Kennedy and Nancy Bernkopf Tucker. Foreign Affairs Oral History Collection, Association for Diplomatic Studies and Training (ADST).

Accessed June 28, 2017, https://www.adst.org/OH%20TOCs/Lord,%20 Winston.pdf.

McNamara, Robert S., and Brian VanDeMark. *In Retrospect: The Tragedy and Lessons of Vietnam*. New York: Vintage Books, 1996.

Marr, David G. *Vietnamese Tradition on Trial, 1920–1945*. CA: University of California Press, 1984.

Minh, Ho Chi. *Ho Chi Minh: Selected Writings 1920–1969*. Hanoi: Foreign Languages Publishing House, 1973.

Minh, Pham Quang. Dean of Faculty, International Relations Department, University of Social Sciences and Humanities, National University of Vietnam Lecture." Princeton Global Summer Seminar in Hanoi, Hanoi, July 6, 2009.

Ngoc, Huu. "Three Thousand Years of Vietnamese History and Culture." Princeton Global Summer Seminar in Hanoi, Van Mieu Confucian Temple , Hanoi.

Nguyen-cao-Kỳ. *How We Lost the Vietnam War*. New York: Cooper Square Press, 2002.

Ninh, Ton Nu Thi. «Princeton Global Summer Seminar Lecture.» Princeton Global Summer Seminar in Hanoi, Hanoi, July 9, 2009.

Nixon, Richard M. *No More Vietnams*. New York: Arbor House, 1985.

Oberdorfer, Don. *Tet!: The turning Point in the Vietnam War*. Baltimore, MD: Johns Hopkins University Press, 2001.

O'Brien, Tim. *If I Die in a Combat Zone*. London: Harper Perennial, 2006.

Olson, Gregory Allen. *Mansfield and Vietnam: A Study in Rhetorical Adaptation*. East Lansing: Michigan State University Press, 1995.

Patti, Archimedes L. A. *Why Viet Nam?: Prelude to America's Albatross*. Berkeley: University of California Press, 1982.

"Presentation in Princeton Global Summer Seminar." Lecture, Princeton Global Summer Seminar in Hanoi , VNU, Hanoi, July 15, 2009.

Quoc, Duong Trung, Secretary General, Vietnam Historical Studies Association Lecture ." Lecture, Princeton Global Summer Seminar in Hanoi, Hanoi, June 9, 2009.

Record, Jeffrey. *The Wrong War: Why We Lost in Vietnam*. Annapolis, MD: Naval Institute Press, 1998.

"Record of the Second Meeting between Premier Zhou and Prime Minister U Nu," June 29, 1954, History and Public Policy Program Digital Archive, PRC FMA 203-00007-03, 46–57. Translated by Jeffrey Wang.

Savaugeot, Andre. "Princeton Global Summer Seminar Lecture." Lecture, Princeton Global Summer Seminar in Hanoi, Hanoi, July 7, 2009.

Solomon, Richard H. Interview by Charles Stewart Kennedy, Foreign Affairs Oral History Collection, Association for Diplomatic Studies and Training (ADST), accessed June 29, 2017, https://www.adst.org/OH%20TOCs/Solomon,%20Richard%20A.toc.pdf?_ga=2.191768169.252048613.1538158566-1561251255.1536867669.

Summers, Harry G. *On Strategy: A Critical Analysis of the Vietnam War*. New York: Presidio Press, 1995.

Tai, Hue-Tam Ho. *Radicalism and the Origins of the Vietnamese Revolution*. Cambridge, MA: Harvard University Press, 1996.

Taylor, Keith Weller. *The Birth of Vietnam*. Berkeley: University of California Press, 1983.

Taylor, Maxwell D. *Swords and Plowshares*. New York: Da Capo Press, 1990.*The Pentagon Papers. Vol. 4*. Boston: Beacon Press, 1971.

The Pentagon Papers. Vol. 2. Boston: Beacon Press, 1975.

Tong, Pham Hong. "Tet." Princeton Global Summer Seminar in Hanoi, University of Social Sciences and Humanities NUV, Hanoi, June 25, 2008.

Webb, James H. *Fields of Fire*. New York, NY: Bantam Books, 2001.

World Bank. *Joint Donor Report to the Vietnam Consultative Group Meeting*. Report no. 65980. Market Economy for a Middle-income Vietnam. Accessed June 29, 2017. Doanh, Le Dang. Lecture, ISEAS Public Seminar, Singapore, June 11, 2015.

Young, Marilyn Blatt. *The Vietnam Wars, 1945–1990*. New York: Harper Perennial, 1991.

Zhai, Qiang. *China and the Vietnam Wars: 1950–1975*. Chapel Hill (etc.): The University of North Carolina Press, 2000.

Index

www.ingramcontent.com/pod-product-compliance
Lightning Source LLC
Chambersburg PA
CBHW050555270326
41926CB00012B/2072